Accounting and Finance in Organisations

third edition

Accounting and Finance in Organisations

accompanying tutor's resources

Tutor's Manual

Pack of support and new material to help tutors explain the main accounting and financial concepts.

Enough material for a two-day short/residential course on key areas of financial & management accounting.

Coloured & b/w OHPs, diagrams / exercises.
A4 looseleaf binder £79.00 ISBN 1 85450 402 9

Overhead Projection Pack

44 overhead projection transparencies
(on coloured backgrounds)
on all the key areas of financial management.

A valuable ready-to-use training resource for short, post-experience courses or for classroom teaching.

A4 looseleaf binder £79.00 ISBN 1 85450 410 X

Accounting
and
Finance
in
Organisations

third edition

Humphrey Shaw

ELM Publications

This third edition of **Accounting and Finance in Organisations** is published September 1998 by ELM Publications, Seaton House, Kings Ripton, Huntingdon PE17 2NJ.

Tel. 01487 773254   Fax: 01487 773359

Printed by St Edmundsbury Press, Bury St Edmunds, Suffolk, England. Bound by Woolnough Bookbinding, Express Works, Church Street, Irthlingborough, Northants, England.

ISBN 1 85450 227 1

British Library Cataloguing-in-Publication Data. A catalogue record for this publication is available from The British Library.

CONTENTS

LIST OF FIGURES

DEDICATION

To my family and friends

ABOUT THE AUTHOR

Humphrey Shaw is a Senior Lecturer in accounting and finance at the University of North London.

He is the author of several books and articles on accounting and finance, including *Strategic Financial Management*, also published by ELM Publications.

A member of the Association of Corporate Treasurers, Humphrey has many years' experience as a lecturer and examiner on a range of post-experience and management courses. He has worked as a consultant lecturing on financial management and his clients include the World Tourist Organisation.

His PhD is from Swansea University.

INTRODUCTION

The study of accountancy and finance is no longer confined to courses in accountancy. The subject is now so important that it is taught on a range of management, business and vocational courses. Many people who once thought that they would never study accountancy now find that they need to be able to understand and interpret financial statements, make financial decisions and understand such terms as shareholder value and corporate governance.

The third edition still seeks to describe the main principles of accounting and finance to anyone studying the subject for the first time. The success of the first two editions has shown that there is a need for a book which provides the reader with a clear descriptive account plus numerical examples which cover all of the main topic areas. This is why each chapter provides the user with examples and diagrams and there are suggested answers, together with a glossary of terms, at the back of the book.

Finally, I would like to thank all the people and organisations who offered advice and gave permission to reproduce information. The following people have all read sections of the book or made valuable comments and suggestions. They are John Syer at Thames Valley University, Dr Helena Shaw of West Herts College, Tony Skone, Director Management and Training Associates, and the following staff at the University of North London: Denise Naylor; Sav Odeva and Rajalingham Nallathamby.

I am also grateful to Boots plc for permission to reproduce part of their annual accounts, the Chartered Institute of Management Accountants for permission to quote their definitions, the Association of Corporate Treasurers to reproduce extracts from their Treasurer's Handbook and for Whitbread plc for permission to reproduce an example of one of their bonds. Special thanks to Cameron de Silva for all his hard work in typesetting the typescript, and to all the people who bought the previous editions and made the book so successful that I was able to write a third edition.

Finally, I would like to thank Sheila Ritchie and all of the staff at ELM Publications for their help and guidance in the writing and production of this book.

Humphrey Shaw PhD, MA., MSc., MCT.

June 1998.

Chapter 1

Financial Management

Introduction

Financial management is the study of money as it applies to business. The financial manager must be able to evaluate the firm's current financial position and determine how future business decisions will affect cash flow, costs and profitability. The role of the financial manager is becoming ever harder because of global competition and the increasing demands of informed and discerning consumers. These new trading conditions have made finance one of the key management disciplines with both financial and non financial managers seeking to improve their understanding and application of financial principles as they progress through their management career.

How Financial Management Differs from Financial Accounting, Cost and Management Accounting and Treasury Management.

Many people use the word finance as a generic term to encompass all aspects of accounting and finance, but this is not correct. Financial management is concerned with interpreting accounting information and using it to make financial decisions. The information will be provided by the financial accountant, the cost accountant and the treasurer. Financial accounting is concerned with the recording and preparation of financial data for it provides information about what has been sold, the expenses incurred and the profit or loss earned during a particular period. It really performs a stewardship role, for it shows the owners how their money has been invested and the returns which the business has made.

All companies must keep accurate financial records in order to comply with the requirements of the Companies' Act 1985. Whilst there is no legal requirement to employ cost accountants and treasurers, many large companies do so because the financial advantages outweigh their costs. Cost accountants ascertain a firm's costs and calculate future profits at different levels of output whilst the treasurer's role is to advise the business about managing risk, financing decisions and cash management.

Financial management is the application of all of these principles with the aim of making decisions which will maximise shareholder wealth without increasing investor risk.

FINANCIAL MANAGEMENT

The Financial Functions of the Firm

	Financial Accounting	Cost Accounting	Treasury Management
Aim	To provide financial information to people outside the organisation, e.g. shareholders, lenders, tax authorities.	To provide cost information to management which can be used for planning, control and decision-making.	To manage the organisation's cash and advise on financing and investment activities.
Focus	Historical	Future	Future
Task	Keep financial records of the whole organisation. Comply with legal requirements relating to the keeping and publication of accounting information To assist in the preparation of the firm's annual accounts.	Cost determination and cost allocation. Preparation, implementation and monitoring of budgeted targets. Preparation of cost information reports to assist management decision-making.	Provision of short and long-term finance. Cash management. Risk management Investment evaluation. Foreign exchange exposure Managing shareholder relations

Corporate Strategy and the Financial Manager

The word strategy comes from the ancient Greek word *strategos* meaning general. Strategic planning should not be concerned with making future decisions, but should consider alternative courses of possible direction for the business. It therefore, looks at questions such as what market is the firm in, what market should it be in and how is the market for its goods and services changing.

There are three key steps to effective strategic planning and these can be categorised as the formulation, the implementation and the evaluation stage.

During the formulation stage management must assess their organisation's external opportunities and threats and evaluate the strengths and weaknesses of their business. Effective strategic planning requires management to reappraise what market they are in, which markets they should be in and whether or not the business should expand, diversify, merge with other organisations or abandon certain markets so that the firm can use its resources more effectively elsewhere. Once these decisions have been made the business can set about deciding its long term objectives.

Even if a business has formulated the correct corporate strategy it will still fail unless it can be implemented. Staff must be motivated, annual objectives set and resources allocated to ensure that the firm can implement its corporate strategy. Financial management is concerned with ensuring that the business has the necessary financial resources to support their long term business plans.

Figure 1:1 The Planning Gap

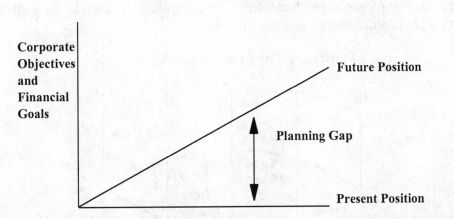

Finally management must constantly evaluate their strategic plans because the business environment is constantly changing. It is during this phase that management performance must be appraised and corrective action taken when actual results fall short of those planned.

In an ever changing market place a business is never where it wants to be and so management must always be planning for the future. Decisions must be made as to where the firm should be, in so many years time, compared with its current position. This is often referred to as its planning gap and is shown in the diagram above.

The diagram shows where the business currently is and where it wants to be in the future. The greater the distance between the lines, the more objectives must be accomplished to achieve the desired goals. These new aims will have to be financed, either by generating sufficient cash from its sales or by raising it from new sources. Any new investment must be appraised to ensure that optimum returns are made. Money once invested cannot usually be recovered, and so the ultimate cost is not just the financial cost but the cost of the other alternatives foregone. Economists call this the opportunity cost and, while it is not shown by traditional accounting records, it must be considered by the financial manager when making decisions.

Markets are constantly changing. New products, new technology and changing consumer tastes and preferences have meant that firms must continually adapt and change their products to meet current consumer demands, or face extinction. This means that management must always be planning for the future because a firm's cash flow and profits are dependent on the goods and services it produces. Marketing textbooks refer to this as the product life cycle. The model charts the different stages of most products from the introductory stages, through to maturity and eventual decline and termination.

Figure 1:2 The Product Life Cycle

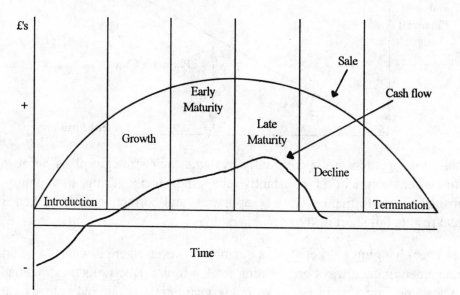

Any firm's profits and cash flows are linked to its product or service mix and their corresponding stage in their life cycle. It is when products are in their maturity stage that they generate their maximum cash flows. During the introductory and decline stages the products can be actual net users of cash because of the high promotional costs of supporting the product in the market

4

place. The key to increasing cash flow and profits is to develop new products which will not only replace existing ones but which have the ability to generate the necessary cash flows to finance further future developments. Figure 1:2 shows the stages in a product life cycle and how a firm's financial fortunes are linked to it.

There is always a danger that, unless new products are launched, the firm will also follow the product life cycle. For many businesses, 80 per cent of sales and profits come from 20 per cent of the products. While the other products are needed to provide a comprehensive product range, their contribution to profits and cash flow is minimal.

Figure 1:3 The Boston Matrix

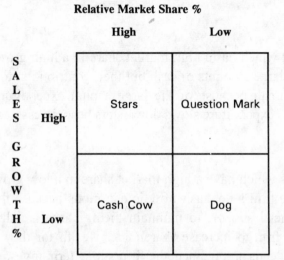

If the business is to survive, new products must be developed and marketed to take the place of those currently producing the company's profits. The aim is to invest the current earnings wisely so that there will always be a stream of new products replacing those at the end of their life cycle.

In recent years there have been two major criticisms of the model. Firstly, the length of the stages in a product's life cycle vary from industry to industry and, secondly, it provides little insight about the competitive processes which accompany the evolution of a market. Whilst there is general agreement that not all products pass through an 'S' shaped curve, its real value lies in making management aware that a firm's profits and cash flows are inexorably linked to effective product management.

Management should think of their current product mix as a portfolio which needs to be managed in terms of the development of new products and the disposal of old ones. The Boston Matrix subscribes to this view for it considers a firm's products as a portfolio instead of a single offering. By viewing products as part of a portfolio, each one can be plotted on a graph to show its growth and profit potential.

The vertical axis shows the market growth rate and the horizontal axis the product's relative market share. By further dividing the graph into four squares, each product can be plotted as a circle with its area being proportional to its sales volume. As a result, each section shows how different products are contributing to the firm's cash flow. Under the Boston Matrix these squares are classified as Stars, Cash Cows, Dogs and Question Marks.

Stars

A star is a product which has a high market share in a high growth market. These products generate large amounts of cash but their contribution to the firm's overall net cash flow is small because of the large capital expenditure which must be undertaken. As this expenditure slows down stars become cash cows.

Cash Cows

These are products which have a high market share in a low growth market. Their contribution to the firm's net cash flow is enormous because their high earnings require little financial support to maintain them. These are the products which should enable the firm to increase shareholder wealth for they produce the cash needed to pay dividends and finance the firm's long term investment plans.

Question Marks

Any product which competes in a big growth market but which has a small market share is called a question mark. These products are net users of cash. The management will have to decide whether it is best to continue to finance the current investment programme in the hope that it will eventually become a star or disinvest.

Dogs

Any product which has a low market share and which is sold in a market which has a slow growth rate is a dog. These generate little cash. Management must decide whether to invest more cash with the aim of securing a high share of the market or to withdraw the product. Dogs tend to arise either when a new brand fails to become established in the market place or when a cash cow's sales fall.

Whilst any firm's financial fortunes are inexorably linked to the effectiveness of its marketing department, it is the financial manager's job to manage and invest these cash flows wisely for the future well being of the business. The key to corporate survival lies in having sound financial management, coupled with a good accounting system, appropriate product range and a committed work force.

Financial Planning

Financial planning is concerned with the overall financial position of the business and the operating results which would be achieved if everything went according to plan. The aim of financial planning is to show the financial results and associated risks from alternative courses of action.

Figure 1:4 The Five Pillars of Financial Planning

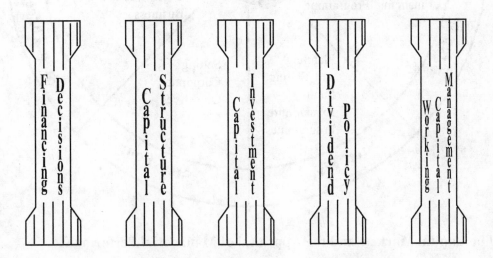

Most financial plans will be prepared to show the long and short term goals for the business. The long term plan will usually be for the next five years, whilst the short term plan will be for the next financial year. The short term plan should show either per quarter or for each month the forecast profit and loss, balance sheet and the projected cash flow position for the business. Management can then evaluate actual performances so that the firm's financial results are consistent with the first year results set out in the five year plan.

FINANCIAL MANAGEMENT

The Eight Stages of Financial Planning

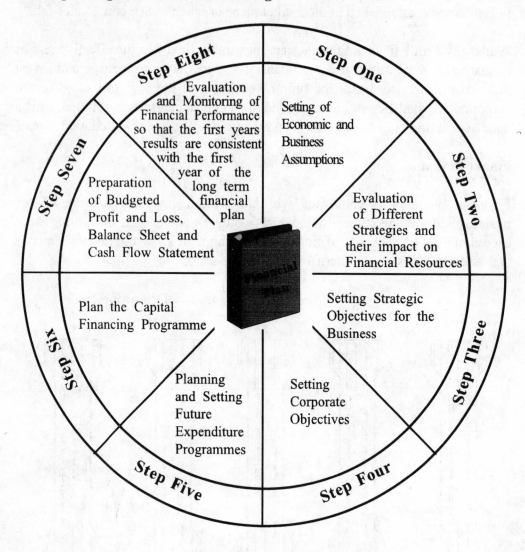

Step Eight — Evaluation and Monitoring of Financial Performance so that the first years results are consistent with the first year of the long term financial plan

Step Seven — Preparation of Budgeted Profit and Loss, Balance Sheet and Cash Flow Statement

Step Six — Plan the Capital Financing Programme

Step Five — Planning and Setting Future Expenditure Programmes

Step One — Setting of Economic and Business Assumptions

Step Two — Evaluation of Different Strategies and their impact on Financial Resources

Step Three — Setting Strategic Objectives for the Business

Step Four — Setting Corporate Objectives

The Capital Markets and the Appraisal of Managerial Performance

In a market economy the shareholders play a key role in providing the necessary capital which finances companies. Whilst the shareholders are the legal owners they delegate the day to day management of their business to a Board of Directors. It is the directors who are accountable to the shareholders and they must by law produce accounts at the end of each year together with a directors' report about the business.

As the shareholders are the owners they need to know whether their business is being effectively managed. From a financial standpoint it is possible to say that a business is well managed if, over time, the wealth of the owners is increased. In a publicly quoted company this will come about in two ways. Firstly, by an increase in the share price and, secondly, by the payment of dividends to the shareholders. This is why many companies set themselves the objective of maximising shareholder wealth.

Investors are only prepared to invest in financial securities because they believe that over time their value will increase. In any economic system resources are limited and capital is a scarce resource. It is important that it is invested wisely so that it will lead to an increase in wealth and living standards for that country's population. In a market economy investors will evaluate different companies, their management and earnings and make their investment decisions accordingly. If a financial manager is to make effective use of the capital markets, then the principles which govern human behaviour and its application to decision making must be understood. There are ten maxims which seek to provide a theoretical framework for understanding the behaviour of investors and collectively they are known as the *principles of finance.*

Self Interested Behaviour

From a financial standpoint the principle merely seeks to establish that each individual to a financial transaction will try to secure the best deal for themselves. It is, therefore, assumed that people do not take into account non financial factors, such as the environment, when making business decisions but simple chose the alternative which will maximise their investment.

Two Sided Transaction

This is very important because there are only four different types of financial transactions and each one is the exact opposite of the other. Whenever goods are bought someone must sell them and, similarly, if someone borrows money another must lend. The principle of two sided transactions is the basis of the double entry book-keeping system which is explained in chapter three. It also explains that if someone makes a profit someone else must have made a loss and it, therefore, follows that one party can only gain at the expense of another. In finance such a transaction is called a zero sum game.

Risk Aversion

Any financial decision exposes its maker to risk but, as a general rule, it is assumed that people prefer the highest return possible coupled with the minimum amount of risk. This is why investors are said to be risk averse, which separates them from risk seekers, such as gamblers and speculators, who are prepared to make financial decisions which expose them to high levels of risk.

Risk Return Trade Off

Ideally investors would like to make high returns whilst exposing themselves to low levels of risk. The principle of risk aversion dictates that those who are prepared to accept high risks expect commensurate returns.

Diversification

This is really the financial equivalent of the old saying 'Don't put all your eggs in one basket'. If investors hold a portfolio of financial securities, such as shares, they will expose themselves to less risk than if they held the shares of just one company.

Incremental Benefit

This principle is very important whenever a financial decision must be made because the important costs and revenues are the ones which will change once the decision is made. This is explained in chapter sixteen.

Capital Market Efficiency

If the capital markets are efficient, the share price will reflect all available information, and so the stock market will have placed an accurate valuation on the security. In the absence of any new information, the share price represents a fair one and price changes will only come about as the market receives new information. The share price in such a market will, therefore, resemble a random walk.

There is a lot of evidence to support the view that the capital markets are efficient and this principle is discussed further in chapter 22.

The Signalling Principle

Information can be conveyed by a variety of means and, when it is communicated by way of actions, it is described as signalling. Actions convey information and so all financial decisions have a signalling effect. For example, if a company borrows money in the capital markets, it signals that it has either found an attractive investment opportunity or that it is short of cash. Investors, therefore, interpret actions and make buying or selling decisions based on the signal which they believe the company has given.

The signalling principle is very important because the actions of individual buyers and sellers of financial securites in the capital markets convey a signal to the issuer of those securities as to the benefits of being a holder. If investors believe that a company has good prospects, they will buy shares in that company but, if it is felt that the management have made wrong strategic decisions or are operating the business inefficiently, they will sell their securities. The collective actions of investors, therefore, appraise a company's management and so changes in the share price act as a signal to managers, lenders and investors.

Valuable Ideas

Inventors of new products and services which are adopted and used by society will earn their owners abnormal returns. Over time these returns will be reduced by competitors so that the owner will only be able to earn a normal return but, in the short-term, these new products and services are said to have an extraordinary positive value. This principle has important implications for financial managers because it shows that shareholder wealth can be increased by investing in new products and services and highlights the importance of investing in research and development.

The Time Value of Money

This principle applies to any investment decision. Money has both an exchange and an earning value because it can be lent, thereby earning interest for its owner. The principle of compound interest holds that interest will be added to capital over time and that the longer the time period the money is lent, the more it will grow. It, therefore, follows that money to be received in the future is worth less because the owner has been deprived of the lost interest. This is known in finance as the principle of discounting.

A business will only be able to increase wealth by investing in projects which can earn a return in excess of the cost of capital which is financing the investment. This is why future cash flows should be discounted so that they take account of the lost interest and therefore, reflect their true value. Investments which can earn a return in excess of their capital cost are said to have a positive net present value and this concept is explained further in chapter 24.

These principles of finance will be referred to throughout this book and explain its format. The first part of the book explains the concept of the two sided transaction, whilst the second section concentrates on the incremental benefit gained from making different financial decisions. The last part of the book considers the other eight principles and how they relate to the work of the financial manager in raising capital, investing it and communicating with investors.

Chapter 2

Recording Financial Information

Introduction

We know from historical records that the early civilisations of the Babylonians and the Egyptians operated a system of recording financial information. While these early systems were important to the merchants of that time, they were not sufficiently advanced to become the foundations of our modern accounting system. Today's methods of recording business transactions are based on the system devised by the Italian merchants. An Italian monk, Pacioli, wrote the first exposition of the double entry method of recording financial information in 1494 and the system has remained unchanged since then.

Although financial management is the study of interpreting and analysing financial data, it is important to understand how financial information is recorded. The main financial statements - the profit and loss account and balance sheet - are prepared from information recorded, using the double entry method of book-keeping.

The Need for Financial Information

The purpose of book-keeping and accounting is to provide financial information about a business. Managers and owners need a wide range of financial information and the accounting system must be such that it shows:

1. whether the business is making a profit or a loss, and whether or not that profit is adequate when one considers the amount of money invested in the business;

2. how much money currently financing the business has been provided by the owners or shareholders and how much has come from outside lenders;

3. whether the business has the ability to repay its short-term and long-term debts (and to pay the necessary interest charges), as and when they fall due for payment;

4. who owes money to the business (debtors) and whether or not the debts are being collected on time;

5. to whom the business owes money for stock which has been bought on credit and how much is owed to each supplier. Management also need to know how long the firm is taking to pay its short-term liabilities (creditors);

6. what the day-to-day running expenses of the business are. Management must know how much money is being spent on electricity, gas, telephone, insurance, wages, rent and whether or not the firm's profit margin is sufficient for the business to be able to meet these costs; and

7. how much money the business has at the bank, where the money has come from and how it has been spent and invested.

The stages of recording financial information are show in figure 2:1 below.

Figure 2:1 Recording Financial Information by the Double Entry Book-keeping System

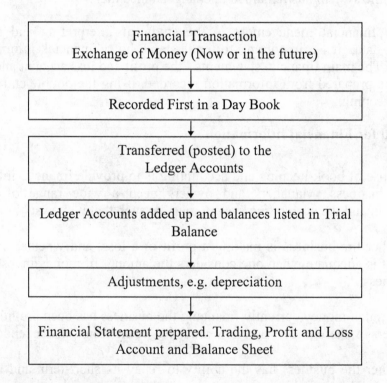

Recording Financial Information

Before explaining the mechanics of the double entry book-keeping system, you need to know what financial records must be kept and the information they contain. With the advent of cheap computing most of this information will now be held on a computer system rather than a manual system.

The Day Books

These are sometimes referred to as the Journals, Subsidiary Books of Account, Books of Original Entry or Books of Prime Entry. The Day Books are used to record daily financial transactions of a business each day. Once this has been done, the transaction is recorded in the firm's ledger accounts.

Figure 2:2 The Day Books

Cash Book	Petty Cash Book	Sales Day Book	Purchase Day Book	Sales Returns Book	Purchase Returns	Journal (Proper)

Sales Day Book: Records goods sold on credit. The book shows when the sale was made, its value, the customer buying the goods and the total credit sales in the accounting period.

Example of a Sales Day Book:

Sales Day Book			
Date	**Customer**	**Folio**	**£ p**
Total			

Sales Returns Book: Sometimes called the Returns Inwards Book. It records the return of goods which had previously been sold to a customer. The goods may be returned because they were faulty or because the goods were sent in error.

Purchases Day Book: Sometimes called the Bought or Day Book. It records goods bought on credit to be resold in the normal course of business.

Example of a Purchases Day Book:

Purchases Day Book				
Date	Supplier	Customer Ref.	Folio	£ p
Total				

Cash Book: Records all cash received and paid out by the business and all payments. The Cash Book will also show money paid into and out of the bank account.

Example of a Two Column Cash Book:

Cash Book							
Date	Transaction	Cash	Bank	Date	Transaction	Cash	Bank
	Records	I N F L O W	I N F L O W		Records	O U T F L O W	O U T F L O W

Note: The two column cash book is just a continuation of the cash and bank ledgers.

Petty Cash Book: This book records small cash payments such as bus fares or payments for tea and coffee.

Example of a Petty Cash Book:

Receipts	Date	Transaction	£ p	Postage	Travel	Tea
£20	3/4	Postage	4.20	4.20		
	5/4	Tea Coffee	2.00			2.00
	6/4	Travel	3.80		3.80	
£20		To Ledger A/C	10.00	4.20	3.80	2.00
£10	6/4	Balance				

Note: Closing Balance = £10.00

The Journal: The Day Book used for recording any transactions which will not fit appropriately into one of the other Day Books, such as correcting errors in the ledger accounts, recording the introduction of new capital and the purchase of assets.

The journal will show the date the transaction took place, which ledger accounts should be debited and credited, the type of transaction invoiced, together with an explanation and the amount of money spent.

Example:

A firm purchased a notebook computer on 1st June for £850. In the journal the entry would be shown as follows:

Journal			
Date	**Detail**	**Dr**	**Cr**
		£	£
1 June	Notebook Computer	850	
	Bank		850
	Bought new computer at Notebook World paid by cheque.		

Once the information has been recorded in the Day Books, it must be posted to the ledger accounts.

The Ledger Accounts

In a manual system, the ledger will either be a large book or a series of loose leaf cards. Today it is far more likely that the information will be stored on a computer disk using one of the many accounting packages which are currently on the market.

Each ledger account only records the financial details of one particular type of transaction. The more financial transactions there are, the more ledger accounts which must be opened. Each ledger account will be given the name of what is being recorded and so the rent will be shown in the rent ledger. Each ledger will show:

1. the date the transaction happened

2. the amount of the transaction in money terms

3. a reference number which can be used to trace the transaction back to the Day Books and, hence, the documentation relating to the transaction

4. the necessary debit and credit entries.

Figure 2:3 A Ledger Account

(Debit) Dr				(Credit) Cr			
Date	**Narrative (details)**	**Folio (reference)**	**£ p**	**Date**	**Narrative (details)**	**Folio (reference)**	**£ p**

Ledger Accounts are often called "T" accounts because they are abbreviated, as in the example below:

Debit	Rent Account	Credit
Dr		Cr

In our examples we will use the simpler T account.

Accountants classify the firm's ledger accounts into different categories. The ledger accounts are split into three sections and these are shown in figure 2:4.

Figure 2:4 Sections of a Ledger Account

Real Accounts	Nominal Accounts	Personal Accounts
Records tangible assets, such as land buildings, motor vehicles and intangible assets such as goodwill. The final balances on these accounts will be shown in the balance sheet.	Records expenses, such as electricity, wages, rent, rates, telephone, travelling expenses. The total balances on these accounts will be shown in the profit and loss account after they have been adjusted for prepayments and accruals.	Records sums of money owed by customers and owing to different suppliers as a result of sales and purchases made on credit. Money owing to the firm is shown as debtors, and money owed as creditors. The total debtor and creditor balances will be shown in the balance sheet.

The Mechanics of Double Entry

The double entry method requires two accounts for each financial transaction. This is why the ledger is divided into two halves. The left hand side of the page is called the debit side and the right hand side the credit side. Double entry involves recording the two parts of every transaction - the giving of a benefit by one party and its receipt by another. The system is a good example of the financial principle called Two-Sided Transaction

The accounting system should be thought of as a camera which takes a picture recording all financial transactions coming into or going out of the business, regardless of whether or not any money is actually exchanged. This is because some goods and services will be bought and sold on credit.

There are only two ways that a business can acquire or sell goods and services and these need to be explained before the transactions can be recorded. Firstly, the goods or services can be bought for cash or they can be acquired on credit. When cash is used to finance the transaction, the firm will gain the benefit of the goods or services bought but will decrease its holding of cash. If they are bought or sold on credit, no money will have changed hands at this point and so the ledger accounts must show either the sum owed to the firm or what is owed to creditors.

The double entry system must record each of these transactions in a way which makes them immediately identifiable, while still only using two sides of the ledger paper. Let us now consider the recording of each of these two transactions in the ledger accounts.

Example:

A firm purchases a van for £1,000 cash from Mr Nawaz on 3rd May.

What has happened?

The business has received a van by giving up some of its cash. The van account has increased while the cash account has decreased.

How is this recorded?

Whenever the transaction involves an exchange of goods or services for money, the account which receives value is debited and the one which gives value is credited.

Which account has received value?

The Van Account has received value because the firm has a van after the purchase and so this account must be debited.

Which account has given value?

The Cash Account has given value because money has been taken from it to pay for the van. The firm's cash deposits have been reduced and this is shown by crediting the Cash Account.

The ledger accounts will now look like this. There must be two accounts to record the two parts of the one transaction.

Van Account and Cash Account

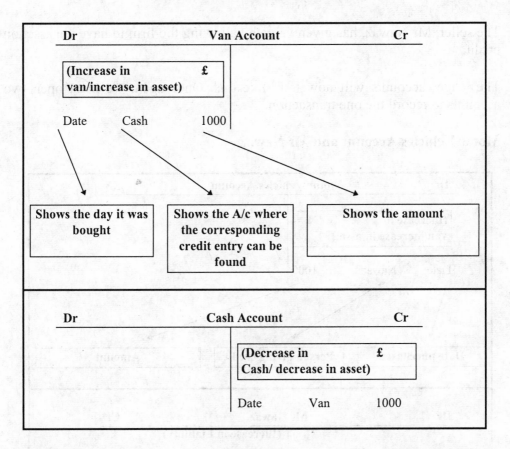

We will now consider the purchase of the van on credit. Let us assume that instead of paying for the asset we are allowed to have them on credit from Mr Nawaz.

How is this recorded?

Whenever the transaction involves an exchange of goods or services on credit, the business which has provided the goods or service is credited and the appropriate goods or service ledger account is debited. In this case Mr Nawaz's account will be credited and the Van Account will be debited.

Which account has received value?

The Van Account has received value because the firm has a van after the purchase. This account must now be debited, even though the goods have not yet been paid for.

Which account has given value?

The seller, Mr Nawaz, has given value by allowing the firm to have the asset on credit.

The ledger accounts will now look like this. Once again we must open two accounts to record the one transaction.

Motor Vehicles Account and Mr Nawaz

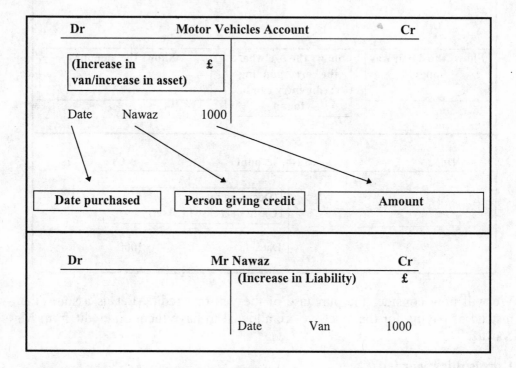

Summary of the Rules of Double Entry

If the transaction refers to:

a)   an increase in an asset expense or loss - **Debit** the asset, expense or loss account.

b)   a decrease in an asset expense or loss - **Credit** the asset, expense or loss account.

Rules (a) and (b) apply for all transactions involving the purchasing of goods or paying for expenses, either by cash or by cheque. Similarly, when goods are sold for cash or a cheque is received, debit the bank or cash account and credit the sales account.

c)   an increase in a liability –**Credit** the liability account.

d)   a decrease in a liability –**Debit** the liability account.

Rules (c) and (d) apply whenever a firm purchases goods on credit, takes out a loan or increases the capital of the business. In such cases the asset or expense gained by the firm will be debited and the account providing the money will be credited.

A Comprehensive Example

Julie Ellis started a floristry business. During the first week of trading the business entered into the following financial transactions:

Day	Transaction
1	Started the business with £5,000 in cash.
2	Bought stock for £100 paid cash.
3	Sold goods on credit to AB Ltd for £150.
3	Bought motor van for £2,000 paid cash.
3	Bought petrol paid cash £15.
4	Bought stock for £50 on credit from JHL Supplies.
5	Paid wages in cash £600.
5	Paid electricity bill £50 cash.
6	Sold goods for £150 received cash.
7	Paid the rent on the shop £500 in cash.

Before posting each transaction to the correct side of the ledger account, it is often best to consider the effect of the financial transaction and which account must be debited and credited.

Date	Effect of the financial transaction	Account to be debited	Account to be credited
1	**Increase in Asset (cash)** **Increase in Liability (capital)**	Debit to Cash Account	Credit Capital Account
2	**Increase in Asset (stock)** **Decrease in Asset (cash))**	Debit Purchases Account	Credit Cash Account
3	**Increase in Asset (debtor)** **Increase Income (sales)**	Debit AB Ltd Account	Credit Sales Account
3	**Increase in Asset (van)** **Decrease in Asset (cash)**	Debit Motor Van Account	Credit Cash Account
3	**Increase in Expense (petrol)** **Decrease in Asset (cash)**	Debit Petrol Account	Credit Cash Account
4	**Increase in Asset (stock)** **Increase in Liability (JHL)**	Debit Purchases Account	Credit JHL Supplies Account
5	**Increase in Expense (wages)** **Decrease in Asset (cash)**	Debit Wages Account	Credit Cash Account
5	**Increase in Expense (elec)** **Decrease in Asset (cash)**	Debit Electricity Account	Credit Cash Account
6	**Increase in Asset (cash)** **Increase in Income (sales)**	Debit Cash Account	Credit Sales Account
6	**Increase in Expense (rent)** **Decrease in Asset (cash)**	Debit Rent Account	Credit Cash Account

While the rules are relatively simple, it takes a while to master the technique of the double entry system. A checklist is provided later in this chapter to act as an aide memoire.

Dr		Cash Account			Cr
Date	**Details**	**Amount [£]**	**Date**	**Details**	**Amount [£]**
Day 1	Capital	5000	Day 2	Purchases	100
Day 6	Sales	150	Day 3	Van	2000
			Day 3	Petrol	15
			Day 5	Wages	600
			Day 5	Electricity	50
			Day 6	Rent	500
	Increase in cash			**Reduction of cash**	

Dr	Capital Account		Cr
	Day 1	Cash	£5000
		Increase in Liability	

Dr	Purchases Account		Cr
		£	
Day 2	Cash	100	
Day 3	AB Ltd	150	
Day 4	JHL	50	
	Increase in Stock		

Dr	AB Ltd Account		Cr
		£	
Day 3	Cash	150	
	Increase in Debtor. Firm owed money therefore an Asset to the firm		

Dr	Van Account		Cr
		£	
Day 3	Cash	2000	
	Increase in Asset		

Dr	Petrol Account		Cr
		£	
Day 3	Cash	15	
	Record of Expense		

RECORDING FINANCIAL INFORMATION

Dr	Wages Account		Cr
	£		
Day 5 Cash	600		
Record of Expense			

Dr	JHL Supplies Account		Cr
			£
	Day 4 Purchases		50
	Increase in Liability. **Goods bought on credit.** **Money still owing.**		

Dr	Electricity Account		Cr
	£		
Day 5 Cash	50		
Record of Expense			

Dr	Sales Account		Cr
			£
	Day 3 AB		150
	Day 6 Cash		150
	Income is always a credit entry.		

Dr	Rent Account		Cr
	£		
Day 6 Cash	500		
Record of Expense			

Balancing the Accounts

As the information is posted to the ledger account, no attempt is made to calculate a final or closing balance on each account. With a manual system this is often done at the end of each month, because of all the work involved. Computerised systems enable the accountant to balance the ledgers quickly and often because computers are excellent at storing and processing large amounts of data.

The Mechanics of Balancing the Ledgers

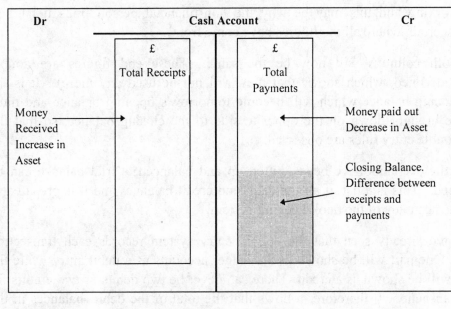

Dr	Cash Account		Cr	
		£		£
Day 1	Capital	5000	Day 2	Purchases	100
Day 6	Sales	150	Day 3	Van	2000
			Day 3	Petrol	15
			Day 5	Wages	600
			Day 5	Electricity	50
			Day 6	Rent	500
		____		Closing balance	1885
		5150			5150
	Opening Balance	1885			

Explanation of Balancing the Cash Account

1. Add up both sides to find the total of each column. One side will have more entries than the other. Do not write down the total yet.

2. Leave a line below the longer column of figures.

3. Insert the larger total at the bottom of both columns.

4. Subtract the smaller number from the larger number and insert the balance in the space which you have left. (Note: accountants do not show any working and this may be why the non-financial person finds it hard to ascertain where all the figures have come from).

5. Both columns will now be the same. (These end figures are double underlined, which shows that they will not be used any more). It is the closing balance which will become tomorrow's opening balance and must be brought down on the opposite side to the closing balance, so that the double entry rules are observed.

Once the accounts have been written up and balanced, a trial balance can be prepared. This is a list of all the debit and credit balances and it is prepared to test the accuracy of the book-keeping system.

We have already seen that the double entry system records each transaction twice. One part will be shown in the ledger accounts as a debit entry while the other will be shown as a credit. There can never be two debits or two credits for one transaction. It therefore, follows that the total of the debit balances in the ledger accounts should be equal to the total of the credit balances. If the totals of the debit and credit balances do not agree, the cause must be found. The main reasons for discrepancy between the debits and credits are listed below:

1. Incorrect addition of the debit and credit columns of the trial balance.

2. A debit balance on one account being entered in error on the credit side of the trial balance and vice versa.

3. Incorrectly recording the amount of a balance in the trial balance.

4. Incorrectly calculating the balance on a ledger account.

5. Not completing the double entry for a transaction.

6. Accidentally recording two debit (or two credit) entries for a transaction.

7. Putting two debits or two credits for one transaction in the ledger accounts.

Trial Balance for Julie Ellis for the First Week of Trading

	Dr £	Cr £
Capital		5,000
Cash	1,885	
Purchases	150	
Petrol	15	
Creditors		50
Debtors	150	
Motor Van	2,000	
Sales		300
Electricity	50	
Wages	600	
Rent	500	
	5,350	5,350

Only now can accounting statements be prepared which will show the firm's assets and liabilities and whether or not a profit or loss has been made during the trading period. Before either of these statements can be prepared, it is necessary to understand the distinction which accountants make between two different types of income and expenditure. These are now explained.

Capital Income

This is income which a business receives on an irregular basis and which is not earned from its normal trading operations. Examples of capital income are funds invested in the business by the owners, or funds it receives in the form of loans. It is also derived from the proceeds of selling fixed assets, such as buildings or plant and machinery.

Revenue Income

Income which is earned by the business on a daily basis, such as income from sales, or income from property (rents received), or income from bank deposits (interest received).

Capital Expenditure

Capital expenditure arises from the acquisition of new fixed assets and its associated costs such as legal expenses or transport costs or from improving the earning capacity of an existing fixed asset. The asset will have a life longer than one year. Capital expenditure enables the firm to earn income because it has invested in long-term assets. An example would be an extension to a factory. The term also applies to the reduction or repayment of loans.

Revenue Expenditure

Revenue expenditure arises from the costs a business incurs when it goes about its normal trading activity, e.g. purchases, rent, electricity, telephone and the maintenance of fixed assets.

Revenue income and expenditure will be recorded in the profit and loss account and capital expenditure will be shown in the balance sheet. In order to calculate whether a business has made a profit or a loss for a particular period, it is necessary to determine the revenue income of the business for that period and to deduct from it the revenue expenditure. Capital expenditure must be separated and will be shown in the balance sheet. Only by keeping records showing the income earned and the costs incurred, is it possible to ascertain whether the business has made a profit or a loss and what assets or liabilities it has. The profit and loss account and the balance sheet are explained in chapter 3.

Ledger Checklist

Recording Liabilities	Debit	Credit
Opening capital	Bank or Cash Account	Capital Account
Additional capital	Bank or Cash Account	Capital Account
Loan	Bank or Cash Account	Loan Account
Repayment of loan	Loan Account	Bank or Cash Account
Owner's drawings	Drawings Account	Bank or Cash Account
Goods bought on credit	Purchases Account	Supplier's Account
Recording Income		
Cash or cheque sales	Cash or Bank Account	Sales Account
Credit sales	Name of Buyer Account	Sales Account
Discount received	Name of Supplier Account	Discount Renewal Account
Rent received	Bank or Cash Account	Rent Received Account
Commission received	Bank or Cash Account	Commission received Account
Recording Assets		
Premises	Premises Account	Bank or Cash Account
Fixtures & fittings	Fixtures & fittings Account	Bank or Cash Account
Plant & machinery	Plant & Machinery Account	Bank or Cash Account
Motor Vehicles	Motor Vehicles Account	Bank or Cash Account
Recording Expenses		
Discount allowed	Discount Allowed Account	Cash Account
Carriage Inwards	Carriage Inwards Account	Cash Account
Wages	Wages Account	Bank or Cash Account
Light & heating	Light & Heating Account	Bank or Cash Account
Postage	Postage Account	Bank or Cash Account
Other Business Expenses	Business Expenses Account	Bank or Cash Account
Carriage Outwards	Carriage Outwards Account	Bank or Cash Account

Trial Balance Check List

Debit	Credit
Bad Debts	Bank Loan
Bank Balance	Bank Overdraft
Carriage Inwards	Capital
Carriage Outwards	Creditors
Cash	Commission Received
Debtors	Debentures
Discount Allowed	Depreciation Provision
Fixtures and Fittings	Discount Received
Heat and Lighting	Interest Received
Investments	Loan
Land and Buildings	Mortgage
Motor Expenses	Ordinary Shares
Motor Vehicles	Preference Shares
Returns Inwards	Reserves
Plant and Machinery	Returns Outwards
Postage	Sales
Purchases	Share Premium
Rates	
Rent	
Stock	
Wages	
Note: Expenses and assets are always debits	**Income and liabilities are always credits**

QUESTIONS

Answers begin page 453

1. Write up the cash book to record the following cash transactions of a small market trader and balance the account for 10 February Year 7.

February		£
1	Opening balance	100
2	Bought stamps	20
3	Cash sales	10
4	Paid rent	15
5	Paid wages	20
6	Bought petrol for van	12
7	Bought office stationery	5
8	Cash sales	30
9	Paid cash into bank	15
10	Cash sales	25

2. Balance the cash book from the information given below:

Cash Book

	£		£
Opening balance	100	Stationery	20
Cash sales	50	Stamps	30

3. Using the spaces provided, write down which account is to be debited and which account should be credited.

		Transaction	Debit	Credit
	a.	Opened a business bank account with cash		
	b.	Bought stationery by cheque		
	c.	Bought stock by cash		
	d.	Sold stock and received payment in cash		
	e.	Bought motor van paid by cheque		
	f.	Bought stock by cheque		
	g.	Bought petrol for van with cash		
	h.	Withdrew cash from the business		
	i.	Sold goods on credit to R. Khan		
	j.	Paid insurance by cheque		
	k.	Paid rent by cheque		

4. Using the spaces provided, write down which account should be debited and credited.

		Transaction	Debit	Credit
	a.	Started a business with £1,000 in cash		
	b.	Opened a business bank account with £500		
	c.	Bought stock for £300, paid by cheque		
	d.	Sold some stock for £200 and was paid in cash		
	e.	Bought a business computer for £600, paid by cheque		
	f.	Sold some stock for £100 received cheque		
	g.	Bought stationery for £50 cash		
	h.	Paid £500 cash into the business		
	i.	Withdrew £30 from the business bank account		
	j.	Paid cleaner £5 in cash		

RECORDING FINANCIAL INFORMATION

5. Complete the following table by stating the type of account which has been affected by the transaction and how it should be recorded in the ledgers. An example is shown below:

	Transaction	Ledgers	Account	Dr/Cr
a.	Bought office computer paid cash	Computer Cash	Real Real	Debit Credit
b.	Paid £50 cash into bank account			
c.	Bought stock on credit from GH Ltd			
d.	Paid wages by writing a cheque			
e.	Bought new premises paid by cheque			
f.	Sold goods for cash to D Patel			
g.	Paid telephone bill with cash			
h.	Bought office computer on credit from KL Supplies			
i.	Sold goods on credit to H Ltd			
j.	Bought stock paid cash			
k.	Withdrew £30 cash from bank account			
l.	Paid insurance by cheque			
m.	Sold office typewriter for cash			

6. In a trial balance, state whether the following balances would be shown as debits or credits.

	Transaction	Debit	Credit
a.	Sales		
b.	Commission received		
c.	Motor vehicles		
d.	Opening stock		
e.	Provision for depreciation		
f.	Bank loan		
g.	Freehold premises		
h.	Purchases		
i.	Drawings		
j.	Office furniture		
k.	Insurance		
l.	Cash		
m.	Carriage inwards		
n.	Carriage outwards		
o.	Office wages		
p.	Warehouse wages		
q.	Debtors		
r.	Returns inwards		
s.	Returns outwards		
t.	Rent and rates		
u.	Debenture		
v.	Plant and machinery		
w.	Light and heating		
x.	Telephone charges		
y.	Motor vehicle repairs		
z.	Capital		

7. Brian Hawkins has been in business for one year selling a range of hand tools. Unfortunately he has not kept a record of the amount of money which he has invested in the business. He has extracted a list of ledger balances but has sent them to you because they do not balance. Using the information below, draw up the firm's Trial Balance for 5 April year 1 and calculate its capital.

	£
Sales	45,890
Commission received	1,540
Freehold premises	73,000
Purchases	22,583
Motor van	800
Heat and light	300
Wages	7,000
Carriage inwards	200
Office cleaning	340
Rent and rates	1,350
Discount received	400
Discount allowed	230
Fixtures and fittings	2,560
Debtors	8,300
Creditors	22,000
Bank loan	1,500
Motor expenses	400
Returns inwards	100
Capital	?

Chapter 3

Understanding Financial Statements

Introduction

Once a year all businesses must produce a set of accounts which show the profit
or loss from trading activities together with a statement of assets and liabilities.
These two financial statements are often referred to as a set of annual accounts.
The profit and loss account will show the profit or loss made during the last
financial year and the balance sheet will show the firm's assets and liabilities at
the year end.

These two financial statements seek to summarise the day-to-day business
transactions, thereby showing the overall financial position at a particular date.
In this way the financial data describes the business just as an ordnance survey
map portrays a picture of the countryside, by using a variety of symbols. The
key to mastering finance is first to understand the meaning of these two
accounting statements.

The Profit and Loss Account

People start businesses for a variety of reasons. They all believe that they can
sell their product or service at a profit, but they need to know how much profit
they are making. During the year stock is purchased and sold and expenses are
paid without the owner being certain how much profit is being made. The profit
and loss account summarises all these transactions into a single statement. It
shows the gross profit made before expenses are paid and the net profit after
they are paid.

What is Profit?

Profit is the money surplus made from selling a product or service for more than
it originally cost. The profit will be used to pay the business costs, pay a return
to the people who have financed the firm and provide funds which can be reinvested to provide the future profits. Profits are, therefore, the life blood of any

37

business, but they should not be thought of as being a cash surplus at the end of a year because the profit and loss account is not prepared on a cash basis. This means that a sale and an expense is recorded as soon as it has been made or incurred, and not when the cash is received or paid. Also in many firms the cash will have been spent either in paying expenses or in acquiring additional assets such as stock. It is for this reason that sometimes profitable firms are forced to cease trading because they have been unable to keep sufficient profits in cash to meet their day-to-day expenses.

How are Profits Calculated

One way of calculating the profit made each year would be to keep a record of all items sold together with the profit margin put on each article or service. At the end of the year the total profit could be added up and the expenses subtracted to yield the annual profit.

While this method would work in theory, it would be impracticable in many businesses. Imagine a modern supermarket checkout person having to record the margin on every item as well as the selling price. It would just take too long and so a simpler method is needed. Provided a record is kept of all stock purchased and all sales, it is possible to calculate the total profit made by subtracting the cost of goods bought from the sales figure.

Figure 3:1 The Calculation of Profit

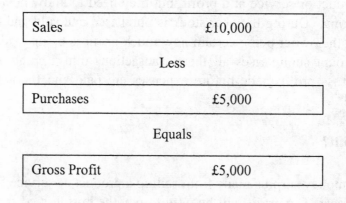

Sales	£10,000

Less

Purchases	£5,000

Equals

Gross Profit	£5,000

In a Profit and Loss Account this would be recorded as:

Profit and Loss for the year ended 5th April Year One

	£
Sales	10,000
Less Purchases	5,000
Gross Profit	5,000

This is a very simple example for it assumes that all purchases are sold during the year. This is unlikely to happen for the end of a financial year must not affect trading. Some stock is likely to remain unsold and must be accounted for.

Cost of Goods Sold

Imagine a sweet shop selling a range of confectionery. The shop's customers always want to be able to buy sweets and so the shop must always carry sufficient stock.

The profit and loss account is drawn up at the end of the shop's financial year. If the owner could so arrange things that on that date all stock had been sold, it would be simple to calculate the cost of the goods sold as it would just be the invoice value of goods purchased. If the owner subtracted this figure from the sales figure, the gross profit or loss could be calculated.

This situation does not often happen because the owner knows that, regardless of the end of the financial year, the shop must be fully stocked so that customers can always buy their sweets. For this reason, there will always be some stock unsold at the end of the year which must be valued and which will be called *closing stock*. The next day, on the start of the new financial year, it will become the firm's *opening stock*. If this closing stock were not included, the profit would be understated for, once this stock is sold, profit will be earned. The stock which has not been sold at the end of the financial year must be valued at the lower of cost or its net realisable value. This means that all firms will apply the same policy when valuing stock. If this were not done, profits could be distorted by applying different valuations to the final stock figure.

In most businesses there will always be some unsold stock at the end of the year which is still of merchantable quality and which can be sold during the following financial year. An adjustment to the year's purchases figure must be made in the accounts, by adding opening stock to purchases and then subtracting closing stock. This will show how much the goods sold during the accounting period actually cost the firm and are shown in the accounts as the cost of goods sold. This information is shown in a trading account which precedes the profit and loss account.

Figure 3:2 Calculating Gross Profit with Unsold Stock Remaining

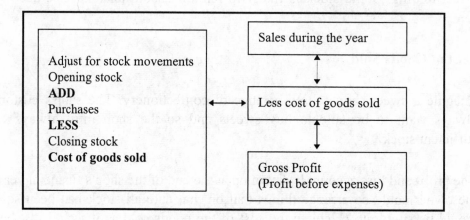

In a Trading Account this would be recorded as:

Trading Account for the Year Ended Year Two

	£	£
Sales		12,000
Opening Stock	1,000	
Add Purchases	5,000	
	6,000	
Less Closing Stock	2,000	
Cost of Goods Sold		**4,000**
Gross Profit		8,000

Note: Arithmetic signs are not shown in the accounts. Instead lines are drawn underneath the figures to be added or subtracted and the total is then displayed to the right. The numbers at the extreme right hand page are always the final figures while the ones to the left show the calculation. Final figures are always double underlined.

Figure 3:3 Flow Diagram of a Trading Account

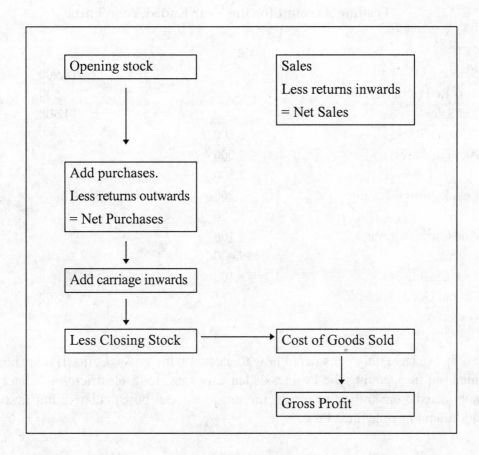

During the year the firm is also likely to have returned some goods to suppliers. These returns are called *returns outwards* and must be deducted from the purchases figure. Similarly, some customers will return their purchases and this will reduce the firm's sales. They are called *returns inwards*.

Whenever goods are bought they must be delivered to the customer. This cost must be paid either by the purchaser (*carriage inwards*) or by the seller (*carriage outwards*). Carriage inwards is shown in the Trading Account and is added to purchases because it has increased the cost of the goods bought. When the firm agrees to pay the delivery cost for the purchaser, the cost, carriage outwards, is shown as an expenses in the Profit and Loss Account and no entry is made in the Trading Account.

Calculating the Gross Profit with Adjustments for Stock Returns

Trading Account for the Year Ended Year Three

	£	£
Sales		15,000
Less Returns Inwards		500
Net Sales		14,500
Opening Stock	1,500	
Add Purchases	4,000	
	5,500	
Less Returns Outwards	200	
	5,300	
Add Carriage Inwards	100	
	5,400	
Less Closing Stock	1,100	
Cost of Goods Sold		4,300
Gross Profit		10,200

So far we have only considered how to calculate the gross profit. If all expenses incurred in operating the business such as wages, rent, electricity and rates are subtracted from the gross profit, the net profit can be calculated, but first any additional income must be shown.

Explanation of Terms - Revenue Income

Discount Received: When a bill is paid early, a sum of money may be offered off the invoice price by the seller as an inducement to pay the bill promptly. Accountants treat this as money earned and call it discount received. It is shown in the profit and loss account as additional income.

Commission Received: Income earned from selling goods on someone else's behalf.

Rents Received: Rental income earned.

Interest Earned: Interest earned on monetary deposits.

Figure 3.4 Calculating Gross and Net Profit

Step 1	**Calculate the Sales Figure**	
	Sales (Less Returns Inwards) =	Net Sales
Step 2	**Calculate the Cost of Goods sold**	
	Opening Stock Add Purchases Less Returns Outwards Add Carriage Inwards Less Closing Stock =	Less Cost of Goods Sold
Step 3	**Subtract Cost of Goods Sold from Sales to Calculate Gross Profits**	
Step 4	**Add Any Additional Revenue Income to Gross Profit**	Gross Profit
	Discounts Received, Commission Received Interest earned Profit on Sale of Fixed Assets	Gross Profit Plus Additional Income
Step 5	**Add up all Expenditure to Calculate Total Revenue Expenditure**	
	Wages Rent Depreciation Carriage Overheads Discounts Allowed etc.	Less Total Expenses
Step 6	**Subtract Total Expenses from Gross Profit Plus Additional Income to Calculate Net Profit**	Net Profit

Example of a Profit and Loss Account for the year ended Year Five

	£	£
Sales		65,000
Less Returns Inwards		1,500
Net Sales		63,500
Opening Stock	7,000	
Add Purchases	20,000	
	27,000	
Less Returns Outwards	400	
Net Purchases	26,600	
Add Carriage Inwards	400	
	27,000	
Less Closing Stock	6,000	
Cost of Goods Sold		21,000
Gross Profit		42,500
Add Discount Received		400
Gross Profit plus Additional Income		42,900

Less Expenses:

Wages	3,000	
Rent	1,000	
Heating	2,000	
Postage and stationery	1,000	
Rates	500	
Travelling expenses	500	
Total expenses		8,000
Net Profit		34,900

If taxation and dividends payments are ignored, the net profit of £34,900 would enable the business to grow because the profit would be kept within the firm. In order to calculate the profit, a time period must be chosen which takes into account the seasonal fluctuations of the trading cycle. For most businesses this is twelve months, although a profit and loss account can be drawn up more frequently to see how the business is performing.

The sales figure in the profit and loss account shows the total sales value of goods delivered to customers. It is the total sum of all invoices during the financial year. Unless the firm is a retailer selling goods only on a cash basis, the sales figure does not represent the amount of cash actually received. Most sales are on credit and so the sales figure simply shows the figure for invoiced goods irrespective of whether the cash has actually been paid.

The profit and loss account shows that the amount of goods sold is not the same thing as the purchases during the year. Similarly, the cash outflow and expenses in the profit and loss account are not the same thing. Some of the purchases are likely to have been made on credit and, at the end of the financial year, they may not have been paid. Any money owed to the business will be shown as a debtor in the balance sheet and any money owed by the business as a creditor.

The Balance Sheet

If we consider our example of the sweet shop, the owner has to have premises, fixtures and fittings, a van, stock and some money for paying the day-to-day expenses. We would expect a sweet shop to possess all of these assets. The balance sheet is simply a statement showing the assets which a business has at a particular time and how they have been financed. It records all capital income (shares and loans) and capital expenditure (fixed assets) and this is why these financial transactions are excluded from the trading and profit and loss account.

The balance sheet gets it name because the total assets must equal the total liabilities and hence the two sides always equal each other, or balance. This is so because the liabilities show where the finance has come from to pay for the assets which have been acquired.

Assets	Liabilities
Possessions which the business needs for trading.	Money financing the business.
Examples: Premises, Fixtures & Fittings, Stock	*Examples:* Owner's Capital, Loans, Creditors

Figure 3:5 The Balance Sheet - Liabilities equal Assets

Balance Sheet (a Business as at Year One)

CAPITAL	FIXED ASSETS
Long-term money used to finance the business. Shown as Share Capital Past Profits Long-term Loans	Assets acquired for long-term use such as buildings, machines and motor vehicles. They are shown in order of permanence and are not primarily for resale. The assets must be shown at their cost price or valuation less depreciation

Assets and liabilities which will have a life longer than 12 months

---

Assets and liabilities which will have a life less than 12 months

CURRENT LIABILITIES	CURRENT ASSETS
Short term liabilities which must be repaid within 12 months. *Examples:* Creditors Bank Overdraft Taxation Owing Dividends	Short-term assets which the business uses to trade and from which it derives its profit. Current Assets are always shown in order of liquidity (how quickly the asset can be turned into cash) with the most illiquid being shown first. The order is stock, debtors, bank and cash balances.
Total Liabilities =	**Total Assets**

Figure 3:6 Horizontal Format of a Balance Sheet

Figure 3:7 Example of Balance Sheet in Horizontal Format as at Year One

CAPITAL	£	£	FIXED ASSETS	£	£
Capital	10,000		Premises	5,000	
Add Profit	9,000		Fixtures	4,000	
	19,000		Motor Car	2,000	11,000
Less Drawings	4,000				
Owner's Equity		15,000			
CURRENT LIABILITIES			**CURRENT ASSETS**		
Creditors		3,000	Stock	4,000	
			Debtors	2,000	
			Bank	1,000	7,000
		18,000			18,000

When a balance sheet is prepared in horizontal format it shows the total assets and liabilities. Sometimes balance sheets are prepared in what is called vertical format. While they still show the assets and liabilities, a different final figure will result, because instead of showing total assets and liabilities, the vertical balance sheet shows the net assets of the business which will equal the capital. Net assets are calculated by adding together the fixed and the current assets and subtracting the current liabilities, thereby showing the net assets owned by the firm.

We have already seen that assets equal liabilities and so the net assets must equal the capital which is financing the firm.

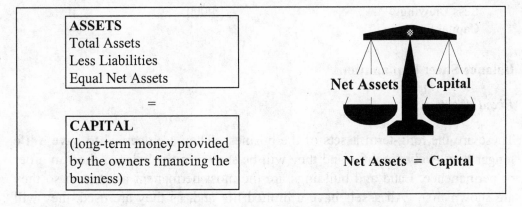

Figure 3:8 Balance Sheet in Vertical Format as at Year One

A balance sheet can be prepared in either horizontal or vertical format. Both are correct but, as a general rule, the horizontal format is used for sole traders and partnerships while most companies prefer the vertical format. This is mainly for presentation reasons as it fits neatly on an A4 page. Some people also believe that the information in this format is easier to understand.

Figure 3:9 Example of Balance Sheet in Vertical Format as at Year One

Fixed Assets	£	£	£
Premises	5,000		
Fixtures	4,000		
Motor Car	2,000		
			11,000
Current Assets			
Stock	4,000		
Debtors	2,000		
Bank	1,000		7,000
			18,000
Less Current Liabilities			
Creditors			3,000
Net Assets			15,000
Capital			
Capital	10,000		
Add Profit	9,000		
		19,000	
Less Drawings		4,000	
Capital Employed			15,000

Balance Sheet Explanation

Fixed Assets

These are the long-term assets of the business. They are deemed to have a life longer than twelve months and they will be shown in the balance sheet in order of permanence. Land and buildings are the most permanent assets and so they are shown first. All assets have a limited life and, as they are used, they will gradually wear out. In recent years buildings have proved to be an exception to this rule for property prices have tended to rise, thereby increasing the asset value of property. Nevertheless old property needs more repairing and so a cost of using the asset should be charged as an expense in operating the business. This cost is called depreciation and will be shown in both the profit and loss account and balance sheet. In the profit and loss account it will be shown as an expense against profit and in the balance sheet it will be shown as a reduction in the asset's value to reflect the cost of its use. Depreciation, therefore, reduces the initial cost of the asset. The cost price of the assets less the total depreciation is referred to as the assets' net book value.

Figure 3:10 Depreciation Shown in a Balance Sheet

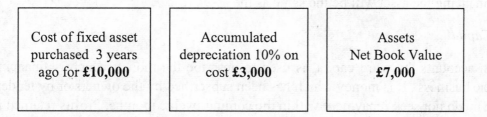

| Cost of fixed asset purchased 3 years ago for **£10,000** | Accumulated depreciation 10% on cost **£3,000** | Assets Net Book Value **£7,000** |

Valuation of Fixed Assets

The balance sheet shows what fixed assets the firm has. Although they will be shown at their cost price, or valuation less depreciation, a balance sheet should not be taken as a guide to the assets' market value. This is because the business is viewed as a going concern, which means that the owners have no intention of ceasing trading and so there is no need to sell the assets and to seek a current market valuation of them.

Current Assets

These are the short-term trading assets of the business. They are shown in order of liquidity. The word liquidity refers to the ease with which the asset can be turned into cash. Stock is the most illiquid asset and so it is shown first.

The word debtor is used to describe someone who owes money to the firm. Most of this money will be owed by individuals and companies who have bought goods on credit. We saw that the profit and loss account shows the total sales from invoices and not the amount of cash received. The balance sheet makes this position clearer by recording, under debtors, the amount of money still owed. This money is expected during the next twelve months, unless a provision for bad debts has been declared, which would reduce the debtors figure in the balance sheet.

Bank and cash balances show the firm's liquid assets at a particular date. They are shown last because they are the most liquid assets.

These then are the assets owned by the firm. How they have been financed will be seen from the other side of the balance sheet. Basically the money will have been provided on a long-term or short-term basis, either by the owners or by lenders to the business. The important thing to remember is that the two sides will always balance because assets must equal liabilities. This is so because the balance sheet shows how the assets have been financed and so the money financing the asset will be the same as the asset.

Capital

In accounts the word capital is used to describe the money which is financing the business. It is money which has been subscribed by the owners or by lenders who do not seek repayment within the coming twelve months. Profits retained in the business will increase the firm's capital just as losses will reduce it.

Drawings

During the year the owner has to pay bills and so s/he takes money out of the business. The amount of money taken out is called drawings and reduces the amount of profit which the business has made. This is why it is not shown in the profit and loss account as an expense, for it is a use of profit. It is shown in the balance sheet because drawings reduce the amount of capital in the business. It is a use of profit which could otherwise be re-invested in the firm.

Current Liabilities

These are short-term debts which the business owes. The money must be repaid within one year from the balance sheet date. If purchases have been made on credit and they have not yet been paid for, then the amount owing will be listed under the heading creditors. Any other money owing because bills have not yet been paid will similarly be shown under this heading as creditors.

Preparation of Final Accounts

By balancing all of the firm's ledger accounts and extracting a Trial Balance the firm's Profit and Loss Account and Balance Sheet can be prepared.

Example   Trial Balance for the Old Sweet Shop as at 31.12 Year Three

	£	£
Creditors		20,000
Sales		50,000
Returns Inwards	2,000	
Opening Stock	3,000	
Purchases	20,000	
Carriage Inwards	1,000	
Returns Outwards		5,000
Discount Received		500
Commission Received		1,000
Rents Received		2,000
Interest Received		500
Wages	2,800	
Discount Allowed	200	
Rent	1,000	
Rates	800	
Bank Interest	400	
Heating	100	
Motor Expenses	400	
Bad Debts	100	
Stationery	300	
Postage	600	
Carriage Outwards	100	
Telephone	200	
Premises	80,000	
Fixtures & Fittings	10,000	
Fixtures & Fittings Depreciation Provision		2,000
Debtors	15,000	
Bank	9,000	
Cash	2,000	
Capital		80,000
Drawings	12,000	
	161,000	161,000

Notes: The firm's closing stock was valued at £5,000. Fixtures and Fittings are depreciated at 10 per cent on cost.

Prepare the Old Sweet Shop's Profit and Loss Account and Balance Sheet for the Year Ending 31st December Year 3.

Before preparing a set of final accounts it is a good idea to remember that it is made up of three parts:

UNDERSTANDING FINANCIAL STATEMENTS

1.   The Trading Account,

2.   The Profit and Loss Account,

3.   The Balance Sheet,

and that it is helpful to write by each item in the Trial Balance where it is recorded. Only closing stock and depreciation will be shown in two of the sections. Closing stock in the Trading Account and the Balance Sheet and depreciation in the Profit and Loss Account and the Balance Sheet.

Creditors	Balance Sheet
Sales	Trading Account
Returns Inwards	Trading Account
Opening Stock	Trading Account
Purchases	Trading Account
Carriage Inwards	Trading Account
Returns Outwards	Trading Account
Discount Received	Profit and Loss
Commission Received	Profit and Loss
Rates Received	Profit and Loss
Interest Received	Profit and Loss
Wages	Profit and Loss
Discount Allowed	Profit and Loss
Rent	Profit and Loss
Rates	Profit and Loss
Bank Interest	Profit and Loss
Heating	Profit and Loss
Motor Expenses	Profit and Loss
Bad Debts	Profit and Loss
Stationery	Profit and Loss
Postage	Profit and Loss
Carriage Outwards	Profit and Loss
Telephone	Profit and Loss
Premises	Balance Sheet
Fixtures & Fittings	Balance Sheet
Fixtures & Fittings Depreciation	Profit and Loss and Balance Sheet
Debtors	Balance Sheet
Bank	Balance Sheet
Cash	Balance Sheet
Capital	Balance Sheet
Drawings	Balance Sheet
Closing Stock	Trading Account and Balance Sheet

A Comprehensive Example:

Trading and Profit and Loss Account and Balance Sheet for The Old Sweet Shop Year Ending 31 December Year Three.

Trading Account

	£	£
Sales		50,000
Less Returns Inwards		2,000
Net Sales		48,000
Opening Stock	3,000	
Add Purchases	20,000	
	23,000	
Add Carriage Inwards	1,000	
	24,000	
Less Returns Outwards	5,000	
Net Purchases	19,000	
Less Closing Stock	5,000	
Cost of Goods Sold		14,000
Gross Profit		34,000

Profit and Loss Account

	£	£
Gross Profit		34,000
Add Discount Received	500	
Commission Received	1,000	
Rents Received	2,000	
Interest Earned	500	
Gross Profit Plus Additional Income		4,000
		38,000
Less Expenses		
Discount Allowed	200	
Wages	2,800	
Rent	1,000	
Rates	800	
Bank Interest	400	
Heating	100	
Motor Expenses	400	
Depreciation	1,000	
Bad Debts	100	
Stationery	300	
Postage	600	
Carriage Outwards	100	
Telephone	200	
Total Expenses		8,000
Net Profit		30,000

Note: Depreciation of Fixtures and Fittings 10 per cent on cost £10,000 = £1,000.

Balance Sheet as at 31 December Year Three

Fixed Assets	Cost/Valuation	Depreciation to Date	Net Book Value
	£	£	£
Premises	80,000	-	80,000
Fixtures and Fittings	10,000	3,000 *	7,000
	90,000	3,000	87,000

Current Assets

Stock	5,000	
Debtors	15,000	
Bank	9,000	
Cash	2,000	
	31,000	

Less Current Liabilities

Creditors	20,000

If applicable Bank Overdraft and Long-term Loans

Working Capital	11,000
Net Assets	98,000

Financed by
Capital

Capital	80,000
Add Profit	30,000
	110,000
Less Drawings	12,000
Capital Employed	98,000

Note: £2,000 depreciation already provided plus £1,000 depreciation for this financial year = £3,000.

QUESTIONS

Answers begin page 456

1. State which of the following would be shown as assets or liabilities in a balance sheet.

		Asset	Liability
a.	Fixtures and fittings		
b.	Debentures		
c.	Prepayments		
d.	Retained profit		
e.	Plant and machinery		
f.	Insurance prepaid		
g.	Stock		
h.	Debtors		
i.	Bank overdraft		
j.	Cash		
k.	Wages owing		
l.	Land and buildings		
m.	Accruals		
n.	Creditors		
o.	Bank loan		
p.	Office computer		
q.	Rent prepaid		

UNDERSTANDING FINANCIAL STATEMENTS

2. Where would one find the following information in a balance sheet?

		Capital	Liability	Fixed Asset	Current Asset
a	Creditors				
b	Premises				
c	Land				
d	Stock				
e	Operating Theatre				
f	Profit				
g	Debtors				
h	Bank Overdraft				
i	Debenture				
j	Hotel				
k	Ambulance				
l	Cash				
m	Machinery				
n	Bank Balance				

3. From the following information calculate the missing figure.

	Capital £	Current Liabilities £	Fixed Assets £	Current Assets £
A	12,500	7,500	15,000	
B		15,000	20,000	10,000
C	30,000		80,000	30,000
D	70,000	45,000	90,000	
E	54,000	28,000		20,000

4.   From the following information calculate the missing figures.

	Capital £	Current Liabilities £	Fixed Assets £	Current Assets £	Net Assets £
A	20,000	10,000	17,500	12,500	
B	80,000	40,000	70,000	50,000	
C	40,000	11,000	25,000		
D		20,000	31,500	25,000	
E	23,000		17,000	12,500	

5.   Calculate the capital for the following firms.

	£	£	£	£
Firm	**A**	**B**	**C**	**D**
Total assets	25,000	40,000	80,000	50,000
Total liabilities	11,000	17,000	50,000	15,000
Capital				

6.   Calculate the amount of capital financing each business.

	£	£	£	£
Firm	**A**	**B**	**C**	**D**
Net Assets	15,000	22,000	37,000	42,000
Capital				

7.   Calculate the capital and net assets for the following different firms from the information given below:

	£	£	£	£
Firm	**A**	**B**	**C**	**D**
Fixed assets	15,000	22,000	30,000	45,000
Current assets	8,000	11,000	14,000	20,000
Liabilities	6,000	9,000	7,000	12,000
Net assets				
Capital				

8.   State whether the following information would be found in a firm's trading or profit and loss account.

	Transaction	Trading Account	Profit & Loss
A	Warehouse wages		
B	Depreciation		
C	Returns outwards		
D	Closing stock		
E	Bank interest		
F	Motor repairs		
G	Heating and Lighting		
H	Bank charges		
I	Motor expenses		
J	Discount allowed		
K	Office cleaning		
L	Carriage inwards		
M	Returns outwards		
N	Insurance		
O	Purchases		
P	Commission paid		
Q	Bad Debts		
R	Returns inwards		
S	Wages		
T	Interest payments		

9. In a set of final accounts state how the following transactions would be classified.

	Transaction	Income	Expense	Asset	Liability
A	Rent received				
B	Rent				
C	Rates				
D	Discount allowed				
E	Premises				
F	Sales				
G	Interest received				
H	Wages				
I	Debtors				
J	Insurance				
K	Loan				
L	Carriage outwards				
M	Laundry expenses				
N	Office cleaning				
O	Cash				
P	Motor van				
Q	Fixtures and fittings				
R	Interest payments				
S	Creditors				
T	Stock				
U	Work in progress				

10. In a set of final accounts state whether the following information would be shown in the trading account, profit and loss account or balance sheet.

	Transaction	Trading Account	Profit & Loss Account	Balance Sheet
A	Carriage Inwards			
B	Debtors			
C	Depreciation			
D	Creditors			
E	Share capital			
F	Debenture			
G	Heating			
H	Wages			
I	Cash			
J	Bank overdraft			
K	Computer			
L	Discount allowed			
M	Returns inwards			
N	Closing stock			
O	Telephone costs			
P	Land & buildings			
Q	Purchases			
R	Returns outwards			
S	Carriage outwards			
T	Premises			
U	Insurance			
V	Advertising			

11. From the following information calculate each firm's net sales.

Firm	A	B	C	D
	£	£	£	£
Sales	45,000	80,000	75,000	65,000
Returns inwards	3,000	8,000	5,000	2,500
Net sales				

12. From the following information calculate each firm's net purchases.

Firm	A	B	C	D
	£	£	£	£
Purchases	23,000	18,500	36,700	43,000
Returns outwards	1,500	2,000	3,400	1,800
Net purchases				

13. From the following information calculate the amount of stock each firm has purchased.

Firm	A	B	C	D
	£	£	£	£
Purchases	15,600	32,400	42,900	37,721
Carriage inwards	500	1,200	1,400	2,000
Returns outwards	1,000	800	700	300
Net Purchases				

14. From the following information calculate each chemist's cost of goods sold.

Chemist	A	B	C	D
	£	£	£	£
Opening stock	4,000	12,000	16,000	24,000
Purchases	9,000	45,000	52,000	70,000
Closing stock	2,000	9,000	12,000	15,000
Cost of goods sold				

UNDERSTANDING FINANCIAL STATEMENTS

15. From the following information calculate each medical centre's profit.

Centre	A	B	C	D
	£	£	£	£
Sales	34,000	89,000	100,000	75,000
Cost of goods sold	14,000	45,000	72,500	35,000
Gross profit				

16. From the following information calculate each firm's cost of goods sold.

Firm	A	B	C	D
	£	£	£	£
Opening stock	15,000	34,000	42,000	56,000
Purchases	35,000	80,000	70,000	90,000
Carriage inwards	7,000	5,000	6,000	8,000
Closing stock	12,000	28,000	35,000	24,000
Cost of goods sold				

17. From the following information calculate each firm's cost of goods sold and gross profit.

Firm	A	B	C	D
	£	£	£	£
Sales	35,000	45,000	84,000	72,000
Returns inwards	2,000	1,000	2,000	1,500
Opening stock	6,000	5,000	14,000	9,000
Purchases	15,000	20,000	45,000	34,000
Carriage inwards	500	800	200	300
Closing stock	4,000	2,000	7,000	6,000
Net Sales				
Cost of goods sold				
Gross profit				

18. Which of the following would be shown as capital expenditure and which as revenue expenditure?

		Capital Expenditure	Revenue Expenditure
a.	Wages		
b.	Purchase of Motor Vehicle		
c.	Office Cleaning		
d.	Factory Extension		
e.	Spare Replacement Engine		
f.	Survey fee for purchase of new office		
g.	Heating and Lighting		
h.	Depreciation of fixed assets		
i	Postage and Telephone		
j.	Leasehold Premises		
k.	Office Carpet		
l.	Insurance		

19. Mountain Biker. Mr Killick set up Mountain Biker this year and has just finished his first year of trading. He has asked you to prepare his trading and Profit and Loss account for the year ending 31 March, year 1.

Trial Balance for the year ending 31 March year 1		
	Dr	Cr
	£	£
Sales		60,000
Purchases	35,500	
Closing stock	7,000	
Wages	10,000	
Light and heating	3,000	
Postage and telephone	1,500	
Cleaning	1,000	
Motor expenses	700	
Repairs to shop	500	
General expenses	800	
	60,000	60,000

63

20. Gardens and Lawns. John Mahoney is a landscape gardener and has just finished his first year in business. He is anxious to know whether or not he has made a profit and has asked you to prepare his Trading Account, Profit and Loss Account and Balance Sheet for the year ending 5 April year 1.

	Dr	Cr
	£	£
Sales		101,160
Purchases	54,225	
Wages	31,230	
Office expenses	4,410	
Motor expenses	2,565	
Office cleaning	855	
Advertising	2,025	
Insurance	1,125	
Capital		20,000
Bank overdraft		7,000
Creditors		14,445
Debtors	46,170	
	142,605	142,605

Closing stock at the year end was valued at £13,275.

Chapter 4

Accounting Concepts and Conventions

Introduction

If every business was allowed to prepare its final accounts based upon its own assumptions it would not be possible to compare one firm's accounts with another for both profits and assets employed could be over or understated. Worse still, firms could change their accounting methods each financial year making it impossible to monitor past performance. This is why there is a need for a conceptual framework for published accounts which covers existing and new developments in financial reporting.

An important part of this regulatory framework is the accounting conventions which have evolved to ensure consistent treatment of financial information. The underlying objective of financial statements is to provide information about a business. This information should be relevant, comprehensible, reliable, complete, timely, comparable and objective. It is, therefore, important that financial statements are prepared in such a way that they can be compared on an equitable basis with those of previous years.

Financial reporting is governed by legislation, financial reporting standards and, where applicable, the requirements of the Stock Exchange. This area of accountancy is constantly changing and it is beyond the scope of this book to explain all of the financial areas relating to the regulatory framework of accounting. This chapter seeks to explain the main accounting concepts and conventions which govern the preparation of a set of annual accounts.

The Need for Accounting Concepts

This is best illustrated by an example:

The Furniture Company and Wooden Furniture Limited are two hypothetical businesses engaged in manufacturing tables. During the last financial year they each bought the same quantity of wood from the same supplier at a cost of £20,000. Both companies made the same number of tables and sold them for £50,000.

The Wooden Furniture Company had collected all of the money from its sales and had paid all of its suppliers. The Furniture Company however at the year end was still owed £2,000 from its debtors and owed £6,000 to suppliers.

The managers of both companies prepared their companies' accounts prior to having them audited but both managed to declare a different profit. This is shown below:

Profit and Loss Accounts for the year ended Year Two for the Furniture Company and Wooden Furniture

Furniture Company	£	Wooden Furniture	£
Cash received from sales	48,000	Actual sales made	50,000
Less cash paid to suppliers	14,000	Less cost of materials used	20,000
Profit	34,000	Profit	30,000

If every business were allowed to prepare its accounts in whichever way they wished, financial statements would be meaningless. With firms using different methods to calculate their profits, inter-firm comparisons would be impossible. The accounting conventions seek to limit this type of situation so that all users of financial information can be assured as to its accuracy and that financial matters have been treated consistently and reliably. The rules which ensure that these standards are adhered to are known as the accounting concepts, principles, postulates, standards or conventions. This chapter seeks to explain the main concepts as they apply to the study of financial management.

The Entity Concept

In accounting a business is always treated as a separate entity from its owners. This is most clearly illustrated in the case of a limited company where the owners (the shareholders) enjoy limited liability status for the debts of the business. If a limited company is forced into liquidation because it has insufficient funds to pay its creditors, the maximum loss which the shareholders can sustain is the value of their shares.

This concept also holds true for sole traders and partnerships. Although in law the business is not treated as a separate legal entity, in accounts the business and the owner are still treated as separate entities. Consider, for example, a small family-owned hairdressing salon called Hair Style. The two owners have subscribed all of the capital and the business has no other shareholders. Nevertheless, the owners' private financial transactions must be kept separate from the business.

The Going Concern Concept

It is a convention that a business will continue unless there is information to the contrary. The owners might be getting close to retirement and may consider ceasing trading, in which case this fact must be shown as a note in the accounts. Otherwise it will be assumed that the business will continue indefinitely. It is this concept which governs the treatment of fixed assets in the final accounts.

An understanding of this concept helps to explain why a business shows fixed assets in a balance sheet at their cost price rather than their current market value. Firms purchase fixed assets with the intention of using them for a number of years. They are not bought with the intention of selling them quickly for a profit and so it is logical to show them at their cost price instead of their market value.

The Money Measurement Concept

The accounts only record items which have a monetary value and so place no value on the non monetary assets of the business such as a loyal workforce or an excellent management team. The money measurement concept also ignores the effects of inflation for assets are shown in the accounts at their cost price. Similarly, liabilities are shown as the amount borrowed or owed and fail to show current purchasing power. This is considered in more detail in chapter 12 which looks at the problems of accounting for inflation.

The Prudence Concept

This concept dictates that when accounts are prepared, which could contain either an optimistic or prudent approach to the presentation of the information, the prudence concept should prevail. A business should recognise losses as soon as the management are aware of them and profits should never be anticipated. For example, if a firm was paid £100,000 for a contract but the management are certain that the final cost will be £120,000, they should charge the £20,000 loss to this year's profit and loss account. If, however, the management believe that the work will be completed for £80,000 then the £20,000 profit should not be shown in the profit and loss account until it has been earned.

The Realisation Concept

As a general rule, a business is said to earn its income, and hence, its profit when a sale is made and the goods are passed to the customer (who then incurs a liability to pay for them). In accounting income is not considered earned just because a customer has placed an order, signed a contract or actually paid for the goods. This is why revenue and profits may only be included in a firm's accounts either when the cash is actually received or the firm is reasonably certain of receiving payment from the person or business owing the money (referred to in accounts as a debtor.). Finally, a provision must be made if it is considered likely that any debtors will not pay their debts and will in fact become bad debts for the firm.

As a result of this concept the profit and loss account shows how much the business has earned from its sales in a particular period and, therefore, supports the accruals concept which states that the firm's expenses must be matched with the income which has arisen from that expenditure.

One disadvantage of the realisation concept is that the profit and loss account may not take account of returned goods for which an allowance has been made in a different accounting period. Although this type of situation may arise, it is unlikely that the amounts involved will be so significant as to materially affect the profit figure, which could mislead users of financial information.

The Accruals Concept

This is a very important accounting concept for it governs the way in which a profit and loss account is prepared. In accounts sales and expenses are shown when the sale is made or the expense incurred and not when the money is received or paid. If a business incurs an expense at the end of its financial year, it will be shown as an expense in the profit and loss account, even though the bill has not yet been paid. The amount owing will then be shown as an accrual or lumped together with creditors and shown as a current liability in the balance sheet. Likewise, any sale made before the receipt of cash will be shown as a sale in the profit and loss account. The amount owed must then be shown as a prepayment or included with the debtors and shown in the balance sheet.

Lastly, any sum of money paid in advance must be deducted from the amount shown in the profit and loss account, for it does not relate to this financial year and must be shown as a prepayment or debtor in the balance sheet.

The Consistency Concept

Once a particular accounting method has been adopted, it should not be changed from one accounting period to another, unless there is a very good reason. For instance the firm may decide to calculate an asset's depreciation on its cost price. If this is done, it is said to be using the straight line method, and so should not alter to another method because it would increase or decrease profits. If a change is made, a note must be made in the accounts stating that a change has been made and the reason for it. Only by applying this concept, can a firm's accounts be compared with previous years' figures.

The Materiality Concept

This refers to the relative importance of an item or an event. Accounts are primarily concerned with significant information and not with those items which have little effect on the financial statements. If a firm decides to purchase some new calculators for £50, a decision must be made as to whether this should be shown as an asset in the balance sheet or just written off as an expense against profit. There is no hard and fast rule. It really depends upon the size of the firm and the amount of the purchase. The materiality concept allows a firm to treat such expenditure as seems most appropriate. Generally an asset will not be treated as capital expenditure if it would be too costly to depreciate it each year and the expenditure would not materially alter the final accounts.

Separate Valuation Principle

This is a new principle introduced by the 1985 Companies' Act which states that when calculating assets or liabilities, which are made up of more than one asset or liability, each must be separately valued or determined before being shown in aggregate in the annual accounts.

By applying these concepts or principles when preparing financial statements, the users can be assured that the accounts have been prepared in a consistent manner. The accounts can then be used for comparative purposes. This information is useful for managers and outside bodies such as investors, trade creditors and bankers who need to assess the firm's financial stability and viability.

This chapter has explained the main accounting concepts and conventions which are part of the conceptual framework of financial reporting. In July 1991 the Accounting Standards Board which took over the role of regulating financial statements from the Accounting Standards Committee has set itself the task of establishing and improving standards of financial accounting and reporting for the benefit of users, preparers and auditors of financial information. This is done by issuing Financial Reporting Standards which are gradually taking over from the Standard Statements of Accounting Practice issued by the former Accounting Standards Committee. The main UK Accounting Standards are listed below and they will be referred to in the following chapters where appropriate.

ACCOUNTING CONCEPTS AND CONVENTIONS

Current UK Accounting Standards

FRS	1	Cash flow statements
FRS	2	Accounting for subsidiary undertakings
FRS	3	Reporting financial performance
FRS	4	Capital instruments
FRS	5	Reporting the substance of transactions
FRS	6	Acquisitions and mergers
FRS	7	Fair values in acquisition accounting
FRS	8	Related party disclosures
FRS	9	Associates and joint ventures
FRS	10	Goodwill and intangible assets

For a comprehensive text on all of these statements and related matters the reader should refer to:

UK Generally Accepted Practice in the United Kingdom, Miles Davies, Ron Paterson and Allister Wilson, published by Ernst and Young.

SSAP	1	Accounting for associated companies
SSAP	2	Disclosure of accounting policies
SSAP	3	Earnings per share
SSAP	4	Accounting for government grants
SSAP	5	Accounting for Value Added Tax
SSAP	8	The treatment of taxation under the imputation system in the accounts of companies
SSAP	9	Stocks and long-term contracts
SSAP	12	Accounting for depreciation
SSAP	13	Accounting for research and development
SSAP	15	Accounting for deferred tax
SSAP	17	Accounting for post balance sheet events
SSAP	18	Accounting for contingencies
SSAP	19	Accounting for investment properties
SSAP	20	Foreign currency translation
SSAP	21	Accounting for leases and time purchase contracts
SSAP	22	Accounting for goodwill
SSAP	23	Accounting for acquisitions and mergers
SSAP	24	Accounting for pensions
SSAP	25	Segmental reporting

QUESTIONS

Answers begin on page 460

1. **R and J Builders**

R and J Builders is a small firm situated in Ludlow. Two brothers, Robert and John Lepley, manage the business. They have submitted their ledgers to their accountant and have written asking for the following matters to be reflected in their final accounts:

a. In May £5,000 was spent on an advertising campaign and we would like to spread this cost over the next three financial years.

b. Our headquarters were revalued in January of this year by a chartered surveyor. When the business was started in 1979 we paid £25,000 for the premises which has now been revalued at £37,000. Is it possible for this gain to be included in this year's profit and loss account?

c. In June of last year we became a subcontractor on a new housing development on the outskirts of Ludlow. Unfortunately planning permission problems has delayed work and, as a result, a loss of £7,000 is expected when the contract is completed during the next financial year. Is it possible to charge this loss to this year's accounts?

As accounts assistant, you have received the following memo:

Memo

To: **Accounts Assistant**
From: **Senior Partner**

I am preparing the accounts for the Lepley brothers and should be pleased if you would draft a letter to them explaining how their proposals must be treated in order that their accounts comply with current accounting concepts and conventions.

2. Executive Stationery Supplies

Anita Sanders has been in business for one year selling office stationery. Last week she received her annual accounts but cannot understand why some expenses have not been shown in the profit and loss account. You are currently working at the store, as part of your work experience, and she has sent you the following memo.

Memo

To: **Trainee**

From: **Anita**

Re: **Annual Accounts**

I need to know why the following information has not been treated as expenses in the firm's profit and loss account:

a.   A van purchased for £12,000 has not been shown as an expense.

b.   My office computer has been depreciated on its cost price, even though I enclosed a note saying that its market value is £200 more than the cost price.

c.   The legal costs of purchasing the shop lease have not been shown in the profit and loss account, even though I sent a copy of the invoice to the accountants.

Chapter 5

Final Accounts - Accounting for Adjustments

Introduction

The two previous chapters have shown the layout and presentation of a profit and loss account and balance sheet together with an explanation of the main accounting concepts and conventions which govern their preparation. This is why a number of adjustments must be made to the firm's profit and loss and balance sheet so that they reflect the main accounting concepts and conventions which are set out in SSAP 2. These are the going concern concept, the consistency concept, the accruals concept and the prudence concept. As a result the final accounts must be adjusted to show the effects of money owing and prepaid, the depreciation of fixed assets and how bad debts are likely to affect the profitability of the business. The aim is to present reliable and relevant information to people who need to use the final accounts for making decisions such as the owners, tax authorities, lenders and suppliers.

Preparation of a Profit and Loss Account and Balance Sheet

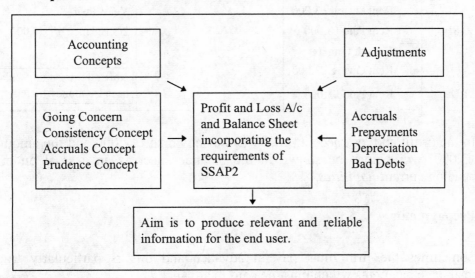

Accrued Expenses

At the end of the firm's financial year some bills may remain unpaid and payment will not be made until the next financial year. The amount of money owing must be added to that already paid and shown first in the profit and loss account and then in the balance sheet as an accrual under the heading current liability. The following example shows how an accrual is shown in the accounts.

The Shoe Shop

The Shoe Shop has just completed its first year of trading in a new shopping centre. The landlord offered an incentive to the new tenant which enabled The Shoe Shop to pay the rent in arrears on a quarterly basis. This can be seen in the diagram below:

	Rent	Rent Account		
1 Jan	**First Quarter**	**Year One**	**£**	**£**
	Rent Owing £3,000	1/4 Bank	3,000	
31 Mar	Rent Paid NIL	1/7 Bank	3,000	
	Second Quarter	1/10 Bank	3,000	
	Rent Owing £3,000	31/12 Balance c/f 3,000		31/12 Profit & Loss 12,000
30 Jun	Rent Paid £3,000		12,000	12,000
	Third Quarter			
	Rent Owing £3,000			**Year Two**
30 Sep	Rent Paid £3,000			2/1 Balance b/f 3,000
	Fourth Quarter			
	Rent Owing £3,000			**Note**: Rent a credit balance because money owing
31 Dec	Rent Paid £3,000			

In the profit and loss account rent will be shown as £12,000 and the amount of £3,000 owing must be shown in the balance sheet as an accrual under the heading current *liabilities*.

Prepayments

Sometimes the firm must pay in advance and this is particularly true of insurance payments which must be paid in advance.

Example:

The Shoe Shop must pay £1,500 per annum for insurance in two half-yearly instalments of £750 in advance starting in January.

Insurance

1 Jan		**First half**
		Insurance paid £750 on 2/1 for period ending 30th June
30th Jun		Insurance paid £750 on 20/6 for period 1st July - 31st December
		Second half
		Insurance paid £750 on 10.12 for period 1st January - 30th June Year Two
31 Dec		

Year One   **Insurance Account**

			£		£
1	Jan	Bank	750	31 Dec Profit & Loss	1,500
20	Jun	Bank	750	31 Dec Balance c/f	750
10	Dec	Bank	750		
			2,250		2,250

Year Two

	£
1 Jan balance b/f	750

When preparing the firm's profit and loss account the prepayment must be deducted from the total amount paid. The profit and loss account will show insurance paid as £1,500. The additional £750 must be shown in the balance sheet as a prepayment under the heading *current assets*.

Accrued Income

A similar adjustment must be made for any income such as rent received in advance or owing. Money received in advance must be deducted from miscellaneous income received and the amount must be shown as a liability under the firm's *current liabilities*.

Similarly any money owed in arrears must be added to the firm's income and shown as an asset in the balance sheet under the heading *current assets*.

Accounting for Bad Debts

Whenever a firm sells goods on credit there is a risk that the buyer will default and never pay the sum owed. This is a loss to the firm for in effect the goods have been given to the buyer. In accounting such a debt is called a bad debt and must be recorded in the ledgers and shown in the profit and loss account.

Example:

The Pasta House supplied a buffet for a local company called Roberts Engineering. The sale was made in accordance with the Pasta House's credit sales policy but it is now six months later and the restaurant owner believes that she has lost £80. She has decided to write the amount off as a bad debt. The accounting entries are:

Roberts Engineering Account

2 Jan	Sales	£80	2 June	Bad Debts	£80

Bad Debts Account

2 June	Roberts Engineering	£80

This bad debt must be treated as any other general expense and must be shown in the firm's profit and loss account. The necessary ledger entries are:

Bad Debts Account

2 June	Roberts Engineering	£80	31 Dec	Profit and Loss	£80

Profit and Loss Account

31 Dec	Bad Debts	£80

If this is the only firm's bad debt then the amount of money shown in the profit and loss account for bad debts will be £80.

Creating a Provision for Doubtful Debts

It is an accounting principle that financial statements should reflect a conservative view of the firm's financial position. This concept is called the Prudence Concept and must be applied to the amount of money invested in debtors as shown in the firm's balance sheet.

At the end of a firm's financial year its unpaid credit sales reflects its investment in debtors and the amount will be shown as a current asset in the firm's balance sheet. Whenever money is owed there is a risk that some of the debtors may not pay and so prudence dictates that a provision should be made for possible non payment. For established firms this is a relatively easy task because doubtful debts generally represent a given percentage of sales. Whatever provision is made it must be shown in the profit and loss account and balance sheet. The necessary accounting entries can be seen in the next example.

H and L Builders

The firm has been trading for ten years but for the last three years the business has been engaged as a sub contractor for some large building companies. As a result the firm has had to give credit. Investment in debtors for the last three years is shown below. H and L Builders always makes a 5 per cent provision for doubtful debts.

31 December	Year 8 [£]	Year 9 [£]	Year 10 [£]
Debtors	20,000	32,000	24,000
5 % provision for doubtful debts	1,000	1,600	1,200
Revised debtors	19,000	30,400	22,800

Between years eight and nine the level of debtors increased and so the firm had to increase its provision for doubtful debts but, as the level of debtors decreased, the business was able to reduce its provision for doubtful debts.

In the ledgers the accounting entries would be shown as follows:

Year Eight

Provision for Doubtful Debts Account

31 Dec	Balance c/f	£1,000	31 Dec	Profit and Loss	£1,000
			Note:	The provision will reduce the debtors figure. Debtors will be a debit entry and so the provision must be a credit entry.	

Profit and Loss Account

31 Dec	Provision for doubtful debts	£1,000

£1,000 must be shown as an expense in the profit and loss account and the firm's debtors must be reduced by £1,000 in the balance sheet.

FINAL ACCOUNTS - ACCOUNTING FOR ADJUSTMENTS

Year Nine

Provision for Doubtful Debts Account

31 Dec	Balance	£1,600	1 Jan	Balance	£1,000
				Profit and Loss	600
		£1,600			£1,600

Profit and Loss Account

31 Dec	Increase in provision for doubtful debts	£600

Note: Between years eight and nine H and L Builders has increased the risk of the business incurring a doubtful debt from £1,000 to £1,600, an increase of £600.

Year Ten

Provision for Doubtful Debts Account

31 Dec	Profit and Loss	£400	1 Jan	Balance b/f	£1,600
31 Dec	Balance	1,200			
		£1,600			£1,600

Profit and Loss Account

31 Dec	Decrease in Provision for doubtful debts	£400

Note: Between years nine and ten H and L Builders has reduced its risk of incurring a doubtful debt from £1,600 to £1,200 a difference of £400. This is why the reduction in the provision for doubtful debts must be shown on the credit side of the profit and loss account.

Bad Debts Received

Sometimes a firm will write off a debt because it believes that as the debtor has been forced into liquidation the sum owed will never be paid. It is the liquidator's task to sell the debtor's assets and use the proceeds to repay the creditors. Usually payments are made based on a percentage in the pound so, for example, the liquidator may pay 10p for every pound owed. When such a payment is received the firm's accounts must be adjusted because if no account was made of this money the firm's profits would be understated.

Example:

The Pasta House was owed £80. When no payment was received within six months the amount was written off as a bad debt. The restaurant has just received £20 from the liquidator as full and final payment. In the firm's ledger the amount will be shown as:

Year Two

Bank Account

1 Sept	Bad debts recovered	£20	

Year Two

Bad Debts Recovered Account

31 Dec	Profit and Loss	£20	1 Sept	Bank	£20

Year Two

Profit and Loss Account

		31 Dec	Bad debts recovered £20

The £20 is additional income for the restaurant and must be shown as an addition to gross profit in the profit and loss account.

Depreciation

Any fixed asset which over time wears out or becomes obsolete, such as a computer, is said in accounting terminology to depreciate. Some assets depreciate more than others. Motor vehicles lose their value quickly whilst buildings depreciate slowly.

If a firm made no allowance for the use of an asset its profit figure would be overstated because no cost would have been charged against profit for the wear and tear of using the asset. This is why a provision for depreciation must be provided for the use of fixed assets. The principle of making a provision for depreciation in the accounts is not to reflect the asset's market value because of the going concern concept, but to ensure that the profit figure is not overstated by charging an amount for its use over the asset's life. There are two main methods. These are the straight line method and the reducing balance method. The consistency concept is applicable to depreciation because the firm should not change its method of depreciation unless there is a very good reason for the change. The matching principle is also relevant because, in using the asset to generate income, costs have been incurred. This reconciles SSAP 12 with SSAP 2.

The Straight Line Method of Depreciation

Whichever method of depreciation is used the firm must know the cost of the asset and make an assessment of its useful life and its possible resale value at the end of its useful life. In accounting this is called the asset's residual value.

The formula for calculating the straight line method of depreciation is:

$$\underline{\textbf{Cost Price less Estimated Residual Value}}$$
$$\textbf{Estimated Economic Life of Asset}$$

Example:

Truck costing	£80,000
Est. Residual Value	£10,000
Expected Economic Life	7 years

Annual depreciation £80,000 - £10,000 = $\dfrac{£70,000}{7 \text{ years}}$ = £10,000 per annum

Reducing Balance Method

This is the second main method for calculating the provision for depreciation. The method calculated the provision for depreciation by spreading the annual amount for depreciation of the diminished value of the asset. This means that the depreciation is calculated on the asset's net book value (cost price less depreciation = net book value). The formula for calculating depreciation is:

$$r = 1 - \sqrt[n]{\frac{s}{a}} \; \times 100$$

where
n = life of the asset
s = residual value
a = cost of the asset
r = rate of depreciation to be applied

Example:

A company purchases a computer for £180,000. The firm's managers have estimated that it will have a life of four years and that its residual value will be £11,250. Calculate the firm's depreciation provision for the next four years.

$$1 - \sqrt[4]{\frac{£11,250}{£180,000}} = 1 - 0.5 = 0.5 \text{ or } 50\%$$

Year One   Depreciation at 50% x £180,000 = £90,000
£180,000 – £90,000 = £90,000 net book value.

Year Two   Depreciation at 50% x £90,000 = £45,000
£90,000 – £45,000 = £45,000 net book value.

Year Three   Depreciation at 50% x £45,000 = £22,500
£45,000 – £22,500 = £22,500 net book value.

Year Four   Depreciation at 50% x £22,500 = £11,250
£22,500 – £11,250 = £11,250 net book value.

The Accounting Entries for Recording Depreciation

Whichever method of depreciation is used, the ledger accounts must show the cost price of the asset and the amount provided for depreciation.

Example:

Memory Lane Antiques has purchased a new delivery van for £11,000. The owners intend to keep the van for 10 years and believe that its residual value will be £1,000. Memory Lane depreciates all motor vehicles using the straight line method. Show the necessary entries in the firm's ledgers.

Motor Vehicles Account

1 Jan	Bank	£11,000		

Provision for Depreciation Account

		31 Dec	Profit and Loss	£1,000
		Note:	Cost price £11,000 less residual value £1,000 = £10,000 ÷10 years = £1,000 depreciation provision per annum.	

The profit and loss account will show £1,000 depreciation as an expense. In the firm's balance sheet at the end of Year One the asset will be shown:

Fixed Assets	Cost [£]	Depreciation to date [£]	Net book value [£]
Motor vehicle	11,000	1,000	10,000

Note: For taxation purposes net book value is sometimes called write down allowance.

Sale of Fixed Assets

Sometimes a firm will sell a fixed asset before it has been used for its estimated full working life. If the sale proceeds do not equal the asset's net book value then the firm will have made either a profit or a loss from the sale. This profit or loss must be shown in the profit and loss account and the asset will no longer appear in the balance sheet. The profit or loss is calculated by the following formula:

Profit/Loss = Selling Price less Fixed Asset's Net Book Value

Example:

MacDonald Engineering

During the last three years the company has bought and sold the following machines:

Year One   1 January bought machine costing £1,800
1 October bought machine costing £1,200

Year Two   1 July bought machine costing £1,100

Year Three   1 September sold machine bought in January year one for £1,800 for £550.

It is company policy to depreciate machinery at 20 per cent on the cost price. Show how these transactions would be recorded in the firm's ledgers.

This information must be recorded in the following ledgers:

Purchase of machinery   -   Plant account.

Depreciation   -   Provision for depreciation account.

Sale of machine   -   Sale of asset account.

Plant Account

Year 1					
1 Jan	Bank	£1,800			
1 Oct	Bank	£1,200	31 Dec	Balance c/d	£3,000
		£3,000			£3,000
Year 2					
1 Jan	Balance b/d	£3,000			
1 July	Bank	£1,100	31 Dec	Balance c/d	£4,100
		£4,100			£4,100
Year 3					
1 Jan	Balance b/d	£4,100	1 Sept	Sale of asset a/c	£1,800
			31 Dec	Balance c/d	£2,300
		£4,100			£4,100

Provision for Depreciation

			Year 1		
31 Dec	Balance c/d	£420	31 Dec	Profit and loss a/c	£420
			Year 2		
			1 Jan	Balance b/d	£420
31 Dec	Balance c/d	£1,130	31 Dec	Profit and loss a/c	£710
		£1,130			£1,130
			Year 3		
1 Sept	Sale of asset	£990	1 Jan	Balance b/d	£1,130
	Balance c/d	£870	1 Sept	Profit and loss a/c	£270
			31 Dec	Profit and loss a/c	£460
		£1,860			£1,860

Note: The calculation of the figures shown in this account are explained after the Sale of Asset Account.

Sale of Asset Account

Sept 1	Plant account	£1,800	1 Sept	Provision for depreciation a/c	£990
				Cash	£550
				Profit & loss (loss on disposal)	260
		£1,800			£1,800

FINAL ACCOUNTS - ACCOUNTING FOR ADJUSTMENTS

Calculation of Depreciation

Year One

Jan 1 Machine £1,800 - held for 12 months.   Depreciation rate 20% =   £360

Oct 1 Machine £1,200 - held for 3 months.   Depreciation rate 20% =   £60

£420

Year Two

Existing machine £1,800 one full year's depreciation at 20%   £360

Existing machine £1,200 one full year's depreciation at 20%   £240

New machine July 1 six month's depreciation at 20%   £100

£710

Year Three

9 months' depreciation on machine sold 20% depreciation on £1,800   £270

12 months' depreciation on remaining machine (£1,200 + £1,100) 20% Dep.£460

Note: Sale of asset = 2 years' depreciation £360 + £360 plus 9 months' depreciation £270 = £990.

All of these adjustments must now be incorporated into the firm's final accounts. How these adjustments affect the preparation of a set of final accounts is shown below.

Example:

Village Farm has just finished its eleventh year of trading. Prepare the farm's trading and profit and loss account and balance sheet for the year ending 31st December Year 11 from the trial balance as at that date.

84

Village Farm, Trial Balance as at 31 December Year 11

	£	£
Bank	2,160	
Fixtures and Fittings	4,080	
Returns Inwards and Outwards	760	500
Travelling Expenses	440	
Leasing Payments	680	
Purchases	72,480	
Land and Buildings	84,000	
Debtors and Creditors	21,400	16,640
Farm Machinery	9,700	
Farm Machinery Provision for Depreciation		970
Bad Debts	240	
Cash	60	
Wages	20,480	
Opening Stock	24,440	
Sales		132,440
Discounts Allowed and Received	2,140	2,310
Heating and Lighting	1,120	
Bad Debt Provision January 1st		1,160
Audit Fee	4,000	
Insurance	840	
Drawings	8,000	
Office Expenses	4,000	
Capital		107,000
	261,020	261,020

Notes to the Accounts

1. Farm machinery is to be depreciated on the straight line basis at the rate of 5 per cent on cost.

2. Closing stock £8,560.

3. Office expenses owing £70.

4. Insurance prepaid £50.

5. The provision for doubtful debts is to be adjusted to 5 per cent of debtors.

6. There were no movements in fixed assets during the year.

Village Farm, Trading and Profit and Loss Account for the year ended 31st December Year 11

	£	£
Sales		132,440
Less Returns Inwards		760
Net Sales		131,680
Opening Stock	24,440	
Add Purchases	72,480	
	96,920	
Less Returns Outwards	500	
Net Purchases	96,420	
Less Closing Stock	8,560	
Cost of Goods Sold		87,860
Gross Profit		43,820
Add Discount Received		2,310
Add Reduction in Doubtful Debts Provision		90
Gross Profit plus Additional Income		46,220
Office Expenses	4,070	
Insurance	790	
Depreciation Farm Machinery	485	
Bad Debts	240	
Travelling Expenses	440	
Leasing Payments	680	
Wages	20,480	
Discounts Allowed	2,140	
Heating and Lighting	1,120	
Audit Fee	4,000	
Total Expenses		34,445
Net Profit		11,775

Village Farm's Balance Sheet as at 31 December Year 11

Fixed Assets	Cost	Depreciation to Date	Net Book Value
	£	£	£
Land and Buildings	84,000	-	84,000
Fixtures and Fittings	4,080	-	4,080
Farm Machinery	9,700	1,455	8,245
	97,780	1,455	96,325
Current Assets			
Stock		8,560	
Debtors	21,400		
Less Provision	1,070	20,330	
Add Prepayments		50	
Bank		2,160	
Cash		60	
		31,160	
Current Liabilities			
Creditors	16,640		
Add Accruals	70	16,710	
Working Capital			14,450
Net Assets			110,775
Capital			
Capital		107,000	
Add Net Profit		11,775	
		118,775	
Less Drawings		8,000	
Capital Employed			110,775

QUESTIONS

Answers begin page 461

1. Prepare the Trading, Profit and Loss Account and Balance Sheet for Woodland Furniture for the year ending 30 September Year 3.

	Dr £	Cr £
Purchases	96,600	
Returns outwards		2,800
Sales		162,740
Returns Inwards	5,200	
Debtors and Creditors	12,800	14,900
Discounts allowed and received	2,480	1,560
Drawings	8,560	
Capital		56,000
Stock	12,260	
Wages	25,640	
Premises	40,000	
Bank	5,620	
Motor vehicles	6,400	
Fixtures and fittings	2,840	
Sundry Expenses	4,620	
Insurance	1,680	
Travelling	6,980	
Advertising	6,320	
	238,000	238,000

Additional Information:

a. Closing Stock £11,160.

b. Provide 10 per cent depreciation on fixtures and fittings and 15 per cent on motor vehicles using the straight line method.

c. Insurance prepaid £80.

2. Prepare RJ Landscape's Trading, Profit and Loss Account and Balance Sheet from the Trial Balance on 31 December Year 3.

	Dr £	Cr £
Capital		35,400
Drawings	8,970	
Furniture and fittings	3,720	
Opening stock	20,100	
Purchases	145,050	
Sales		182,400
Debtors	16,290	
Creditors		14,610
Discount allowed	3,945	
Discount received		2,952
Bad debts	1,701	
Provision for bad debts Jan 1 Year 3		600
Wages	20,340	
Rent	5,247	
Insurance	816	
Advertising	429	
Rates	1,800	
Bank	7,554	
	235,962	235,962

Notes to the Accounts:

a. Closing stock £24,750.

b. Rent owing £600.

c. Insurance prepaid £162.

d. The provision for bad debts to be reduced to £390.

e. Depreciation provision fixtures and fittings £372.

3. From the Trial Balance of Jonquil Fashions on 30 June Year 8 prepare the firm's Trading, Profit and Loss Account and Balance Sheet as at that date.

	£	£
Capital		280,000
Drawings	56,400	
Returns	29,200	24,800
Sales		2,071,600
Purchases	1,473,600	
Opening stock	137,200	
Buildings	184,000	
Furniture and fittings	10,000	
Furniture & fittings depreciation provision		4,000
Cash at bank	70,600	
Cash	5,000	
Discount allowed and received	40,800	33,600
Debtors and creditors	180,000	228,400
Carriage inwards	88,800	
Carriage outwards	41,200	
Wages	144,400	
Advertising	32,400	
Rates	19,600	
Insurance	45,600	
Heating and lighting	66,400	
Stationery and printing	14,400	
Provision for bad debts		800
Bad debts written off	1,600	
Commission received		78,000
Treasury stock 6%	80,000	
	2,721,200	2,721,200

Notes to Accounts

a. Closing stock 30 June year 8 = £127,200
b. Expenses owing - Wages - £7,200, Rates £320
c. Pre-Payments - Insurance £3,600
d. Depreciate Furniture and fittings 10% using reducing balance method
e. Commission received in advance £200
f. Interest owing on treasury stock £4,800
g. Unused stationery £1,000
h. Adjust provision for bad debts to 2% of debtors

Chapter 6

Control Accounts

Introduction

The accounting system must be capable of recording accurately all of the firm's transactions. The largest number of entries during any accounting period will be the record of sales and purchases. The more entries which are recorded the greater the probability that mistakes will be made. Although the trial balance provides a check on the accuracy of the book-keeping system, on a manual system it is produced infrequently and only shows that there is an error somewhere in the system. This is why many firms choose to set up an additional control mechanism.

Control accounts provide a way of checking the accuracy of the firm's sales and purchases. As these accounts have the largest number of entries, a mistake is most likely to be contained in this section of the ledgers. The other accounts usually contain only a small number of entries and so it is a relatively easy task to check their accuracy.

The Book-Keeping System

It is possible to divide a firm's book-keeping system into three sections. These are the record of credit sales, credit purchases and all other transactions. This can be seen in the diagram below:

Figure 6:1 Classification of the book-keeping system

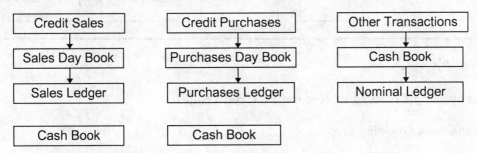

By separating the book-keeping system in this way it is possible to check the accuracy of each section. For instance, if there is no mistake in the credit sales accounting section, then the error must be contained in one or both of the other two sections. Control accounts show the total amount the firm is owed and what it itself owes. The sales ledger control account will show the total debtors figure and the purchase ledger control account the total amount owed to creditors. Control accounts are sometimes called *total accounts* for this reason.

Recording Credit Sales and Purchases

Figure 6:2 Accounting entries to record credit sales and purchases

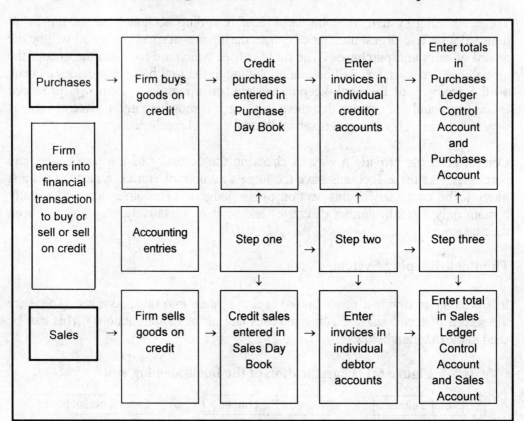

Example

Accounting Entries For Recording Credit Sales

Heating and Plumbing Supplies

In January the following credit sales were made:

January 10	RKL Builders	£4,000
January 16	Therm Heating	£2,000

This information must be recorded first in the firm's Sales Day Book.

This information must be recorded first in the firm's Sales Day Book.

Sales Day Book			
Date	Customer	Reference	£
Jan 10	RKL Builders	RKL/121	4,000
Jan 16	Therm Heating	TH/912	2,000
			6,000

Once the necessary entries have been made in the Sales Day Book the invoices must be recorded in the individual debtors' accounts.

RKL Builders	
	£
Jan 10 Sales	4,000 dr

Therm Heating	
	£
Jan 16 Sales	2,000 dr

The last task is to record the entries in the Sales Ledger Control Account and the Sales Account.

Sales Ledger Control Account	
	£
Sales Day Book	6,000 dr

Sales Account	
	£
Sales Day Book	6,000 cr

Example

Accounting Entries For Recording Credit Purchases

Heating and Plumbing Supplies

In January the following credit purchases were made:

January 7	Building Supplies	£3,000
January 11	Heating Supplies	£1,200

This information must be recorded first in the firm's Purchases Day Book.

Purchases Day Book			
Date	Supplier	Reference	£
Jan 7	Building Supplies	BS/009	3,000
Jan 11	Heating Supplies	HS/006	1,200
			4,200

CONTROL ACCOUNTS

Once the necessary entries have been made in the Purchases Day Book the invoices must be recorded in the individual creditor accounts.

Building Supplies	
	£
Jan 7 Purchases	3,000 cr

Heating Supplies	
	£
Jan 11 Purchases	1,200 cr

The last task is to record the entries in the Purchases Ledger Control Account and the Purchases Account.

Purchases Ledger Control Account	
	£
Purchases Day Book	4,200 cr

Purchases Account	
	£
Purchases Day Book	4,200 dr

The Purchases and the Sales Ledger Control Accounts are updated from the books of prime entry. The Purchase Ledger and Sales Ledger are subsidiary records. Control accounts serve as a check on the arithmetic of the accounting entries. The benefits of using control accounts to trace errors can be seen in the following example.

Example

The Carpet Warehouse

The Carpet Warehouse has just extracted its trial balance but it fails to agree by £234. The accountant believes that the error is in either the sales or purchases ledger and she has decided to prepare control accounts from the following information so that the error can be found.

	£
Purchase Ledger Opening Balance	18,801
Purchases	243,186
Returns Inwards	7,248
Cheques to Suppliers	225,783
Returns Outwards	2,376
Discount Allowed	9,048
Cheques from Customers	283,851
Discounts Received	3,069
Sales Ledger Opening Balance	33,504
Sales	307,239
Balances in Sales Ledger set off against balances in Purchases Ledger	2,157
Bad Debts	651
Dishonoured Cheque	294

The balances on the personal ledgers were:

Creditors £28,602 and Debtors £37,848.

Solution

The Carpet Warehouse

Purchases Ledger Control Account			
	£		**£**
Cash Paid to Suppliers	225,783	Opening Balance	18,801
Returns Outwards	2,376	Purchases	243,186
Discount Received	3,069		
Contra Sales Ledger	2,157		
Balance c/d	28,602		
	261,987		261,987
Sales Ledger Control Account			
	£		**£**
Opening Balance	33,504	Cash From Debtors	283,851
Sales	307,239	Bad Debts	651
Dishonoured Cheque	294	Returns Inwards	7,248
		Discounts Allowed	9,048
		Contra Purchases Ledger	2,157
		DIFFERENCE	234
		Balance c/d	37,848
	341,037		341,037

Note: If a firm buys goods and also sells goods to a supplier it is normal practice to net off the amount owed instead of both parties sending each other cheques for the balance. In accounting this is called a contra entry.

This example shows how control accounts help detect errors and in this case the difference of £234 will be found in the firm's sales ledger.

CONTROL ACCOUNTS

Control Account Check List

Purchases Ledger Control Account	
Dr. Entries	**Cr. Entries**
Personal A/C Debit Balances	Personal A/C Credit Balances
Cash Paid to Suppliers	Total Credit Purchases
Discount Received	Interest on Overdue Accounts
Returns Outwards	
Bills payable	
Sales Ledger Contras	

Sales Ledger Control Account	
Dr. Entries	**Cr. Entries**
Personal A/C Debit balances	Personal Account Credit Balances
Total Credit Sales	Cash From Debtors
Dishonoured Cheques	Discounts Allowed
Interest on Overdue Accounts	Returns Inwards
	Bad Debts
	Purchase Ledger Contra Entries

QUESTIONS

Answers begin page 467

1. What are the main advantages to a business in keeping Control Accounts?

2. From the following information prepare the firm's Sales Ledger Control Account for 31 November Year 7.

		£
Nov 1	Sales ledger debit balance	11,448
Nov 1	Sales ledger credit balance	66
Nov 31	Total transactions	
	Cash received	1,312
	Cheques received	17,717
	Sales	21,270
	Bad debts	700
	Discount allowed	1,112
	Returns inwards	492
	Cash refund	198
Nov 31	Sales ledger debit balance	11,637
	Sales ledger credit balance	120

3. The following balances have been taken from the books of Runa Ltd as at 31 December Year 7.

	£
Sales ledger balances at 1 December Year 7	38,984
Purchase ledger balances at 1 December Year 7	19,200
Sales	183,280
Purchases	148,400
Cash from debtors	168,016
Cash paid to creditors	145,520
Discounts allowed	3,280
Discounts received	2,808
Bad debts written off	120

Prepare the firm's sales and purchases ledger control accounts for the month ended 31 December Year 7.

CONTROL ACCOUNTS

4.   The following balances have been taken from the books of Solfona Ltd as at 31 December Year 6.

	£
Sales on credit	10,032
Purchases	8,796
Opening debtor balances 1 December Year 6	16,068
Opening creditor balances 1 December Year 6	11,274
Returns inwards	378
Returns outwards	222
Cash from debtors	12,912
Dishonoured cheque from debtor	480
Discounts allowed	678
Bad debts	384
Cash paid to creditors	7,776
Discounts received	372
Bills of exchange payable	990

Prepare the firm's sales and purchases ledger control accounts for the month ended 31 December Year 6.

5.   The following balances have been taken from the books of Kalliopi Ltd as at December Year 5.

	£
Sales ledger balances as at 1 December Year 5	32,136
Purchase ledger balances as at 1 December Year 5	22,548
Sales	20,064
Purchases	17,592
Cash from debtors	25,824
Discount allowed	1,356
Bad debts	768
Cash paid to creditors	15,552
Bill of exchange receivable	2,400
Bill of exchange payable	1,980
Discount received	744

Prepare the firm's sales and purchases ledger control accounts for the month ended 31 December Year 5.

Chapter 7

Bank Reconciliation

Introduction

The preparation of a bank reconciliation statement fulfils two important functions. Firstly, it provides a check on the accuracy of the cash book and secondly it shows the amount of available funds at the bank.

All receipts and payments be they in cash or by cheque must be recorded in the cash book. The business therefore, has a record of its transactions with its bankers. The bank will also keep a record of all transactions between itself and the business and will periodically send a statement outlining all transactions. Large companies will require a daily statement but most small and medium sized firms will receive their statement on a monthly basis. As the bank statement is the mirror image of the cash book the two accounting statements should have the same balance. This is rarely the case and so a bank reconciliation statement must be prepared.

Differences Between the Cash Book and the Bank Statement

There are five reasons why the two statements will not show the same balance and they can be put into three categories. Firstly, differences caused by time as when a cheque has not yet been credited or debited to the account. Secondly, an error made either by the bank or the firm in recording financial information. Lastly, errors of omission where the bank has paid a standing order but no entry has yet been recorded in the firm's cash book.

Examples of Differences Between the Cash Book and the Bank Statement

Differences which are time related

Unpresented Cheques: Cheques which have been written, entered in the cash book and sent as settlement of the debt but which have not yet been presented to the bank for payment.

Uncredited Items: Cheques which have been received by the business and entered in the cash book but which have not yet been credited to the firm's account by the bank.

BANK RECONCILIATION

Differences which have been caused by errors

Bank Errors: The bank has made a mistake in the amount debited or credited to the account.

Cash Book Errors: There may be an error in the arithmetic or an entry may have been made on the wrong side of the ledger.

Differences which have been caused by omissions

Omissions: These will be transactions which have been recorded on the bank statement but not in the cash book. They are:

- Interest charged by the bank.
- Bank Charges.
- Standing Orders and Direct Debits.
- Dishonoured Cheques.

Preparing a Bank Reconciliation Statement

The first task is to identify differences between the cash book and the bank statement. If any errors are found they must be corrected and then the cash book must be credited with any unknown payments such as bank charges. Once this has been done a bank reconciliation statement can be prepared. This can be seen in the next example.

Example

Kelso Trading's cash book had a debit balance of £680 but the balance on the bank statement showed a credit balance of £820. On checking the bank statement the following differences were found.

The bank had paid £20 by standing order for a trade journal. No entry has yet been made in the cash book.

The bank has debited the account with a £40 fee for holding documents in its safe and no entry has yet been made in the cash book.

A £400 cheque received on the 30 June from a customer has been entered in the cash book but has yet not been credited by the bank to Kelso's bank account.

A customer has paid £80 into Kelso's bank account but no entry has yet been made in the cash book.

A cheque for £520 drawn on the 30 June and recorded in the cash book has not yet been presented for payment.

From the following information adjust Kelso's cash book and prepare a bank reconciliation statement as at 30 June Year 12.

Solution

Cash Book					
		£			**£**
June 30	Balance	680	June 30	Subscription	20
	Bank Credit	80		Bank Charges	40
				Balance	700
		760			760

Bank Reconciliation 30 June Year Twelve	
	£
Balance as per Cash Book	700
Add Unpresented Cheques	520
	1,220
Less Cheques Not Yet Credited	400
Balance as per Bank Statement	820

In this example the firm had a credit balance at the bank which means that the bank owes the business money. When an account is overdrawn the bank statement will show a debit balance which means that the firm owes the bank money. Whether the bank account is in credit or overdrawn the statement is always prepared in the same format. This is shown in the following diagram.

Bank Reconciliation Arithmetic

Balance as per Cash Book	Add	Unpresented cheques	Less	Cheques not yet credited	Equals	Balance as per Bank Statement

Finally when the bank account is overdrawn the cash book will show a credit balance and so in the bank reconciliation statement the cash book balance will be negative. This can be seen in the example below:

Example

Caprella Limited

On the 31 January Caprella's cash book showed a credit balance of £670 whilst the bank statement showed that the firm's account was overdrawn by £500. A cheque for £300 had not been presented even though it had been recorded in the cash book and a cheque for £130 although entered in the cash book has not yet been credited to the bank account. Prepare the firm's bank reconciliation statement for the 31 January Year Seven.

Solution

Bank Reconciliation Statement 31 January Year Seven	
	£
Balance as per Cash Book	(670)
Add Unpresented Cheques	300
	(370)
Less cheques Not Credited	(130)
Balance as per Bank Statement	(500)

This example shows that care must always be taken when preparing a bank reconciliation statement when the account is overdrawn because an arithmetical error would mean that the cash book could not be reconciled with the bank statement.

QUESTIONS

Answers begin page 469

1. a. State four entries which might appear in a firm's bank statement but which are unlikely to have been recorded in the cash book.

    b. State two entries which should be recorded in the firm's cash book but which may not appear on the bank statement.

2. The cash book of Candmar Ltd had a debit balance of £1,876 on 30 May Year 7. On the same date the firm's bank statement showed a credit balance of £2,248. The following difference has been discovered.

    a. The company deposited cheques worth £628 on 30 May and these have not been shown on the bank statement.

    b. Cheques written and sent to suppliers for £1,052.80 have not yet been presented for payment.

    c. Bank charges of £13.60 appeared on the statement.

    d. The bank has paid £400 by standing order to the General Leasing Company.

    e. £360.80 has been credited to the firm's bank account by the General Mutual Insurance Company as settlement of a claim.

    Required:

    Write up Candmar's cash book and prepare a bank reconciliation statement for 30 May Year 7.

3. The cash book of Nadime Traders had a credit balance of £1,347.60 on 1 June Year 2. The bank statement for the same date showed a debit balance of £7,156.72. On investigation the following difference were discovered.

    a. A cheque sent to a supplier for £4,889.28, although entered in the cash book, has not yet appeared on the bank statement.

    b. Bank charges of £56.40 have not been entered in the cash book.

    c. A debtor has paid £600 direct into the company's bank account.

d. Interest of £2,500 charged on the bank overdraft has been deducted from the company's account but not entered in the cash book.

e. A cheque received from a debtor for £3,060 has been returned by the bank marked Refer to Drawer. No entry has yet been made in the cash book.

f. A cheque received from a debtor for £5,682 has not yet been credited to the firm's bank account although it has been entered in the cash book.

Required:

Show the necessary entries in the firm's cash book and prepare a bank reconciliation statement.

4. The cash book of the Rose Garden had a credit balance of £449.20 on 1 June Year 2. The bank statement for the same date showed a debit balance of £1,392.24. The following differences have been found by the firm's accounts clerk.

a. Two cheques for £1,210.96 and £418.80, although entered in the cash book, have not yet appeared on the bank statement.

b. Bank charges of £78.80 have not been entered in the cash book.

c. A debtor has paid £200 direct into the firm's bank account.

d. A cheque banked for £1,894 has not yet been credited to the account.

e. Interest owed on the bank overdraft £800 has been charged to the firm's account.

Prepared the cash book entries and the bank reconciliation statement to reflect the above information.

Chapter 8

Correction of Errors

Introduction

The accounting system forms an important part of any organisation's management information system and it is vital that this information is accurate. Correct information is essential for managerial control, assessing profitability and decision making. Unfortunately the sheer mass of data which must be processed means that some errors are inevitable. Whether the accounts are held on a manual or computerised system the errors once detected must be located and corrected. The longer the errors remain in the system the greater the risk that wrong decisions will be made and that money will be lost because the amounts owed and owing are incorrect.

The Trial Balance

The trial balance performs a key role in the detection of errors because total debit entries must equal total credit entries. If the two sides do not agree there must be an error in the system. Unfortunately the trial balance does not detect all errors but it provides the first line of defence in error detection.

The trial balance and the detection of errors

There are two types of errors. Those which affect the balancing of a trial balance and those which do not. This can be seen in the diagram below:

Errors and Omissions

Affect Trial Balance	Do not affect Trial Balance
Arithmetic Error	Error of Omission
Only one part of double entry completed	Original Error Reversal of Entries
Wrong calculation of balance brought forward from ledger accounts	Error of Comission Error of Principle Compensating Error

CORRECTION OF ERRORS

Explanation of errors which do not affect the trial balance

Error of Omission:	There is no record in the accounting system of the financial transaction which has taken place.
Error of Original:	The principles of double entry are correct but the transaction has been entered wrongly. For example, £170 has been entered as £710.
Reversal of Entries:	Although the entry has been made in the correct accounts each item has been shown on the wrong side. For example, credit purchases and debit cash account.
Error of Comission:	The correct amount has been posted but to the wrong account. For example, a cheque received from D Brown has been posted to A Brown's account.
Error of Principle:	This type of error occurs whenever revenue expenditure is recorded as capital expenditure or vice versa. Such an error will affect the profit and loss account.
Compensating Error:	This type of error rarely happens in practice but when it does occur the errors cancel each other out and so the trial balance still balances.

Correction of Errors

Final accounts should not be prepared until the trial balance agrees, but practical necessities may mean that the profit and loss account and balance sheet must be prepared before the errors are found. In such cases the difference is placed in a suspense account, thereby making the two sides balance.

A suspense account is opened in the general ledger. Once the errors are found they must be corrected. The first task is to correct the account where the error was made and then make the necessary entries in the suspense account and journal.

Correcting errors requires a thorough understanding of the principles of double entry. The first task is to look at the entries which have been made in the accounts and then work out how these entries should have been recorded. Only then can the relevant accounts be adjusted and the errors eliminated.

The following two examples illustrate the use of suspense accounts and the journal in the correction of errors.

Example

Correction of errors before the preparation of the annual accounts

The Ski Shop

When the trial balance for the Ski Shop was prepared the debit side was £380 greater than the credit side and the difference was posted to a suspense account. It has been decided to find the error before preparing the firm's profit and loss account and balance sheet.

Later the following three errors were found:

1. Purchases for £200 had been debited to Alpine Products Account.

2. The returns inwards account was undercast by £20.

3. Sales for £240 have been debited to Master's Account instead of Bedford's Account.

These errors must now be corrected by making the necessary entries in the firm's journal and suspense account.

Solution

Journal	Dr	Cr
	£	£
Suspense Account	400	
Alpine Products		400
Being the correction of posting £200 debited instead of credited to Alpine Products		

Journal	Dr	Cr
	£	£
Returns Inwards	20	
Suspense Account		20
Being the correction to returns inwards book wrongly cast by £20		
	£	£
Master's Account	240	
Bedford's Account		240
Being the correction of posting to wrong account		

Suspense Account			
	£		£
Alpine Products	400	Difference	380
		Returns Inwards	20
	400		400

Now that the errors have been located and corrected the annual accounts can be prepared.

Sometimes a decision is made to prepare the accounts before the errors have been found. Once the errors have been located the necessary corrections must be made together with any adjustments to the draft profits. This is shown in the next example.

Example

Giralda Trading

Giralda Trading's trial balance does not agree. The debit side is £400 more than the credit side and so the difference has been placed in a suspense account until the errors can be found. A draft profit and loss account has been prepared and it shows that the business made a profit of £30,000.

The following errors have now been located in the accounts and you have been asked to show the necessary entries in the journal and suspense account together with a statement of revised profit.

Errors

1.   Goods sold to AK Ltd for £800 had not been entered in the books.

2.   £300 for the payment of rent had been debited to the rates account.

3.   A motor van for £5,000 had been entered on the debit side of the Motor Van Repair Account.

4.   Cash received from A Patel £150 had been entered in her account as £510.

5. The discount allowed column in the firm's cash book had been undercast by £10.

6. A cheque for £340 from A Walker had been debited to his account as £430.

Solution

Journal	Dr	Cr
	£	£
AK Ltd	800	
Sales Account		800
Entry not written in ledgers		

Journal	Dr	Cr
	£	£
Rent Account	300	
Rates Account		300
Payment of rent wrongly debited to rates account		

Journal	Dr	Cr
	£	£
Motor Van Account	5,000	
Motor Van Repair Account		5,000
Purchase of Motor Van wrongly entered on debit side of Motor Van Repair Account		

Journal	Dr	Cr
	£	£
A Patel	360	
Suspense Account		360
Being the receipt of £150 wrongly credited to A Patel's account as £510		

Journal	Dr	Cr
	£	£
Discount Allowed Account	10	
Suspense Account		10
Being the discount Allowed undercast in Cash Book by £10		

Journal	Dr	Cr
	£	£
Suspense Account	770	
A Walker		770
Being the money received from A Walker £340 wrongly posted to debit side of account as £430. [£340+£430 =£770]		

Suspense Account			
	£		£
A Walker	770	Difference	400
		A Patel	360
		Discount Allowed	10
	770		770

Statement of Revised Profits		
	£	£
Draft profit		30,000
Add Sales	800	
Motor Vehicle	5,000	
	5,800	
Less		
Discount Allowed	10	
		5,790
Adjusted Profit		35,790

It is best practice to find any errors before preparing the final accounts but if this is not possible then the balance on the suspense account must be shown in the balance sheet together with a supporting note to the accounts. It should never be included in the balance sheet as part of the firm's creditors.

However, if it cannot be found, a debit balance should be written off to profit and loss, whereas a credit balance will appear on the balance sheet. This follows the prudence concept.

QUESTIONS

Answers begin page 470

1. Explain the following terms:

   a. Error of omission.

   b. Error of original entry.

   c. Error of principle.

2. State whether the following errors will affect the trial balance.

   a. Error in balancing account.

   b. Error of principle.

   c. Compensating error.

   d. Posting a figure on the wrong side of an account.

   e. Errors in original entry.

3. Show how the following errors would be corrected by journal entries.

   June 1 Motor van repairs of £110 posted to the debit side of Motor Vehicles Account.

   June 7 Discount shown as £200 on the credit side of the Cash Book recorded as a credit in the Discount Allowed Account.

   June 10 The purchase of a van from All Vehicles Ltd by cheque of £3,000.

CORRECTION OF ERRORS

4. The following errors have been found in the accounts of Ashby Traders. Prepare the necessary journal entries.

   a. Cash received from Welcome Stores £200 was entered in the cash book correctly but was wrongly posted to the debit side of their account.

   b. A credit note for £80 issued to Clea Ltd was entered in the firm's Returns Outwards Book.

   c. Sales book overcast by £400.

   d. An invoice for £462 issued to Mansell Traders was recorded in the Sales Book as £426.

Chapter 9

Company Accounts

Introduction

Anyone who has ever looked at a set of company accounts could be forgiven for saying that they can be split into two halves. The first, containing the chair's statement, photographs of directors and buildings, together with graphs showing sales and other financial data, is reasonably comprehensible. The second half, showing the accounts together with the relevant accounting notes, is a complete mystery made even more baffling by the fact that so many numbers seem to balance with each other. Unfortunately it is the second half of the report which contains the annual accounts but, before it can be understood, certain facts relating to companies and their accounts must be explained.

Before studying company accounts, one needs to understand how companies are formed and the legal terminology which applies to them. This chapter seeks to introduce you to the main legal requirements and explains the technical terms relating to company accounts.

Every year companies are required by law to maintain administrative and accounting records, to publish their annual accounts and to send a copy to every shareholder and debenture holder. A copy must also be filed with the Registrar of Companies at Companies' House. The Companies' Act 1985 consolidated the previous acts and lays down what information must be disclosed, how it must be presented and when it must be published.

Many people who decide to start their own business form a company. As a result they range in size from the small family firm, employing a few people, to the large multi-national companies such as Marks and Spencers, ICI and British Petroleum. Although companies differ in size, they all have two things in common. Firstly, they owe their origin to an act of Parliament and, secondly, they must comply with the legal requirements of the Companies' Act 1985 as amended by the Companies' Act 1989.

COMPANY ACCOUNTS

What is a Company?

Companies are an invention of Acts of Parliament. During the 19th century entrepreneurs were forming businesses at a very fast rate but it was felt that their growth could be further increased if two obstacles were removed. The first problem was raising sufficient funds to start. Sole Traders and Partnerships often lacked sufficient capital and found it difficult to raise further capital from outside sources. The second main problem was that the owners were responsible for their business' debts. A business failure could therefore lead to bankruptcy, making many people reluctant to invest in commercial ventures.

In 1855 Parliament sought to remove these two obstacles by creating a new business organisation called the limited company. This meant that the members' liability for company debts would not extend beyond the amount of their shareholdings. This made company shares an attractive form of investment for, although there was risk involved, a shareholder could only lose the monetary value of the shares. Companies could now raise funds from investors who were prepared to accept a limited risk in return for what they considered to be an acceptable return.

Another advantage for the shareholders is that they can delegate the management function to directors who will manage the company on their behalf. The directors are appointed by the shareholders at the firm's annual general meeting and companies are required by law to hold such a meeting of shareholders.

The privilege of limited liability is subject to strict rules and regulations, as laid down in the Companies' Acts. These are designed to protect investors and lenders of money who are not allowed to sue the owners in the case of a company defaulting on its debts.

Different Types of Company

When a company is formed it is said to be incorporated and it may have either limited or unlimited liability. Incorporation means that a company has most of the benefits, rights and responsibilities of an individual in law and is often referred to as being a legal entity. This means that it has an identity of its own apart from the people who own it. This allows the company to make contracts in its own name, employ people and own property. There are two main types of company as defined by the Companies' Act 1985. These are private companies and public companies. There are also companies limited by guarantee and unlimited companies.

A Private Company Limited by Shares

This is the most common type of company and is favoured by many small businesses as it has no minimum requirement for issued share capital.. The owners' liability is limited to the amount of share capital its members have agreed to pay, but the company is not allowed to advertise the sale of its shares to the general public.

A Public Company Limited by Shares

In order to be a public company, a company must be incorporated with a share capital of at least the authorised minimum £50,000 and at least a quarter of this must be paid up when the company is formed. Such companies may raise capital by selling their shares on a recognised stock exchange and have the letters plc in their title.

Before either of these companies can be formed, certain documents must be filed with the Registrar of Companies. The two main documents are the Memorandum of Association and the Articles of Association.

Memorandum of Association

This is a document drawn up by a solicitor which governs the company's dealings with the outside world. It must contain the following information:

a)   the name of the company.

b)   the company's registered office.

c)   the objective of the company.

d)   the amount of the company's share capital.

e)   a statement that the liability of the company's members is limited.

f)   the maximum limit of the company's borrowing powers.

COMPANY ACCOUNTS

Articles of Association

This document covers the internal constitution of the company and must contain the following information:

a)   the rights of different types of shareholders.

b)   how shares can be issued and transferred.

c)   when company meetings must be held.

d)   the powers of the directors.

Once these documents have been submitted, together with the other necessary information, the Registrar will issue a Certificate of Incorporation which gives the company its legal identity. The certificate will show the date of incorporation and the company name. Once a private company has received its certificate of incorporation, it can commence trading, but a public company wishing to raise funds must first issue a prospectus outlining its assets, past profitability and its future prospects so that subscribers can decide whether or not to invest. As soon as the prospectus has been registered and approved a Certificate of Trading will be issued by the Registrar of Companies and the firm can commence trading.

The Published Accounts of Companies

Every private and public company must keep accounting records which will give a true and fair view of its financial position. Once a year it must have its accounts audited and it must send a copy to every shareholder and debenture holder before its annual meeting. A copy must also be kept at its registered office.

The Companies Act 1985 states what information must be included and which accounting statements must be prepared. All public companies must publish a profit and loss account a balance sheet and a director's report. This is the minimum information which must be published, but many public companies use this opportunity as a public relations exercise and publish relevant information about their company, its products and staff. By doing this they seek to make their shareholders, employees and other interested parties more aware about the company and its future developments.

Private companies rarely produce more than the statutory minimum information and are of little interest to outside parties because of the small scale of the business. Larger private companies employing more than five hundred people may attract more attention if it is thought likely that they will consider a stock market listing. If this is the case, the accounts will often be more akin to those of a public company for the directors will wish to gain as much valuable publicity as possible before bringing their company to the Stock Market.

Consolidated Accounts

Companies often expand by purchasing or controlling other companies. Sometimes they will purchase all of the shares, in which case the other company becomes a wholly-owned subsidiary. In other cases, a controlling interest, (over 50 per cent of the voting shares) or a percentage of the shares, will be acquired.

In such cases the accounts must reflect the profits earned by the subsidiaries, and the assets and liabilities which they have. There are two ways that this accounting information could be shown. The first is called the Entity Concept, which treats the minority interests as co-owners and the latter is called the Parent Company Concept, which regards the holding company as the main shareholder.

In Britain the accounts are always prepared under the Parent Company Concept, and the Standard Statement of Accounting Practice 14, (SSAP14) states that, when preparing Consolidated Company accounts they must be prepared to show a true and fair view from the viewpoint of the shareholders of the holding company.

Most large plc's either own or control subsidiaries, and so their accounts always reflect the fact that their profits and assets derive from the holding and subsidiary companies.

The Profit and Loss Account

Companies are not required to publish details of all their expenses against profit but must summarise the main items. In this way, the owners and outside interested parties have access to useful information, whilst not forcing the company to publish material which could be useful to competitors or costly to produce. The following information must be disclosed and the Companies Act

1985 allows two different formats to be used. Whichever one is adopted, it is helpful to classify the information under four different headings as this makes it easier to remember.

1.   Income

The company must provide details about its:

a)   Turnover (sales).

b)   Income from investments.

c)   Rental income received (rents received).

d)   Profit or loss on the sale of fixed assets.

2.   Expenses Against Profit

a)   Staff costs.

b)   Directors' emoluments (income).

c)   Employees' emoluments.

d)   Interest payments.

e)   Hire of plant.

f)   Auditing fees.

g)   Depreciation.

h)   Reduction in the value of investments (write-downs).

3.   Appropriation of Profit (How profit is used)

a)   Taxation (Corporation Tax).

b)   Reduction in goodwill.

c)   Transfer to reserves.

d)   Dividends paid.

4.   Notes to the Accounts

a)   Extraordinary items and abnormal items.

b)   Changes in accounting procedures.

The two formats prescribed by the Companies' Act 1985 are shown below. Format One is the most commonly used and shows cost to sales, whereas Format Two shows changes in stock.

Format One	Format Two
1. Turnover	1. Turnover
2. Cost of sales	2. Change in stock of finished goods and in work in progress
3. Gross profit or loss	3. Own work capitalised
4. Distribution costs	4. Other operating income
5. Administration expenses	5. (a) Raw materials and consumables (b) Other external charges
6. Other operating income	6. Staff costs: (a) wages and salaries (b) social security costs (c) other pension costs
7. Income from shares in group companies	7. (a) Depreciation and other amounts written if tangible and intangible fixed assets (b) Exceptional amounts written off current assets
8. Income from shares in related companies	8. Other operating charges
9. Income from other fixed asset investments	9. Income from shares in group companies
10. Other interest receivable and similar income	10. Income from shares in related companies
11. Amounts written off investments	11. Income from other fixed asset investments
12. Interest payable and similar charges	12. Other interest receivable and similar charges
13. Tax on profit or loss on ordinary activities	13. Amounts written off investments
14. Profit or loss on ordinary activities after taxation	14. Interest payable and similar charges
15. Extraordinary income	15. Tax on profit or loss on ordinary activities
16. *Extraordinary charges	16. Profit or loss on ordinary activities after taxation
17. Extraordinary profit or loss	17. Extraordinary income
18. Tax on extraordinary profit or loss	18. Extraordinary charges*
19. Other taxes not shown under the above items	19. Extraordinary profit or loss
20. Profit or loss for the financial year	20. Tax on extraordinary profit or loss
	21. Other taxes not shown under the above items
	22. Profit or loss for the financial year

* As amended by FRS 3.

The rest of this chapter explains the main terms contained in a set of company accounts. Where appropriate examples have been taken from Boots plc to illustrate how such information is presented.

Example of the Boots Company plc Group Profit and Loss Account for the year ended 31 March 1997

Explanation of the information contained in the Profit and Loss Account.

	Before exceptional items 1997 £m	Exceptional items (note 3) 1997 £m	Total 1997 £m	Before exceptional items 1996 £m	Exceptional items (note 3) 1996 £m	Total 1996 £m
Turnover						
Continuing operations						
- excluding acquisitions	**4,291.8**	--	**4,291.8**	4,010.4	--	4,010.4
- acquisitions	**273.3**	--	**273.3**	--	--	--
Turnover from continuing operations	**4,565.1**	--	**4,565.1**	4,010.4	--	4010.4
Discontinued operation	**12.9**	--	**12.9**	114.3	--	114.3
Total turnover	**4,578.0**	--	**4,578.0**	4,124.7	--	4,124.7
Operating profit						
Continuing operations						
- excluding acquisitions	**496.4**	**8.6**	**505.0**	444.0	12.8	456.8
- acquisitions	**(4.7)**	--	**(4.7)**	--	--	--
Operating profit from continuing operations	**491.7**	**8.6**	**500.3**	444.0	12.8	456.8
Discontinued operation	**0.1**	--	**0.1**	(1.4)	--	(1.4)
Total operating profit	**491.8**	**8.6**	**500.4**	442.6	12.8	455.4
Profit /(loss) on disposal of fixed assets						
Continuing operations	--	**11.3**	**11.3**	--	1.2	1.2
Profit on disposal of businesses						
Continuing operations	--			--	0.2	0.2
Discontinued operation	--	**15.0**	**15.0**	--	--	--
Profit on ordinary activities before interest	**491.8**	**34.9**	**526.7**	442.6	14.2	456.8
Net interest	**44.4**	--	**44.4**	50.9	--	50.9
Profit on ordinary activities before taxation	**536.2**	**34.9**	**571.1**	493.5	14.2	507.7
tax on profit on ordinary activities	**(175.0)**	**(3.3)**	**(178.3)**	(163.4)	(3.7)	(167.1)
Profit on ordinary activities after taxation	**361.2**	**31.6**	**392.8**	330.1	10.5	340.6
Equity minority interests	**0.5**	--	**0.5**	--	--	--
Profit for the financial year attributable to shareholders	**361.7**	**31.6**	**393.3**	330.1	10.5	340.6
Dividends			**(586.1)**			(176.4)
(Loss)/ profit retained			**(192.8)**			164.2
Earnings per share	**39.5p**	**3.4p**	**42.9p**	34.7p	1.1p	35.8p

Explanation of the Main Terms in a Company Profit and Loss Account

1.   Turnover

The total sales (net of returns and taxation including UK VAT) made during the year must be shown, together with information about the source of the sales and the geographical markets where they were made. This latter information may be omitted if the directors believe that it would be against the company's interest, in which case a note must be made in the accounts stating the reason for non-disclosure.

2.   Investment Income

If a company has surplus funds, it may choose to invest them in other companies' shares and fixed interest loan stocks or in Government Securities. If the shares are quoted on a recognised stock exchange, they are referred to as listed investments and, if not, they are called unlisted investments. Short-term deposits refers to cash held in interest-bearing deposits where the money can be withdrawn relatively quickly.

3.   Rental Income

If the company owns any property which it has let during the year, the amount received in rent must be shown as a separate category in the profit and loss account.

4.   Profit or Loss on the Sale of a Fixed Asset

During the financial year, the company may decide to sell certain fixed assets which are surplus to requirements. The profit and loss account must show any profit or loss recorded on the sale of the asset.

5.   Staff Costs, Directors' Emoluments and Employee Emoluments

Staff Costs

The amount paid in wages and salaries to staff, together with social security payments (National Insurance and State Pensions) and any contributions to company pension schemes, must be disclosed.

Directors' Emoluments

The accounts must show the total amount paid to directors inclusive of expenses, pension contributions and benefits, such as company cars. The amount of money paid as pension income to former directors from company pension schemes, together with any amount paid to a director for 'loss of office', must also be shown.

If the amount paid to directors exceeds £60,000 the following information must be shown:

a)   the number of directors whose emoluments fall within the range of £0-5,000, £5,001 - £10,000, £10,001 - £15,000 and so on in bands of £5,000.

b)   the chair's emoluments.

c)   the emoluments of the highest paid director, if they are not the chair, their name does not have to be disclosed.

d)   the number of directors who asked not to be paid any emoluments during the year.

Employee Emoluments

The accounts must also show the number of employees resident mainly in the UK earning over £30,000 a year in bands of £5,000.

6.   Interest Payments

If money is borrowed, interest will have to be paid on the amount borrowed and the total interest payments made must be shown.

7.   Hire of Plant

If any machinery has been hired during the year, the amount paid must be disclosed.

8.   Auditors' Fees

All companies must have their accounts audited. This means that their books of accounts must, with a few exceptions, be checked by either a Chartered or Certified Accountant. The accounts must then be signed by the auditors, subject to any qualification, that the accounts show a true and fair view of the company's financial position.

9.   Taxation

Companies pay Corporation Tax on their profits and are also liable for Capital Gains tax arising out of any monetary gain from the sale of a fixed asset. Firms may mitigate their tax liability by claiming capital allowances from their investment in fixed assets. Deferred taxation reconciles the notional tax in the accounting profit with the actual tax assessment on the taxable profit because not all expenses are tax deductible. The firm may also be able to affect its tax payments by using tax allowances, such as capital allowance relief from investing in fixed assets.

10. Goodwill

Goodwill arises when groups of assets are bought for more than the sum of their market value. The difference between the purchase price and the asset value is called goodwill. Although goodwill is shown as an asset in the balance sheet, firms often seek to reduce the value of this intangible asset by writing it off against profit. The profit and loss account must show any amount written off for goodwill. (see SSAP22).

11. Reserves

A reserve is created whenever profit is kept within the company and is not distributed as dividends to the shareholders. The amount transferred to the reserves must be shown in the profit and loss account and will be discussed further when we look at company balance sheets.

12. Dividends

Dividends represent a share of the company's profits and are paid to the shareholders. There are two types of dividend which may be paid by companies. Preference dividends are paid to the holders of preference shares and these are fixed in advance as a certain percentage, so the holder always knows the amount of money which will be received, provided the company has earned sufficient profit. Ordinary dividends, on the other hand, vary. If profits are good, the dividend may be increased and, if poor, they may be reduced. The amount paid will either be shown in pence per ordinary share, or as a percentage of the company's issued ordinary share capital.

Preference shares carry a fixed rate of dividend and so they are really more akin to a loan stock. Their value will be affected by current market interest rates and the company's overall credit rating.

Large companies often pay an interim dividend before they know their final year's profit and then a final payment once the total profit has been ascertained. This means that a shareholder will receive two payments during the year. If this was not done, a shareholder would have to wait until after the company's year end before receiving a dividend payment. The interim payment acts as a signal that all is well and enables the company to provide the Stock Market with more information about its trading activities.

13. Extraordinary and Exceptional Items

An item is classified as extraordinary when it does not relate to the ordinary activities of the business. In order to be classified as extraordinary, it must derive from events or transactions outside the ordinary activities of the business, be material and must not be expected to reoccur frequently. A good example of an extraordinary item is the profit or loss arising from the sale of a fixed asset.

An exceptional item arises out of the ordinary trading activities of the business. The sum involved must be material and so its non-disclosure would mean that the accounts did not give a true and fair view of the business's financial position. An example of an exceptional item would be reorganisation costs.

The way companies report extraordinary and exceptional items has in recent years been an area of concern because sometimes company directors have chosen to deduct expenditure from the company's brought forward accumulated profits instead of deducting it from the profits of the current year. This practice distorts the profit figure shown in the accounts and presents investors and shareholders with a false profit figure. The practice has become known as reserve accounting and FRS 3 was introduced to present the users of accounting information with a truer and fairer view. As a result of FRS 3 the following information must be disclosed in the profit and loss account after the operating profit and before interest, the profit or losses on the sale or ceasing of operation, the costs of major reorganisation and restructuring, and the profits or losses on the sale of fixed assets.

14.   Changes in Accounting Procedures

A note must be made to the accounts if a change has been made to the accounting procedures in previous years, such as a change in the method of calculating depreciation or valuing closing stocks, and the effect of the change.

Company Balance Sheet

A company balance sheet follows the same principles as any balance sheet in that it shows company assets and liabilities. Companies however, have to show their assets and liabilities in greater detail and the Companies' Act 1985 specifies what must be shown and in what order.

Companies may choose either the vertical or horizontal method of presentation. Today most companies produce their annual accounts in A4 format and therefore choose the vertical format. The horizontal format is now considered old fashioned and in our example we will use Boots plc which has chosen the vertical method of presentation. If the other method is chosen, the information will be the same, although the final figures will differ. This is because the vertical balance sheet will show the net assets equalling capital, whereas the horizontal balance sheet will show total assets and total liabilities. Both answers are correct and the difference in final figures is due solely to the method of presentation adopted.

124

Balance Sheet Format as defined by the Companies' Act 1985

Balance sheet - format 1

A.   **Called up share capital not paid**

B.   **Fixed assets**
I   **Intangible assets**
    1. Development costs
    2. Concessions, patents, licences, trade marks and similar rights and assets.
    3. Goodwill
    4. Payments on account

II   **Tangible assets**
    1. Land and buildings
    2. Plant and machinery
    3. Fixtures, fittings, tools and equipment
    4. Payments on account and assets in course of construction

III   **Investments**
    1. Shares in group companies
    2. Loans to group companies
    3. Shares in related companies
    4. Loans to related companies
    5. Other investments other than loans
    6. Other loans
    7. Own shares

C.   **Current assets**
I   **Stocks**
    1. Raw materials and consumables
    2. Work in progress
    3. Finished goods and goods for resale
    4. Payments on account

II   **Debtors**
    1. Trade debtors
    2. Amounts owned by group companies
    3. Amounts owned by related companies
    4. Other debtors
    5. Called up share capital not paid
    6. Prepayments and accrued income

III   **Investments**
    1. Shares in group companies
    2. Own shares
    3. Other investments

IV   **Cash at bank and in hand**

D.   **Prepayments and accrued income**

E.   **Creditors: amounts falling due within one year**
1. Debenture loans
2. Bank loans and overdrafts
3. Payments received on account
4. Trade creditors
5. Bills of exchange payable
6. Amounts owed to group companies
7. Amounts owed to related companies
8. Other creditors including taxation and social security
9. Accruals and deferred income

F.   **Net current assets (liabilities)**

G.   **Total assets less current liabilities**

H.   **Creditors: amounts falling due after more than one year**
1. Debenture loans
2. Bank loans and overdrafts
3. Payments received on account
4. Trade creditors
6. Amounts owed to group companies
7. Amounts owed to related companies
8. Other creditors including taxation and social security
9. Accruals and deferred income

I   **Provisions for liabilities and charges**
1. Pensions and similar obligations
2. Taxation, including deferred taxation
3. Other provisions

J   **Accruals and deferred income**
Minority Interests

K   **Capital and reserves**

I   **Called up share capital**

II   **Share premium account**

III   **Revaluation reserve**

IV   **Other reserves**
1. Capital redemption reserve
2. Reserve for own shares
3. Reserves provided for by the articles of association
4. Other reserves

V   **Profit and loss account**

Example of Boots PLC Balance Sheet for the Year ending 31 March 1997

	Group 1997 £m	Group 1996 £m	Parent 1997 £m	Parent 1996 £m
Fixed assets				
Intangible assets	33.8	26.6	3.2	2.6
Tangible assets	1,769.7	1,624.4	584.8	205.2
Investments	0.5	46.4	944.3	962.2
	1,804.0	1,697.4	1,532.3	1,170.0
Current assets				
Stocks	667.3	522.1	186.1	168.4
Debtors falling due within one year	347.2	358..9	54537	735.3
Debtors falling due after more than one year	133.2	2.2	293.9	186.0
Investments and deposits	603.0	893.9	584.0	868.6
Cash at bank and in hand	30.9	15.3	119.0	0.1
	1,781.6	1,792.6	1,728.7	1,958.4
Creditors: Amounts falling due within one year	(1,597.2)	(1,092.1)	(1,075.8)	(1,264.1)
Net Current assets	184.4	700.3	652.9	694.3
Total assets less current liabilities	1,988.4	2,397.7	2,185.2	1,864.3
Creditors: Amounts falling due after more than one year	(274.9)	(150.5)	(1,162.5)	(562.5)
Provisions for liabilities and charges	(92.0)	(45.7)	(12.8)	(15.8)
Net assets	1,621.5	2,201.5	1,009.9	1,286.0
Capital and reserves				
Called up share capital	226.5	238.4	226.9	238.4
Share premium account	233.4	226.9	233.7	226.9
Revaluation reserve	351.9	321.4	--	--
Capital redemption reserve	36.8	24.0	34.8	24.0
Profit and loss account	772.7	1,390.8	512.9	796.7
Equity shareholders' funds	1,621.6	2,201.5	1009.9	1,286.0
Equity minority interests	(0.1)	--	--	--
	1,621.5	2,201.5	1009.9	1,286.0

Explanation of the Main Terms in a Company Balance Sheet

Fixed Assets

The Companies' Act 1985 distinguishes between three different types of fixed assets – intangible assets, fixed assets and investments. An asset is classified as a fixed asset, if it is held for use rather than exchange.

Intangible Assets

These are assets which represent money spent by the company to acquire a long-term benefit. They are called intangible assets because they lack a physical identity. Goodwill, development costs, patents and trademarks are all good examples of intangible assets. These assets must be shown in the balance sheet at cost less depreciation. If any fixed asset has been revalued during the year, a note must be made to the accounts and the name and qualification of the valuer, together with the method used to value the asset.

Tangible Assets

These are the long-term assets of the business which have not been purchased primarily for resale and which are needed for carrying out the company's business. In a balance sheet they are shown in order of permanence. These assets must be shown at their cost price or valuation, less any amount charged for depreciation. The accounts will then show the asset's net book value, which is unlikely to be its market value because, as we have already seen, the accounts are prepared under the going concern concept. Examples of fixed assets are land and buildings, plant and machinery and motor vehicles.

Investments

Investments refers to paper assets such as shares, loan stocks or other fiduciary issues. It is the length of time which the company intends to hold these investments which determine whether or not they are fixed assets. If the intention is to keep them longer than twelve months, they are classified as fixed assets and, if they are to be held for a shorter period, they are classified as current assets.

Current Assets

These are the short-term trading assets of the company. They are shown in reverse order of liquidity with the most illiquid shown first.

Stock

If the company is a manufacturing business, the accounts must show the amount of raw materials, work in progress and the stock of finished goods. A retailing business will just show its stock of goods for resale. The stocks must be valued according to the prudence concept, which means that they will be valued at the lower of cost or net realisable value (market price).

Debtors

The amount of money owed to the company within the next twelve months by its trade debtors must be shown, together with any money owed by related companies. This could be net of provision for doubtful debts and discounts allowable, but we do not know as there is no need to disclose this. If the money is to be repaid later than one year from the balance sheet date, the amount must be shown under a separate heading. Examples of such debtors would be money owed by related companies or loans made to directors.

Liabilities

The balance sheet must show liabilities due within twelve months and those due after twelve months.

Creditors and amounts falling due within 1 year

Any money which must be repaid during the next twelve months must be shown in the balance sheet. Examples are trade creditors, bank overdraft, bills of exchange payable, dividends, taxation and any other liability which must be repaid within the coming twelve months.

Creditors and amounts falling due after more than one year

This section will generally show the long-term loans which the company owes, as well as payments for taxation and creditors where the amount paid will be settled after one year from the balance sheet date.

Companies can raise additional funds by selling long-term fixed debt securities to investors. The investor is paid a given rate of interest during the life of the bond and, on redemption, will receive repayment of the loan. These loans may be secured on the company's assets, or they may be unsecured, in which case an investor cannot sell company assets in the event of the firm defaulting on its debts. Examples of such loans are debentures and secured or unsecured loan stock. The balance sheet must show the amount of the loan, the interest rate payable and the date the loan must be repaid, the interest rate and the date of redemption.

Provisions for liabilities and charges

Any amounts of money (provisions) set aside for pension or tax must be disclosed in the balance sheet.

Share Capital

The shareholders are the owners of the business and the amount of share capital which they have subscribed must be stated in the balance sheet. There are a number of terms which relate to share capital and these are now explained.

COMPANY ACCOUNTS

Ordinary Shares

The owners of these shares are entitled to receive a share of the profits after all expenses have been paid. The amount of dividend will vary according to the profits of the firm. Ordinary shareholders are usually entitled to voting rights, although some companies do issue non-voting ordinary shares. If this is done, the shares are generally distinguished by calling one the A shares and the others the B shares. The voting shares are normally more expensive because they allow the holder to vote on issues affecting the company.

Preference Shares

Preference shares also form part of the company's capital. The holders of these shares receive a fixed rate of dividend, once all the expenses have been paid, and often enjoy preferential rights over the ordinary shareholders with respect to dividend payments and when the company is wound up. If the shares are cumulative preference shares, the holders have the right to have any unpaid dividend paid to them as soon as the firm has remade sufficient profits. In such cases, the preference shareholders will receive their dividend, even if other shareholders receive nothing.

Lastly, a firm may have issued participating preference shares. These entitle the holder to receive an extra dividend, once the ordinary share holders have received more than a stated return on the capital and the preference dividend has been paid.

Authorised Capital

This is the amount of share capital a company is authorised to raise when it is first incorporated. The company's memorandum of association must state the number, value and type of shares which the company intends to issue. Once the company is registered, this becomes its authorised share capital, and the amount must be shown in the balance sheet or in the notes to the accounts.

Issued Capital

This is the amount of share capital which the company has issued to shareholders. The amount of issued capital may be less than the authorised capital if the directors believe that they do not yet need to raise the amount of share capital they were authorised to issue.

Called Up Capital

When shares are issued, the purchase price is often not payable in one amount. By allowing the shareholder to pay by instalments, it allows the investor time to either earn extra income or liquidate other investments. When a company asks for the next instalment, it is said to be making a call. The amount of called up and fully paid up capital is the same as the company's issued capital.

Issued and Partly Paid

This term is used to describe shares which have been sold to shareholders but which have not yet been fully paid for. The amount owing will be shown as a current asset in the firm's balance sheet.

Reserves

There are two types of reserves and both belong to the shareholders for they represent either past undistributed profits, or surpluses made and kept within the business.

Revenue Reserve

A revenue reserve arises when an amount of profit is retained within the company. It may be kept for a particular purpose, such as a Foreign Exchange Reserve, or it may be kept for a general purpose, such as a General Reserve. These revenue reserves can be used to pay dividends to the shareholders and are mainly called upon to maintain the dividend payments when company profits fall. With the exception of the profit and loss account, all other revenue reserves have the word *reserve* in their title. The retained profit is treated as a reserve because it represents small amounts of profits which have not been distributed as dividends to the shareholders, but which have been kept within the company. The main reason for this is that there are insufficient profits to pay a reasonable dividend to each shareholder, and so the balance is kept for possible later distribution.

Capital Reserves

A capital reserve cannot be used to make dividend payments to shareholders but the proceeds may be distributed by way of bonus shares and will then rank as equal with the other ordinary share capital. A good example of a capital reserve is the share premium account which arises when shares are sold for more that their nominal value. This surplus is shown as a capital reserve under the heading *share premium*. These reserves are sometimes called statutory reserves.

The Directors' Report and Responsibility Statement

The Companies' Acts have made it a legal requirement for the directors to produce financial statements for each year which give a true and fair view of the company's financial position and its profit or loss. This means that when the accounts are prepared the directors must ensure that they:

1.   use suitable accounting policies and apply them consistently.

2.   make reasonable and prudent judgements and estimates.

3.   apply the relevant accounting standards where applicable or provide information about any material departures from the relevant standard.

4.   prepare the accounts on the going concern basis.

This is why most company accounts now contain a directors' responsibility statement which confirms that the accounts have been prepared according to the Companies' Act 1985.

The directors' report must contain the following information:

1.   **Review of the business** – the principal activities of the company and any changes which have taken place during the year. The report must give a fair review of the company's development during the year and its position at the year end.

2.   **Results and Dividends** – the after tax profit, amount of money transferred to reserves and the recommended dividend.

3.   **Share Capital** – details of the number of transactions in the firm's shares, their nominal value, aggregate consideration and the percentage of the called up capital represented by the shares purchased.

4.   **Market Value of Land and Buildings** – the difference between market value and book value should be shown if it is significant and the directors believe it is of significance to members (shareholders).

5.   **Political and Charitable Contributions** – if the company has donated £200 to charities or political parties it must disclose separate totals for each, together with the name of the recipient of each political contribution over £200.

6.   **Fixed Assets** – details of any significant changes in the company's or subsidiary's fixed assets during the last financial year.

7. **Disabled Persons** – this information does not have to be given unless the firm employs more than 250 staff. If it does, the company must state its policy with regard to recruitment, employment and training of disabled persons.

8. **Directors** – the names of directors during the last financial year, together with a statement showing their interests in shares and debentures of the company and other group companies at the start of the year or, if later, their appointment date.

9. **Events Since the Year End** – the report must supply details of any important event affecting the company which has occurred since the end of the financial year.

10. **Future Developments** – an indication of the future developments for the company.

11. **Research and Development** – information about the company's research and development programme.

12. **Employee Information** – the report must state what action has been taken to introduce, maintain or develop employee information, consultation, involvement and company performance during the year.

13. **Health and Safety** – the directors' report must state arrangements for securing the health, safety and welfare at work of employees and other persons connected with the work activities of their employees.

The Corporate Report

During the last twenty years there has been a great deal of discussion as to how corporate reports can be made more informative to what is often referred to as the end user.

The process can be traced back to August 1975 when the then Accounting Standards Committee issued a discussion paper entitled the Corporate Report. The report addressed itself to the main issues of corporate reports and the information which they should contain.

The main users were defined as investors, lenders, employees, financial advisors, government, the public and interest corporate bodies such as suppliers.

The Committee's main recommendations were that the report should be relevant, understandable, reliable, completely objective, timely and comparable, and that an additional financial statement should be included called a Statement of Added Value. Such a statement shows the wealth which has been created by the owners, capital, employees and government. It is a broad based measure of wealth creation and therefore differs from the profit and loss account because it only shows the wealth created by the owners of capital.

What is added value?

It is the difference between what a company is paid for its products, and the cost of material and services. It represents, therefore, the value of the conversion process.

	£
Sales	300
Less materials and bought in parts and services	130
Leaving Added Value	170

The wealth credited from this process has to be used to reward the providers of this wealth. They are:

1. Employees who require wages, salaries, pensions and other benefits.

2. Providers of capital who require dividends and interest.

3. Government which requires taxation for the benefit of the nation.

4. The company which requires re-investment for the replacement of existing assets and for growth.

Example of a Value Added Statement for the Year Ending Year Six

	£	£
Sales		350,000
Less: Bought in goods and services		190,000
Value added by the company		160,000
To employees:		
Wages and Benefits		45,000
To providers of Capital:		
Interest	15,000	
Dividends	20,000	35,000
To government:		
Taxation		20,000
To finance and maintain fixed assets:		
Depreciation		20,000
Retained Profits		40,000
Valued Added		160,000

How can Value be Increased?

1. By increasing the selling prices, providing it exceeds any increases in costs and does not affect the volume.

2. By buying in raw materials and services at more competitive rates.

3. By reducing wastage and encouraging greater efficiency.

4. By increasing productivity through capital expenditure and by having a motivated and loyal workforce.

The Companies' Acts 1985 and 1989 have not incorporated any of the Committee's proposals although some companies do show Value Added Statements.

The late 1980's saw a number of large corporate failures such as Polly Peck and this intensified the debate about what information should be shown in the corporate report. This led to the setting up of the Cadbury Committee which reported in November 1994 and set out a framework for what in accounting is called 'good corporate governance'. The aim of the Cadbury Report has been to set out a code of best practice. This code requires directors to state that the company is a *'going concern'* and that the directors *'have a reasonable expectation that the company has adequate resources to continue in operational existence for the foreseeable future'*. Readers should also refer to the recommendation of the Hampel Committee which seeks to address a wider range of issues and risks than those which are usually classified under a financial regulatory framework. The aim of the Hampel Report is to restrict inappropriate management action thereby creating the right environment for sound decision making.

Both the Cadbury and the Hampel Report place further responsibilities on directors, who must have sufficient information about the type and level of financial risk which the company faces during the next twelve months before they can make any statement in the Corporate Report. In addition to the Cadbury and the Hampel Report the Accounting Standards Board has issued Financial Reporting Exposure Draft 13 (FRED). This proposes further disclosure of information regarding asset and liability reporting. FRED 13 seeks to provide users of corporate reports with more information about risk issues and the objectives, policies and strategies currently being adopted by the directors. It is likely that in the future the Corporate Treasurer will have an important role to play in assessing financing risks, interest rate risk, foreign exchange exposure and use of derivatives and how they affect the company's future financial viability.

Whilst these additional measures should avert the fears of investors, lenders and other interested parties, the sudden collapse of Barings has once again highlighted the importance of up-to-date information and accurate risk assessment measures as a means of averting financial failure.

QUESTIONS

Answers begin page 472

1. **The General Trading Company Limited**

   a.   The company is about to publish its annual accounts. What four pieces of information must the accounts show in relation to the income which the company has earned during the last financial year?

   b.   What are the eight expenses that must be shown against the firm's profits?

   c.   What are the four pieces of information that must be shown in the accounts as to how the company appropriated its profit?

2. **Plumbing Supplies Limited**

   The company has just prepared its annual accounts and the directors have decided to include a Value Added Statement. You have been given the following information and have been asked to prepare the statement for 31 March Year 4.

	£
Taxation	40,000
Sales	324,000
Wages and employee benefits	75,000
Cost of goods sold	120,500
Interest payments	14,000
Dividends	22,000
Depreciation of fixed assets	17,000
Retained profits	35,000

3.   **Transic plc**

The Transic Group have just placed an advertisement in the national papers to advertise the group's results.

Extract from Chair's Statement

"Profits and sales continue to rise in a year when trading conditions have been badly affected by the recession."

Summary of the Group's Results

	Last Year £	This Year £
Turnover	3,500,000	4,250,000
Trading Profit	800,000	910,000
Net Interest	40,000	65,000
Profit on ordinary activities before taxation	760,000	845,000
Taxation	250,000	300,000
Profit for the financial year attributable to shareholders	510,000	545,000
Dividend	80,000	90,000
Profit retained	470,000	455,000
Earnings per share	17p	18.25p

The company have decided to send a brief explanation to all shareholders before the published accounts are despatched. You have been asked to explain the information shown in the above advertisement.

Chapter 10

Cash Flow Statements

Introduction

A business must be able to generate cash from its trading operations so that it can pay its operating expenses, interest payments, tax and dividends as and when they fall due. Cash is also needed to finance investment programmes which will generate future cash flows.

During the last few years investors, lenders and financial analysts have begun to place more importance on a firm's ability to generate cash from its operating activities than on its ability to build profits or add value. There are two main reasons for this change in emphasis. Firstly, it is possible for a business to be profitable and yet have a negative cash flow which may threaten its future survival. Secondly, many finance practitioners subscribe to the view that a company's share price reflects the present value of its future cash payments to shareholders. These cash payments may be in the form of dividends or capital payments and so companies need to prepare a financial statement which shows how cash resources have changed over a financial period. During the last thirty years there has been a great deal of debate as to how the information should be presented. This chapter seeks to explain the changes in reporting movements in cash and the reasons why they have come about.

Profitability and Cash Flow

We have already seen that profits are not the same as cash. The profit and loss account and balance sheet do not show a firm's cash inflows and outflows. This is because the profit and loss account and balance sheet are not prepared on a cash basis but according to the accruals concept. Sales and expenses are recorded as soon as they are made or incurred and not when the cash is actually received or paid. Any money owing is then shown in the balance sheet as a current liability and any money owed is recorded as a current asset. A firm's debtors therefore, represent the amount of sales for which cash has not yet been received and, similarly, the creditors figure shows the amount of money owing at the end of the financial year.

CASH FLOW STATEMENTS

By analysing two sets of final accounts, it is possible to prepare either a source and application of funds statement or a cash flow statement. The source and application of funds statement is a very broad measure of liquidity because it shows the change in a firm's working capital. The cash flow statement shows the change in net cash flows and is a much narrower measure of liquidity.

The Difference Between Liquidity and Cash Flow

It is possible for a business to improve its overall level of liquidity by increasing its working capital whilst still having a negative cash flow. This can be seen in the following example.

Julie's Boat Yard

Julie has just started a small business building river boats. All materials are bought on credit from local suppliers and a boat yard has agreed to buy the first boat for £1,200 so long as they receive two months' credit. During the first year of trading the business was only able to make one boat.

Julie's Boat Yard
Extract Profit and Loss Account for the Year Ending Year One

	£
Sales	1,200
Less Cost of Sales	800
Gross Profit	400

Extract Balance Sheet as at Year One

Current Assets	£
Debtors	1,200
Current Liabilities	
Creditors	800
Working Capital	400

The change in the firm's working capital can be shown by preparing a source and application of funds statement for Julie's Boat Yard.

Source and Application of Funds Statement as at Year One

Source of Funds	£
Profit	400
Increase/decrease in working capital	
Increase in Debtors	1,200
Increase in Creditors	(800)
Increase in Working Capital	400

This example shows that it is possible for a business to increase its profits and working capital and yet experience a negative cash flow. In this case the firm cannot pay its creditors until the debtor settles his account. As a result Julie's Boat Yard is insolvent and would be forced to cease trading even though it is profitable unless it can raise additional sources of credit.

Although this is a simple example it is possible for large public companies to be profitable and yet have a negative cash flow. The sudden collapse of Polly Peck illustrated this point with devastating effect to both investors and the wider financial community even thought the firm was profitable and liquid. This can be seen in the table below:

Extract of Accounts for Polly Peck

Year	1989 £'000	1988 £'000	1987 £'000
Sales Turnover	1,162,300	967,100	380,846
Profit For The Financial Year	137,700	117,000	69,436
Net Current Assets	231,700	179,000	111,300
Net Assets	843,700	386,200	197,233
Net Cash Flow Before Financing	(982,340)	(206,915)	(47,560)

The table shows why the company was popular with investors. Its turnover, profitability, liquidity and net assets were rapidly increasing but these financial gains were won at the expense of cash flow. Once the company's overall cash flow position was taken into account, it could be seen that the business although profitable and liquid, was consuming more cash than it could generate from its trading activities. During each of the last three years it had a negative cash flow before financing and the increased turnover simply aggravated the company's cash shortages.

Converting a Trading and Profit and Loss Account From an Accruals Basis to a Cash Basis

There are three major adjustments which must be made. These are now explained.

Adjusting Sales

The sales figure will often contain both cash and credit sales and so the first task is to subtract the cash sales. Once this has been done the amount of cash received from credit sales must be calculated. This is done by calculating the increase or decrease in the firm's debtors during the last financial year. Add a decrease in debtors to credit sales and subtract an increase.

Figure 10:1 How to Convert Credit Sales to a Cash Basis

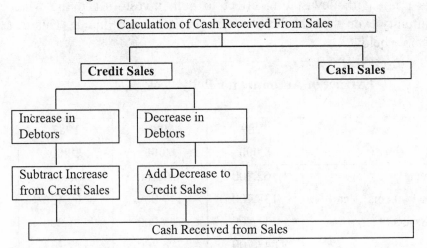

Adjustments to Cost of Goods Sold

The trading account will show how much the firm paid for the goods before they were sold. If the goods have been bought on credit then this will not be the amount of cash paid to suppliers. Two adjustments are necessary to convert the accounts from an accruals to a cash basis.

The first adjustment is for stock. If the amount of stock held by the firm between two accounting periods has increased then this increase in stock must be added to the cost of goods sold figure shown in the trading account. Any decrease in stock must be subtracted.

The second adjustment must consider the amount owed to creditors. A decrease in creditors must be added to the cost of goods sold figure and an increase must be deducted.

Figure 10:2 How to Convert Cost of Goods Sold to a Cash Basis

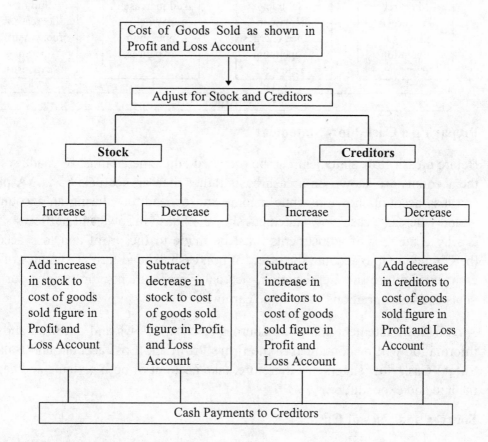

Adjustments to Operating Expenses

The operating expenses in the profit and loss account such as insurance, wages and rent must be adjusted to take account of prepayments and accruals.

Accruals: Add a decrease in accrued charges to operating expenses and subtract an increase.

Prepayments: Add an increase in prepayments and subtract a decrease.

Figure 10:3 How to Convert Operating Expenses to a Cash Basis

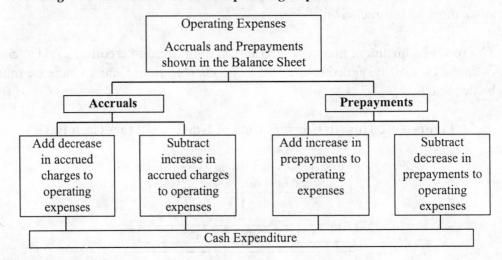

Preparing a Cash Flow Statement

Before a cash flow statement can be prepared adjustments must be made so that the accounts are shown on a cash basis rather than an accruals basis. A profit and loss account shows revenue income and expenditure during an accounting period whereas a cash flow statement shows all cash inflows and outflows. This is why a number of adjustments must be made to the profit and loss account thereby taking into account the effect of non cash expenditure. Examples of non cash expenditure are depreciation, accruals, prepayments, provisions for bad debts and appropriations of retained earnings.

A cash flow statement shows all sources of cash inflows and outflows and this information will be contained in the firm's Profit and Loss account and Balance Sheet. Cash flow statements therefore, take account of both revenue and capital income and expenditure.

Sources and Uses of Cash

Information Contained in the Profit and Loss Account

Sources	Uses
Cash Sales	Cash Purchases
Credit Sales	Credit Purchases
Rent Received	Operating Expenses
Income From Investments	Payment of Dividends
Other Sources of Income	Interest Payments
	Taxation

Information Contained in the Balance Sheet

Sources	Uses
Sale of Fixed Assets	Purchase of Fixed Assets
Sale of Investments	Purchase of Investments
Issue of Shares	Redemption of Preference Shares
Issue of Loan Capital	Redemption of Loan Capital
Bank Loan	Repayment of Bank Loan

Cash Flow Statements and Financial Reporting Standards 1

Cash flow statements are very objective and the information contained in them can be verified more easily than accounting statements which have been prepared under the historic cost convention or on a value added basis. They also overcome some of the problems of how inflation affects annual accounts with regard to holding gains, because cash flow statements show all cash receipts and payments as they occur and not when they become due for payment.

In September 1991 the Accounting Standards Board issued their first reporting standard which governed the preparation of cash flow statements. For many years there had been growing criticisms of funds flow statements, mainly because changes in working capital were being used as a measure of cash flows. To make matters worse there were also wide variations in the preparation of funds flow statements and, as a result, it was felt that SSAP 10 should be replaced.

FRS 1 was principally concerned with the format of cash flow statements and allowed a cash flow statement to be prepared according to either the direct or indirect method. The direct method is a very narrow measure of an organisation's liquidity because it is a summary of the receipts and payments account. The direct method calculates cash flows as the difference between cash received and cash payments for supplies and expenses. Advocates of this method believe that it is easier for people who do not have a financial background to understand a statement prepared in this way. Historically in the U.K. the direct method has not proved popular. The second is the indirect method. This is a very broad measure of liquidity and is more akin to the old funds flow statement for it involves calculating cash flows by adjusting operating profit for non-cash items and changes in working capital.

FRS I Revised

The original FRS I required a company to analyse the change in its cash and cash equivalents but the statement did not define the term "cash equivalent".

CASH FLOW STATEMENTS

This was the main reason for reviewing the standard because of inconsistencies in financial reporting when showing cash equivalents.

The new statement requires all entities which must produce financial statements giving a true and fair view to produce a cash flow statement in accordance with FRS I revised. The only exceptions are:

- Subsidiaries where the holding company has at least 90% interest in the voting shares.

- Small companies classified as 'small' under the Companies Act.

- Pension funds, like assurance companies and investment funds.

- Building Societies.

An example complying with the new requirements of FRS I (revised) is shown on the next page.

The new statement has eight new headings.

1. **Cash Flow from Operating Activities**
2. **Taxation**
3. **Return on Investments and Servicing Finance**
4. **Acquisitions and Disposals**
5. **Capital Expenditure and Financial Investments**
6. **Equity Dividends**
7. **Management of Liquid Resources**
8. **Financing**

FRS I Revised requires:

a) Cash flow statements to concentrate on movements in cash only

b) The changes will make it easier to see changes in an entity's treasury policy.

c) Investing activities must show separately movements in liquid resources.

d) Payment of dividends must be shown separately.

e) Capital expenditure must be shown separately.

f) There must be an explanation of how the entity's net debt position has changed during the last reporting period.

FRS 1 (Revised) Cash Flow Statement for the Year Ending 30 Nov Yr 7

	£000	£000
Net cash inflow from operating activities (note 1)		**13,778**
Returns on investments and servicing of finance (note 2)		**5,998**
Corporation tax paid (including advance corporation tax)		**(5,844)**
Capital expenditure		(3,050)
		10,882
Equity dividends paid		(4,834)
		6,048
Management of liquid resources (note 2)		(900)
Financing (note 2)		114
Increase in cash		5,262

Reconciliation of net cash flow to movement in net debt (note 3)

Increase in cash in the period	5,262	
Cash repaying debenture	298	
Cash paid to increase liquid resources	900	
Change in net debt		6,460
Net debt at 1.12, Yr 6		(5,806)
Net debt at 30.1, Yr 7		654

* In this example all changes in net debt are cash flows.

Notes to the cash flow statement

Note 1: Reconciliation of operating profit to net cash inflow from operating activities

Operating profit	12,044
Depreciation charges	1,786
Loss on sale of tangible fixed assets	12
Increase in stock	(388)
Increase in debtors	(144)
Increase in creditors	468
Net cash inflow from operating activities	**13,778**

Note 2: Gross cash flows

Returns of Investments and Servicing of Finance

Interest received	6,022	
Interest paid	(24)	
		5,998

Capital Expenditure

Payments to acquire tangible fixed assets	(171)	
Payments to acquire intangible fixed assets	(2,992)	
Receipts from the sale of tangible fixed assets	84	
		(3,050)

Management of Liquid Resources

Purchase of treasury bills	(1,300)	
Sale of treasury bills	400	
		(900)

Financing

Issue of ordinary share capital	422	
Repurchase of debenture loan	(298)	
Expenses paid in connection with share issues	(10)	
		114

Note 3: Analysis of changes in net debt

	£000 At 1 Dec Yr6	£000 Cash flow	£000 At 30 Nov Yr 7
Cash in hand and at ban	84	1,694	1,778
Overdrafts	(3,568)	3,568	
Debt due within one year	(298)	298	
Debt due after one year	(2,524)		(2,524)
Current asset investment	500	900	1,400
Total	(5,806)	6,460	654

CASH FLOW STATEMENTS

Definitions of Key Terms in FRS 1

Cash: Cash in hand or deposits with qualifying institutions repayable on demand, less overdrafts at qualifying institutions repayable on demand. Cash includes deposits denominated in foreign currencies.

Repayable on Demand: Without giving notice or suffering an interest penalty in the event of withdrawal.

Cash Flow: Increase or decrease in cash. See definition of cash.

Liquid Resources: Current asset investments held as readily marketable stores of wealth which can be realised without disruption to the business entity or which can be traded in an active market.

Net Debt: The borrowings of the entity less cash and liquid resources.

Net Funds: When cash and liquid resources exceed borrowings.

The preparation of a cash flow statement complying with FRS 1 Revised using both the indirect and direct methods is shown in the next example.

Example

Ruckinge's Profit and Loss Account

Extract of Profit and Loss Account for the Year Ended 31 December Year 2

	Year 2		Year 1	
	£'000	£'000	£'000	£'000
Sales		4,760		5,400
Cost of goods sold		3,500		3,726
Gross profit		1,260		1,674
Less expenses				
Wages and salaries	234		340	
Depreciation	240		210	
Other expenses	200		224	
Total expenses		674		774
Trading profit		586		900
Loan interest		46		90
Profit after interest		540		810
Taxation		216		288
Profit after tax		324		522
Proposed dividend		144		210
Retained profit		180		312

Ruckinge's Balance Sheet

Balance Sheet as at 31 December Year 2

	Year 2			Year 1		
	Cost	Dep. to Date	NBV	Cost	Dep. to Date	NBV
Fixed Assets	£'000	£'000	£'000	£'000	£'000	£'000
Land & Buildings	3,000	-	3,000	3,000	-	3,000
Plant & Machinery	2,160	1,230	930	1,710	990	720
Investments	570	-	570	1,290	-	1,290
	5,730	1,230	4,500	6,000	990	5,010
Current Assets						
Stock		1,404			792	
Debtors		540			336	
Bank		100			1,100	
Cash		32			100	
		2,076			2,328	
Less Liabilities						
Creditors	516			420		
Taxation	216			288		
Dividend	144			210		
		876			918	
Working Capital			1,200			1,410
			5,700			6,420
Mortgage			-			900
Net Assets			5,700			5,520
Financed by						
Share Capital		4,000			4,000	
Share Premium		1,000			1,000	
Profit and Loss		700			520	
Shareholders' Funds			5,700			5,520

CASH FLOW STATEMENTS

Ruckinge's Cash Flow Statement for the Year Ending 31st December Year 2

	£'000	£'000
Net Cash Flow from Operating Activities (Note 1)		106
Returns on Investment and Servicing of Finance		
Interest Paid		(46)
Taxation		
Corporation Tax Paid		(288)
Capital Expenditure		
Payments to Acquire Tangible Fixed Assets	(450)	
Receipts from Sales of Tangible Fixed Assets	720	
Net Cash Inflow from Capital Expenditure		270
		42
Equity Dividend Paid		(210)
Net Cash Inflow Before Financing		(168)
Financing		
Issue of Share Capital	------	
Long Term Loans Repaid	(900)	(900)
Decrease in Cash		(1068)

Note 1

	£'000
Operating Profit	586
Depreciation Charges	240
Increase in Stock	(612)
Increase in Debtors	(204)
Increase in Creditors	96
Net Cash Inflow from Operating Activities	106

If the statement was prepared according to the Direct Method it would be shown as:

	£'000
Operating Activities	
Cash Received from Customers	4,556
Cash Payments to Suppliers	(4216)
Cash Paid to and on Behalf of Employers	(234)
Other Cash Payments	---
Net Cash Inflow from Operating Activities	106

Explanation

Note 1: Calculation of Cash From Customers
Sales £4,760 plus Opening Debtors £336 less Closing Debtors £540 = £4,556
Note 2: Calculation of Cash Payments to Suppliers
Opening Creditors £420 plus Purchases £4,112 plus Other Expenses £200 less Closing Creditors £516 = £4,216
Calculation of Purchases
Cost of Goods Sold £3,500 less Opening Stock £792 plus Closing Stock £1,404 =£4,112
Note 3: Dividend Payments
Although the dividend is declared in year 1 it is not paid until year 2.
Note 4: Taxation
Tax is always paid the following year and so the amount owed in year 1 must be paid in year 2.

Note: An increase in stock and debtors is a use of funds because cash is tied up in the increase. This is why an increase in creditors is a source because they are in effect financing the business.

FRS 1 Revised Heading Checklist.

There are Eight New Headings.

Number	Heading	Summary of Contents	
One	Cash flow from Operating Activities	**Indirect Method**	**Direct Method**
		Operating Profit	Cash from Customers
		Depreciation Charges	Cash Payments to Suppliers
		Increase/decrease in stock	Cash paid to and on behalf
		Increase/decrease in debtors	of employees
		Increase/decrease in creditors	Other Cash Payments
		Net Cash Inflow from Operating Activities =	**Net Cash Inflow from Operating Activities** =
Two	Returns on Investment and Servicing Finance.	Interest and Dividends received	
		Interest Paid	
		Interest element of finance lease repayments	
		Preference Share Dividends	
		Dividends to Minority Interest Shareholders	
Three	Taxation	Receipts and Payments of tax - Revenue and Capital	
Four	Capital Expenditure and Financial Investments	Purchase of Fixed Assets	
		Receipts from Sale of Fixed Assets	
Five	Acquisitions and Disposals	Receipts and Payment relating to Acquisitions and Disposals in:	
		Interests in Subsidiaries	
		Associated of Joint Venture	
		Companies Receipts and Payments	
Six	Equity Dividends	Dividends paid to Equity Shareholders	
Seven	Management of Liquid Resources	Marketable Current Assets Investments/their sale or Acquisition	
Eight	Financing	Receipts and Repayments of External Sources of finance such as shares, debentures, bonds and the capital element of finance leases	

QUESTIONS

Answers begin page 473

1. Indicate, in a Cash Flow Statement, whether the following would be shown as a source or an application of funds.

		Source	Application
a.	Decrease in debtors		
b.	Increase in stock		
c.	Reduction in bank overdraft		
d.	Dividend payments		
e.	Corporation tax		
f.	Increase in creditors		
g.	Sale of fixtures and fittings		
h.	Redemption of debentures		
i.	Purchase of new premises		
j.	Issue of shares at a premium		
k.	Depreciation of fixed assets		
l.	Redemption of debentures at a premium		
m.	Issue of new shares		
n.	Decrease in creditors		

2. S & J Industries

Extract of S & J's Profit and Loss Account for the Yr Ending 31 Dec Yr 8

	Year 8		Year 7	
	£	£	£	£
Sales		48,500		45,300
Cost of Goods Sold		33,000		28,000
		15,500		17,300
Less Expenses				
Wages and Salaries	4200		3,800	
Depreciation	1,500		1,300	
Other Expenses	500		500	
		6,200		5,600
Operating Profit		9,300		11,700
Loan Interest		500		700
Profit after Interest		8,800		11,000
Taxation		250		300
Profit after Tax		8,550		10,700
Proposed Dividend		550		700
Retained Profit		8,000		10,000

S & J Industries' Balance Sheet as at 31st December Year 8

	Year 8			Year 7		
	Cost	Dep to Date	NBV	Cost	Dep to Date	NBV
Fixed Assets	£	£	£	£	£	£
Land and Buildings	44,670	---	44,670	40,000	---	40,000
Fixtures and Fittings	15,000	4,500	10,500	13,000	3,000	10,000
	59,670	4,500	55,170	53,000	3,000	50,000
Current Assets						
Stock		15,000			12,000	
Debtors		3,000			2,500	
Bank		400			1,000	
		18,400			15,500	
Less Liabilities						
Creditors	750			480		
Taxation	250			300		
Dividend	550	1,550		700	1,480	
Working Capital			16,850			14,020
			72,020			64,020
Less Mortgage			5,000			5,000
Net Assets			67,020			59,020
Financed by						
Share Capital			45,000			45,000
£1 Ordinary Shares						
Issued and Fully Paid						
Share Premium			2,000			2,000
Profit and Loss			20,020			12,020
Shareholders' Fund			67,020			59,020

Prepare a cash flow statement for the year ended 31 December Yr 8

Chapter 11

Interpreting Financial Statements

Introduction

When a company has drawn up its annual accounts, they should be analysed so that the financial strengths and weaknesses can be assessed, together with any trends which may have led to its current position. The firm's management should be in the unique position of having all the necessary information to assess the financial position of their company and their performance during the year. They should have monthly management accounts, present and future cash forecasts and updated budgets. Management performance measures should concentrate on the return on assets and the return on new investments. Investors are becoming increasingly concerned about the quality and ability of the firm's management as it is they who will determine the company's competitive position, develop new products or services, control costs and increase earnings. The Corporate Report will contain some information but business publications such as *Investors' Chronicle* and *The Financial Times* will provide up to date information about changes in the firm's management. Ultimately it is management who determine the level of a firm's earnings and it is these earnings which affect the share price. This is why investors now place such emphasis on the quality of the firm's management, because they know it is not companies that succeed or fail but their managers.

Unfortunately other interested parties are not privy to the same information and have to rely on the published audited accounts, plus any interim statement issued by the company. The amount of information which can be gained by looking at a set of accounts is limited because companies are only required by law to publish certain details and the directors may decide not to show any additional information which could assist competitors. In order to gain a better insight, it is prudent to compare present performance with past and to compare one company's performance with another operating in the same business. The general state of the economy must also be taken into account and how a change in economic activity would affect corporate earnings. Accounting ratios provide further information about the firm's liquidity, profitability, use of assets, financial structure and the returns paid to investors.

155

Interpretation of Accounts

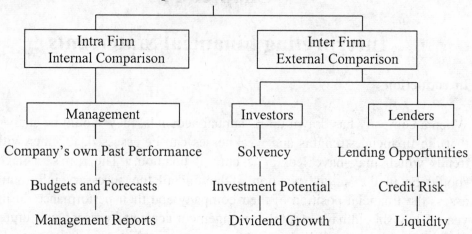

What is an Accounting Ratio?

An accounting ratio is the same as any arithmetic ratio in that it seeks to measure the relationship between two numbers. This information can be presented in several ways and these are now explained.

Example

If a company has £5,000 invested in debtors and owes £1,000 to creditors, the relationship between these two figures can be shown as follows:

a)   The ratio of Debtors to Creditors is 5:1

b)   The ratio of Creditors to Debtors is 1:5

c)   Debtors represent five times (5 x) Creditors

d)   Creditors represent 1/5 of Debtors

e)   Creditors represent 20 per cent of Debtors

It is an accounting convention that ratios are expressed in different ways. While the arithmetical calculation is relatively straightforward, it is the interpretation which is difficult, for it is unlikely that one set of accounts will contain all the information one needs.

When interpreting accounts, the ratios used should follow a logical sequence. If a company is having liquidity problems, its future existence may well be in jeopardy, even if it is profitable. It is, therefore, a good idea to assess its liquidity first, then its profitability and, finally, to see if there is a link between these two factors and how effectively it uses its assets. Lastly the accounts should be analysed so that the firm's capital structure is assessed, together with the risks involved in its chosen method of long-term finance, as this will affect the returns which investors expect.

1. Ratios which Measure Liquidity

One of the main tasks for any financial manager is to maintain a balance between the need for liquidity and the desire for profitability. The aim is to manage the business so that it generates long term profits whilst maintaining short term liquidity.

The word liquidity refers to the firm's ability to meet its short-term liabilities by having sufficient cash or near cash resources. All companies buy and sell on credit. In a competitive market, credit terms have to be offered in order to win contracts and to keep existing customers. At the same time the firm's own liabilities can only be paid in cash. If a firm is unable to pay its liabilities in cash, it may be wound up by its creditors and so management, investors, lenders and employees are all concerned that the firm should have sufficient current assets to meet its current liabilities. There are two ratios which measure a firm's liquidity.

The Current Ratio   = $\dfrac{\text{Current Assets}}{\text{Current Liabilities}}$

This is a broad measure of liquidity. Current assets are assets of a circulating nature which generate the firm's profits. They are stock, debtors and cash and bank deposits. Current liabilities are short-term debts which must be repaid within one year of the balance sheet date. The main components of current liabilities are creditors, bank overdraft, taxation due and proposed dividends.

Caution dictates that current assets should exceed current liabilities, for not all of the current assets will be in cash or near cash, such as debtors.

The speed with which the firm can turn its stock and debtors into cash will determine the amount of money which must be invested in current assets relative to current liabilities. A building company operating in a recession may find it prudent to have a ratio of say 2:1, whereas a fast food chain may operate at 1:1. It is not just the ratio for one year which is important, but the trend for this will show whether the business is maintaining its liquidity ratio or whether it is rising or falling. If the ratio is rising, it would suggest that the business is becoming more liquid and increasing its working capital. Whilst this increase could be as a result of raising new long term finance, if the business can improve its working capital position through trading, it will be in a position where it could pay higher dividends or invest in new projects. A decrease would suggest that the firm is experiencing declining levels of liquidity and it may need new long term finance which can be used to provide additional working capital.

This is why it is important to look at the composition of the current assets and how they have changed during the last financial year. As a general rule cash should make up ten per cent of a firm's current assets, but this figure should include short term investments as today's managers seek to improve earnings by investing all idle cash balances. If the balance sheet shows increasing cash balances, it would suggest that management are considering making a strategic acquisition.

The amount of money invested in stock and debtors should be closely related to the firm's level of sales and compared with the industry average. The higher the ratio of sales to finished stock and the quicker debtors can be converted into cash, the more efficient and liquid the business.

The Acid Test or Quick Ratio $=$ $\dfrac{\text{Current Assets Less Stock}}{\text{Current Liabilities}}$

This is a stricter measurement of a firm's liquidity for it measures its ability to meet its current liabilities out of its cash or near cash current assets. If the managers are totally risk averse, they must have a minimum ratio of 1:1 and would probably prefer a higher one. In this way all liabilities can be met without worry.

Ability to Make Timely Repayment of Liabilities

Time	Nature
Immediate	Pay creditors by end of week
Short Term	Pay dividend, tax and interest payments in six months time
Long term	Repay long term debt in five years' time

Once again the ratio will depend upon the type of business in which the firm is engaged and the ease with which it can convert its stock and debtors into cash.

The quicker this can be done, the less liquid it needs to be and the more it can finance its current assets by borrowing short-term from its creditors. Generally the higher the ratio of current liabilities to current assets, the more profitable the firm as it is able to use its creditors to finance its current assets (usually interest free). Part of the cost of this increased profitability is the increased risk, but ratios of 0.4:1 are not uncommon for the large supermarket chains. These businesses can operate at this level because they can extract advantageous credit terms from their suppliers and can sell the goods quickly to customers for cash. If these same techniques were applied by many manufacturing companies or retailing firms which have a slow stock turnover, they would be in great danger of insolvency and would probably be described as overtrading. This is why the firm's ratio should always be compared with the industry average.

The Four Signs that a Business is Overtrading

£	Increase in stock as a proportion of sales	Increase in debtors as a proportion of sales	**Fast decrease in cash and other liquid assets**	Large and rapid increase in creditors

Time

Overtrading is an accounting term which describes a business which is trying to finance too high a level of trading with too little working capital. Once again, in order to assess whether or not a firm is overtrading, it is necessary to look at the liquidity ratios for several years to see whether its liquidity ratios are relatively stable or deteriorating. Firms which are overtrading normally have increasing stock and debtors balances, coupled with decreasing cash balances and a rapid rise in creditors. If this situation occurs, and cannot be abated by acquiring additional finance, the firm is in danger of imminent collapse as creditors and lenders ask for immediate repayment of their loans. It is not just the firm's current level of liquidity which is important but its ability to generate cash from its trading activities. Before it can be said that a business has sufficient liquidity, information is needed about its future investment in fixed assets and the amount of working capital needed to finance next year's budgeted level of activity together with expected dividend payments and tax liabilities. This is why analysts and investors look for stable current and acid test ratios.

2.   Profitability

In the long run companies must be profitable if they are to survive. There are a number of measures of profitability which calculate the percentage profit made when goods are sold and after all expenses have been made.

It is not possible to say what percentage profit a firm should make for it will depend upon its stock turnover. As a general rule, the higher the stock turnover the smaller the profit margin, and the slower the turnover, the higher the profit margin. In either case sufficient gross profit must be earned so that the business can meet its expenses, pay a reasonable return to its owners and still leave sufficient funds for reinvestment.

The profit margin, whilst important, must not be seen in isolation. Just as important is the growth in expected future sales for this will ultimately determine the firm's future profitability. A firm with a low profit margin but which has a forecast of a large increase in sales will make a better investment than a firm which currently has a high profit margin but is seen as being static in terms of sales growth.

The gross profit percentage should remain reasonably stable but, if a change does occur, this should be investigated. It may have been brought about by heavy discounting, increased production costs caused by price increases in raw materials, excessive wage claims or by changing the firm's product range (usually referred to as its product mix). The published accounts do not usually contain sufficient information to analyse why costs and net profits have increased or decreased. Nevertheless, one should look for large increases in overheads or debt repayments which could cause financial problems if the firm found its sales and profits fall because of a recession.

The two main ratios for calculating the firm's profits from sales are the gross profit and net profit to sales ratio. They are calculated by the following formulae:

Profitability Ratios   = $\dfrac{\text{Gross Profit} \times 100}{\text{Sales}}$ and $\dfrac{\text{Net Profit} \times 100}{\text{Sales}}$

Once the profit percentages earned from each sale have been calculated, managers, investors and lenders need to know the return which the company can make on its capital employed. Capital is a scarce resource and the owners want to earn the maximum return relative to the risk involved. The firm needs to make as high a return as possible so that it can attract investors' funds, which are always seeking a safe and secure investment and this is why many companies set themselves the objective of maximising shareholder wealth.

Profitability ratios are important because they show the returns which the firm can make and, therefore, assess management's ability to use the firm's assets effectively to generate profitable sales. The ratios also provide information on the returns earned from past investment decisions as well as providing information on how effectively the business controls its costs. Good management increases sales whilst keeping costs under control so that increasing costs do not reduce the firm's profitability.

A company cannot be judged financially successful just by the size of its profits for this takes no account of the profit made in relation to its size or capital base. The Return on Capital Employed ratio seeks to measure the firm's earnings power and can be calculated by this formula:

Return on Capital Employed or Primary Ratio $= \dfrac{\text{Profit} \times 100}{\text{Capital Employed}}$

While this ratio shows the return earned from the company's capital, it is not specific as to what capital or profit figure has been used to measure its earnings power. For instance, should the profit be after tax or before interest payments and preference dividends are paid? The answer really lies in how the firm has raised its long-term capital, which can come from two main sources. Firstly, from the shareholders who are the owners of the business and, secondly, from lenders who are not owners, but creditors. If the company has any reserves, these will belong to the shareholders, giving rise to a third possible definition of capital. As a result, three different figures for the return on capital employed can be used, each of which will show a different percentage return.

The broadest definition includes all of the capital financing the business from long-term loans to shareholders' funds and reserves. If this interpretation is applied, the ratio should be called the *Return on Long-Term Capital Employed* and is calculated as follows:

Return on Long-Term Capital Employed $= \dfrac{\text{Profit before Interest and Tax}}{\text{Loan Capital} + \text{Share Capital and Reserves}} \times 100$

It is also possible to calculate the return earned from the shareholders' investment in the business, and so this ratio excludes any debt capital. When this ratio is used, the company's preference shareholders are treated as debt capital, because they receive a fixed rate of dividend, and so the earnings are the profit after tax and preference dividend. This ratio is called the *Return on Equity Capital* and is calculated by using the formula:

Return on Equity Capital $\;=\;$ $\dfrac{\text{Profit after tax and Preference Dividend}}{\text{Ordinary Share Capital plus Reserves}}$ x 100

Lastly, the return on capital employed may be taken as the shareholders' funds, which is made up of both ordinary and preference shares plus reserves. This ratio is called the Return on Shareholders' Capital and is calculated as follows:

Return on Shareholders' Capital $\;=\;$ $\dfrac{\text{Profit after tax}}{\text{Share Capital plus Reserves}}$ x 100

It is important to know which figure has been used to calculate the return on capital employed, as each method will yield a different answer. Most companies seek to increase their return on capital over time and so, whichever method is used, one should look to see if the ratio is increasing. A mere increase on its own should not be immediately regarded as a good sign, for the increase, if adjusted for inflation, may in fact be negative. Similarly, there is also a danger that if the firm's assets have not been recently revalued to reflect the increase in asset values brought about by inflation, the ratio will have been based upon an unrealistic figure for capital and so the returns will be overstated.

Whilst the return and profits made are important, there is always a danger that too much profit may be distributed as dividend to the owners. If the company is to grow and have a secure financial base, it needs to reinvest past profits back into the business. The retained profit to sales and the net working assets to sales ratios show the amount of capital needed to finance extra sales. If the firm lacks the cash to finance these extra sales, it will have to fund them from outside sources, which will involve additional borrowing or issuing more shares.

Retained Profit to Sales $\;=\;$ $\dfrac{\text{Retained Profit}}{\text{Sales}}$

This ratio shows how much new capital each extra sale will generate for the business, while the net working capital to sales ratio measures the amount of additional capital which will be needed to finance extra sales.

Net Working = Net Working Capital (where net working capital = Stock + Debtors - Creditors)
Capital to Sales   Sales

As a general rule, if the net working capital ratio is higher than the retained profit to sales, the business will need additional capital to finance any increase in sales. If this is not provided from a long-term source, there is always a danger that the management will fund it by increasing their creditors, which could lead to financial problems in the future.

Profitable companies enjoy three major advantages. Firstly, they are able to generate equity internally by retaining profits in the form of reserves. Secondly, such companies can raise additional funds in the capital markets and finally, they are better placed to withstand a downturn in business activity should the economy enter a recession. In the long-term it is only profitable companies which can generate the necessary cash flows to meet their liabilities.

3. Use of Assets

Companies seek finance either from the owners (shareholders) or from lenders (loan stock holders) to purchase both fixed and current assets which will make profits for the business. It is by effectively managing the current assets that firms are able to generate profits. The quicker raw materials can be turned into finished goods, sold and the cash received, the greater the profits, for this process can then be undertaken more times each financial year. The use of assets ratio seeks to measure how effectively the firm uses its fixed and current assets.

A firm needs its fixed assets so that it can trade. For instance, a shop cannot exist without a building and fixtures where customers can come and browse before purchasing. All investments in fixed assets must yield returns and one measure of assessing the return is to look at the ratio of sales to fixed assets:

Sales to Fixed Assets =   Sales
                         Fixed Assets

As a general rule the sales should always be higher than the investment in fixed assets for, otherwise, the investment has not been effective; it has failed to generate sales income. When assessing this ratio it is important to look at when the fixed assets were last revalued, the date they were purchased together with the firm's depreciation policies. This is why it is difficult to make inter firm comparisons using this ratio. It is best used for comparing the firm's performance from one year to the next.

Finally, it must be remembered that any new investment takes time to generate returns and so, if the balance sheet shows a large investment in fixed assets, it may not be realistic to see a corresponding increase in sales. Nevertheless, if the ratio of sales to fixed assets is falling, it would suggest that the business is not using its assets effectively and should consider rationalising the scale of its operations.

Another useful ratio is the relationship between a company's fixed and current assets. A large shop with a small amount of stock would be likely to lack customers because most of the firm's capital has been invested in fixed assets which are not for sale. It may be difficult to assess this ratio because of seasonal factors or attempts by the management to destock before the final accounts are prepared, so that the company appears to have a higher liquidity ratio. Nevertheless, if a firm has a high ratio of current assets to fixed assets, coupled with a high stock turnover rate, it will be able to improve its profitability and return on capital employed.

The key to profitability lies in being able to sell the stock as many times as possible in any one financial year and to receive the cash quickly from the debtors so that it can be invested in more stock. The following ratios show how long it takes the business to sell stock or receive cash in days and is referred to as its *cash operating cycle*. Before the cash operating cycle can be calculated, the following ratios must be worked out:

Stock Turnover Ratio $= \dfrac{\text{Average Stock x 365}}{\text{Cost of Goods Sold}} = $ Days to sell stock

The average stock figure is calculated by adding the opening and closing stock together and dividing it by two to find the average. By dividing the number of days taken to sell the stock, it is possible to calculate the number of times the stock is sold during the year.

If the company engages in manufacturing, raw materials must be purchased, turned into finished goods (work in progress) and, finally, kept as finished stock until sold. The following ratios will show how long it takes in days for this to happen. Once again the average stock is found by adding together the opening and closing stock and calculating the mean.

---

a) **Stock Turnover for Raw Materials**

$$\frac{\text{Average Stock of Raw Materials x 365}}{\text{Cost of Raw Materials Consumed}} = \text{Number of days the firm holds its stock of raw materials}$$

b) **Stock Turnover for Work in Progress**

$$\frac{\text{Stock Turnover for Work in Progress x 365}}{\text{Cost of Goods Manufactured}} = \text{Number of days it takes to turn work in progress into finished stock}$$

c) **Stock Turnover for Finished Goods**

$$\frac{\text{Stocks of Finished Goods x 365}}{\text{Costs of Goods Sold}} = \text{Number of days it takes to sell finished goods}$$

If stock is bought on credit, the creditors are in fact financing its purchase. The longer the credit period, the greater the savings, for the firm is often able to use this money interest free. The time taken to pay creditors can again be expressed in days by using this ratio:

d) **Time Taken to pay Creditors**

$$\frac{\text{Trade Creditors x 365}}{\text{Purchases on Credit}} = \text{Number of days credit allowed by trade creditors before payment must be made}$$

Unfortunately this benefit is offset because most firms also sell on credit and so have to give credit to their customers. The length of time which the firm has to wait for payment is calculated by the Sales to Debtors ratio.

e) **Time Taken to Receive Payment from Debtors**

$$\frac{\text{Debtors x 365}}{\text{Credit Sales}} = \text{Days taken to receive payment from credit sales.}$$

The shorter the time period the better, for then the money can be reinvested in more stock. Ideally the firm would like to receive payment before having to pay its creditors so that the money can be invested in interest bearing deposits which will earn the business additional profits.

Once these ratios have been calculated, the firm's cash operating cycle can be worked out. This is best explained by an example.

Example

The Iron and Steel Manufacturing Company has decided to calculate its cash operating cycle from the following information:

	£
Sales	100,000
Cost of Sales	84,000
Purchases	56,000
Debtors	12,000
Creditors	8,000
Stock of Raw Materials	14,000
Work in Progress	7,000
Finished Stock	16,000

Calculation of the Iron and Steel Manufacturing Company's Cash Operating Cycle.

STOCK TURNOVER

RAW MATERIALS

$$= \quad \frac{\text{Stock of Raw Materials} \times 365}{\text{Purchases}} \qquad \frac{£14,000 \times 365}{£56,000} \quad = \quad \textbf{91 days}$$

PRODUCTION TIME

$$= \quad \frac{\text{Work in Progress} \times 365}{\text{Cost of Sales}} \qquad \frac{£7,000 \times 365}{£84,000} \quad = \quad \textbf{30 days}$$

FINISHED GOODS

$$= \quad \frac{\text{Finished Goods} \times 365}{\text{Cost of Sales}} \qquad \frac{£16,000 \times 365}{£84,000} \quad = \quad \textbf{70 days}$$

DEBTOR'S COLLECTION TIME

$$= \quad \frac{\text{Debtors} \times 365}{\text{Sales}} \qquad \frac{£12,000 \times 365}{£100,000} \quad = \quad \textbf{44 days}$$

Less CREDIT RECEIVED

$$= \quad \frac{\text{Creditors} \times 365}{\text{Purchases}} \qquad \frac{£8,000 \times 365}{£56,000} \quad = \quad \textbf{(52) days}$$

Note: All calculations to the nearest whole number.

By adding up the number of days the firm's cash operating cycle can be calculated:

	Days
Holding Time of Raw Materials	91
Time to Make Goods	30
Time to Sell Finished Goods	70
Credit Time given to Debtors	44
	235
Less Credit Time Taken from Suppliers	(52)
Cash Operating Cycle	**183**

If the company is a non manufacturing business then the cash operating cycle is calculated by adding the time finished stock is held, plus the financing time of debtors, less the interest free period taken from creditors.

The cash operating cycle shows the number of days the firm's cash is needed to finance its stock and credit sales. Any extension which can be gained from creditors will help to conserve the firm's cash, as will any reduction in manufacturing time or reduction in the time taken to receive payment. These ratios are useful for they provide further insight as to the firm's liquidity and should be compared with previous years and other companies operating in the same industry.

4.   Capital Ratios

Debt capital is the cheapest form of long term finance, and provided the money is invested in assets which can generate a higher return than the interest payments, there will be a net gain for the shareholders. This is called trading on the equity. The amount of debt which a company should have in its capital structure is partly dependent on the stability of its earnings. Companies which tend to have stable earnings can afford to be more highly geared than those whose earnings fluctuate widely. The effect on a firm's earnings and its level of gearing is discussed further in chapter 23.

Whilst debt finance is an important source of long term finance, its use must not be such that it could have a detrimental effect on the firm's earnings and shareholder interests. The amount of debt should not be excessive when compared with the firm's earnings and total assets.

Capital ratios show who has provided the long-term capital which is financing the firm. The ratio of debt to equity capital is called *gearing* and is explained further in chapter 23. The ratio is:

Gearing Ratio $=$ $\dfrac{\text{Debt Capital}}{\text{Equity Capital}}$ or $\dfrac{\text{Net Debt}}{\text{Share Capital} + \text{Reserves}}$

Note: Net debt equals long and short term debt minus investments

The main problem is – what should be included as debt and equity capital? The simplest method is to divide the ordinary share capital into the long-term debt capital, but stricter measures include all long-term and short-term debt as well as ordinary share capital plus reserves. The problem is made more difficult for two reasons. Firstly, some financial securities, such as convertible loan stock and preference shares, are more akin to debt capital than share capital. Convertible loan stock is debt capital which can, on certain dates, be converted into share capital should the holder choose to exercise their right to convert. Preference shares are normally treated as debt capital because they pay a fixed rate of dividend and so are more akin to debt than equity capital. Secondly, many companies use short-term debt as a permanent means of finance. This money finances not just seasonal fluctuations in trade, but also a significant percentage of the company's asset base and, in such cases, it should be included as debt capital, unless the company has sufficient liquidity to enable short-term borrowings, to be offset from its short-term liquidity. Whichever method is used, the ratio shows who has provided the majority of the money which is financing the business.

This can be calculated by another ratio which measures what percentage of the total assets have been financed by the shareholders.

Shareholder Investment to Total Assets $=$ $\dfrac{\text{Shareholders' Investments}}{\text{Total Assets}}$

Both these ratios provide some indication of the risks involved in investing in the company. The shareholders are the owners and should provide the majority of the money, for all the profits will accrue to them. A loan holder will want to see the majority of the money coming from the shareholders, otherwise the lenders will demand a higher interest rate to compensate for the extra financial risk involved.

The more money is financed by long-term debt, the greater the gearing ratio and the risk to the firm. Highly geared firms have a ratio of 1:1 or even higher. When the level of debt reaches these proportions, the level of risk is increased to both the owners and borrowers for there is always a danger that, if sales and profits fall, the firm will default on its loan and interest payments. If the debts cannot be rescheduled, the firm may be wound up by its creditors who will seek to sell the assets to recover their money. Rescheduling may be a way out for a firm having problems meeting its interest payments, provided it has sufficient assets. When a firm asks to reschedule its debts, it means that it wants its interest payments reduced in the short-term and the difference added to the capital owing. Then, when profits and cash flow improve, it will be able to meet its liabilities. This option may suit both parties if it is felt that the business is only suffering from short-term financial instability.

One way of assessing a firm's stability is to calculate the number of times its loan interest can be met out of profits. The formula is:

Interest Cover $=$ $\dfrac{\text{Net Profit before Interest}}{\text{Interest Charges}}$

The higher the ratio, the less risk involved and this will be reflected in the company's credit rating and in its cost of borrowed capital.

Shareholders benefit whenever a company uses small amounts of debt in its capital structure, because it will increase the value of the business. Large amounts of debt capital should be avoided because they have the potential to damage the long term viability of the business should earnings be insufficient to meet interest and capital repayments.

5. Investment Ratios

Investment ratios are concerned with measuring the returns which a shareholder receives by purchasing shares in one company as opposed to another. Investment ratios show what the firm can earn with its share capital and the returns paid to shareholders.

INTERPRETING FINANCIAL STATEMENTS

Whenever an investor buys a share in a company they have acquired an asset which gives them the right to receive an uncertain amount of future earnings and dividends. If it were possible to predict future earnings for a share with certainty, then the estimated future price and dividend payments for the share could be calculated mathematically. Investors could decide whether or not the current share price would enable them to earn an acceptable return.

This is why investors seek to forecast future earnings by using a range of statistical forecasting techniques, enabling them to estimate the risks and future returns of investing in a company's shares. If management can make decisions which will lead to a strong and stable growth in earnings, the shares will be popular with investors and shareholder wealth will be maximised by an increase in the share price.

An equity investor will want to know what return the company can earn with its share capital. If the return is 12 per cent, it shows that at the end of the financial year the business has earned an additional 12p on every pound invested in it. The formula for calculating the earnings per share is:

Earnings Per Share   = $\dfrac{\text{Profit after tax and Preference Dividend}}{\text{Issued Ordinary Shares}}$

Companies usually only distribute part of their profits as dividends and so a shareholder will not receive a share of the total earnings. Nevertheless, the higher the earnings, the more profit which can be distributed and so investors seek companies making high returns on their issued capital. The problem for investors is that a firm's earnings will only follow an increase in sales provided that there is no change in the ratio of expenses to sales, operating level, product mix and the level of debt in the firm's capital structure. This is why an increase in sales does not automatically lead to an increase in earnings per share and why investors are placing more emphasis on the cash earnings per share.

Cash Earnings Per Share = $\dfrac{\text{Net Profit after Tax} + \text{All Non-Cash Expenditure}}{\text{Number of Ordinary Shares}}$

This ratio shows the funds generated from trading that remain after all cash expenses have been paid. It is an important ratio because it shows how good the firm is at generating finance internally which can be used to expand the business.

Since 22 June 1993 if a figure is given for earnings per share in the annual accounts then, with the exception of accounts prepared under a statutory framework, the calculation must conform to the requirements of FRS 3. This states that the earnings per share must be calculated on the profit attributable to the firm's ordinary shareholders after deducting minority interests, extraordinary items and preference share dividends.

Dividend Payments

The dividend payments are always calculated on the nominal value of the share. This is the price as shown on the share certificate but which is likely to be different from its market value. If a company has £1.00 shares and pays a dividend of 10p per share, the return to a shareholder would be 10 per cent because the market price is the same as the nominal price. This is unlikely to be the case, for the share price will rise if the company is profitable and distributes part of its profits as dividends.

If the market price rose to £2.00, the return to the shareholder would be 5 per cent because, in order to receive the dividend, they have had to pay £2.00 per share. This inevitably reduces their return (in this case by fifty per cent). The dividend payable as a percentage of the share's market price can be calculated by using the Dividend Yield Ratio.

$$\text{Dividend Yield} = \frac{\text{Gross Dividend Per Ordinary Share} \times 100}{\text{Market Price Per Share}}$$

This ratio is useful for making comparisons with other investments and is likely to influence investors' choice about which company's shares they should buy. The dividend yield for a share is similar to the current yield on bonds but it should be remembered that the financial risks of owning a share are higher. The first task is to calculate the gross dividend as the net dividend will be the dividend paid after tax has been deducted.

For example if a share has paid a net dividend of 5.7p per share, calculate the dividend yield if the tax rate is 25% and the share price is £2.29.

Gross Dividend   = $\dfrac{5.7}{0.75}$ = 7.6p per share

The dividend yield is therefore

Dividend yield   = $\dfrac{\text{Gross Dividend Per Share}}{\text{Market Price Per Share}}$ x 100

= $\dfrac{7.6}{229}$ x 100

Dividend Yield = 3.3%

Dividend Cover

The dividend cover shows what proportion of the firm's profit is distributed as profit and how much is retained to finance future investment. It is a useful measure of a company's ability to pay its ordinary shareholders a dividend while, at the same time, withholding sufficient profit for reinvestment. The ratio is:

Dividend Cover   = $\dfrac{\text{Profit after tax, less Preference Dividend}}{\text{Gross Dividend on Ordinary Shares}}$

Price to Earnings Ratio

This ratio is useful to potential investors, for it shows how many years it would take for the earnings per share to equal the ordinary share's market price. The formula is:

Price to Earnings Ratio   = $\dfrac{\text{Market Price Per Share}}{\text{Earnings Per Ordinary Share}}$

Many people believe that a low price to earnings ratio is good because its earnings are a greater proportion of its market price. As a general rule the price of a share is governed by the laws of supply and demand and, if a share is popular, its price will rise as more investors seek to purchase shares in the company's future earnings. Companies which are very profitable, and which pay good dividends, tend to have a high price to earnings ratio because of their expected future earnings potential. A high ratio suggests low financial risk whereas a low ratio tends to be synonymous with high risk.

A company's price to earnings ratio will change once investors expect a change in a firm's expected growth rate of earnings and this is why companies which are expected to have stable growth in earnings per share will experience higher P/E ratios than companies where earnings are cyclical or are considered speculative.

There is a large amount of research which suggests that accounting investment ratios may not be a good way of assessing the future performance of a company's share price. In accounting a value is placed upon a company by capitalising its earnings per share. This is done by using the price/earnings formula so that if a firm's shares sell at ten times these earnings, and if earnings are fifty pence, then the share price according to the accounting model would be five pounds. Whilst this model is easy to calculate, it assumes that price/earnings multiples do not change, whereas in reality they are constantly changing as a result of managerial decisions such as acquisitions, disposals, changes in the level of gearing and new investment announcements. This is why the model is not a good and reliable measure of value.

An alternative model is the economic one which seeks to value a share according to the cash flow which the business can generate and its risk. The economic model values a company by discounting the company's expected future free cash flow to determine its present value, thereby according with the financial principle of time value of money discussed in chapter 1.

Free cash flow is cash which the firm has generated in excess of any immediate liability and so, at the end of a financial year, a business can have either a positive or negative free cash flow position.

In the long term a firm's value will depend upon the return which it can earn from its capital spending and not just its free cash flow position. This is because it is possible for a profitable company, which is investing heavily, to have a negative free cash flow whilst an unprofitable one, which is reducing its asset base, could have a positive free cash flow.

The debate between accounting and economic models of value has recently grown in intensity and this explains the current interest in Economic Value Analysis. Economic Value Analysis estimates a business's true economic profit for the year and highlights operating efficiency and balance sheet management and, therefore, provides another measure of evaluating managerial performance. Economic profit seeks to measure the growth in investment and return, thereby showing the difference between the earnings on the equity capital invested in the company and the cost of that capital. Advocates of economic profit believe that it forces management to consider the long term when making decisions and the expected future cash flows which should result from such decisions. Such a measure of value is not favoured by accountants because it does not meet the criteria as an objective measure of income - SSAP6.

If the capital markets are efficient, then accounting measures of wealth are unlikely to influence the share price because the capital markets will value a share according to the sum of the present value of the company's future cash flow and other benefits discounted at a present value rate. The share price in an efficient market will resemble a *random walk* with the price changing as the market receives new information.

All expectations are based on assumptions about future earnings and new information can have a profound effect on the profitability of a company and its share price. In an efficient market it is possible for a company to increase its profits and earnings per share whilst seeing its share price fall, because new information has changed investor expectations, leading to a corresponding correction in the share price.

In such a market the share price will reflect all available information and so the share price represents a fair price, because it is correctly valued. This explains why past information is unlikely to be of value as it is already incorporated in the share price, thereby making investment ratios based on published annual accounts of limited use or value to investors when making investment decisions.

Limitations of Accounting Ratios

Accounting ratios can only provide a guide to the present and the future. They do not on their own provide answers but they do allow managers, investors and lenders to focus on the financial strengths and weaknesses of the business. Sudden changes in a firm's cash flow, together with an increase in creditors, are worrying signs for they show that the business operates in an unstable trading environment. Any increase in sales should always be matched by a similar increase in stock, debtors and cash. Stable growth is best so that the firm's ratios remain in kilter with last year's ratio, thereby showing that the business can meet its future financial obligations.

Unfortunately the outside investor does not have access to the same amount of information as the internal management and what information there is may not be representative of the company's normal financial position. For instance, stock levels may be unrealistically low and cash deposits artificially high because of the seasonal nature of the business. This is why so much emphasis is now placed on a firm's ability to generate cash. Nevertheless despite these limitations, ratio analysis is an important management tool for it forces managers, investors, and lenders to focus on the future and is a useful attitude development device.

Checklist of the Key Accounting Ratios

Ratios which assess liquidity

Current Ratio
$$\frac{\text{Current Assets}}{\text{Current Liabilities}}$$

Acid Test Ratio or Quick Ratio
$$\frac{\text{Current Assets Less Stock}}{\text{Current Liabilities}}$$

Sales to Working Capital Ratio
$$\frac{\text{Sales}}{\text{Working Capital}}$$

Sales to Capital Employed Ratio
$$\frac{\text{Sales}}{\text{Capital Employed}}$$

Net Working Capital to Sales Ratio
$$\frac{\text{Stock + Debtors - Creditors}}{\text{Sales}}$$

Ratios which assess how effectively a firm uses its assets

Stock Turnover Ratio
$$\frac{\text{Cost of Goods Sold}}{\text{Average Stock}}$$

Debtors Collection Period Ratio
$$\frac{\text{Debtors}}{\text{Credit Sales/365}}$$

Time Taken to Pay Creditors Ratio
$$\frac{\text{Creditors}}{\text{Credit Purchases/365}}$$

Sales to Fixed Assets Ratio
$$\frac{\text{Sales}}{\text{Fixed Assets}}$$

Fixed Assets to Current Assets Ratio
$$\frac{\text{Fixed Assets}}{\text{Current Assets}}$$

Ratios which assess profitability

Primary or Return on Capital Employed Ratio

$$\frac{\text{Profit x 100}}{\text{Capital Employed}}$$

Gross Profit to Sales Ratio

$$\frac{\text{Gross Profit x 100}}{\text{Sales}}$$

Net Profit to Sales Ratio

$$\frac{\text{Net Profit x 100}}{\text{Sales}}$$

Ratios which asses a firm's capital structure

Gearing Ratio

$$\frac{\text{Net Debt}}{\text{Shareholders' Funds}}$$

Shareholders' Investment Ratio

$$\frac{\text{Shareholders' Investment}}{\text{Total Assets}}$$

Interest Cover Ratio

$$\frac{\text{Profit before Interest and Tax}}{\text{Interest Paid}}$$

Ratios which asses the returns paid to investors

Earning Per Share Ratio

$$\frac{\text{Profit after Tax and Preference Share Dividend}}{\text{Number of Issued Ordinary Shares}}$$

Dividend Yield Ratio

$$\frac{\text{Ordinary Dividend Per Share x 100}}{\text{Market Price per Share}}$$

Dividend Cover Ratio

$$\frac{\text{Profit after Tax less Preference Dividend}}{\text{Gross Dividend on Ordinary Shares}}$$

Price Earnings Ratio

$$\frac{\text{Present Market Price per Ordinary Share}}{\text{Annual Earnings per Share}}$$

QUESTIONS

Answers begin page 474

1.   What do the following ratios seek to measure?

	Ratio	Calculation	Assessment
a.	Acid test		
b.	Primary ratio		
c.	Gearing ratio		
d.	Interest cover		
e.	Current ratio		
f.	Dividend yield		
g.	Earnings per share		
h.	Stock turnover		
i.	Debtors' collection period		
j.	Price to earnings ratio		

2. **The Wine Grotto**. The Wine Grotto is a chain of off licences in the north east of England. The directors have just received extracts from the audited accounts and they are shown below:

Profit and Loss Account for the year ending year 5		
	£'000	£'000
Sales		460
Cost of goods sold		220
Gross profit		240
Wages	50	
Overheads	30	
		80
Net Profit		160

Balance Sheet as at end of year 5			
	£'000	£'000	£'000
Fixed assets		400	
Current assets			
Stock	80		
Debtors	120		
Bank	400		
	600		
Less current liabilities			
Creditors	300	300	
Net Assets			700
Financed by			
Share capital			600
Reserves			100
Shareholders' funds			700

The directors have asked you to calculate the firm's:
- a. Current ratio
- b. Acid test ratio
- c. Stock turnover
- d. Debtors' turnover
- e. Return on capital employed.

3. **Traditional Kitchens Ltd**.

From the following information prepare a report outlining the changes in the firm's financial fortunes over the last financial year.

Balance sheet as at 31 December, Year Four

	This Year £		Last Year £	
Fixed Assets				
Land and buildings		60,000		46,000
Fixtures and fittings		42,000		14,000
Plant and machinery		14,000		14,000
		116,000		74,000
Current Assets				
Raw materials	16,000		18,000	
Work in progress	14,000		26,000	
Finished goods	20,000		24,000	
Debtors	56,000		44,000	
Cash/bank balance	4,000		2,000	
	110,000		114,000	
Current liabilities				
Creditors	30,000		41,000	
Bank overdraft	20,000		12,000	
Corporation tax	16,000		15,000	
	66,000		68,000	
Working capital		44,000		46,000
Net assets		160,000		120,000
Financed by				
Share capital				
Ord. shares @ 50p each		80,000		60,000
7% pref. shares @ £1 each		40,000		40,000
Retained profits		40,000		20,000
Shareholders' funds		160,000		120,000

Additional information:

Extract of Profit and Loss Account for the year ended 31 December Year 5

	This Year £	Last Year £
Sales	200,000	140,000
Gross profit	80,000	70,000
Net profit before tax	35,000	15,000

Chapter 12

Accounting for the Effects of Inflation

Introduction

When a firm's accounts are prepared under the historical cost account accounting convention they make no allowance for inflation. Although the accounts comply with the requirements of the Companies' Act 1985 and 1989, the Financial Reporting Standards and the Standard Statements of Accounting Practice, they will generally understate the firm's assets and overstate its profits. By failing to adjust the annual accounts for the effects of inflation, it can be argued that they do not give a true and fair view of the firm's financial position. Inflation accounting seeks to mitigate this defect by amending the accounts, showing managers, investors and lenders how inflation has affected the company's financial performance.

What is Inflation?

Inflation can be defined as a persistent rise in the general price level of goods and purchasing power of a unit of currency over a period of time.

The purchasing power of a Pound is calculated by using index numbers which compare the number of goods which a unit of currency can buy one year with another. An index number is a statistical technique which uses the figures for one year's set of data as a base and then calculates the following year's figures as a percentage of the base. Most indices take the base figure as being one hundred, and so if the price of a good last year was £100 and this year it is £120, the index would be calculated as follows by the formula:

Price Index $\quad \dfrac{\text{Price in Year Two}}{\text{Price in Year One}} \quad \text{x } 100 = \dfrac{£120 \text{ x } 100}{£100} = £120$

The index would then show the information as follows:

Last Year	100
This Year	120

ACCOUNTING FOR THE EFFECTS OF INFLATION

The Retail Price Index is calculated by using a Weighted Average Index which takes into account the movement in price of a number of household items between one year and the next. The Retail Price Index is commonly used as a measure of the rate of inflation and is useful for comparison purposes.

How Does Inflation Affect Financial Statements?

In Britain annual accounts are prepared under the historical cost accounting convention. The Chartered Institute of Management Accountants defines this as a system of accounting in which all values in revenue and capital are based on the costs actually incurred or as revalued from time to time. The final accounts, therefore, ignore the different purchasing power of money, making comparison of past profits, sales and shareholders' funds nearly impossible. Although the accounts may show the business to be profitable, if the profits were adjusted to show the effect of inflation, the profits and returns could turn out to be negative. This can be illustrated by three examples.

Examples of how inflation distorts accounts prepared under the historical cost accounting convention

All of these examples consider the effects of inflation on three hypothetical businesses. They show how inflation affects a firm's fixed assets, stocks of goods and its capital structure.

Example 1

Four years ago a farmer purchased a combine harvester and rented it out to other farmers. The machine cost £80,000 and was depreciated over the four years using the straight line basis. The farmer retained all profits in cash. The profits for each year were as follows:

	Year 1	Year 2	Year 3	Year 4
Retained Profit after Depreciation	£15,000	£25,000	£35,000	£40,000

At the end of the fourth year the combine harvester had been completely depreciated as it had no residual or resale value. In spite of depreciating the full cost of the machine over four years' trading and accumulating profits of

£115,000, the farmer was unable to purchase a new machine because its cost had risen to £150,000.

Although the annual accounts prepared under the historical cost accounting convention show profits of £115,000, these are not enough to purchase a new machine. If one takes the effects of inflation into account, it can be argued that the business has made only £45,000 profit over the four years and that the annual accounts should reflect this fact.

Note: £20,000 depreciation must be added back to the retained profit figure before deducting the cost of the new machine. £195,000 - £150,000 = £45,000

Example 2

At the beginning of the financial year a market trader started a business with £20,000 and bought 20,000 plants at £1.00 each. The business had no other assets and so its opening balance sheet was as follows:

Balance Sheet for Market Trader at start of Year One

Capital		Assets	
Owner's equity	£20,000	Stock	£20,000
	£20,000		£20,000

During the year all of the stock was sold for £40,000 and £5,000 expenses were incurred. The trader decided to purchase a further 20,000 plants before the end of the financial year, but the cost of each plant had risen to £1.75. The trader's profit and loss account prepared under the historical cost accounting convention will look like this:

Profit and Loss Account for the Year Ending Year One

	£
Sales	40,000
Less Cost of Goods Sold	20,000
Gross Profit	20,000
Less Expenses	5,000
Net Profit	15,000

Balance Sheet for Market Trader at Year End

Capital	£	Assets	£
Owner's Equity	20,000	Stock	35,000
Retained profit	15,000		
	35,000		35,000

At the start of the year the firm had a stock of 20,000 plants and it had the same stock at the year end. If the stock had been bought before the price increase, the firm would have made a holding gain by having the stock which had increased in price. Unfortunately the firm placed its order after the price increase and so, although the firm has made profits of £15,000, the price increase has resulted in all the profits being reinvested in stock just to maintain the same level of trading as last year. In such a situation the £15,000 profit ceases to have any real meaning.

Example 3

The Cash Poor Company and the Cash Rich Company

These two companies make similar goods and operate in the same market where the rate of inflation is 10 per cent. The Cash Poor Company has to give credit and is unable to purchase new stock until it has received payment from its debtors. The company is unable to purchase goods on credit because of its poor credit rating which has been brought about by its cash shortages. Unfortunately while it has been waiting to receive payment from its debtors, the price of its raw materials has increased and so it has effectively lost money by not having the cash to purchase the stock before the price increase.

The Cash Rich Company, on the other hand, is able to give and accept credit. As soon as the stock is sold, more is ordered on credit ahead of the price increase, giving the company a holding gain by the time the goods are ready to be sold. This holding gain will inflate the firm's profits.

The last three examples have all illustrated how inflation affects a firm's annual accounts. These gains will be made on fixed assets and on stocks. The problem is to whom do these gains belong? Let us consider two different companies called the Share Capital Trading Company and the Share and Loan Trading Company.

The shareholders are the owners of a company and they are entitled to any profits made after all other expenses and liabilities have been met. The loan holders, on the other hand, do not own the business but will receive interest on the money lent and must have their capital repaid at the end of the loan. If there is inflation, the amount repaid will have had its purchasing power reduced during the life of the loan and the lender must hope that the interest payments have compensated for this. This is the only return which loan holders receive for, not being owners, they are denied any holding gains which accrue from inflation. In the Share Trading Company all of the gains will accrue to the shareholders as they have provided all of the finance. This will also be the case in the Share and Loan Trading Company, because the loan holders receive none of the benefits as they are not owners. During times of inflation, the shareholders see their funds in the company increase through the creation of reserves which show the holding gains at the expense of the loan holders, who see the monetary value of their loan fall as inflation rises.

Limitations of Historical Cost Accounting

When accounts are prepared under the historical cost convention, the assets in the balance sheet are shown at their original cost or revalued amount. Many companies now regularly revalue their property assets, but this is rarely done to the other assets. During times of inflation, the accounts will fail to show the value of the assets employed by the business and, as a consequence, it becomes nearly impossible to measure the business' profitability.

Once fixed assets and stock are incorrectly valued, the profit and loss account will not show the correct profit for it will have under-provided for depreciation and included stock-holding gains as part of its profits. When this is done, the firm is in danger of paying out too high dividends, leaving it short of retained profit which will be needed to finance new investment.

In an attempt to overcome these shortcomings, the accountancy bodies and academics have given much thought as to how accounting information can be presented to show the effects of inflation. Two main methods have been considered. These are the Current Purchasing Power (CPP) and the Current Cost Accounting (CCA) methods.

Both methods seek to measure the effects of inflation by adjusting a unit of currency to show its real purchasing power. The problem is whether to adjust the accounts to show the effect on the shareholders' or the business' purchasing power. The current purchasing power method shows how inflation has affected purchasing goods in general, while current cost accounting will show its effect on the goods and services which the business needs to purchase in order to trade.

The CPP and CCA methods seek to adjust accounts prepared under the historical cost accounting convention by using two different measurements of how inflation affects businesses. The CPP methods seeks to show the effects of inflation on the shareholders' capital base, while CCA explains how it has affected the firm's operating capacity.

In the UK the CPP method was first adopted to try to show how inflation affects accounts prepared under the historical cost convention. This method seeks to make adjustments to monetary values by using index numbers, making comparison of previous financial accounts possible. One of the main problems with this method is that, while it adjusts the value of money brought about by inflation, it does not show the correct value of the firm's assets or liabilities. This makes it difficult to assess the firm's profitability and there is still the danger that the firm will distribute too much of its profits as dividend, because it has underprovided for depreciation and included stock holding gains in its profit calculations.

In an attempt to overcome these limitations, the Accountancy bodies (following the Sandiland's report) introduced a new system of accounting for inflation for a three year trial period, in 1980. The new method was called Current Cost Accounting and applied mainly to the large public limited companies. The method proved unpopular with industrialists and some members of the profession because of the costs involved in preparing the information and the subjectivity of placing correct market values on company fixed assets. Although the accounting standard *Standard Statement of Accounting Practice 16* was finally withdrawn in 1988, the Accounting Standards Committee recommended that the final accounts should show the following when calculating the profit made during a financial year:

a.   whether the firm's assets have been valued on a historical or current cost basis.

b.   the effect of inflation on the firm's working capital and long-term capital which is referred to as the capital maintenance concept.

c.   whether the accounts show just the monetary value of the currency or whether some attempt has been made to calculate the current purchasing power of the currency.

The Principles of Current Cost Accounting

Current cost accounting techniques adjust final accounts prepared under the historical accounting convention to show the effects of inflation. Four adjustments are made and these are known as:

1. Depreciation Adjustment
2. Cost of Sales Adjustment (COSA)
3. Monetary Working Capital Adjustment (MWCA)
4. Gearing Adjustment.

Depreciation Adjustment

During times of high inflation the monetary value of assets increases. If the depreciation provision is not calculated on the replacement cost, the business will not set aside sufficient funds out of profit to be able to purchase new equipment. In order to remedy this situation, current cost accounting charges an additional provision (based on the replacement cost of the asset) and this amount is then deducted from the historical profit.

Cost of Sales Adjustment (COSA)

Under the historic cost convention the profit and loss account does not distinguish between a stock operating and holding gain. An operating gain occurs when the stock is sold in the course of trading for a higher price, while a holding gain is made when stock increases in value because of inflation before the stock can be sold. Under the system of current cost accounting, this holding gain is calculated by using index numbers for the opening and closing stock. This is done by applying the following formula:

Opening Stock   x $\dfrac{\text{Average Index During the Accounting Period}}{\text{Index at the start of the year}}$

Closing Stock   x $\dfrac{\text{Average Index for Financial Period}}{\text{Index at the end of the year}}$

Monetary Working Capital Adjustment

When stock prices rise because of inflation, a company needs more capital to purchase the same amount of stock. This cost can be offset if the firm is able to purchase the goods on credit, for then it is the creditor who is financing the extra cost. Unfortunately, when the firm sells goods, it will also have to give credit and so part of this gain will be lost to its debtors. As a result, a further adjustment is needed to the cost of sales adjustment, depending on whether debtors exceed creditors or vice versa. If debtors exceed creditors, then the firm is in effect giving away money to its debtors and this fact must be reflected by adding the cost to the cost of sales adjustment. If creditors exceed debtors, the firm is saving money and this saving should be deducted from the cost of sales adjustment, increasing the current cost profit. Once again the calculation is made using index numbers and the formula is:

$$\frac{\text{Closing Monetary Working Capital}}{\text{Closing Index Number}} \quad \text{x} \quad \frac{\text{Average Index Number}}{1}$$

$$\frac{\text{Opening Monetary Working Capital}}{\text{Opening Index Number}} \quad \text{x} \quad \frac{\text{Average Index Number}}{1}$$

Adjustments for Stock and Monetary Working Capital

Both of these adjustments will either reduce or increase the historical profit, depending upon whether or not trade has expanded or decreased. If trade has expanded, one would expect larger stocks and monetary working capital at the end of the year than at the beginning. In times of high inflation this would also be the case, even if the volume of trading remained at the same level – because inflation will increase its monetary value. Unless there is a fairly dramatic down-turn in business activity, the end of year figure should be higher than that at the beginning and so the adjustment will be shown as a deduction from profits.

Gearing Adjustment

The gearing adjustment seeks to measure the gain to the business from being financed partly by long-term debt capital instead of being financed entirely from share capital. This is because any unrealised holding gains, such as the revaluation of fixed assets, or realised holding gain, such as the sale of stock, will be shown as a reserve in the current cost balance sheet.

While current cost accounting seeks to amend the historical accounts so as to show the effects of inflation, it has proved to be a most contentious subject. The Accounting Standards Committee, on withdrawing their *Statement of Accounting Practice 16*, were only able to recommend that some attempt be made to consider how inflation can distort accounts prepared on a historical cost basis.

Although it is no longer a legal requirement to adjust final accounts for the effects of inflation, the problem cannot be ignored because inflation makes financial analysis over a period of time very difficult. The central problem still remains unsolved which is how to adjust a firm's annual accounts for the effects of inflation without making them incomprehensible to all but accountants, corporate treasurers and financial analysts.

QUESTIONS

Answers begin page 476

1. **Plumbing Supplies**

It is 8 o'clock in the morning and George Turner has just taken the shutters down before serving his first customer. Five minutes later Linda enters the shop clutching a piece of paper and they engage in the following conversation:

George: Hello Linda, you look worried.

Linda: Just started a massive job. I will need a central heating boiler, seven radiators together with all the copper piping and fittings. Look, can I come back and collect them in an hour?

George: Yes, that's no problem. I assume you want your standard order.

Linda: Yes, that should do it. Just put it all on my account and I will settle up with you at the end of the month.

George: You know you already owe me £2,000 from last month and this little order will nearly double it. I'm afraid I will have to ask you for £500. Unfortunately the business just cannot afford to be owed so much money.

Linda: Look, here is £300. I'm sorry but I have no more cash on me at the moment. There was a time when this amount of money would have bought all my supplies but now I never know what it's going to cost.

George: Well it's the same for me. Every month the wholesaler puts up his prices. The stock costs more and more and so I end up being owed a small fortune. The trouble is while I give credit I'm often having to borrow the money myself on overdraft from my bank. My accountant keeps telling me that it is bad business but she does not have the problem of trying to sell the stuff. You know the little van I have, three years ago I paid £8,000 for it and the other day I thought I would buy a new one, but when the garage only offered me £2,000 for it, and

189

wanted £12,000 for a new one, I decided not to proceed. The real joke is that the van is valued at £6,000 in the accounts.

Linda: You are right. Same thing happened to me when I changed by van, except I had to because it was so old. It took nearly all my cash to replace it. I must rush. See you in an hour.

a. How does inflation affect George and Linda's businesses?

b. Why do George's accounts not show the effects of inflation?

c. What adjustments would be necessary to George's accounts to take account of the effects of inflation?

Chapter 13

Introduction to Cost Accounting

Introduction

Management have to make decisions about what products to manufacture, their selling price, the number to be sold and the profits required to ensure that the firm earns a reasonable return on its capital employed. Cost and Management Accounting techniques provide management with information about the costs and the estimated profits at different levels of output, enabling them to make better business decisions. The long-term aim should be to make the business more cost effective and this can only be achieved by controlling the activities which give rise to costs. Information is, therefore, the key to cost control and this is why many firms have invested heavily in information technology so that the business has an effective management information system.

The Accounting Function and a Firm's Management Information System

The accounting function provides management with a large data base of financial information. An effective accounting system not only records this information but processes it in such a way that it assists management in their task of planning, controlling costs and decision making as well as being able to communicate effectively with outside bodies. The revolution in information technology has meant that organisations can have more powerful computer systems, at an ever decreasing cost. This has led to business systems such as accounting, production, stock control and marketing becoming integrated, thereby providing management with better information about the entire operation of their business. A good management information system is one which will increase net cash flows because the cash inflows from improved decision making outweigh the cash flows from providing it. Such a system can be said to have a positive net cash flow value of information.

Differences Between Financial and Management Accounting

Companies are required by law to keep accurate records of their financial affairs which show their sales, purchases, expenses, assets and liabilities. Once a year the firm must have its accounts audited and prepare a profit and loss account and balance sheet. The Companies' Act 1985 requires all companies to keep a system of financial accounting which will give a *true and fair view* of the business. It is from these accounts that the Inland Revenue will be able to calculate the amount of tax owed, and shareholders and lenders of funds to the business will be able to monitor its performance.

Financial accounting is concerned with the past and present. While this information is important, the main problem with it is that it tends to be out of date by the time it has been produced. As a result, management only know their costs and profits after they have been incurred.

Management accounting uses the information recorded by the financial accounting system to produce financial statements which assist management in their task of controlling and monitoring financial performance, decision making and planning.

Cost accounting is part of management accounting, but it is narrower in its focus as it concentrates on the cost of producing a product or service. It also serves as an important bridge between financial and management accounting when it provides cost information concerned with product costs as this is used for stock control purposes. This information is used to show the value of stock in the firm's balance sheet, thereby assisting the work of the financial accountant as well as providing information about inventory levels which assist the management accountant determine optimum stock levels.

Any system of management accounting must supply information which is relevant to management and which takes account of the changes which are taking place in what is now commonly referred to as the global market place. Today's business climate is one characterised by constant change coupled with an ever increasing demand from customers for quality products and services, often at ever decreasing prices. This has forced managers to consider how their business creates customer value and explains why many firms have adopted the Japanese system of Total Quality Management (TQM). Such a system seeks to bring about continuous improvement in the way an organisation conducts its business operations.

In today's market place where competition amongst firms is intense, management must focus on their customers in terms of how customer expectations are changing and what the business needs to do in order to meet customer demands. Customers are becoming ever more value conscious and better informed before making their purchasing decisions, so that they consider the value of a product or service and its price when compared with other brands and models. In such a market place management accounting techniques help a firm gain a competitive advantage by enabling it to market products and services which offer the highest ratio of value to price. This is why many businesses now consider the strategic aspects of management accounting when determining their overall corporate strategy.

Benefits of Operating a Cost Accounting System

Unlike financial accounting, there is no legal requirement to produce cost accounts but, if they are kept, the benefits from producing them must exceed their costs. If a business has an efficient and accurate cost accounting system, costs can be ascertained before they are incurred. This information can then be used for planning and control purposes. Unless this information is available, management will not know whether they are selling the product for a profit or at a loss. The main benefit of operating a cost accounting system is that it is immediately apparent which products contribute most to the firm's profits and which products or services have the highest costs in relation to their selling price. There are other benefits of introducing a cost accounting system. They are:

1. The departments which are operating efficiently and inefficiently are identified.

2. Stock control is done earlier.

3. The firm can accurately estimate its costs, which will help them set their prices.

4. The firm can compare costs from one period to another.

5. Budgeted accounts can be prepared so that management can compare actual results with budgeted.

An effective cost accounting system is one which improves the firm's cash flow and profitability by providing information which enables prices to be set more effectively.

What is Meant by the Term Cost?

Whenever an organisation provides a service or makes a product it incurs an expense and so the broadest definition embraces this monetary cost. The real cost of any decision is the cost of the alternative foregone or what economists call the *opportunity cost*. Resources such as materials, labour and cash are scarce and so management should realise that, in addition to their monetary cost, there is the other cost that once used they cannot generally be used for another purpose. By seeing costs in this way, management are forced to evaluate different courses of action. In accounting there are many different cost terms and these are now explained.

Cost Centre

In cost accounting each activity of the business should be divided into cost centres so that costs can be ascertained. Examples of a cost centre are departments, equipment, such as a print centre, a person or a physical part of the business such as a paint shop.

Cost Unit

A cost unit is an accounting term for describing whatever it is that a firm produces. In a paint factory the cost units would be tins of paint.

Cost Allocation

Some costs will be incurred either by the cost centre or be part of the cost of making a particular cost unit. Cost allocation describes the process of allotting whole items of cost to cost centres or cost units.

Cost Apportionment

Not all costs will relate directly to the cost centre or cost unit. In such cases the correct procedure is to allot a proportion of the relevant cost to either the cost centre or cost unit. This is an important concept and their different treatment will be explained in more detail in the next chapter.

Cost Absorption

Some costs, such as building insurance, relate to the whole firm and not just a particular department. These costs must be apportioned to the relevant cost centre. Cost absorption is the term for allotting overhead costs to cost units.

Classification of Expenditure

In cost accounting expenditure which can be identified as having been incurred in the production of a cost unit is called a direct cost. Any cost which is indirectly incurred is called an indirect cost.

Is the Cost Direct or Indirect?

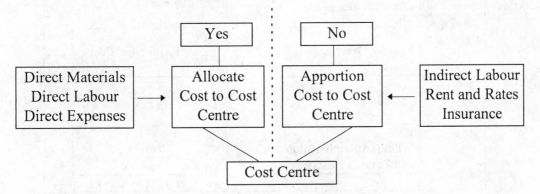

Figure 13:1 Allocation of Costs to Production

Direct Costs

These are costs which are incurred as the product is made. They include the cost of the materials used in production, plus the wages of the workers directly involved in manufacturing, together with any other direct costs of production. Collectively these costs are referred to as the *prime costs*.

Indirect Costs

Direct costs are not the only ones involved in making a product. Other costs, such as indirect materials, indirect labour, rent, factory insurance and cleaning, will also be incurred and these must be accounted for. Any cost which is not directly related to production is referred to as an *indirect cost*. These costs are not charged directly to the product or cost unit but are shared amongst them by, firstly, apportioning the overheads to cost centres, and then by absorbing them into the cost units.

The cost will be made up of all the direct cost plus any indirect costs which are incurred in producing the good or service.

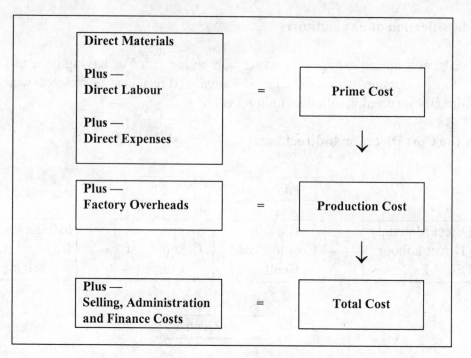

Figure 13:2 Costs of Making a Product

The cost of making a cost unit, such as a barrel of beer, would be shown as in the following financial statement:

The Cost of Making a Cost Unit

	£
Direct Materials	5
Direct Labour	3
Direct Expenses	1
Prime Cost	9
Proportion of Production Overhead	7
Factory cost of making Cost Unit	16
Proportion of administration, selling and distribution overhead	5
Total Cost of Cost Unit	21

At the end of the financial year a Manufacturing Account must be prepared which will show the cost of the firm's output and this figure is transferred to the firm's Trading Account. The Profit and Loss Account and Balance Sheet are then prepared in the usual way.

Example of a Manufacturing Account and a Trading Account for the year ending 31 December Year 7

	£	£
Opening stock of raw materials	8,000	
Add purchase of raw materials	50,000	
	58,000	
Less closing stock of raw materials	12,000	
Raw materials used in production	46,000	
Factory wages	10,000	
Prime Cost		56,000
Factory rent and rates	3,000	
Factory heat, light and power	2,000	
Plant repairs	1,000	
Depreciation on factory plant	1,000	
Factory cost		63,000
Add opening stock of work in progress	2,500	
		65,500
Less closing stock of work in progress		1,500
Factory cost of finished goods		
transferred to Trading Account		64,000

	£	£
Sales		300,000
Less:		
Finished Goods - opening stock 1/1 yr7		46,000
Cost of Goods Manufactured transferred		
from Manufacturing Account		64,000
		190,000
Less Closing Stock of Finished Goods		
31/12 yr7		40,000
		150,000
Gross Profit		150,000
Less Non-Manufacturing Costs:	35,000	
Administration Expenses	60,000	
Selling Expenses	10,000	
Finance Costs		**105,000**
		45,000

The Preparation of a Manufacturing Account for External Publication

When a manufacturing account is prepared for external publication, a distinction is made between costs which relate to production, product costs and those which do not, known as period costs.

Product costs include all production costs of making a product such as material, direct and indirect product wages and depreciation of plant and equipment. Such costs are treated as an asset until sold.

Period costs are non-production costs such as administration, selling and the costs of loans and finance, and are always treated as an expense. Such costs must never be treated as an asset, and once written off, as an expense in the profit and loss account. Product and period costs are explained further in chapter 16.

Figure 13:3 Treatment of Products and Period Costs for External Publication

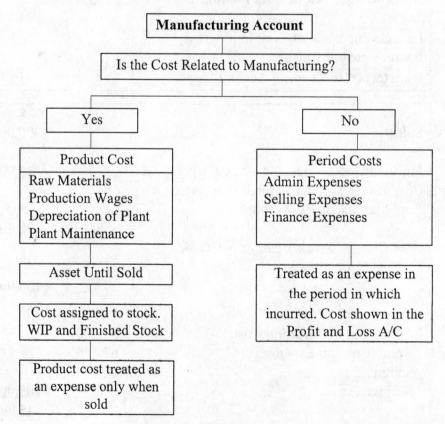

Classification of Costs

Accountants classify costs according to their nature, function and behaviour. The nature defines the type of cost, such as the cost of the raw material needed to make the product, whereas functional classification describes the area of the business which has incurred the cost, such as the sales department.

Once management know the nature and function of their costs, they need to know how they alter according to different levels of activity. Some costs will remain unchanged, while others will vary proportionately to output. This is what is meant by the term *cost behaviour.*

How Costs Alter According to the Level of Activity

Fixed Costs

These are costs which remain constant at a given level of activity. The cost of renting a building is an example of a fixed cost because the amount of rent paid will depend upon the space rented and not on the level of output or sales. So long as the firm does not need any additional space, this cost will remain fixed and this is why they are said to be independent of activity.

Example of Fixed Costs

Management can expect the following costs to remain relatively stable regardless of the level of output within the organisation: rent, rates, road tax, depreciation, advertising and insurance payments. These do not move in sympathy with production and sales but are unavoidable and are incurred even when the business is not working.

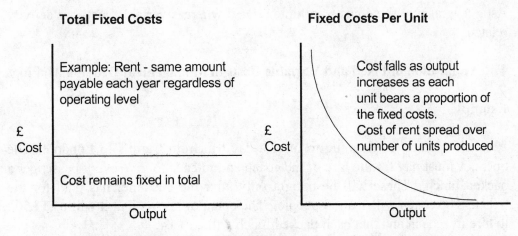

Figure 13:4 How Fixed Costs Behave According to Activity

Variable Costs

These are costs which vary with changes in the level of output. Such costs change in direct proportion to changes in volume and so a firm making shirts will have to purchase enough cloth to make each shirt, and the more shirts it makes the greater the cost of the material. Any cost which increases with output is a variable cost, and so any change in output will have a direct effect on the firm's costs. For example the more shirts that are made, the greater the total material cost, although in cost accounting the material cost per shirt is assumed to remain constant. Quantity discounts are, therefore, ignored.

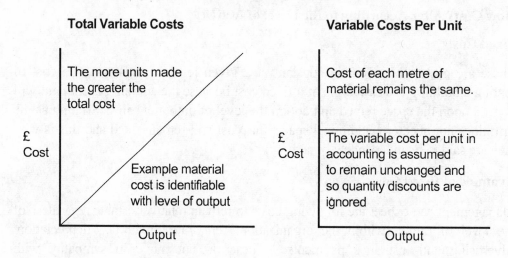

Figure 13:5 How Variable Costs Behave According to Activity

As a general rule fixed costs are time related whereas variable costs are activity related.

The Application of Fixed and Variable Costs in Management Decision Making

Example

A coach operator is planning to offer a day trip from Cardiff to London. The operator must pay for the hire of the coach and intends to give every passenger a packed lunch. These will be bought only after the customer has paid for the ticket. The coach will seat 50 people. The operator knows that it will cost £500 to hire the coach and that each packed lunch will cost £4.

In this example the hire of the coach is a fixed cost. Once it is booked, the hirer must pay for it, even if there are no passengers. On the other hand, the packed lunches are a variable cost for they will only be provided to passengers who have booked a place. The tour operator will need £500 to cover the hire cost and will need an additional £200 to provide all travellers with a packed lunch (£4 x 50). If there are any unbooked places on the coach the operator will save the £4 cost of the packed lunch as it is a variable cost.

The problem for the operator is to decide what price to charge for the journey. The price must be competitive with other forms of transport as well as covering costs and providing a profit.

The cost of the packed lunch is variable and so, the more people who travel, the greater the cost. As each packed lunch costs £4 the total variable cost will be the number of people requiring lunch multiplied by the price. The £500 cost of the coach, however, is fixed and so, although this cost is fixed, the cost for each passenger will fall as more people travel. This is so because the fixed cost is shared between the number of travellers. This can be seen from the following table:

Cost of the coach trip to London

Number of passengers	Fixed cost per person £	Variable cost per person £	Total cost £
0	500	-	500
1	500	4	504
10	50	40	540
20	25	80	580
40	12.50	160	660
50	10	200	700

The table shows that as more passengers travel on the coach the fixed cost per passenger falls, even though the total sum required to hire the coach remains at £500. The cost of the packed lunch is variable and so, the more people travelling, the greater the cost to the operator. It is the variable cost which increases the total cost. If the total cost is divided by the number of passengers, the total cost per passenger can be calculated. The more passengers, the more competitive the operator can be on price and the greater the likelihood of selling all the seats on the coach.

The table also shows that if 40 people travel they must each pay £12.50 to cover their fixed costs but if 50 people travel the fixed cost per person will fall to £10. This example shows that although fixed costs remain fixed in total they fall as output increases, whereas variable costs increase in proportion to output.

We have already seen that fixed costs are unaffected by changes in activity while variable costs increase proportionately as output increases. This is important to management when considering what price to charge for a product or service, as the different costs will require different treatment. The fixed costs must be paid regardless of the level of activity, while the variable costs will only be incurred once production begins.

Consider a hotel which has been asked to quote for a firm's annual dinner. The company would like the use of a function room with a buffet reception for about 200 guests. The hotel's management must decide what the costs of providing the service are and then set a price which will cover its costs and leave a profit.

The hotel's management must charge for all the direct and indirect costs be they fixed or variable. Costs, such as the food, its preparation and service, will be direct costs and can be allocated to each person served. The indirect costs, such as supervisors' wages, hotel rent and rates, must be apportioned first to the function room (which is the cost centre) and then shared amongst each meal (which is the cost unit).

If the hotel can cover all of its direct variable costs plus any variable indirect costs, the balance which is left over can be used to pay the fixed costs. The surplus which is left after paying the variable costs is called contribution, for it will contribute to the firm's fixed costs and, ultimately, to its profits.

Accounts can then be drawn up to show the variable costs of providing a service, the contribution earned from different selling prices and the profit or loss which will be made after paying the fixed costs.

Example

Income Statement showing the Variable and Fixed costs of the function evening

	£	£
Sales		3,000
Less Variable Costs		
Food	1,200	
Direct Labour	600	
Direct Variable Overhead	200	
Prime Cost		2,000
Contribution		1,000
Less Fixed Costs		700
Profit		300

By using this format instead of the traditional profit and loss layout, management can see immediately the detailed break-down of the costs involved in providing the product or service. Assuming that the fixed and variable overheads have been allocated and apportioned correctly, the hotel will know exactly the cost of providing the function. This greatly assists management when tendering for orders as they know their costs and required profit margins to meet financial targets.

QUESTIONS

Answers begin page 477

1. State which of the following costs should be classified as being direct or indirect.

	Cost	Direct	Indirect
a.	Materials		
b.	Rent		
c.	Direct labour		
d.	Supervisors' wages		
e.	Factory insurance		
f.	Rates		

2. Calculate the variable cost per unit for product X.

	£	£	£	£
Prime cost	54,000	43,200	129,000	91,800
Output	10,000	8,000	24,000	8,500
Cost per unit				

3. Calculate the material cost per unit for Product Y.

	£	£	£	£
Materials	6,750	13,500	33,750	19,125
Output	3,000	6,000	15,000	8,500
Cost per unit				

4. Calculate the direct labour cost per unit of Product Z.

	£	£	£	£
Labour cost	44,100	31,500	75,600	94,500
Output	7,000	5,000	12,000	15,000

5. If a firm has a productive capacity of 10,000 units per week and fixed costs of £10,000 what are its fixed costs per unit of output if the factory is operating at quarter capacity?

6. You are working as a trainee in the cost accounting department and have been told that the variable cost per unit of output is £5.00. What will the unit variable cost be at the following levels of output? 300, 800, 1000.

7. A travel company knows that the variable cost of travel is £10. What will be the total variable cost if it sells the following number of tickets? 50, 100, 150 and 200.

8. **Zolan Limited**. The company manufacture springs which are used in the motor industry. The firm's new factory can manufacture 20,000 springs per month. The firm's fixed costs are £40,000 per month. Recently the firm has been experiencing an erratic demand for its products. The firm's costs are shown below.

    Calculate the firm's total costs at the different levels of output.

	50%	60%	70%	80%	90%	100%
Direct materials (£6 per unit)						
Direct labour (£4 per unit)						
Variable overheads (£1.50 per unit)						
Fixed costs						

9. **The Electric Motor Company**. Electric Motors manufacture a range of motors which are used in consumer appliances. The company has just built a modern factory close to one of its other plants to manufacture engines for lawn mowers. The costs and output figures are shown below.

	£
Fixed costs per quarter	250,000
Direct materials	50.00
Direct labour	28.00

The directors have asked you to calculate the costs per quarter for the following levels of output.

Output Per Month	Total Fixed Cost	Fixed Cost Per Unit	Total Variable Cost	Variable Cost Per Unit
	£	£	£	£
0				
500				
1,000				
3,000				
6,000				
10,000				
15,000				
30,000				
45,000				
50,000				
60,000				

Note: Round all numbers to the nearest whole number.

10. **Zoraq Limited**. Zoraq manufacture components for the computer industry. One of their small industrial units has fixed costs of £20,000 per month. The firm's variable costs are £3 per unit and each one sells for £8. The management need to know how their costs and profits are affected by changes in output. The firm's output levels are shown below.

Output	Fixed Costs	Variable Cost	Sales	Profit
1,000				
2,000				
3,000				
4,000				
5,000				
6,000				
7,000				
8,000				
9,000				
10,000				
11,000				
12,000				
13,000				
14,000				
15,000				

Chapter 14

Accounting For Overheads

Introduction

There are two main reasons why management need information about their product or service costs. Firstly the information is required by law and must be shown in the corporate report and secondly management need such information to control and monitor their activities and for price setting. The law states how product costs should be reported and the aim of the regulating authorities is to provide consistency and compatibility with regard to external reporting, but this may not be sufficiently detailed for internal control. Managers know that it is not possible to know exactly what their product costs are but that they must have a system which provides reliable cost estimates. This is best achieved whenever a cost such as materials can be directly traced to a particular job or service. The problem with overhead costs is that, although they cannot be directly traced to a particular job or service, they must still be accounted for. This is why many firms now use a different system for internal reporting from that used for external reporting.

We have already seen that accountants distinguish between direct costs which are related to production, such as materials, and indirect costs which are not directly related to production. The total of indirect materials, indirect wages and indirect expenses are collectively known as *overheads*.

All firms incur overheads be they manufacturing, retailing or service sector businesses and, because indirect costs do not relate to a particular cost unit, they cannot be charged directly to them. Instead they must be shared, or to use the accounting term *apportioned*, on a fair basis to cost centres where the cost can then be absorbed into cost units.

ACCOUNTING FOR OVERHEADS

Classification of overheads

Overheads are generally classified into four main headings:

Type of Overhead	Example
Production Overhead	Factory rent
	Factory maintenance
	Depreciation of plant
	Insurance of plant
	Indirect factory wages
Administration Overhead	Printing and stationery
	Rent and rates of office
	Office salaries
	Heat and light of office
	Audit fees
Selling Overhead	Salesperson's salaries
	Advertising
	Training and conferences
	Travelling expenses
	Sales promotions
Distribution	Warehouse wages
	Transport costs
	Warehouse rent and rates
	Warehouse heat and light
	Insurance

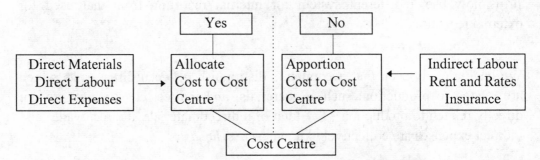

Figure 14:1 Allocation of Costs to Production

Analysis of Overhead - Cost Allocation and Cost Apportionment

Once the cost of an overhead has been calculated, the cost must be either allocated or apportioned to the relevant cost centre. An overhead can only ever be allocated to a cost centre if it, firstly, relates solely to a particular cost centre and, secondly, is for a definite sum. For example, indirect wages will generally relate to a particular cost centre and so the cost will meet the criteria for allocating overheads to a cost centre. If, however, the indirect labour was related to a supervisor who had responsibility for several cost centres, then the cost must not be allocated because it does not relate to a particular cost centre.

Whenever an overhead cannot be allocated to a cost centre it must be apportioned and this is done by preparing an overhead analysis sheet which shows the overhead charged to each cost centre. The exact basis used for apportioning the cost will differ from firm to firm but the important factor is that the basis used for apportioning the overhead must be representative of the overhead being apportioned. For example rent and rates would usually be apportioned according to area and maintenance costs according to the number of machine hours. This can be seen in the next example.

Mumfords Limited

Mumfords manufacture car speakers and the company is divided into four cost centres. One, two and three are Production Cost Centres but four is a Service Cost Centre which provides maintenance to the other three cost centres. The actual costs for the last quarter are as follows:

	£
Power	3,600
Rent	2,600
Rates	1,400
Depreciation of Plant	1,800
Heat and Light	2,400
Supervision	6,600
Insurance	2,000

The following information relates to the four cost centres:

	One	Two	Three	Four
Area in Metres	3,000	2,200	1,800	1,000
Number of Employees	40	30	20	10
Value of Plant	£48,000	£36,000	£24,000	£12,000
Value of Stock	£30,000	£18,000	£12,000	---
Machine Hours	8,550	4,050	5,400	---
Maintenance Hours	380	180	240	---

From the above information, prepare an overhead analysis sheet which shows how the overheads, including the service cost centres, should be apportioned to the relevant cost centres.

The first task is to define the basis for apportionment.

Overhead	Basis of Apportionment
Power	Machine Hours
Rent	Area
Rates	Area
Depreciation of Plant	Value of Plant
Heat and Light	Area
Supervision	No of Employees
Insurance	Value of Stock

Overhead Analysis Statement Showing the Apportionment of Service Cost Centre.

Overhead	Method of Apportionment	Production cost centres			Service Cost Centre	
		One	Two	Three	Four	Total
		£	£	£	£	£
Power (note 1)	Machine hours	1,710	810	1,080		3,600
Rent	Area	975	715	585	325	2,600
Rates	Area	525	385	315	175	1,400
Plant	Depreciation	720	540	360	180	1,800
Heat and Light	Area	900	660	540	300	2,400
Supervision	No. of employees	2,640	1,980	1,320	660	6,600
Insurance	Stock value	1,000	600	400		2,000
		8,470	5,690	4,600	1,640	
Re Apportionment of Production Overhead Service Cost Centre Overhead (note 2)		779	369	492	(1640)	
		9,249	6,059	5,092	--	20,400

Note 1.   Total Machine Hours 18,000.   8,550 hours = 47.5%
47.5% of £3,600 = 1710

Note 2.   Total Maintenance Hours 800. Cost Centre One 380 hours as a % of 800
= 47.5% 1,640 x 47.5% = 779

Once the total production overhead has been either allocated or apportioned to the relevant cost centre, the cost must be absorbed into the individual cost units. This is done by calculating an overhead absorption rate. Most firms use a pre-determined overhead rate fixed upon the budgeted overhead cost divided by the budgeted level of activity. The formula is:

Pre-determined Overhead Rate $\quad = \quad \dfrac{\text{Budgeted Overhead Cost}}{\text{Budgeted Level of Activity}}$

Most firms prefer to use a pre-determined rate rather than an actual overhead cost for three reasons. Firstly, if a firm uses actual costs then these cannot be applied until after the costs, which relate to that period, have been incurred. By using a pre-determined rate overhead, costs can be assigned to cost units during the production period rather than at the end of it. Secondly, pre-determined overhead rates can take account of different levels of activity brought about by seasonal fluctuations. Finally, pre-determined rates take account of the behaviour of costs where, although fixed costs, in total, remain the same, fixed costs per unit will alter with activity.

Methods of Cost Apportionment

Whatever system of apportionment is chosen it must be fair, practicable and cost effective to implement. In theory each cost could be worked out in minute detail and charged accordingly. Such detail would defeat the object of setting up such a system because the costs involved would outweigh the benefits gained. The firm needs a method which is not too costly to calculate and install but which will allocate the costs to each department on a reasonable basis, according to the benefit which it receives.

There are three main methods of apportioning costs. They are according to the amount produced, the hours worked and the machine hours used, but other methods may also be appropriate, such as the quantity sold or the amount of materials used.

Whichever method is used, it is vital that the overhead cost is charged to the cost unit so that it bears both its direct costs plus its fair share of overheads. This process is referred to as *overhead absorption* and involves the calculation of an overhead absorption rate. The following example shows how overhead costs can be charged to cost units.

Example

A firm knows that its overheads for a year amount to £35,000 and that it makes 10,000 hand saws per year (cost unit). The direct costs allocated to each saw are £7, but the firm needs to know how much to charge for the overheads incurred in production. The firm can use 2,500 labour hours and 2,000 machine hours on saw production.

The firm's management must decide how to absorb the overhead cost into the cost unit. In this way they will know the actual cost of producing a saw. The three main methods used are the *output*, *labour* and *machine output* methods. Whichever method is chosen, the overhead absorption rate is calculated by dividing the total overhead cost by the level of activity. Examples of each method follow.

Calculation of the *overhead absorption rate* using the *output method*

This is calculated by the formula:

$$\frac{\text{Total Overheads for Cost Centre}}{\text{Number of Cost Units Produced}} = \frac{£25,000}{10,000} = £2.50$$

Cost of manufacturing a saw:

	£
Direct Costs	7.00
Overheads	2.50
Total Cost	9.50

Calculation of the *overhead absorption rate* using the *labour hour method*

This is calculated by the formula:

$$\frac{\text{Total Overheads for Cost Centre}}{\text{Number of Labour Hours}} = \frac{£25,000}{2,500} = £10.00$$

Cost of manufacturing a saw:

	£
Direct Costs	7.00
Overheads	10.00
Total Cost	17.00

Calculation of the *overhead absorption method* using the *machine hour method*

This is calculated by the formula:

$$\frac{\text{Total Overheads for Cost Centre}}{\text{Number of Machine Hours}} = \frac{£25,000}{2,000} = £12.50$$

Cost of manufacturing a saw:

	£
Direct Costs	7.00
Overheads	12.50
Total Costs	19.50

Choosing the Most Appropriate Method

These examples show how the cost will vary according to the method used to allocate overheads to cost units. The firm should chose a method which is appropriate and which reflects the level of activity. This can be a problem if production is seasonal, because the overhead absorption rate will change from one period to another, thereby making comparison difficult. This is why an overhead absorption rate based upon the firm's budgeted level of activity is most common in industry and commerce.

Activity Based Costing

In recent years there has been a revolution in manufacturing processes and this has lead to a re-appraisal of how overheads should be absorbed into cost units. Today's manufacturing processes are very capital intensive using a large amount of machine time, with the result that firms tend to have low direct labour costs but high overhead costs. This is a familiar problem for hi-tech manufacturing companies and explains why activity-based costing may under certain conditions offer advantages over traditional costing systems because the method takes account of how costs change with activity.

Value and Non Value Added Activity

Activity Based Costing forces management to review all of their operating procedures by analysing all of their activities. This is referred to as activity based management and its aim is to improve the service offered to customers, and the overall profitability of the organisation. Any activity which increases the value of any product or service is called a *value added activity* and those activities which lead to no extra value are referred to as *non value added activities*. The aim is to remove all non value added activities because such activities simply increase production or service time, without bringing any additional benefits which a customer would be willing to pay extra for.

ACCOUNTING FOR OVERHEADS

Once all non value added activities have been eliminated and the relevant costs recorded, the next task is to group the costs according to activity into cost pools. Such costs are known as *cost drivers* and once accumulated into activity pools, can be assigned to the firm's products or services.

Firms changing from a traditional costing to activity based costing often notice that there is a discrepancy between the two systems. As a general rule activity based costing systems shift a high proportion of overhead costs away from high volume products to low volume products, which are both time consuming and complex to manufacture. If the new method is to be successfully introduced, management must be prepared to accept the additional costs in staff training and time to ensure that the system works properly.

The problem for managers is that they now operate in a highly competitive market place, whether they be in manufacturing, retailing or the service sector. In this new market place prices are being increasingly set by the market, forcing firms to supply at prices which consumers are happy and willing to pay. For many businesses this has meant decreasing prices over time and this can only be achieved by cost reduction programmes. Advocates of activity based costing believe that it helps a firm reduce its costs by changing the activities which incur costs, thereby making the business more efficient. The firm is then able to reduce its costs in the long run instead of merely achieving short- term gains.

QUESTIONS

Answers begin on page 479

1. State how the following overheads should be allocated to cost centres.

    a. Rent
    b. Depreciation
    c. Rates
    d. National Insurance
    e. General Administration
    f. Canteen
    g. Maintenance

2. **Ramal Engineering.** The company has its own conference centre which caters for both in-house and outside events. During the last month the conference centre has worked on six jobs for Ramal Engineering's marketing department. Past accounting records show that the centre incurred overheads of £30,000 during the month and used 6,000 hours of direct labour on the following jobs:

Job	Hours
A171	700
A191	400
B200	1,500
B242	1,000
C314	1,800
C318	600

Required:

a. Calculate the historical overhead rate per direct labour hour.

b. Prepare a statement showing how the conference overhead should be charged to each job.

c. What are the disadvantages of using historical overhead rates?

215

3. **Alpine Skis** is a small company. The firm has two main departments. These are a production department which manufactures skies and a customer service department which services customer's skis. The overheads for the customer service department and the production department are shown below.

Service Department	£
Customer Services	800,000
Engineering	200,000
Production Department	**£**
Machinery	600,000
Assembly	200,000

The customer service department spends 20 per cent of its time on engineering matters, 30 percent on machinery and 50 per cent on assembly. The engineering department spends 40 per cent of its time on machinery and 60 per cent on assembly.

Production	Machinery	Assembly
Machine Hours	30,000	8,000
Labour hours	6,000	20,000
Wage costs	£36,000	£120,000

Advise the company as to how it should calculate its overhead absorption rate.

Chapter 15

Profit and Output Decisions

Introduction

The aim of a cost accounting system is to provide relevant cost information to management so that decisions can be made about which products should be produced, in what quantity and at what price they should be sold. By using cost accounting techniques firms are able to make the best use of their resources, thereby optimising the return which can be made from their capital employed.

Cost and Output Decisions

We have already seen that costs can be classified according to their behaviour. Within a relevant range the fixed costs will remain unchanged with variations in output, while the variable costs will vary proportionately. Once the costs are known, decisions can be made on how to maximise the earnings potential of the business in relation to its costs. The aim is to operate at the highest level of output so that the firm's total fixed costs are spread over the maximum number of outputs (cost units). The firm is then able to maximise its earnings from its current level of resources.

The Concept of Contribution

All firms must pay their fixed costs regardless of their level of activity, but the variable costs will only be incurred as goods are produced or a service provided. If the selling price is greater than the variable cost, a surplus will be made on each sale. This surplus is called *contribution* because it can be used to contribute towards the fixed costs of the firm. Once these have been covered, the additional contribution from each sale will make profits for the firm.

Example

A furniture factory makes 1,200 wooden book cases. The variable cost of making each one is as follows.

Variable Cost of Production	£
Wood used in production	30
Direct Labour	15
Variable Direct Overheads	<u>10</u>
Prime Cost	<u>55</u>

Each book case costs the firm £55 to make, before any fixed costs are apportioned to it. If the fixed costs are £30,000 and the book cases sell for £85 each the firm will make a £30 contribution on each book case sold.

How to calculate contribution

	£
Selling Price	85
Less Variable Costs	<u>55</u>
Contribution	<u>30</u>

On each sale the firm now receives £30 which can be used to pay the fixed costs. Once these have been paid the firm will start to make a profit.

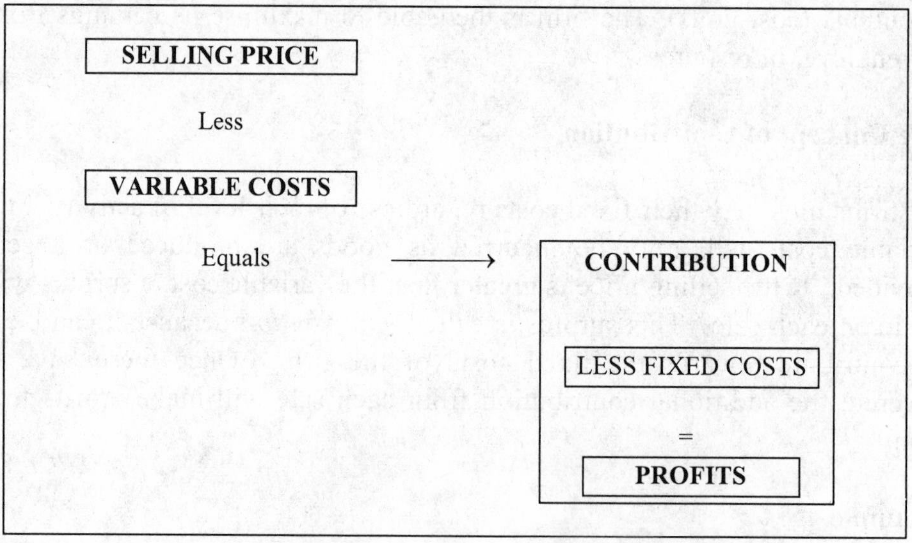

Figure 15:1 The Inflow and Uses of Contribution

Each £30 contributes to the fixed costs and, as soon as these have been covered, builds profits for the business.

Contribution and Profit

Contribution is not profit. This is because only the variable costs have been covered. The fixed costs have yet to be paid. Once these are covered the firm makes its profit, which is the surplus of money received over its costs.

The Break Even Concept

As long as the selling price is higher than the variable cost of the product or service sold, a contribution will be made. While this information is important, the management need to know how many sales have to be made for the business to cover its own costs and then move into profit. There is always a danger that the profits earned are insufficient to cover all the firm's costs, leading to the business making a loss at the end of the financial year. Management need to consider both their fixed and variable costs, together with their planned level of sales, before setting realistic output and profit levels.

Break even analysis provides this information by showing the level of sales needed to cover the firm's fixed and variable costs. Once the firm has reached its break even point any sales above this point will create profits for the firm. Sales managers then know how much stock they have to sell just to cover the firm's own costs, but it is important that they remember that any change in costs and revenues will alter the break even point.

How to Calculate the Break Even Point

Once the selling price exceeds the variable costs, contribution will be earned which can be used to meet the fixed costs. If a firm makes £10 contribution on each sale and has fixed costs of £1,000, it will reach its break even point once one hundred units have been sold. This is so because the variable costs have already been covered and so each £10 reduces the fixed costs, until they have all been covered.

If the fixed costs are divided by the contribution from each sale, the number of cost units which must be sold to break even can be calculated. This is often shown as a formula:

PROFIT AND OUTPUT DECISIONS

Output level to break even = **Fixed Costs** = Number of units to break even
Total Contribution

Contribution = Unit Selling Price, less unit Variable Cost.

Using the same figures as in the previous example the break even point in units is:

   Fixed Costs   £30,000   =   1,000 book cases to break even
Unit Contribution   30

Another way of calculating the break even point is to work out the level of sales which must be made in order to break even. The formula is:

Level of sales to = **Total Sales Value x Fixed Costs** = Sales to Break Even
break even   **Total Contribution**

Contribution = Total Sales, less Total Variable Costs.

Using the same figures the break even point in terms of sales is:

Total Sales Value x Fixed Costs   =   £102,000 x £30,000
      Total Contribution   £36,000

The firm must have sales of £85,000 if it is to break even. The greater the contribution earned in relation to the selling price, the less units which must be sold for the firm to break even. Once the firm knows its break even point, the management can calculate the profit the firm will earn at a given level of output.

Profit Earned at Output of 1,200 Book Cases

	£
Total Contribution (£30 x 1,200 units)	36,000
Less Fixed Costs	30,000
Profit	6,000

Graphical Presentation of this Information

It is also possible to calculate the break even point by plotting costs and sales on a graph. The fixed costs will be shown as a straight line because at that level of activity these costs will remain unchanged. The variable costs will increase the total costs as output increases and so these should be plotted above the fixed cost line which will show the total cost line. The break even point occurs where the sales line crosses the total cost line.

The break even chart allows the relationship between costs, profits and volume to be shown as a graph. By using this method of presentation, it is immediately apparent what level of sales must be achieved if the firm is to break even.

Example of a Break Even Chart

Using the same figures as in the previous example, the break even point can now be shown graphically. It is a good idea to work out the break even point arithmetically before plotting the information as it will assist in calculating the best scale to use for the graph.

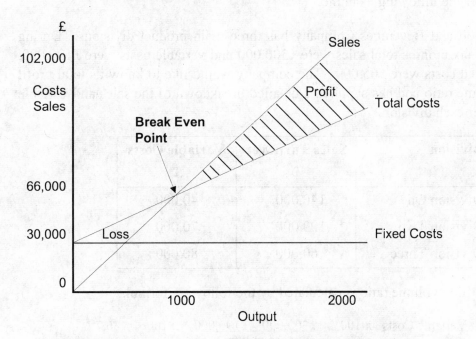

Figure 15:2 Example of a Break Even Chart

The chart shows that at the break even point contribution equals the firm's total costs. The difference between sales achieved and the sales needed to break even is called the *margin of safety* and, by multiplying the margin of safety by the contribution per sale, the firm's profit can be calculated. Once this is known it is possible to calculate the profit at any level of sales and the percentage contribution earned from each sale generated. This can be seen from the following example.

Consider the following Income Statement.

	£	Percentage
Sales	100	100
Less Variable Costs	60	60
Contribution	40	40
Less Fixed Costs	20	
Profit	20	

In this example the contribution percentage of sales is £40 or 40 per cent and it is possible to present this information by drawing a profit to volume graph. Consider the following example.

The Food and Beverages Company has three main product divisions. During the last six months total sales were £300,000 and variable costs were £190,000. The fixed costs were £65,000. The company would like to know its total profit to volume ratio and has supplied a detailed breakdown of the sales and variable costs for each division.

Division	Sales Turnover £	Variable Costs £
Division One	140,000	40,000
Division Two	100,000	70,000
Division Three	60,000	80,000

The profit to volume ratio is calculated by the following formula:

$$\frac{\text{Sales} - \text{Variable Costs}}{\text{Sales}} \times 100 = \frac{£300,000 - £190,000}{£300,000} \times 100 = 36.7\%$$

This ratio shows the relationship between contribution and sales. The contribution first covers the fixed costs of £65,000 and then goes on to yield a profit of £45,000. This information can be presented as a graph by first calculating the profit to volume ratio for each division and then plotting the information on graph paper. The individual contributions are:

Division	Sales £	Variables Costs £	Contribution £	P/V Ratio %
One	140,000	40,000	100,000	71
Two	100,000	70,000	30,000	30.0
Three	60,000	80,000	(20,000)	(33.3)
	300,000	190,000	110,000	37
Fixed Overheads			65,000	
Profit			45,000	

The individual and total contributions can now be plotted. The steepness of the curve will show the total contribution.

Profit to Volume Graph for the Food and Beverage Company

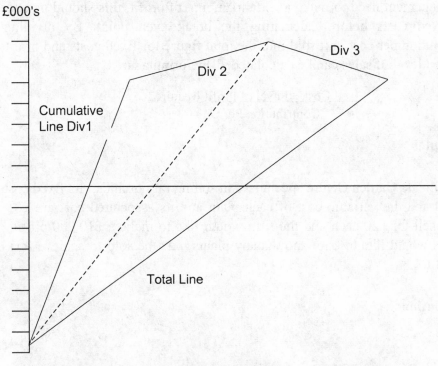

Figure 15:3 Example of a Profit to Volume Graph

Explanation of the Profit to Volume Graph

The profit to volume graph shows the contribution to fixed costs from each product and the total contribution for all three divisions. The horizontal line is the fixed cost line and the first sale yields contribution which will go towards the fixed costs. As sales increase, so does the amount of contribution, until it crosses the fixed cost line and goes on to show the profit from a given level of sales.

In our example the chart shows that division three fails to make a contribution as it does not even cover its variable costs. In such a case, management must consider whether or not the price could be increased or the variable costs reduced. Unless the product assists in selling the other two products, the firm should consider launching a new product or rationalising the business so that the costs of the third division can be eliminated. This may prove to be a difficult task if the three divisions are inter-related because the costs cannot be isolated. In such a case, it would be a better strategy to launch a new product which can earn a contribution towards the firm's fixed costs.

If management need to make a certain amount of profit, this should be added to the fixed costs before calculating the break even point. By dividing the contribution per cost unit sold into the total figure for fixed costs and profits the required level of sales can be calculated. The formula is:

$$\frac{\text{Fixed Cost} + \text{Level of Profit Required}}{\text{Contribution Per Unit}}$$

Example

The Hillside Garden Centre specialises in selling rare orchids. Its fixed costs are £8,000 and the variable cost of each plant and its associated cost are £8. The plants sell for £20 each and the firm would like to make a £10,000 profit. The owners would like to know how many plants must be sold to achieve this level of profit.

Calculation:

	£
Selling Price	20.00
Less Variable Cost	8.00
Contribution	12.00

$$\frac{\text{Fixed Costs} + \text{Profit}}{\text{Unit Contribution}} = \text{Number of plants which must be sold to cover costs and achieve the desired profit.}$$

224

	£
Fixed Costs	8,000
Profit	10,000
Total	18,000

$$\frac{\text{Fixed Costs} + \text{Profit}}{\text{Contribution}} = \frac{£18,000}{£12} = 1,500$$

One thousand and five hundred plants must be sold if the garden centre is to cover its costs and reach its profit target.

Most firms make a number of products and so they need to know the break even point for their current product mix. This is shown in the next example.

The Electric Power Drill Company

Product	Professional	Craft	Standard
	£	£	£
Unit Selling Price	70	50	40
Variable Cost	40	30	21

The Sales Manager has told you that they sell in a ratio of three Professional, five Craft and two Standard. The firm has fixed costs of £23,000. Calculate the firm's break even point.

Solution

First calculate the unit contribution

	Professional	Craft	Standard
	£	£	£
Selling Price	70	50	40
Less Variable Cost	40	30	21
Unit Contribution	30	20	19

Then calculate the weighted average contribution

225

Product	(a) Weighting	(b) Contribution per Product	a & b Weighted Contribution
		£	£
Professional	3/10	30	9
Craft	5/10	20	10
Standard	2/10	19	4
	Weighted Average Contribution	**=**	**23**

Weighted Average Contribution $\dfrac{£69}{3}$ =   £23

$\dfrac{\text{Fixed Costs}}{\text{Weighted Average Contribution}}$ $\dfrac{£23,000}{£23}$ =   1,000 units to break even

	Professional	Craft	Standard
Ratio	3:10	5:10	2:10
Break Even in units	300	500	200

Note: Professional = 1000/10 =100 x 3 = 300
All calculations to nearest whole number.

Limitations of Break Even Analysis

While it is important for management to know the level of sales needed to break even, the calculations are based on a number of assumptions and, if these change, different break even points will occur. The assumptions can be categorised into two main areas – those relating to costs and those relating to sales and output.

The first assumption refers to the firm's costs. It is always assumed that both fixed and variable costs increase in a straight line as output increases. This will not happen, for many firms' costs are not linear with volume. If this is the case, the firm will move in and out of break even, even though its sales are increasing.

Assumptions are also made about the firm's costs because, in break even analysis, they are always neatly separated into their fixed and variable elements. In practice this may not be as easy because some costs are in fact semi-variable, having both a fixed and variable element. An example of such a cost is electricity which has a fixed standing charge plus a charge for each unit used, which is variable. It may be difficult for a business to separate its semi-variable costs. Break even analysis further assumes that fixed costs will remain constant at that level of output whereas, in practice, they might increase, as might variable costs.

The second set of assumptions refer to the level of sales and the product mix of the firm, which is expected not to change. In practice the selling price may well be altered to gain additional sales and the product mix may be altered as new products are launched and old ones withdrawn.

Thirdly, it is taken for granted that sales and production will always be in balance, although this may not be the case.

Finally, the break even model assumes that there will be no change in the level of inflation and that the firm's level of productivity and market share will also remain constant.

It is important to remember that costs can only be separated into their fixed and variable elements in the short term. Management decisions can reduce a firm's fixed costs by closing plant and cutting staffing levels, just as they are increased by new investment decisions such as the acquisition of new premises and plant. Any of these examples will alter a firm's fixed costs and this is why management should, from a planning perspective, regard fixed costs as long term variable costs. Unless management consider how their business decisions will affect operating costs, they will be incorrect in their assumptions about future profits. This will be the case because costs, output and profits will no longer be based upon the assumption of how costs behave within a relevant range.

In spite of these limitations, break even is still a useful concept for it helps management determine output levels and selling prices. Ideally the firm should seek products which have a high contribution to sales ratio and which have a low break even point. Unfortunately this last fact is often determined by the industry in which the firm operates. For example, hotels and transport operators tend to have high fixed costs and low variable costs and the nature of the business means that this cannot be altered. Nevertheless break even is still useful in helping management to set prices which will maximise the contribution earned from each journey or each hotel bedroom occupied. In this way the firm may be able to reduce its losses, even if it cannot make a profit for, if no one travels on a train or stays at an hotel, that sale can never be regained – so any contribution which can be earned by altering the price will help to pay the fixed costs.

QUESTIONS

Answers begin page 480

1. Calculate the contribution and profit earned from the following information.

Firm	A	B	C	D
	£	£	£	£
Sales	70,000	65,000	70,000	80,000
Prime cost	20,000	15,000	40,000	29,000
Contribution				
Fixed costs	15,000	25,000	30,000	35,000
Profit				

2. Calculate the contribution from the following information.

Firm	A	B	C	D
	£	£	£	£
Sales	30,000	250,000	17,900	65,000
Prime cost	15,000	149,000	12,000	43,000
Contribution	?	?	?	?

3. Calculate the contribution from the following information.

Firm	A	B	C	D	E
	£	£	£	£	£
Sales	84,000	72,000	90,000	43,000	29,000
Materials	15,000	20,000	30,000	13,000	7,000
Direct labour	20,000	15,000	40,000	10,000	12,000
Variable overheads	4,000	6,000	12,000	9,000	3,000
Contribution	?	?	?	?	?

4. Calculate the break even point in units from the following information.

	£	£	£	£
Fixed costs	45,000	30,000	27,000	48,000
Contribution	5	10	9	12
Units to break even				

5. From the following information calculate the firm's margin of safety.

Firm	A	B	C	D
	£	£	£	£
Sales	65,600	121,000	69,000	53,000
Break even in sales	34,000	55,000	28,000	39,000
Margin of safety				

6. A firm can only market one new product next year. The selling price per unit and the prime cost per unit are shown below. Which product should the firm market?

Product	A	B	C	D
	£	£	£	£
Selling price	28.00	24.00	26.00	30.00
Prime cost	10.00	15,00	12.00	24.00

7. A laundry has fixed costs of £40,000 a month. If it earns £8 contribution on each unit washed, how many units must be produced for the business to achieve its break even point?

8. **Geoff's Garage**

Geoffrey Roland has been self-employed for ten years. He owns a small garage which services all makes of cars and is currently considering buying an additional hydraulic ramp to undertake routine oil and filter changes as part of a while-you-wait service for customers.

A new ramp will cost £5,000 and will last five years. A good quality oil can be purchased at £5 for 5 litres and the average price of an oil filter is £3.50. A new employee will have to be recruited, which will cost £12,000 in wages, and other overheads will amount to £5,000. Customers will pay £14.50 per service and Geoffrey has approached his bank manager to ask for permission to increase his overdraft.

The bank manager has agreed to lend the money, once she knows the contribution earned from each service, and the number of filter changes required for the business to break even. Geoffrey has asked you for advice and would like you to:

a. explain to him what is meant by the term break even?

b. to calculate the firm's break even point?

9. **Metal Forge Masters**

Metal Forge Masters have been invited to submit a tender to supply a new component for a series of cranes currently being manufactured in Germany. The contract requires the firm to deliver 100 components per month for three months and specifies that the unit cost should be in the price range of £600 - £650. The costs of manufacturing each component are as follows:

	£
Direct materials	200
Direct labour	75
Variable overheads	30

The firm has estimated that the fixed costs of production are £25,000 per month and the directors are anxious to secure the contract because the firm's order book is low. As a result, the directors have decided to submit a selling price of 5 per cent above the minimum tender price.

You have been asked to calculate:

a. the marginal cost of making each component.

b. the contribution earned from each sale.

c. the number of components which must be made each month if the firm is to break even.

10. The Interior Door Company

The company manufacture wooden doors and its costs and estimated sales for any given month are shown below.

Output	Selling Price £	Total Sales £	Total Costs £	Profit £	ATC £	MC £	IR £
0	48		75,000				
1000	45		105,000				
2000	42		123,000				
3000	39		135,000				
4000	36		141,000				
5000	33		147,000				
6000	30		156,000				
7000	27		171,000				
8000	24		195,000				
9000	21		237,000				
10000	18		300,000				

Note: ATC = Average Total Cost
MC = Marginal Cost
IR = Incremental Revenue

Calculate the most profitable level of output for the firm.

Chapter 16

Absorption and Marginal Costing

Introduction

Any business must cover both its fixed and variable costs if it is to make a profit. Absorption costing charges both the fixed and variable costs involved in making a product or providing a service. Marginal costing separates the fixed costs and only calculates the variable cost. Once the variable or marginal cost has been determined, this is subtracted from the selling price to find the contribution. The fixed costs are then subtracted from the contribution, thereby showing the firm's profit.

Marginal costing is, therefore, not a costing method but a costing technique for it does not calculate all of the costs in making or providing a service. Its real importance lies in the way it can be used to assist decision making, by showing the contribution which can be earned in different circumstances, which can then be used to pay the firm's fixed costs.

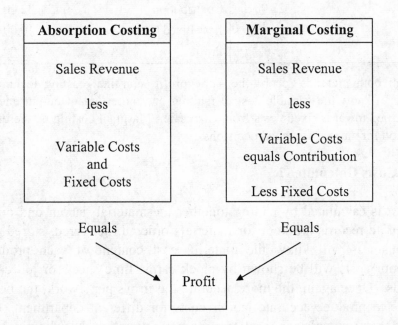

Figure 16:1 Comparison of Absorption and Marginal Costing

ABSORPTION AND MARGINAL COSTING

The different treatment of costs by the two methods can be seen by preparing a statement showing the absorption and marginal cost of making a pullover.

Cost of Manufacturing a Woollen Pullover

Absorption Costing	£	£	Marginal Costing	£	£
Selling Price		50.00	Selling Price		50.00
Direct Materials	6.00		Direct Materials	6.00	
Direct Labour	8.00		Direct Labour	8.00	
Direct Expenses	2.00		Direct Expenses	2.00	
Prime Cost	16.00		Prime Cost	16.00	
Variable Overhead	2.00		Variable Overhead	2.00	
Fixed Overhead	10.00		Fixed Overhead	-	
Total Cost		28.00	Marginal Cost		18.00
Profit		22.00	Contribution		32.00
			Less Fixed Costs		10.00
			Profit		22.00

Note: Although both methods record the same profit, marginal costing techniques enable the firm to know the variable cost of making one more unit of output and the contribution earned towards fixed costs from each sale. Marginal costing is, therefore, the better method for making financial decisions.

How are the Costs Calculated?

The *prime cost* is calculated by adding together the material, labour and direct costs. If accurate records are kept for materials ordered, delivered, stored and issued, the business will know the material cost content of each product. Similarly, labour costs will be shown by clock cards, time sheets or job cards and route cards. Once again, the more accurate the firm's paperwork, the better it will be able to produce accurate labour costs for different departments and products. The factory overheads are determined by estimating the following:

1.   Estimated Total Factory Overheads.

2.   Estimated Level of Activity.

By dividing 1 by 2, the firm's recovery or absorption rate can be calculated. In this example the figures are:

$$\frac{\text{Estimated Factory Overheads}}{\text{Estimated Labour Hours}} \qquad \frac{£60,000}{10,000}$$

$$\text{Absorption Rate} \quad = \quad \frac{£60,000}{10,000} \quad = \quad £6.00 \text{ per Direct Labour Hour}$$

If it takes two hours to manufacture the pullover, the indirect factory overheads are £12. The accuracy of this figure is, therefore, determined by the accuracy of our estimates of cost and activity and by the suitability of our choice of activity. Other bases of activity are:

- Direct Labour Cost

- Machine Hours

- Prime Cost

- Direct Material Cost

- Number of Units

It is important to remember that the marginal or variable costs do not depend on the estimation of overheads and activity. They move in sympathy with production and sales. In this example, the cost of producing one extra pullover is £18.00 and so ten extra pullovers would cost the firm another £180.

The difference between the selling price and the variable cost is known as *contribution*. Each time a pullover is sold, £32 of the contribution is earned to meet fixed costs. Each sale will build a fund of contribution which can be used to pay fixed costs and which, we hope, will be sufficient to yield profits for the business.

Marginal Costing

As stated earlier, marginal costing is not a cost accounting method as it only considers the variable costs involved in making a product or providing a service. The fixed costs are considered at a later stage in the calculation whereas in absorption or full costing they are considered alongside the variable costs. By separating the fixed and variable costs into their separate elements, management can make decisions about pricing strategies, output levels and predicted profit levels.

How Marginal Costs Behave with Changes in Output

Marginal or variable costs do not depend on the estimation of overheads and activity because they move in sympathy with production and sales. As long as a firm operates within its current operating capacity, called its *relevant range*, its fixed costs will not change. The total variable costs will increase in proportion to output, but the cost per unit will fall as the total fixed costs are spread over an increasing number of units. If management consider both the fixed and variable costs, profitability will fluctuate with changes in output because increases in output will reduce the cost per unit. This makes it difficult for management to know the costs involved before setting selling prices. There is always a danger that, if output falls, the firm may sell its products at a loss, because of the increase in fixed cost per unit produced as output levels fall. This can be seen from the following example.

The High Output Company

The managers at the High Output Company always try to produce as many units as possible so that they can keep the fixed cost per unit as low as possible. Unfortunately the firm's sales are seasonal, and so they suffer from an erratic demand for their products. During the first quarter its output and costs have been as follows:

	January		February		March	
Output (units)	500		1,000		2,000	
Variable Cost	£		£		£	
£2 per unit	1,000		2,000		4,000	
Fixed Costs	4,000		4,000		4,000	
Total Cost	5,000		6,000		8,000	
		£		£		£
Cost Per Unit		10.00		6.00		4.00
Selling Price		8.00		8.00		8.00
Profit/loss		£(1,000)		£2,000		£8,000

(Profit per unit times output)

This example shows how the cost of the product varies according to output. This makes it difficult to set selling prices and predict profit levels, even though the managers know all of the firm's costs. When output falls to 500 units, the firm makes a loss of £2.00 on each one sold, but once output increases to 2,000 an £8,000 profit is achieved.

Marginal costing techniques assume that the unit variable costs of production will remain unaltered regardless of the level of activity. It is this assumption which makes it a useful technique for appraising pricing strategies and determining output levels. The marginal or variable cost can then be subtracted from the selling price so that the contribution from each sale can be calculated. This can be seen by preparing the High Output Company's costs in marginal costing format.

	January	February	March
Output (units)	500	1,000	2,000
Selling Price	£	£	£
Per Unit	8	8	8
Less Variable Cost per Unit	2	2	2
Contribution per Unit	6	6	6
	£	£	£
Total Contribution	3,000	6,000	12,000
Less Fixed Costs	4,000	4,000	4,000
Profit/Loss	(1,000)	2,000	8,000

Note: Total contribution equals contribution per unit times output.

By preparing the information in this way, management can see the contribution earned from each sale. Contribution is not profit, because the fixed costs have not yet been covered, but it can be used to pay the fixed costs and any surplus after paying them will give rise to profits. Any change in selling price will, therefore, affect the amount of contribution earned per unit, but the variable cost per unit of production will be unaffected by the level of activity. The total contribution is calculated by multiplying the output by the contribution per unit. The aim is to increase the total contribution by selling at a price which maximises sales. In this way the fixed costs will be covered and any surplus will be profits.

The Separation of Costs into their Fixed and Variable Elements

In the last three examples the management have known the costs involved because accurate cost records have been kept. These costs may not always be available and must be calculated. This can be seen in the following example.

Muddling Through Limited

The manager at Muddling Through Limited do not keep accurate cost records but they do keep records of output levels, prime costs and overheads. For the last three months the costs have been as follows:

	January	February	March
Output	7,000	11,000	16,000
Costs	£	£	£
Prime Cost	30,450	47,850	69,600
Production Overhead	43,440	51,120	60,720

Selling Price £12 per unit

Before separating the costs, it is important to remember how different costs behave according to different levels of activity.

Variable Costs: These remain fixed per unit, but the total variable cost will increase with activity.

Fixed Costs: These remain fixed in total, but fall per unit as output is increased.

Separation of Costs into their Fixed and Variable Components

Prime Cost

We have already seen that the prime cost is a variable cost, but this can be proved. The figures show that the costs increase with output but, if the cost per unit remains constant when the total prime cost is divided by output, it is a variable cost.

Calculation of Prime Cost

	January	February	March
	£	£	£
Prime Cost	30,450	47,850	69,600
Output	7,000	11,000	16,000
Cost Per Unit	£4.35	£4.35	£4.35

The prime cost is, therefore, a variable cost.

Production overhead

A fixed cost remains the same in total provided the form operates at an activity level within its relevant range. In this example the production overhead cost increases with output and so the production overhead must contain a fixed and variable element. This can be proved again by dividing the highest and lowest production overhead costs by the output figure. If the cost per unit falls, there must be a fixed cost element which is bringing down the cost per unit. It is possible that the overhead cost could be completely variable. If this is the case, the cost per unit will be the same, even though output has increased, for variable costs per unit do not change with output levels.

Calculation of the variable element of the Production Overhead

Production Overhead	Cost £	Output	Cost Per Unit
Highest Level of Activity	60,720	16,000	£3.80
Lowest Level of Activity	43,440	7,000	£6.21
Change in cost/output	17,280	9,000	

This shows that the cost per unit falls as output increases and so the production overhead must be made up of fixed and variable costs. These must now be separated.

If the change in output is divided by the change in cost, the variable cost per unit can be calculated. This can best be explained by a diagram showing the production overheads and fixed and total costs. The difference between the two lines is the variable cost and, as output increases, the distance between the two lines increases.

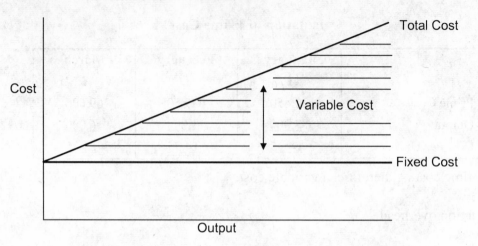

Figure 16:2 Production Overhead – Fixed and Total Costs

Change in Cost $\quad$ £17,280 $\quad$ = £1.92 is the variable cost per unit of overhead
Change in Activity $\quad$ 9,000

Once the variable cost of the production overhead has been determined, the fixed cost can be calculated. This is done by multiplying output by the unit variable production overhead cost, thereby calculating the variable part of the overhead cost. If this is then subtracted from the total cost, the fixed costs can be determined. If there have been no additional fixed costs, they should remain unaltered in total, even though output has increased. This is because the business is still operating within its relevant range.

Calculation of the fixed element of the Production Overhead

Production Overhead	Jan	Feb	Mar
	£	£	£
Total Cost	43,440	51,120	60,720
Less variable cost per unit £1.92 multiplied by output	13,440	21,120	30,720
Fixed Cost	30,000	30,000	30,000

The costs have now been separated into their fixed and variable components and a profit statement can now be prepared in either marginal or absorption costing techniques.

Muddling Through Limited Profit Statement – Marginal Costing

	January £	February £	March £
Sales	84,000	132,000	192,000
Less Variable Costs			
Prime Costs	30,450	47,850	69,600
Variable Overheads	13,440	21,120	30,720
Total Variable Cost	43,890	68,970	100,320
Contributions	40,110	63,030	91,680
Less Fixed Costs	30,000	30,000	30,000
Profit	10,110	33,030	61,680

Muddling Though Limited Profit Statement – Absorption Costing

	January £	February £	March £
Sales	84,000	132,000	192,000
Less Costs			
Prime Costs	30,450	47,850	69,600
Variable Overheads	13,440	21,120	30,720
Fixed Costs	30,000	30,000	30,000
Total Costs	73,890	98,970	130,320
Profit	10,110	33,030	61,680

Comparison of Marginal and Absorption Costing

The two accounting systems can, in certain circumstances, give rise to different profit figures, even though the same figures are being used. This is because the two systems treat costs differently.

In the last example the profit figure was the same regardless of the method used, because the firm sold everything it produced. Whenever sales and production do not equal each other, stock will be held by the firm and this must be valued.

Accountants use two terms which must first be explained. These are *product costs* and *period costs*. In absorption costing all production costs of making the product, be they fixed or variable, are called *product costs* and they are

241

treated as an asset until sold. Non production costs such as selling, administration and research and development costs are called *period costs* because they are not related to the production process. These costs are written off as they are incurred to the profit and loss account and are never treated as assets.

When financial statements are prepared under absorption costing, the figures for work in progress, finished stock and cost of goods sold will be made up of the unit variable cost of production together with a unit allocation of the product overhead.

Marginal costing, however, only treats the variable costs of production as product costs. Fixed costs are never treated as product costs but are written off as period costs, just as selling, administration and research and development costs are treated as period costs. Internal reports are often prepared on a marginal cost basis to assist management decision making because, in the short term, variable costs are generally easier than fixed costs to control.

The fundamental difference between the two methods is that fixed costs of producing the product are treated as a product cost under absorption costing. Until the goods are sold, they remain an asset of the company and the fixed costs are only written off in the profit and loss account as period costs when they are sold. Marginal costing, however, treats all fixed production costs as period costs and they are written off as they are incurred. This is why absorption costing will show a greater profit than marginal costing when stock levels are increasing and the opposite will be the case when stock levels are reduced.

This different treatment of costs highlights the difference between the two methods. Marginal costing treats manufacturing fixed costs as an expense as soon as they are incurred, but absorption costing allocates the fixed cost on sale. Absorption costing is based on the functional classification of costs whereas marginal costing is based on the behaviour of costs and is, therefore, better for decision making and financial control.

Although both methods use the same cost data, marginal costing is a better method for planning and decision making because it shows how costs will change in the short term with changes in output. The method also shows the income earned from a decision because the non-variable product costs are written off as an expense when incurred. As a result, the firm's income cannot be manipulated as is possible under absorption costing if management decide to increase output, thereby treating some fixed costs as product costs instead of showing them as an expense. If this is done it is possible for a company to show a profit even though its sales are below its break even point.

QUESTIONS

Answers begin page 482

1. **Leaded Lights**. The company specialise in making stained glass windows which are sold to numerous double glazing firms. During the last six months the firm has received unprecedented orders and the owner would like to use part of the profits to build an extension. Unfortunately he has been so busy that he has not been able to keep a tight control on costs but has, nevertheless, been able to supply you with the following information.

	May	June	July	Aug	Sept	Oct
Units made	500	620	700	840	900	940
	£	£	£	£	£	£
Glass	4,500	5,580	6,300	7,560	8,100	8,460
Direct labour	2,315	2,871	3,241	3,889	4,167	4,352
Overheads	11,285	11,593	11,799	12,159	12,313	12,416

   a.   What are the firm's unit variable costs of production?

   b.   What are the fixed costs?

2. **Bridge Hotel**. You have just been appointed the manager of the Bridge Hotel which has a large restaurant. At present the firm has no system of cost accounting but you have been able to ascertain the following information.

	Jan	Feb	March	April	May
Number of meals served	20,000	25,000	33,000	40,000	45,000
	£	£	£	£	£
Cost of food	94,800	118,500	156,420	189,600	213,300
Cost of labour	25,800	32,250	42,570	51,600	58,050
Overheads	82,400	91,750	106,710	119,800	129,150

The average selling price of a meal in the restaurant is £12.50.

You are required to calculate:

   a.   the variable unit costs of the restaurant

   b.   the fixed costs of the restaurant.

   c.   the contribution per meal sold.

   d.   the number of meals which must be sold for the restaurant to break even.

3. **Hi Slope Skis**. The firm is small and the owner does not understand cost accounting techniques but has supplied you with the following information.

	October £	November £	December £
Materials	255,000	289,000	340,000
Labour	180,000	204,000	240,000
Overheads	93,500	101,500	113,500
Output	15,000	17,000	20,000
Selling price	50	50	50

Task

The owner would like to know:
a. The unit variable cost of making a pair of skis for each month.
b. The cost of manufacturing 25,000 skis.
c. The break even point for the months of October, November and December if the skis sell for £53 per pair.

4. **Manakos Limited**. Manakos is a small engineering firm. The company makes a range of steel tubing. Product line Z196A sells for £9.00 per one metre unit. Unfortunately the firm's accountant has been taken ill but you have been able to find out the first quarter's production and costs of Z196A.

First Quarter Production and Costs for Product Z196A

	January £	February £	March £
Prime cost	83,000	99,600	106,240
Production overhead	44,750	50,600	52,940
Output in units	25,000	30,000	32,000

The marketing manager has received an additional order for 12,000 bars from a French firm provided that the selling price can be reduced by 15 per cent. He would like you to send him a memo showing a break down of the costs of production and a statement saying whether or not the order should be accepted.

5.   The Fireworks Party

The social secretary of the Wattleton Tennis Club has been asked to organise a fireworks party which will be open to both club and non club members. The club has 400 members and it is estimated that 60 per cent will attend and that 100 non members will also come to the function. The tickets will be sold to members for £6 and non members will pay £7.

After the fireworks display there will be a free barbecue and disco. The food cost has been estimated at £2 per person and beverages will cost a further 40p.

At the end of the evening each guest will be given a magazine outlining future events and how to join the club. The club has 500 copies printed by a local printer who charged £320. Any programmes left over will be used in other marketing campaigns.

The club will employ a local firm to build the bonfire at a cost of £70 and the disco will cost a further £120. In addition, the club must carry insurance for the evening, which will cost £50 and the hire of equipment will cost £70. The club plans to spend £400 on fireworks.

The club's secretary has asked you to prepare a flexible budget showing the costs and revenues which the club will earn at 50, 60, 70, 80 and 100 per cent level of activity.

Chapter 17

Accounting for Decision Making

Introduction

In the long run a firm's costs are variable. It is the time factor which makes these costs variable because management can change its investment in fixed assets and the number of people employed in the business in response to changes in its level of sales. If there is a large increase in demand, the business will have to invest in more premises and plant but, if demand is declining, decisions will have to be made about how the firm should rationalise its activities by disposing of surplus operating capacity.

In the short run, however, some of the firm's operating costs will change directly as a result of increases or decreases in the level of sales. These costs are called variable costs and good examples are raw materials used in production and direct labour. Both of these costs will alter with any change in output and so they are affected by output decisions rather than time.

There is another type of cost which, in the short run, is not affected by a change in output. These are fixed costs such as rent and insurance. These costs are time rather than output related. As a result they are incurred every minute of the day that the firm is in business, regardless of the firm's output level. For example, if a restaurant is closed for a public holiday, its fixed costs such as insurance must still be paid, but it will not incur any food costs because all cooking has stopped for the holiday.

In the short run a firm must make the best use of its resources, as seen in Figure 17:1 Financial Aspects of Short-Term Decision Making, on page 248, overleaf.

Any change in its operating capacity will affect profitability and cash flow. The correct decision will be the one which maximises the firm's cash flow and profit by considering the costs and revenues which are affected by the decision.

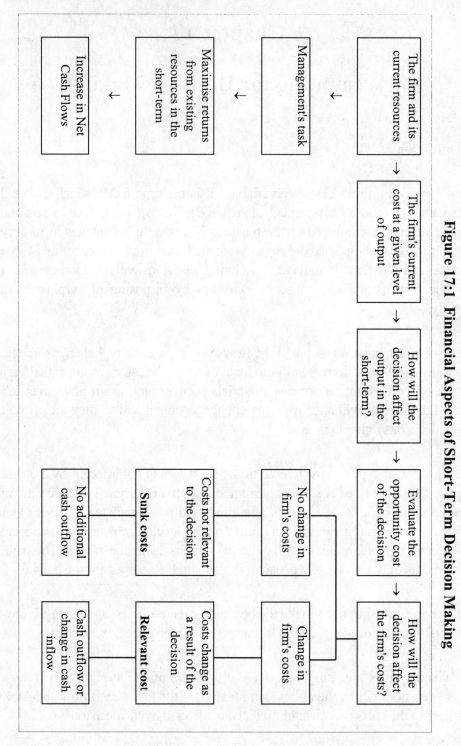

Figure 17:1 Financial Aspects of Short-Term Decision Making

Financial Aspects of Short-Term Decision Making

Whenever there are alternative courses of action, a decision must be made. Short-term financial decision making is concerned with maximising the return from a given level of resources and requires a thorough understanding of what cost accountants call *relevant costs*. Whether or not a cost is relevant depends on how it is affected by the decision being made.

What Costs are Relevant to the Decision?

For a cost to be relevant it must satisfy two conditions. Firstly, it must relate to an expected future cost and, secondly, the cost must be one which will change according to the decision being made. The aim is to make a decision which will increase the firm's cash flow and profit. This is illustrated in the next example.

Example

Waverley Engineering

Last year Waverley Engineering bought a machine tool which cost £75,000. The asset's current net book value is £60,000. Although the machine has a further working life of four years, the company is considering selling it for a new one. A local dealer has offered £15,000 for the machine if it is taken in part exchange for a new one.

The Production Director would like to purchase a new machine because it would reduce variable operating costs from £250,000 to £220,000. The new machine would cost £90,000 and have a life of four years.

The Sales Director believes that the new machine should not be bought for two reasons and the majority of the firm's directors agree with him. Firstly, the firm's sales will remain static at £280,000 and, secondly, a new machine will result in a £45,000 loss.

The company must, therefore, make a decision whether it should keep its existing machine or invest in a new one.

The correct decision is the one which considers the relevant costs involved in this decision. When considering this type of problem, it is helpful to tabulate all of the costs involved in the decision.

Solution

Table of Costs

	Keep machine £	Purchase machine £
Purchase Price	75,000	90,000
Assets Net Book Value	60,000	--
Trade in Value	15,000	--
Sales	280,000	280,000
Variable Operating Costs	250,000	220,000
Useful Life	4 years	4 years

The next step is to analyse how the decision will affect the firm's net cash flow. The decision making process is shown in the following diagram.

How Relevant Costs Affect the Decision Making Process

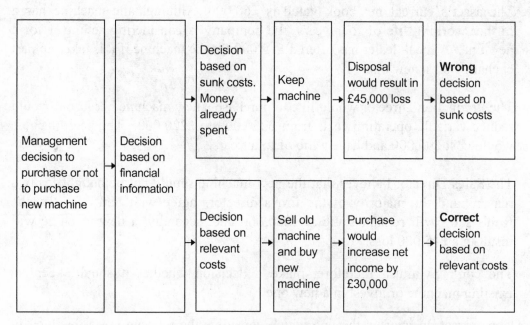

Note: Old Machine's Net Book Value £60,000 less Trade in Allowance £15,000 = £45,000.

Solution

Net Cash Flow Analysis

Immediate Capital Cash Outflow	£
Cash Purchase Price of New Machine	90,000
Less: Trade in Value	(15,000)
Expected Cash Outflow	75,000

Annual Operating of Cash Flow

	Keep	Buy	Difference
	£	£	£
Sales	280,000	280,000	---
Less: Variable Cost	250,000	220,000	
Contribution	30,000	60,000	30,000

The company is expecting to save £30,000 each year for the next four years and so net cash flows over that period will be increased by £45,000 (Cash Inflows £120,000 less £75,000 Outflows = £45,000). It, therefore, makes financial sense to purchase the new machine. **Note:** New machine, less trade in = £75,000.

The book value of the old machine, £60,000, is a sunk cost and is, therefore, not relevant to the decision. In this example the only relevant cost is the machine's trade in value of £15,000.

The only costs which are relevant to a decision are those that affect future cash flows as soon as the decision has been made. This is why marginal costing techniques are appropriate when making decisions, for marginal costing considers the additional cost of making one more unit. Before explaining how marginal costing techniques can be applied to short-term decision making, it is necessary to explain the following terms.

Sunk Cost: Any expenditure which has already taken place in the past and which will not be affected by a particular decision under consideration can be ignored. Sunk costs cannot be changed or recovered and are, therefore, not relevant to the decision making process.

Incremental Cost: If a cost will be incurred if a particular course of action is taken, but avoided if the action is not taken, the cost is said to be incremental. Specific fixed costs appropriate to the decision may also be incremental if, as a result of not taking the action contemplated, they can be avoided. For example, if a decision to increase output results in the firm having to rent additional premises, then the cost of the rent would be an incremental fixed cost. Incremental costs are sometimes called differential costs.

Committed Cost: This is a cost which has its origin in a previous decision. For example, if a firm decided to rent a warehouse last year, then this years rent is a committed cost.

Discretionary Cost: Such a cost does not have to be made immediately, such as the re-decorating of the firm's offices. Management can choose the best time to do the work and when to spend the money. This is why it is called a discretionary cost, although sometimes it is referred to as a programmed or managed cost.

Opportunity Cost: If the firm's resources could be put to an alternative use, then the opportunity cost is the opportunity foregone. This is the true cost of any decision.

How Marginal Costing Techniques Assist Managerial Decision Making

Whilst a firm must cover its fixed and variable costs if it is to be profitable, a study of total costs does not always provide a sound basis for decision making. Many fixed costs, such as fixed manufacturing overheads, have to be allocated by absorbing the fixed costs over every unit made. As a result, the unit cost will alter with output. If fixed costs are £100,000 and 50,000 units are made, then the fixed cost per unit will be £2 but, if only 10,000 are made, then the cost will rise to £10. The following example shows how wrong decisions can be made if management consider the total costs involved in making an additional order instead of the cost changes which result from the new order.

Example

D and K Electrics

D and K Electrics is a small manufacturing company. The business currently manufactures 60,000 electric motors which are sold for £30 a unit. The manufacturing costs are shown below.

	£
Materials	14
Direct Labour	6
Variable Production Overhead	1
Unit Variable Cost	21
Fixed Costs	£110,000

The Sales Director believes that the company could sell an additional 12,000 units to an export customer if the selling price was reduced to £22. The company makes its financial decisions after considering the firm's full costs and is about to reject the export order.

Solution

Financial Statement Based on Full Costs

	£	£
Sales 12,000 units at £22		264,000
Less Prime Cost £20 x 12,000	240,000	
Variable Production Overhead	12,000	
Fixed Production Overhead	21,960	
Total Cost		273,960
Loss		(9,960)

Note: Calculation of overhead using a predetermined rate of absorption Fixed Costs £110,000/60,000 units = £1.83 per unit.

Differential Cost Statement

	Without Order £	With Order £	Total £
Sales	1,800,000	264,000	2,064,000
Prime Cost	1,200,000	240,000	1,440,000
Variable Production Overhead	60,000	12,000	72,000
Contribution	540,000	12,000	552,000
Fixed Costs	110,000	None	110,000
Profit	430,000	12,000	442,000

By considering only the relevant costs the firm will increase its profits by £12,000 and so the new order is financially viable.

This example shows why managers must consider the change in costs and income which result from any decision to alter output levels. Marginal costing shows how the variable costs alter with any change in output and the contribution which will be earned from each sale. The variable cost represents a cash outflow to the firm, for goods cannot be made without raw materials being purchased and direct labour being employed. The contribution shows the cash inflow earned from each sale, and so the difference between the selling price and the variable costs represents the cash gain to the firm, called *contribution*.

The Marginal Cost Approach to Decision Making

Whenever short-term decisions have to be made, marginal costing techniques should be employed to see how the decision will affect the amount of contribution which the firm will earn. The following examples show how marginal costing techniques can assist management to make non routine decisions.

Making Decisions when there are Limiting Factors

A limiting factor is an accounting term to describe a factor which will affect output such as a shortage of materials, or a maximum number of labour hours which can be worked.

Example

The Radio Company manufacture two small circuit boards. The variable costs of manufacture are:

	Small £	Large £
Direct Materials	1	3
Direct Labour (3 hours)	6	3
Variable Overhead	1	1
Marginal Cost	8	7

The small circuit board sells for £14 and the large one for £11. During August the firm has only 8,000 hours of direct labour and the management need to know which product should have priority, so that the business can maximise its profits.

Solution

Here, labour is the limiting factor, and so priority should be given to the circuit board, which earns the maximum contribution from each direct labour hour.

	Small £	Large £
Selling Price	14	11
Less Variable Cost	8	7
Unit Contribution	6	4
Labour Hours Per Unit	2 Hours	1 Hour
Contribution Per Labour Hour	3	4

Because labour is in short supply, it is more profitable to give priority to the large circuit board. The unit contribution is only relevant when there are no limiting factors. In this case unit contribution is not the correct way to decide priorities because it takes two hours to earn £6 from the small circuit board and only one hour to earn £4 from the large circuit board.

Close a Department or Cost Centre

It does not always follow that, if a loss making department or division is closed, a firm's profits will improve. In the short-term the firm may still have to pay the fixed costs, even though production has ceased. This is why it is important that idle productive resources are put to profitable use, as shown in the next example.

Example

The Glass Tower Hotel

The Glass Tower Hotel has three bars on the ground floor. The management are considering closing one of the bars, because it is losing money, and converting the area into a reading room for guests. The costs and revenues for the three bars are as follows:

	Caribbean Bar £	Glass Tower Bar £	Bar by the Pool £	Total £
Sales	30,000	12,000	18,000	60,000
Marginal Cost	18,000	7,000	11,000	36,000
Contribution	12,000	5,000	7,000	24,000
Fixed Costs	6,000	6,000	6,000	18,000
Profit/(Loss)	6,000	(1,000)	1,000	6,000

These figures can now be used to see what would happen to the hotel's overall profitability if the Glass Tower Bar is shut or kept open.

	Close One Bar £	Keep All Bars £	Change in Sales Costs & Profits £
Sales	48,000	60,000	12,000
Marginal Cost	29,000	36,000	7,000
Contribution	19,000	24,000	5,000
Fixed Costs	18,000	18,000	Nil
Profit	1,000	6,000	5,000

The hotel should not close the Glass Tower Bar, unless the area can be used to generate an additional source of revenue.

Make or Buy Decisions

Manufacturing companies sometimes receive quotes from suppliers for components. If the quote is below the firm's current cost for making the product, a decision must be made whether or not to buy in the component or continue making it. From a financial viewpoint the quote should be accepted if the cost of the bought-in product is less than the firm's variable cost of manufacture. This rule only applies if the idle factors of production can then be applied to more profitable work.

Example

Motor Components

Motor Components specialise in manufacturing filters for British, European and Japanese cars. One particular filter is used extensively in British cars and the firm has received a quote from another supplier at a cost of £8. The firm's management are currently considering whether or not to accept the order and its costs and production are shown below.

Production 30,000 units

	Unit Cost of Manufacture £	Total Cost of manufacture £
Direct Materials	3	90,000
Direct Labour	2	60,000
Variable Overheads Per Unit	1	30,000
Fixed Cost Per Unit	4	120,000
Total	10	300,000

If production ceased the firm would save £15,000 in fixed costs.

256

Solution

	£	£
Purchase Cost (30,000 units x £8)	240,000	
Manufacturing Cost		
Direct Materials	90,000	
Direct Labour	60,000	
Variable Overheads	30,000	
Fixed Costs	15,000	
	195,000	
Cost Savings By Manufacturing		45,000

Note: The variable costs of production are always relevant to the decision, whereas the fixed costs will only be a relevant cost if they can be avoided by stopping production.

It would initially appear that the firm's net income would increase by £60,000 because the purchase price is £2 below the firm's current manufacturing cost. Once, however, all of the relevant costs are taken into consideration, the firm's net income would decrease by £45,000. This is because only £15,000 of Motor Component's fixed costs would be avoided by purchasing the components from an outside supplier, and is a relevant cost. The £105,000 is a committed fixed cost, such as rent and rates, and these costs must be paid regardless of whether anything is produced.

A business should only ever buy in components if the variable cost, plus the incremental fixed cost and the opportunity cost, when added together are less than the supplier's price. The opportunity cost of a make or buy decision occurs whenever a firm sacrifices contribution by displacing an existing product.

A make or buy decision should not be based just on financial factors, for the decision has wider implications such as quality control, buyer reaction and finally how the news will affect sales.

Accept or Reject an Order

If a business has spare capacity which is not being used, then it may be able to operate at a higher level of output by accepting orders at reduced prices.

Example

The Hand Soap Company

The Hand Soap Company is currently operating at only 50 per cent capacity. The firm produces boxed soap sets but has found that demand has fallen. The firm has just received an export order from an overseas customer, provided that the price can be reduced from the normal selling price of £5 to £3. If the order is accepted, the company would be able to operate at 100 per cent capacity, but the management are worried that they may lose money by accepting the order. The firm's fixed costs are £50,000 and the variable costs per unit of production are £2.

Solution

	Existing orders £	Export Orders £	Combined Orders £
Sales (50,000 units)	250,000	150,000	400,000
Marginal Cost	100,000	100,000	200,000
Contribution	150,000	50,000	200,000
Fixed Costs	50,000	Nil	50,000
Profit	100,000	50,000	150,000

The order should be accepted because the firm will make an extra £50,000 profit. An order should never be accepted just because the unit cost decreases. The important consideration is whether the total contribution increases or decreases as a result of the additional business, In this case the company has increased its profits by £50,000, and so the order should be accepted.

All of these examples show how marginal costing techniques can assist short-term decision making. This is generally defined as up to six months. During this time period it is unlikely that the firm's cost structure will alter and the interest lost by not receiving the money immediately will be insignificant.

Before making any non routine decision, management must consider its opportunity cost and how else the firm's resources could be used. Any productive capacity which could be used for another purpose has an opportunity cost, and it is unusual for assets not to have an opportunity cost, because of the enterprise of managers and entrepreneurs. The short-term gains in contribution which a firm may make by using its short-term resources more effectively must be balanced against the long-term goals of the firm. Short-term price cutting can damage a firm's brands, revenues and can result in the business losing its pricing authority, thereby damaging its profitability. There is also the additional danger that the business will not cover all of its costs and that it will be forced into liquidation. This is why the best short-term decisions are the ones which increase the firm's earnings in the short-term without damaging its long-term goals.

QUESTIONS

Answers begin page 488

1. **The Potter's Wheel**

Last year Julie Young decided to set up a small business making and selling a range of clay flowerpots. Recently the firm has been experiencing cash flow problems and her bank manager has advised her to concentrate on making her best selling lines. Julie knows that each month she sells 200 units of her brightly coloured patio pots but she is uncertain which one contributes the most to the firm's profits and cash flow. The costs, selling prices and time taken to manufacture the patio flower pots are shown below.

	Small	**Medium**	**Large**
	£	£	£
Selling price	7.00	9.00	11.00
Clay	1.50	2.00	2.50
Paint	0.75	1.10	2.00
Variable overheads	1.00	1.25	1.50
Manufacturing time	2 hours	3 hours	4 hours

a. What is the marginal cost of each patio flower pot?

b. What is the contribution earned from each product sold?

c. Which product should Julie concentrate on making?

2. **Central Theme Parks**

The Central Theme Park company has invested in three major attractions at their new site in Leicestershire. Unfortunately one of the attractions has been operating at a loss. The management are currently below their budgeted profit targets and are keen to eliminate any loss-making facilities. They would like you to prepare a financial statement showing whether or not they should close the loss-making attraction and have presented you with the following information.

Attraction	Shark Ride	The Swamp	The Tunnel
	£	£	£
Sales	130,000	90,000	225,000
Variable costs	50,000	35,000	70,000
Direct labour	35,000	15,000	40,000
Fixed overheads	65,000	20,000	55,000

3. Southern Cross Hotel

Last year the Southern Cross Hotel chain opened a new hotel in Dockland. The hotel is currently losing money on some of its restaurants and the sales and costs are shown below.

	Docklands Restaurant £	City Life Restaurant £	Waterside Restaurant £
Sales	80,000	150,000	197,000
Food costs	25,000	45,000	63,000
Labour	25,000	35,000	45,000
Overheads	40,000	40,000	40,000

The company has calculated that 30 per cent of its overhead costs are variable. The owners would like to know:

a. The profit currently earned from each restaurant.

b. Whether or not they should close one restaurant.

Chapter 18

Budgetary Control

Introduction

One of a manager's main tasks is to plan the future level of business activity. It is the establishment of a plan which is the critical phase for, once this is done, actual performance can be compared with planned performance. Corrective action can then be taken to ensure that future activities conform to planned results. Budgeting can assist managers in their planning role and they should regard it as a management tool rather than just a mere accounting exercise. If this approach is adopted, accounting ceases to be just a method of recording financial information but evolves into part of the decision making process within the organisation. By establishing such a system, it will assist management in their task of planning, controlling and co-ordinating the different functions of the firm. Each business function, such as marketing, sales, production, finance and personnel, has its own objectives, but these must interrelate with the other functions if the business is to meet its declared aims and objectives.

What is a Budget?

The Chartered Institute of Management Accountants define a budget as:

> *a plan quantified in monetary terms, prepared and approved prior to a defined period of time, usually showing planned income to be generated and/or expenditure to be incurred during that period and the capital to be employed to attain a given objective.*

This definition highlights the three essential characteristics of the budgeting process. Firstly, there must be a plan. Secondly, the objectives must be quantifiable. They should be set either in terms of money or activity such as the number of units to be produced or sold. Lastly, the budget period must be for a certain period of time which can then be sub-divided into control periods.

Budgeting and the Strategic Planning Process

Strategic planning seeks to set out the long term goals for a business and how they can be achieved. In most organisations this task is performed by senior managers, after considering the firm's external environment and its current resources.

Strategic planning is not concerned with day-to-day operational management for it seeks to steer the organisation in a way which will enable it to maximise its potential in the market place in terms of profit and market share.

Once a business has agreed a strategy, management must prepare and set objectives which will enable the business to implement its strategy. This is usually referred to as tactical or operational planning. A company's annual budget is a good example of a tactical plan because it translates an organisation's strategic objectives into a quantifiable set of objectives to be achieved during a given time period.

The Budgetary Process and Staff Participation

An effective system of budgeting is one which communicates the organisation's objectives, limiting factors and budgeted targets so that the entire work force is aware and committed to their achievement. It is for management to decide how best to introduce their annual budgeting process and there are broadly two schools of thought as to how this should be done. Firstly, the budgeting process can be imposed by top management onto the organisation or, secondly, the process can start from lower levels in the organisation, in which case they are called participatory budgets.

Imposing budgets on an organisation is generally unsatisfactory, particularly for businesses, because the system can generate a lot of dissatisfaction amongst employees making them demotivated and reluctant to work as a team, thereby reducing communication between employees and managers.

This is why most managers opt for a system of participatory budgeting. The degree of participation can vary widely, from just the right to be consulted on the budget before it is implemented, to actually having the authority to set budgeted targets. Management should seek a level of participation which will encourage staff to participate and use their initiative, whilst still providing co-operation and communication between the different functional areas which make up the business.

How to establish a system of budgetary control

The starting point for any budgetary control system is the actual preparation of the budget, within the guidelines as defined by the firm's corporate objectives. The budgeting process cannot begin until the firm's corporate strategy and objectives have been agreed, otherwise it is impossible to formulate a budget for the business. As soon as the budget has been prepared, agreed and issued, actual results can be compared with budgeted. Management can then review and investigate the reasons for the deviations from the planned, budgeted results. This is a very important part of the budgeting process for management gain vital information about variations from the budgeted target. If the variation has been caused by inefficiency, this must be corrected and any savings which are cost effective must be made. Whenever there is likely to be permanent changes to the original plan, such as the increase in price of essential raw materials, the loss of major customers or other uncontrollable events, the original plan and budget should be revised.

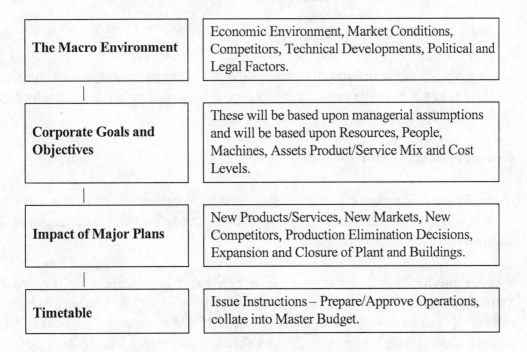

Figure 18:1 The Stages in the Budget Process

Once the corporate goals and objectives have been set, the next step is to set up a budget committee which will be responsible for overseeing the budgeting process. This committee is usually chaired by an accountant with the other members being co-opted from the different business functions. The committee's task is to advise departmental managers about the budgeting process, to co-ordinate activity and ensure that the planning process is completed to its planned timetable.

Purpose of Drawing up Budgets

Apart from the control aspect, it is vital that each of the functional budgets is compatible with one another. For instance, the sales department may estimate that they could sell 10,000 cost units of a certain product, while the production department only have the resources to manufacture 7,000. When this situation occurs, a decision must be taken either to increase capacity or to accept the limitation and lose the possible sales income. These limiting factors are referred to as either internal or external principal budget factors.

Internal Principal Budget Factor

This occurs when the limiting factor is inside the company where, for instance, the firm does not have the productive capacity to manufacture the amount which could probably be sold.

External Budget Factor

If the firm could make 3,000 units but the sales department knows that only 2,000 could be sold, the limit on activity is from outside the business and so it is known as an external budget factor.

Whether the limiting factor is internal or external it is important for it to be ascertained before the start of the coming financial year so that production and sales levels can be co-ordinated and controlled. If this is not done, the firm will produce stock which cannot be sold and this will inevitably lead to cash flow problems as too much working capital will be held in illiquid stock. On the other hand, if the sales department promote products which cannot be made, customers will be disappointed and future orders could be lost because of past supply problems.

Example of an Internal Principal Budget Factor

Budgeted Sales Product X1	7,000	units
Productive Capacity Product X1	5,000	units
Internal limitation	2,000	units

Preparing the Budgets

Figure 18:2, below, shows the stages in the budgetary process, the budgets which have to be prepared and the information needed for their preparation.

Figure 18:2 Preparing Budgets

Step One	Sales Budget	Based on the firm's products Sales Territories Customers
Step Two	Manufacturing / Retailing/Services Production Budget / Purchases Budget	Plant utilisation Production costs Purchases Stock
Step Three	Operating Budgets	Cost of sales Distribution costs Administration Finance Research & Development
Step Four	Capital Expenditure Budget	Land and buildings Plant and equipment
Step Five	Cash Budget	Opening cash balance Projected cash receipts Projected cash balances
Step Six	Preparation of Master Budget	Supports firm's strategic goals Communicates budgeted targets Evaluates management performance
Step Seven	Review, Monitor and Control so these achievements are the same as budgeted	Corrective action is the key to effective budgeting

BUDGETARY CONTROL

The first budget to be prepared should always be the sales budget as this will affect all the other departments. The expected level of sales can be calculated by looking at past years' results and then estimating the likely level of sales by considering the firm's product mix and the level of demand in the economy. This method is particularly suitable for companies operating in the fast moving consumer goods market where large databases can be built up showing sales by product and region.

For companies operating in the non fast moving consumer goods market, such as construction and engineering, this method is not really appropriate. In such cases it is better to set targets based on market share. By knowing the size of the market, it is possible to estimate the share of that market which will be captured by the company. The sales budget can then be ascertained.

Once the sales budget has been agreed, the production budget can be completed. The production budget must show the type of products required, the number to be made and the sell-by-date. Management can only schedule production effectively once sales and inventory levels are known. In a manufacturing company the next task is to break the products down into their component parts so that the purchases budget can be prepared, which will show the exact quantities of direct materials needed for production.

When these two budgets have been prepared, the manufacturing wages budget can be drawn up. The job cards will provide information about the time taken to do a job, the rates per hour and the quantity produced, so that future costs can be forecast. The next step is to prepare the overhead budget which will be based upon the best way of predicting overhead costs, such as direct labour or machine hours.

Lastly, the operating budgets must be prepared by departmental managers, such as Accounting, Marketing, Transport and Distribution and Research and Development.

The last two budgets to be prepared are the Capital Expenditure Budget, if applicable, and the Cash Budget. The capital budget should be prepared separately from the master budget, but its expenditure will affect the master budget and so its major impact will be on the cash budget. The cash budget is arguably the most important, because the business cannot continue once it does not have sufficient cash to finance its day to day trading activities.

If the totals of each individual group of budgets are added together, the master budget can be prepared. The master budget is really a projected profit and loss account and balance sheet which will show the business' position if its sales and costs are as budgeted. It is always prepared for a specific time period and it is based on a static level of demand which would enable the business to achieve an optimum profit.

The master budget will show the budgeted profit but, as we have already seen, profit is unlikely to be in cash. There is no point in setting a budgeted profit if no account is taken of the firm's cash position. A budget must be prepared showing the future cash receipts and payments. This will ensure that there is always sufficient cash for the firm to meet its day-to-day trading obligations. A cash flow forecast will indicate the business' ability to finance its future activities. If the budget shows cumulative deficits, then there will not be sufficient funds to finance its level of trading operations and ways must be considered of either rescheduling payments or raising additional finance to cover them.

Finally, once the budget has been prepared, actual performance must be compared with budgeted performance. In this way corrective action can be taken so that actual results conform to budgeted targets. If this is not done, the budget will cease to be a control document and will be of limited use to the organisation.

To illustrate the principles and explain the mechanics of preparing a functional and a master budget, we will now consider the following example.

Example

IMD Manufacturing Limited

IMD manufacturing Limited are planning their next six months' business activity. The balance sheet for the last six months is as follows:

IMD Balance Sheet as at 31 December Year 5

Fixed Assets	Cost £	Depreciation to date £	Net Book Value £
Land and Buildings	45,000	-	45,000
Plant and Machinery	30,000	3,000	27,000
	75,000	3,000	72,000
Current Assets			
Stock/Raw Materials		2,000	
Finished Goods		1,800	
Debtors		5,000	
Bank		15,000	
		23,800	
Less Current Liabilities			
Creditors		600	
Working Capital			23,200
Net Assets			95,200
Financed by			
Share Capital		60,000	
Reserves		35,200	
Shareholder's Funds			95,200

Budgeted expenditure and income for the next six months:

a. The unit costs of production are – £5 per unit direct material and direct labour – £4 per unit. Finished goods are valued on a prime cost (material + direct labour only) basis.

The sales manager expects the following sales volumes at a constant price of £20 per unit.

Jan	Feb	March	April	May	June
200	250	300	250	200	270

b. Production is planned at 150 units in the first two months rising to 300 for March and April and falling back to 200 units for May and June. It is expected that July will also be 200 units.

c. To reduce working capital requirements, the accountant has recommended that raw material for only one month's production should be held.

d.   All material is bought on one month's credit. Labour costs are incurred in line with production and paid during the month.

e.   Variable overhead is £2 per unit produced from January to April, and £4 from May onwards. Fixed overheads are £700 per month. Both are payable in the month in which they are incurred. There is £1,500 of depreciation in the fixed overhead.

f.   The directors intend to spend £10,000 on plant in March, £7,000 in May and £3,000 in June. Depreciation will not be charged on these items until the end of the year.

g.   The company will take a term loan for £12,000 on 1st February. Interest at 15 per cent is payable every six months, the first payment being on 30 June.

h.   Vehicle leasing payments cost £600 per month.

i.   Depreciation of plant and machinery is 5 per cent on cost price.

j.   Debtors pay their accounts two months after the sale is made. In the balance sheet the £5,000 balance is made up of £2,000 in November and £3,000 in December.

From this information it is possible to prepare the firm's functional budgets and a budgeted profit and loss account and balance sheet.

Preparation of the Function Budgets

In this example the functional budgets are:

1.   the sales budget
2.   the production budget
3.   the purchases budget
4.   the production cost budget
5.   the cash budget

Solution

1. The Sales Budget

	Jan	Feb	March	April	May	June	Total
Planned sales units	200	250	300	250	200	270	
Value £20 per unit	4,000	5,000	6,000	5,000	4,000	5,400	29,400
Materials (£5)	1,000	1,250	1,500	1,250	1,000	1,350	(7,350)
Labour (£4)	800	1,000	1,200	1,000	800	1,080	(5,880)
Gross Profit							16,170

2. Production Budget

From the balance sheet value of £1,800 and the detail in note (a) £1,800/£9 (materials £5 and Labour £4) = 200 units of opening finished goods.

	Jan	Feb	March	April	May	June
Opening stock (units)	200	150	50	50	100	100
Production (note b)	150	150	300	300	200	200
Sales (note a)	200	250	300	250	200	270
Closing stock	150	50	50	100	100	30

Note: Closing stock = 30 units and is calculated by adding the opening stock and production and then subtracting it from the number sold. The June figure (30) will later be shown in the budgeted profit and loss account and balance sheet. The value of the closing stock will be 30 x £9 (£5 materials and £4 labour) = £270.

3. The Purchases Budget

The opening balance sheet shows 400 units (£2,000/£5 per unit of raw materials).

	Jan	Feb	March	April	May	June
Opening Stock	400	250	300	300	200	200
Production	150	150	300	300	200	200
Purchases	-	200	300	200	200	200
Closing Stock	250	300	300	200	200	200

Note: Closing stock = 200
  a. To reflect policy, no stocks were bought in January (note c).
  b. The closing raw material stock must equate with the July planned production.
  c. The closing stock is calculated by subtracting the production from the opening stock.

4. Production Cost Budget

	Jan	Feb	March	April	May	June
Volume (note b)	150	150	300	300	200	200
Materials	750	750	1500	1500	1000	1000
Labour	600	600	1200	1200	800	800
Prime Cost	1350	1350	2700	2700	1800	1800
Variable Overhead	300	300	600	600	800	800

5. Cash Budget

	Jan	Feb	March	April	May	June
Receipts	£	£	£	£	£	£
Debtors (j) (i)	2,000	3,000	4,000	5,000	6,000	5,000
Loan		12,000				
Total Receipts	2,000	15,000	4,000	5,000	6,000	5,000
Payments						
Material (d)(iii)	600	-	1,000	1,500	1,000	1,000
Labour (iv)	600	600	1,200	1,200	800	800
Variable Overhead (iv)	300	300	600	600	800	800
Fixed Overhead (e)	575	575	575	575	575	575
(NB no depreciation)						
Lease	600	600	600	600	600	600
Capital Equipment			10,000		7,000	3,000
Interest (6 months)						900
Total Payments	2,675	2,075	13,975	4,475	10,775	7,675
Opening Balance	15,000	14,325	27,250	17,275	17,800	13,025
Net Receipts	(675)	12,925	(9,975)	525	(4,775)	(2,675)
Closing Balance	**14,325**	**27,250**	**17,275**	**17,800**	**13,025**	**10,350**

Note: The opening balance is taken from the balance sheet. Cash budgets are explained further in Chapter 28.

Once the functional budgets have been prepared the master budget can be drawn up.

Budget Profit and Loss Account for IMD Manufacturing
for the period January to June Year 6

[Figures in brackets ( ) indicate source of information]

	£	£
Sales (i) 1,470 units @ £20		29,400
Direct material (i)		(7,350)
Direct labour (ii)		(5,880)
Gross profit		16,170
Expenses		
Variable overheads (iv)	3,400	
Fixed overheads including depreciation	4,200	
Lease payments (h)	3,600	
Interest (5 months)	750	
		(11,950)
Net profit		£4,220

We can now do the budgeted balance sheet.

IMD Budgeted Balance Sheet as at 30 June Year 6

Fixed assets	Cost £	Depreciation	Net Book
Land and buildings	45,000	-	45,000
Plant and machinery	50,000	3,750	46,250
(e) (f)	95,000	3,750	91,250
Current assets			
Stock (iii) Raw materials (220x5)		1,000	
(iv) Finished goods (30x9)		270	
Debtors (i)		9,400	
Prepayments		150	
Bank (v)		10,350	
		21,170	
Current Liabilities			
Trade creditors (200 x 5)		(1,000)	
Net current assets			20,170
			111,420
Loan			(12,000)
Total Net Assets			99,420
Financed by:			
Capital			60,000
Profit brought forward			35,200
Profit from six months trading			4,220
Shareholders' funds			99,420

Flexible Budgets

Flexible budgets take account of the behaviour of costs and how they change at different levels of activity. By preparing budgets in this way, management can see how the firm's costs will change with different levels of activity, and can use them for decision making.

In chapter 13 we saw that fixed costs tend to be time related, whereas variable costs are activity based. Fixed costs will, therefore, remain the same within the firm's current operating capacity whilst the variable costs will alter with the different levels of activity.

It is because the fixed cost per unit of output changes with levels of activity that management select a pre-determined activity rate and use this output level to calculate a fixed overhead rate per unit of output for costing purposes.

Example

The Universal Clothing Company

The company's budgeted level of output for the coming quarter is 20,000 direct labour hours, which means that the firm can produce 40,000 cost units. The company's costs are:

Direct labour	£4 per hour
Materials	£7 a unit
Factory Consumables	20p per direct labour hour
Factory power	£1 per direct labour hour
Rent and Rates	£30,000
Insurance	£10,000
Other fixed overheads	£40,000

The management have asked you to prepare a flexible budget for the firm at the following levels of activity:

50%   60%   70%   80%   90%   and 100%

273

Flexible Budget for the Universal Clothing Company

Activity	50%	60%	70%	80%	90%	100%
Output (units)	20,000	24,000	28,000	32,000	36,000	40,000
	£	£	£	£	£	£
Direct labour	80,000	96,000	112,000	128,000	144,000	160,000
Materials	140,000	168,000	196,000	224,000	252,000	280,000
Factory Consumables	4,000	4,800	5,600	6,400	7,200	8,000
Factory Power	20,000	24,000	28,000	32,000	36,000	40,000
Rent & Rates	30,000	30,000	30,000	30,000	30,000	30,000
Insurance	10,000	10,000	10,000	10,000	10,000	10,000
Fixed Overheads	40,000	40,000	40,000	40,000	40,000	40,000
Total cost	324,000	372,800	421,600	470,400	519,200	568,000

Incremental and Zero Based Budgeting

There are two main methods of budgeting expenses for the coming year *incremental budgeting* and *zero based budgeting*. Incremental budgeting is the most popular method and uses last year's costs as the basis for next year's budget. These costs are then adjusted for any change in output plus expected inflation. Such a system provides management with little control, for costs can escalate from year to year because there has been no systematic review as to whether such costs could be reduced or eliminated by new working procedures.

Zero based budgeting ignores last year's costs and requires managers to justify their budgeted figures by concentrating on the organisation's objectives. This method of budgeting makes managers consider other ways of achieving the same result. Advocates of zero based budgeting believe that the method makes the organisation more efficient because managers cannot build slack into their budgets. This forces managers to consider the organisation's objectives and evaluate all operations of the business. Whilst this method of budgeting can be used by any business, it is particularly relevant for service areas. Unfortunately zero based budgeting is expensive, time-consuming to introduce and does not provide a measure of efficiency. Ultimately management must decide whether the benefit of ZBB will exceed the cost of using the system.

The Benefits of Budgetary Control

If a system of budgetary control is to be effective, the whole organisation must be involved in the process. Budgets must be prepared by the operating divisions and it is essential that each functional area must believe in the budget which has been set. This can only be achieved if the operational areas are given guidelines as to how to prepare their budgets. In this way staff feel responsible for their budgets and are more likely to be motivated to achieve the targets. This is the major benefit from the process for it forces both management and staff to consider the future, determine planned output levels and compare actual results with budgeted results.

If the budgetary process can be presented in this way, instead of as an accounting exercise, the firm will have an effective budgetary control system and will benefit from having a clear set of goals which all staff are committed to and which can be regularly reviewed throughout the year. Otherwise, the process will become a meaningless accounting exercise with unmotivated staff believing that the budgeted output, sales and profit targets are unrealistic and unfair.

Controlling the Budgeting Process

Once the budget has been agreed and implemented, management must compare actual results with their budgeted results. If the budgeting process is to be more than an accounting exercise, management must have an effective control system where actual costs and revenues are compared with those budgeted for. The control process should aim to determine the cause for the variances from the budgeted targets and, once discovered, it should be communicated to operational managers. Managers should be held accountable for the costs and revenues of any operating area for which they have responsibility.

Calculation of Revenue and Cost Variance

Sales Price Variance

This is calculated by taking the difference between the budgeted selling price and the actual selling price and multiplying that figure by the number of units sold. This will then highlight the variance which has been brought about by a change in the selling price.

Sales Value Variance

This is the difference between the actual and budgeted sales value. It is calculated by taking the difference between actual and budgeted sales value and multiplying that figure by the budgeted selling price. Once management have investigated the cause of the sales variance they must consider cost variances.

Cost Variance

It is essential that management always analyse costs in relation to the actual volume of sales rather than the budgeted volume of sales. This can be seen in the next example.

The Value Radio Company

At the end of each quarter the company produces a responsibility report which compares actual results with those budgeted. The firm's responsibility report for the last quarter is shown below:

The Value Radio Company Budget Report for the Quarter Ending 31st March, Year 7.

	Actual	Budget	Variance Favourable/ Adverse
Output	1910	1800	110
Variable Cost of Production			
	£	£	£
Direct Materials	53,480	51,300	(2180)
Direct Labour	59,210	55,080	(4130)
Variable Overhead	38,200	36,450	(1750)
	150,890	142,830	
Fixed Production Costs			
Depreciation	10,000	10,000	
Indirect Labour	19,500	20,000	500
Corporate Costs			
Quality Selling and Admin Costs	35,000	32,000	(3,000)
	215,390	204,830	10,560

Note: Budgeted Unit Cost Direct Materials £28.50, Direct Labour £30.60, Variable Overhead £20.25. These figures are calculated by dividing total cost by budgeted output.

This example highlights two major deficiencies. Firstly, the report compares actual costs with static budget costs instead of comparing actual costs with flexible budget costs. For evaluation and control purposes management should never compare costs based on two different activity levels. Secondly, a manager should only be responsible for costs which are within their control and corporate

276

costs, such as quality, selling and administration, are not within the control of a production manager and should not be included.

The information should be presented so that it reflects these two principles, and the next example incorporates them.

Volume	Actual 1910 Units		Budgeted 1910 Units		Variance Favourable/ Adverse
	Per Unit	Total	Per Unit	Total	
	£	£	£	£	£
Variable Production Costs	28	53,480	28.50	54,435	955
Direct Materials					
Direct Labour	31	59,210	30.60	58,446	(764)
Variable Overheads	20	38,200	20.25	38,678	478
Fixed Production Costs					
Depreciation		10,000		10,000	
Indirect Labour		19,500		20,000	500
Total Production Costs		180,390		181559	1,169

QUESTIONS

Answers begin page 490

1. **The South West Brewing Company**. The firm is a small family-owned brewery. It sells its products under own-label as well as brewing own-label brands for several of the large supermarket chains. The brewery is currently operating at 100 per cent capacity but demand is seasonal. The directors have decided to adopt a flexible budgeting system so that they can ascertain costs at different levels of activity.

Cost	£
Rent	70,000
Rates	15,000
Prime costs	90,000
Insurance	10,000
Indirect labour	20,000
Advertising	5,000

You work for the company and have been asked to prepare a flexible budget for the firm showing its costs at the following levels of activity: 70, 80, 90, and 100 per cent.

2. **The Wooden Fencing Company**. A company manufactures a range of ready-assembled wooden fences. It is currently operating at 100 per cent capacity, but the management know that demand for its products are very dependent upon the weather. As a result they have decided to prepare a flexible budget for different levels of possible activity. The costs below show the firm's annual operating costs at 100 per cent activity, but for short periods the firm can operate at 110 per cent capacity by working overtime.

	£
Rent	100,000
Rates	20,000
Direct materials	600,000
Direct labour	450,000
Power	120,000
Factor insurance	20,000
Indirect labour	30,000

You work for the company and have been asked to prepare a flexible budget showing costs at the following levels of activity: 80, 90, 100, and 110 per cent.

3. Electric Motors Limited.

Electric Motors Limited manufactures electric motors which it sells both at home and abroad. Last month the firm heard that it had lost an export tender and, as a result, has had to sell some surplus plant and reduce productive capacity to 7650 units, which represents 90 per cent of the maximum.

You work in the costing department at Electric Motors and have already prepared a flexible budget covering 80, 90 and 100 per cent activity levels for the firm.

Flexible Budget			
	80% £	90% £	100% £
Direct materials	115,600	130,050	144,500
Direct labour	74,800	84,150	93,500
Overheads	143,800	146,775	149,750
Sales	353,600	397,800	442,000

You have just received a memo from the marketing director informing you that since losing the export order the projected sales figures for the coming year has been reduced to 70 per cent level of activity. As a result she has asked you to prepare a statement in marginal costing form showing the forecast profit for the coming year.

4. R and H Metal Manufacturers.

The company produce metal springs used in the car industry and face fierce competition from both Far Eastern and European manufacturers. The firm's management believe that, if fixed costs could be reduced by 3 per cent, sales could be increased by 9 per cent. During the coming year raw materials are expected to rise by 5 per cent and wages by 7 per cent. Variable overhead costs are expected to increase by 6 per cent.

Last year's profit and loss account is shown below.

R and H Metal Manufacturing Profit and Loss Account for the year ending 4 April year 7		
	£	£
Sales		870,000
Less costs		
Raw materials	155,000	
Wages	130,000	
Variable overheads	37,000	
Fixed overheads	52,000	374,000
Profit		496,000

Based on their forecasts the directors would like you to prepare the budgeted profit and loss account for the company.

5.   **The Malaysian Restaurant** specialises in selling Malaysian food in North London. The owner faces fierce competition from other restaurants in the area and believes that, if his restaurant prices could be reduced by 5 per cent, his sales could be increased by 12 per cent.

During the coming year food costs are expected to rise by 4 per cent and wages by 6.1 per cent. The restaurant also faces a £2,000 increase in its rent. Last year's profit and loss account is shown below

The Malaysian Restaurant Profit and Loss Account for the year ending 31 January Year 5		
	£	£
Sales		100,000
Less costs		
Food costs	30,000	
Wages	25,000	
Variable overheads	7,000	
Fixed overheads	20,000	82,000
Profit		18,000

You are required to:

a.   Prepare a forecast budgeted profit and loss account.

b.   Write a report outlining how a system of budgetary control can help a business to control its costs.

6.   **Ankar Limited** are about to enter into a local productivity agreement. The management and union negotiators have asked for an adjournment and you have been asked to calculate whether or not the firm should agree to the union's proposal or stick to its offer of a straightforward 10 per cent pay rise. The union's proposal is as follows:

Every direct worker would receive a bonus of £0.16 for every good unit produced, thereby enabling the firm to increase production by 12½ per cent. The marketing director has confirmed that the increased output can be sold if the selling price of all sales is reduced by £0.20 per unit.

You have just been given next year's budget which has not taken account of any salary or wage rise.

	£000	£000
Sales (400,000) units		1,600
Direct materials	320	
Direct wages	480	
Variable production overhead	72	
Fixed production overhead	134	
Variable selling overhead (5% of sales value)	80	
Fixed selling overhead	53	
Variable distribution overhead	64	
Fixed distribution and administration overhead	183	
		1,386
Profit		214

7. **Rolan Industries**. The firm's planned output and sales are shown below.

a. Sales £160 per unit. Debtors to settle accounts 1 month after sale.

	January	February	March
Units	320	240	600

b. Purchases are made on one month's credit.

January £	February £	March £
6000	8000	10000

c. Labour costs and overheads are paid in the month of production. Fixed overheads are £3,600 per month paid in the month of production.

d. Unit production costs:

	£
Direct materials	20
Direct labour	24
Variable overheads	10
Unit variable cost	54

Rolan Industries plan to produce 140 units in January, 300 in February and 600 in March.

e. **Notes to the accounts:**

Stock of raw materials	31 December	£3,000
Stock of finished goods	31 December	£10,800
Debtors	31 December	£14,600
Creditors	31 December	£4,000
Bank	31 December	£12,000 Dr

Prepare the following budgets for Rolan Industries

Materials Budget   Creditors Budget

Production Budget   Debtors Budget

Production Cost Budget   Cash Budget

Chapter 19

Standard Costing

Introduction

The Chartered Institute of Management Accounts defines a standard cost as a predetermined calculation of how much costs should be under specified working conditions. A standard costing system assesses what the cost should be to make a product before actually making it. The actual cost can then be compared with the standard cost, enabling management to investigate why a difference or variance has occurred.

How a System of Standard Costing Supports the Budgetary Control Process

The establishment of a standard costing system allows greater control of costs within the business for the differences between actual costs and standard costs can be detected as they are incurred, allowing management to take corrective action.

Standard costing systems, therefore, support the budgetary control process but, unlike budgets, comparisons can be made with standard costs as the firm is producing the goods. If the business only has a system of budgetary control, management can only compare actual results with budgeted performance at the end of the budgeted period. This is a major limitation of budgeting because new control procedures cannot be instigated immediately. Often budgets focus on future planned activity levels in fairly broad terms, such as production and sales, rather than the costs involved of making a particular product.

Standard costing also assists management decision making, particularly with regard to pricing decisions because management know their costs based on an expected level of operating efficiency.

The system can also be used to evaluate management performance because the actual costs of operations can be compared with the standard cost.

The Control Process

If standards are set for a firm's direct and indirect costs, comparisons can be made with actual and planned results. Standards can be set for direct materials, both price and usage, for direct labour and for indirect fixed or variable overheads. The difference between the goal set and the results achieved can then be analysed and the reason communicated to the relevant departments. A standard costing system will only be effective in controlling costs if management analyse the reason for the variance. In itself the variance just shows that a difference has occurred. It is the analysis of the variance which will reveal the reason for the difference and it is only then that management are able to decide what action to take. This can be seen from the following diagram.

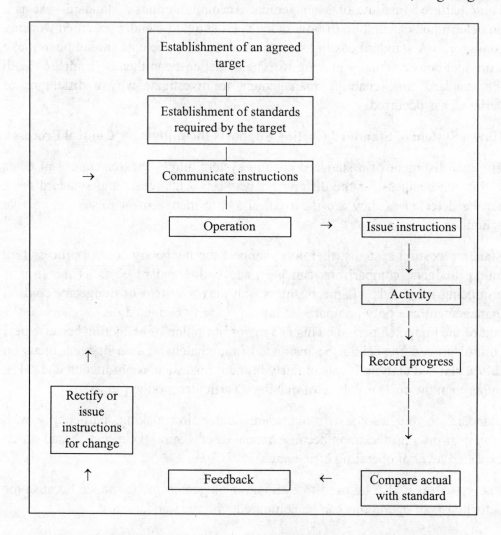

Figure 19:1 Cycle of Actions for a Standard Costing System

The diagram shows that corrective action is not automatic but depends upon identifying the variance. This may be adverse, meaning that the costs or usage are more than the standard envisaged, or less, in which case they are referred to as *favourable*. In this way standard costing monitors performance against expectation and so any variance from standard must be investigated by management.

The Benefits of a Standard Costing System

It is expensive and time consuming to install a system of standard costing and, if the costs involved are to be justified, the firm must gain the following benefits.

1. Unit costs should be reduced because of improvements made in controlling costs.

2. Stock control procedures should be simplified because stock and work in progress can be valued at its standard cost. This makes stock control easier because stock need not be valued on a *last in first out* basis (LIFO) or on a first in first out basis (FIFO) or any other method such as average cost.

3. Price setting should be improved because the firm has accurate details about its costs.

4. The system highlights variances from standards and so management are able to concentrate on that analysis. There is, therefore, no need to spend time in analysing costs which are performing to standard and so the system is often said to allow management by exception.

5. The business can benefit from establishing new working practices by reconsidering working practices before the standards are set.

Setting Standards

The Chartered Institute of Management Accountants defines four different types of standard. They are the *basic standard, ideal standard, normal standard* and the *current standard*. It is the firm's management who must decide which is the most appropriate for their business.

Basic standard

This is defined as *a standard established for use over a long period from which a current standard can be developed*. Such a standard could remain unchanged for a long time but, if this is the case, it will be useless as an effective short-term attention-directing control tool. Inflation, competition and new technology have meant that management must adapt to a changing business environment if their company is to survive today's competitive pressures. While a basic standard may be of interest to see what extent prices of commodities, goods or services have changed over a period of time, it is ineffective as a meaningful control tool unless coupled to a costly and complicated two-tier standard costing system. Some firms set a base standard for long-term comparisons while, at the same time, using a current standard for current operational control.

Ideal Standard

A standard which can be attained under the most favourable conditions. Some managers believe that if a standard is set, assuming that all waste and inefficiency have been eliminated from the system, that the actual costs should be the same as the standard cost. No allowance is made for human error, machine breakdowns or wastage. Advocates of such a system believe that the resulting unfavourable variances will remind management of the on-going continual need for improvement in all phases of operations and that there can be no room for complacency within the organisation.

This approach contradicts many behavioural scientists' views that the setting of such variances is self destructive and dysfunctional since they actually remove motivation, for workers believe that the targets are unrealistic and unachievable.

The use of ideal standards may, however, be appropriate in new hi-tech factories where highly automated production processes controlled by computers can virtually guarantee continuous high quality output. In such cases adverse variances are likely to be reduced to levels which are almost immaterial and may be so small as not to need investigating.

Normal Standard

A standard which can be attained if a standard unit of work is carried out efficiently, a machine properly operated or material properly used. Such a standard makes allowances for normal wastage, machine breakdown and operator failure. This standard represents future performance and objectives which are reasonably attainable and is sometimes called the *attainable standard*. It has the added benefit in that it can be used for other purposes such as budgeting and inventory control. This is possible because the standard is attainable under normal circumstances and can, therefore, be legitimately used for other purposes.

The Current Standard

This is defined as *a standard established for the use over a short period of time, related to current conditions*. Many business people use the term *current standards* for the standard currently used by the firm but this is incorrect. The current operations standards which are used during the accounting or budget period will be the *attainable* or *normal standards*; while the current standard is the one used in abnormal operating conditions, as it recognises current problems and works within the present conditions.

The Standard Cost Card

At the heart of any standard costing system is the standard cost card which sets out details relating to the standard quantities and standard prices for producing a cost unit. The exact format differs from firm to firm but an example of the layout of a standard cost card is shown below.

Figure 19:2 Example of a Standard Cost Card

Product RQT Quantity - one unit	Current Standard £	Ideal Standard £	Normal Standard £
Direct materials			
10 KG at £20	200	-	-
9 kg at £16	-	144	-
10 Kg at £18	-	180	
Direct labour			
30 hours at £6	180		
25 hours at £5		125	
30 hours at £5.50			165
Overheads			
15 hours at £18	270		
10 hours at £16		160	
15 hours at £17			255
Standard Production Cost	650	429	600

Note: How the standard cost is dependent upon the standard being used.

Setting Standards

Before a standard costing system can be installed, it is necessary to build up the costs for each individual component or product. Once this has been done standard cost cards can be produced which will establish and itemise the individual cost components of direct materials, direct or conversion labour and overheads. It will be against these standards that actual costs are compared. Each standard must provide a target for achievement, provide a yardstick which can be used to evaluate performance and, lastly, must highlight the aspects of the business not operating according to plan.

The standards can only be set via liaison and discussion of costs with the various function heads and their staff. This is shown below.

Data Source	Information required	Data analysis/cost accountant
Production specifications	Technical	Output levels
Financial Accountant	Overheads	Expenses
Purchasing	Material prices	Costs
Personnel	Pay Rates	Costs

Figure 19:3 Information Needed for a Standard Costing System

The figure shows that the cost accountant must gather a great deal of detailed information from various sources before the standards can be set. Once this has been done further information will be required because the standards will have to be reviewed to take account of the firm's product mix, changes in material and labour costs and productivity improvements. Setting standards is an on-going process because the standards must reflect the current costs and operating efficiencies.

We have already seen that in cost accounting there are three elements to the word *cost*, this is also the case when setting standard costs and they are materials, labour and overheads. These can be further broken down into two parts as shown below.

Element	Materials	Labour	Overhead
Possible variance	Price and usage	Rate & efficiency	Spend & efficiency

Figure 19:4 The Three Elements of a Firm's Costs

Direct Materials

Before a standard cost for materials can be set management must know four things. They are:

A. What materials are needed for production.

B. Their quality.

C. The quality needed.

D. Their price.

The price standard will be made up of prices obtained, negotiated and agreed with suppliers. This agreed price may take into account any future short-term price increase. If this is the case the final standard will be based on the mean of a range of prices likely to prevail during the time that the standard is operational.

The standard must also make allowances for normal loss, defective material, storage, deterioration, theft and wastage that may occur during the production process. This amount should be added to the figure for planned usage.

Lastly, for many firms operating in the fast moving consumer goods market, the packaging forms an important part of the promotional mix and this added cost must be taken into consideration when setting the standard cost.

Direct Wage Cost

Most large firms set their wage costs after negotiations with the relevant trade union. With the introduction of two year agreements this part of the standard setting process has become easier because the labour rate is already known. However, the main problem occurs when calculating the time needed to perform a task as this varies according to worker motivation and level of skill, together with the type of machinery used.

If a firm is to control its labour costs the time taken to complete a task should be recorded. An allowance must be built into the labour cost standard to take account of operator fatigue, together with a contingency allowance for reading diagrams and cleaning machinery. If new products are being made the firm should also set a reject allowance to take account of problems brought about by the introduction of new manufacturing processes. When making these allowances care must be taken that they are set at an equitable level or cost overruns will be incurred which could add between 10 and 15 per cent to total labour costs.

Conversion Overhead

It is possible to split the conversion overhead into its fixed and variable components, although in practice this is rarely done. This is because most overheads are time related and few vary materially with actual production or activity. As a result most businesses work only on fixed overhead controls and are determined by:

1. Calculating the cost of the conversion overhead, such as factory rent.

2. Selecting the base by which it is to be recovered, such as standard labour production hours, or machine produced hours, or a percentage on standard direct materials.

3. Once the method for absorbing the overhead has been established, the rate is calculated by using the following formula:

$$\frac{\text{Conversion overhead cost}}{\text{Produced hours (or other appropriate method)}} = \text{Standard overhead rate}$$

Once all the information has been collected and staff have been consulted and involved in the process, the firm's management can compare actual costs with standard costs. This process is referred to as *variance analysis* which is explained fully in chapter 20.

Recently the usefulness of standard costing as a cost control technique has been criticised for two main reasons. Firstly, activity based costing has highlighted how costs change with activity and, secondly, target costing, sometimes called *Kaizen* costing has proved to be very effective in controlling costs in new product design and development.

Kaizen costing seeks to reduce actual costs to below their standard costs and is, therefore, the exact opposite of standard costing which seeks to ensure that actual costs are the same as standard. There is a danger that standard costing systems fail to reduce costs in the long-term, thereby depriving the firm of a cost competitive advantage in the market place.

In contrast to standard costing Kaizen costing sets a cost reduction target and then sets out to achieve it. Managers can then be assessed as to how well they are performing to meet these new cost challenges.

Chapter 20

Variance Analysis

Introduction

The previous chapter explained the principles of standard costing, but the system is only effective in monitoring costs if the variances are calculated correctly and their cause analysed. A variance is the difference between planned, budgeted or standard cost and the actual costs or revenues received. When the variance is worse than the budgeted or standard cost, it is said to be *adverse* and it is an accounting convention that adverse variances are shown in brackets. If the costs and revenues are better than the budgeted or standard cost, the variance is deemed to be *favourable* and is shown without brackets.

Whilst it is possible to calculate the total variance for each cost element of production, be it materials, labour or overheads, it is of limited use for control purposes because it does not explain why the variance has occurred. This is why the total variance for materials and labour are further sub-divided into price and quantity variances. Price variances show the difference between what the firm paid for its imports and the firm's expected purchase price. Quantity variances show the difference between a firm's actual and standard output and highlight levels of operating efficiency.

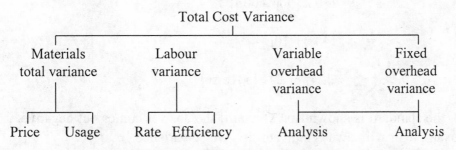

Figure 20:1 The Composition of Variance Analysis

Figure 20:1 shows the total cost variance (the sum of all the cost variances that can be identified). In other words it is the total standard cost less the total actual cost. The variances for materials, labour and overheads can now be computed. It is a good idea when calculating the standard cost with the actual cost to calculate the standard first. By putting the standard first, if there is an adverse variance the answer will be negative and is then automatically shown in brackets.

Direct Materials Price Variance

This is defined as *the difference between the standard price and the actual purchase price for the actual quantity of the material*. This can be calculated at the time of delivery or at the time of usage. It is best to calculate whether or not a variance has occurred when the material is delivered. It is also good accounting practice to write off or add to profit any variance which has occurred at the earliest opportunity. The formula for calculating whether or not a variance has occurred is:

Actual Quantity Purchased x [Standard Price - Actual Price]

Example

A restaurant has set a standard cost of 50p per kg of sugar and a standard usage per month of 200 kgs. The head chef has ordered 240 kg at 60p per kg. Calculate the direct material price variance.

Formula:

Actual Quantity Purchased x [Standard Price - Actual Price]

$$240 \times [50p - 60p]$$

$$= \quad 240 \times [-10p]$$

$$= \quad £[24] \text{ or } £24 \text{ [adverse]}$$

Note: the standard is shown first so that if the answer comes out negative, as in this example, it will always indicate an adverse variance.

Causes of Material Price Variances

In the case of materials, an adverse price variance usually means that a supplier has increased the price of the goods after the standard has been set. If prices are rising because of inflation there is little the firm can do. Whenever the purchasing department place a large order with one supplier an attempt should be made to fix a price for the life of the contract. This may not always be possible, sometimes the firm cannot meet the supplier's minimum order quantities and is, therefore, unable to take advantage of price freezes or discounts. Unfortunately this type of situation reinforces the criticism levelled at standards, that they are little more than measures of prediction rather than a measure of bargaining expertise. They are a measure of forecasting rather than a measure of operating efficiency.

The price may also be higher because a different supplier has been used or because a different quality of material has been purchased. Whatever the reason for the variance management must analyse the cause and then decide what action to take.

Direct Material Usage Variance

This is *the difference between the standard quantity specified for the actual production, and the actual quantity used, at standard purchase price.* It is calculated using the following formula:

[Standard Quantity specified for actual production - Actual Quantity used] x Standard Price

Example

Using the same information as in the previous example it is possible to calculate the direct material usage variance. A restaurant has set a standard cost of 50p per kg of cane based sugar and a standard usage per day of 200 kgs. The head chef has ordered a poorer quality beet sugar and 240 kgs are needed to provide the same degree of sweetness. Applying the formula quoted above:

$$[200 - 240] \times 50$$
$$= [40] \times 50$$
$$= £[20] \text{ or } £20 \text{ [adverse]}$$

Causes of Usage Variances

Management should be able to control usage variances because the difference will have taken place within the firm. Often the variance has been brought about by carelessness, e.g. incorrect storage, which could lead to spillage or deterioration. It may also have occurred because of careless usage or because the workforce is unskilled or inexperienced in using the material. Lastly, the materials used may have been of poor quality. This often brings about a high usage variance as many of the units produced will fail to meet the required quality levels and will, therefore, have to be scrapped.

Management can combine the two variances to form the direct material total variance.

$$
\begin{aligned}
&\quad [200 \times 50p] - [240 \times 60p] \\
&= \quad 100 - 144 \\
&= \quad 44 \text{ i.e. £44 [adverse]}
\end{aligned}
$$

Note: The adverse variance is bigger than before because it includes both the increase in price and the increase in quantity.

Direct Labour Variance

This is *the difference between the standard direct labour cost and the actual direct labour cost incurred for the production achieved.* By doing this, the hours worked or actually booked to the job can be compared with the actual standard hours produced at the end of the programme of work. The variance is calculated by the following formula:

[Standard direct labour hours produced x Standard rate per hour]
less
[Actual direct labour hours worked x Actual rate per hour]

Example

The General Building Company

The company have set a standard labour cost for building a brick wall around a business park. The firm set a standard time of 300 hours at £9 per hour. The work was completed in 270 hours at a cost of £9 per hour.

Formula:

Standard direct labour hours produced x Standard rate per hour = 300 x £9 = £2,700

Less Actual direct labour hours worked x Actual rate per hour = 270 x £9 = £2,430

	£	
Standard cost	2,700	
Actual cost	2,430	
	270	Favourable

Direct Labour Rate Variance

This is defined as *the difference between the standard and the actual direct labour rate per hour of the total hours worked/paid.* The variance is calculated by the following formula:

[Standard rate per hour - Actual rate per hour] x Actual hours worked/paid

Example

The Precision Engineering Company

The Precision Engineering Company has set a standard for 100 direct labour hours at an hourly rate of £5.00 per hour. The work was completed in 110 hours but the rate of pay was lower than expected at £4.50 (because of a lower than expected rate of wage inflation).

Formula:

[Standard rate per hour - Actual rate per hour] x Actual hours worked/paid

$$[5 - 4.5] \times 110$$
$$= \quad 0.50 \times 110$$
$$= \quad £55 \text{ favourable}$$

Causes of Labour Rate Variances

Labour rate variances need not arise if standards are based on the current union negotiated pay rates. Sometimes the standards are set before the pay rates have been negotiated and so it is important for management to identify the difference between the standard rate and the agreed settled rate. If this is not the case other causes must be investigated. Temporary labour may also have been used and they may be paid at a different rate. Lastly, special allowances may have been paid to staff which will effectively increase the hourly rate.

Direct Labour Efficiency Variance

This is *the difference between the standard hours for the actual production achieved and the hours actually worked, valued at the standard labour rate.* It is calculated by the formula:

[Standard hours produced - Actual hours worked] x Standard rate per hour

VARIANCE ANALYSIS

Example

The Precision Engineering Company has set a standard for 100 direct labour hours at an hourly rate of £5.00 per hour. The work was completed in 110 hours but the rate of pay was lower than expected at £4.50 (because of a lower than expected rate of wage inflation).

Formula

[Standard hours produced - Actual hours worked] x Standard rate per hour

Using the data in the example:

$$[100 - 110] \text{ x } 5$$
$$= \quad [-10] \text{ x } 5 \text{ (10 hours at £5)}$$
$$= \quad £50 \text{ [adverse]}$$

Causes of Efficiency Variances

Inadequate training may be responsible for the variance. If the workers are inexperienced they usually take longer to do the job or there may be quality problems resulting in more rejects being produced. The cause could also be due to poor quality materials being purchased because the usual source is temporarily out of stock. Whenever there is a variance management must correctly identify the cause so that corrective action can be taken.

Overhead Variances

We have already seen that standards can be set for variable and fixed overheads. The variable overheads will be activity related whereas the fixed overheads will be time related. An overhead expenditure variance is defined as *the difference between budgeted and actual overhead expenditure.*

Fixed overheads are calculated by the following formula:

Fixed overhead budgeted cost - Actual conversion overhead incurred

Variable overheads are calculated:

[Actual units produced x Variable overhead absorption rate per unit] less actual cost

296

Example

The Precision Engineering Company has just drawn up the following budget:

Budgeted fixed overhead = £288,000 per annum over a 48 week year = £6,000 per week.

Budgeted Production = 96,000 units per annum over 48 weeks = 2,000 units per week.

Variable overhead for the year was expected to be £48,000.

Actual output for the week under review was 2020 units and the actual fixed over head cost was £6,200.

The actual variable overhead expenditure was £1,250.

The directors would like you to calculate the two overhead expense variances.

Suggested Solution

The first task when calculating the variable overhead expense variance is to calculate the unit rate. Using the information in the question:

Budgeted Cost

Units of output [be it hours or units]

$$\frac{£48,000}{96,000 \text{ units}} \quad = \quad £0.50 \text{ per unit}$$

It is now possible to calculate the individual variances starting with the fixed overhead expenditure variance. The formula for calculating this variance is:

Fixed conversion overhead budgets - Actual fixed conversion overhead incurred

6,000 - 6,200 = £200 [adverse]

The variable overhead is calculated using the formula:

[Actual units produced x variable overhead absorption rate] - Actual cost

(2020 x 0.50) = 1010 - 1250 = £[240] [adverse]

The variable overhead expense variance is based upon actual output and recognises that the expenditure is likely to change with output. The example shows that there were 20 more units produced which required the firm to spend an extra £10 on variable overheads.

Whenever a firm has a difference between its actual and standard overhead, management must investigate the reason for the under or over absorption of overhead costs. Managers should only be held responsible for costs which they can control but different management skills are required for controlling overhead costs, depending on whether the firm uses a predetermined variable or fixed overhead rate.

Variable overheads will change with different levels of operating activity and so these costs can only be controlled if management can achieve two goals. First, the actual costs must be the same as planned costs for any given level of activity and, secondly, managers must achieve the same output as planned. Any change in an uncontrollable cost, such as an increase in the indirect labour rate, will affect the variable overhead rate and will necessitate a change in the standard rate.

Managers should be held accountable for costs which they can control, such as the use of indirect materials. This is a cost which can be controlled and highlights the level of operating efficiency.

Fixed overheads however, within a relevant range, are unaffected by changes in output. The fixed overhead cost will be determined as a set sum for a given period of time. Once this cost has been agreed, it will be unchangeable in the short term and so, if managers are to control fixed overhead costs this must be done before production begins. This is why it is so important to consider all aspects of production with the aim of eliminating activities which do not add value, thereby reducing the firm's fixed overhead cost.

So far we have treated variance analysis as a fairly mechanical task by calculating the different variances for materials, labour and overheads. Once these have been calculated, they need to be summarised and compared with the budgeted figure so that managerial decisions can be taken to ensure that actual costs are the same as the standard cost. The next example will show how this can be done.

Example

The Edwardian Carpet Company

The Edwardian Carpet Company manufactures a range of woollen rugs. The company operates a standard costing system and has set the quarterly output level together with the standard costs for one of their products. The costs are shown below.

	Budgeted Output	Standard Cost £	Actual Cost £
Sales	10,000	15	9,000
Materials		8	68,000
Labour		4	41,000
Factory overheads fixed		2	16,000

The directors have asked you to prepare the firm's costing trading and profit and loss account and to compare the budgeted profit with the actual profit.

The first task is to prepare the firm's budged profit and loss account.

Edwardian Carpet Company Budgeted Profit and Loss Account for the Quarter Ending Year Seven

	£	£
Sales (10,000 units at £15 per unit)		150,000
Less Variable Costs:		
Materials	80,000	
Labour	40,000	
		120,000
Contribution		30,000
Less Fixed Costs		20,000
Profit		10,000

Note: Budgeted Profit and Loss prepared using Standard Costs.

As there has been no alteration in the selling price there is no need to calculate the sales variance. The actual costs for materials, labour and overheads are different from the standard cost and so the variance, be it favourable or fixed, must be calculated.

Material Price Variance

Standard price of materials	**£**	
(£8 per unit x 9000 units)	72,000	
Actual cost	68,000	
	4,000	Favourable
Labour Rate Variance	**£**	
Standard wage rate	36,000	
Actual wage rate	41,000	
	(5,000)	Adverse
Factory Overhead	**£**	
Standard overhead	18,000	
Actual overhead	16,000	
	2,000	Favourable

Once the variances have been calculated the costing profit and loss account can be prepared.

Edwardian Carpet Company Profit and Loss Account for the Quarter Ending Year Seven

	Adverse	**Favourable**	**£**	
	£	**£**	10,000	
Budgeted Profit			10,000	
Variances				
Materials		4,000		
Labour	(5,000)			
Fixed Overheads		2,000		
	(5,000)	6,000	1,000	Favourable
Actual Net Profit			11,000	

The company has made a bigger profit than that estimated when the standards were set. The difference has occurred because materials and overheads were less than the standard cost, which offset the increase in wage costs. The reasons for these variances must be analysed by management and, if need be, the standards must be reset. If the standards have been set correctly any variance shows a flaw in the system and its cause must be investigated and analysed if the business is to keep a proper check and control on its costs.

The quicker a variance is recorded the easier it will be for management to discover its cause. A standard costing system will only be effective in controlling costs and evaluating management performance if the standards are, first, up to date and, second, reflect the firm's operational expectations.

Whilst effective cost control techniques are important they will not, on their own, ensure the future survival of the firm for ultimately that depends on generating sufficient profits and cash flows by producing products or services which the market wants.

Checklist for Key Variances

Variance	Formula
Material Price	Expected price of material used less actual price of material used.
Material Usage	(Expected quantity of material used less actual quantity of material used) multiplied by standard price.
Labour Rate	Expected cost of hours worked less actual cost.
Variable Overhead Expenditure	Expected cost of hours worked less actual cost.
Variable Overhead Efficiency	(Expected hours worked less actual hours worked) multiplied by standard rate.
Fixed Overhead Volume	Budgeted fixed overheads less expected fixed overhead for the actual production.
Sales Price	Expected revenue from units sold less actual revenue.
Sales Volume	(Expected sales (units) less actual sales) multiplied by standard profit/unit.

QUESTIONS

Answers begin page 495

1. Calculate the following variances.

   a. A bakery has set a standard cost of 30p per kg of flour and a standard usage of 1,000 kg per week. The bakery manager has used 1,200 kg at 33p per kg. Calculate the direct usage variance.

   b. A property company has set a standard cost of 40p per brick and a standard usage of 3,000 bricks per week. The site manager has used 2,700 bricks. Calculate the direct usage variance.

   c. A shipping company has set a standard cost of 46p per litre of gas oil and a standard usage of 8,000 litres per week. The master has used 9,000 litres. Calculate the direct usage variance.

2. Calculate the following variances.

   a. A garage has set a standard cost for servicing a car of 3 hours at £17 per hour. The work was completed in 2 hours at a cost of £15 an hour. Calculate the direct labour variance.

   b. A dry cleaners has set a standard time of cleaning a suit of one hour at £3 an hour. The work was completed in 1½ hours at a cost of £2 per hour. Calculate the direct labour variance.

   c. A carpet factory has set a standard time of making a roll of carpet at 5 hours at £10 per hour. The work was completed in 11 hours at £9 per hour. Calculate the direct labour variance.

3. Calculate the following variances.

   a. A bakery has set a standard cost of 30p per kg of flour and a standard usage per week of 1,000 kg. The bakery manager has ordered 1,200 kg at 33p per kg. Calculate the direct material price variance.

   b. A property company has set a standard cost of 40p per brick and a standard usage of 3,000 bricks per week. The site manager has ordered 2,700 bricks at a cost of 38p per brick. Calculate the direct material price variance.

   c. A shipping company has set a standard cost of 46p per litre of gas oil and a standard usage of 8,000 litres per week. The master has ordered 9,000 litres at 47p per litre. Calculate the direct material price variance.

4. **The Executive Traveller**. The company manufacture a range of expensive leather cases and holdalls. The firm has experienced record growth but the directors are anxious to monitor costs and have set up a standard costing system. The costs for their best selling range are shown below.

	Budgeted Output	Standard Cost £	Actual Cost £
Sales	25,000	45	950,000
Materials		20	450,000
Labour		10	300,000
Variable overheads		7	175,000
Fixed overheads		4	112,500

You work for the firm as a trainee accountant and have been asked to calculate the costing trading and profit and loss account and to compare the budgeted with the actual profit.

5. **The Kitchen Mouldings Company**. The company manufactures a range of kitchen accessories for both the consumer and the industrial market. A standard costing system is in operation and the half yearly output level, together with the standard costs for one product, is shown below.

	Budgeted Output	Standard Cost £	Actual Cost £
Sales	15,000	10	130,000
Materials		3	48,500
Labour		2	27,000
Factory variable overheads		1	15,000
Factory overheads fixed		1	14,000

The directors have asked you to prepare the firm's costing trading and profit and loss account and to compare the budgeted with the actual profit.

Chapter 21

Raising Finance

Introduction

A business must consider additional sources of capital if it lacks the finance to invest in the necessary fixed and current assets which allow it to trade at its optimum level. Fast growing businesses often find that their growth plans exceed their ability to generate profits which could be used to fulfil such plans. Once management know that the business will require additional outside sources of finance they must consider the precise amount to be raised, the various sources and the cost of such capital.

Sources of Capital

Publicly quoted companies have access to the capital markets and so, theoretically, it is easier for them to raise capital than private limited companies, partnerships or sole traders. Nevertheless, once a public company announces that it intends to raise additional capital the news will affect the share price. Management inevitably possess information which the market does not yet know and so, before the announcement, the share price does not incorporate this information. Once an announcement is made the market must assess how it will affect the company's cash flows, capital structure and possible changes in ownership. Unanticipated announcements will make the share price more volatile and, in the absence of information, the market must interpret why it thinks the company needs more money. Raising more capital signals either that the company has discovered new investment opportunities which will yield positive net present values or that the business is likely to expect a reduction in future earnings and, therefore, seeks additional outside sources of finance to cover its current earnings deficit.

Capital can be raised either from the owners, who are the shareholders, or from outside lenders, called *long term creditors*. Raising long term capital is an extremely complicated area of finance and, before any decision is taken, management must consider how the new capital will affect the existing owners in terms of earnings and control.

Raising Equity Finance

A firm raises equity capital whenever it sells shares to investors who then become the owners of the business. A company will find it easier to sell its shares if investors can trade them in a stock market. If a company's shares are traded on a recognised stock market it is called a *quoted company*. An example is Boots plc. Quoted companies find it easier to raise finance than non quoted ones because their shares can be quickly converted into cash.

Unquoted companies can still raise finance by issuing new shares but most will seek to be listed on a stock exchange because it gives them access to the capital markets. When a private company decides to obtain a stock market listing it is referred to as *going public*. Before becoming a publicly quoted company a firm must comply with the requirements of the Companies' Acts and the strict rules of the Stock Exchange.

Although the requirements for a full listing are strict and exacting, the Stock Exchange has sought, since setting up the Unlisted Securities Market in 1980, to provide specialists markets, with the aim of helping small entrepreneurial businesses raise capital. Initially the USM was very successful but, with the loss of its special status as a result of compliance with European legislation, the market declined. Before its closure on 31 December 1996, the London Stock Exchange, on the 19 June 1995, opened the Alternative Investment Market. The AIM seeks to provide finance for small and developing companies although some large established companies have sought a listing on this market. In order for a company to be able to seek a listing on the AIM, it must be a company registered in the United Kingdom, have produced and published audited accounts which comply with the relevant accounting standards, and it must have appointed both a nominated advisor and broker to support its application. In addition the company must be a public limited company and its securities must be freely transferable between shareholders. As a general rule it takes between three and six months of legal work for a company to become quoted on this market.

Whenever, a company decides to raise additional capital by issuing more shares, there is a danger for current investors that earnings per share will be diluted in the short term, together with a lower return on equity capital. In an efficient market investors will consider the present value of the company's after tax cash flows and will then decide whether to invest or disinvest. The share price will then reflect the market's expectations as to the return which the new money will make to the company's earnings. This is why it is so important that the money is invested in new projects which can earn a positive net present value.

Once a company has gone public and achieved a listing, it can raise further capital by announcing a *rights issue*. A rights issue allows existing shareholders to purchase additional shares based on a declared ratio of their existing holding. Thus a one for four rights issue would enable an existing shareholder to purchase one new share for every four which they already own.

Rights issues offer existing shareholders an inducement to subscribe for more shares because the rights issue price will be below the current price quoted on the stock market. Existing shareholders are, therefore, able to acquire further shares in proportion to their existing shares at a discount. For the company there is the added benefit that the new money will not lead to a change in ownership, so long as existing shareholders take up the rights issue. This is important because, if a large percentage of a firm's shares are acquired by one owner, there is a danger of a takeover bid. Such a bid may be regarded as hostile by the existing management and would threaten the firm's very survival.

How a Rights Issue Affects a Share's Market Price.

When a company announces a rights issue the share price will generally fall. This is because more shareholders will now share in the profits of the company and so there is a danger that the new shareholders will lead to a dilution in the company's earnings. This is why as a general rule a rights issue has a negative impact on a firm's share price.

The company wants the rights issue to be a success and so it must declare a rights issue price which will induce shareholders to subscribe for additional shares, whilst ensuring that there is not an excessive dilution in the company's earnings per share.

Raising Additional Debt Finance

Debt is an important source of corporate finance and publicly quoted companies have two main ways of raising debt finance in addition to borrowing from financial institutions, such as banks and leasing companies. Firstly, they can borrow from financial institutions in the money market and secondly they can sell a range of debt securities, such as debentures and loan stock, to investors in the capital markets. Before a company decides to borrow money from any source, management need to consider three questions. Firstly, how long will the money be needed, secondly, what will the new money finance and, finally, how will the firm repay the debt.

Any increase in a firm's debt capital, be it short or long term, will affect its gearing ratio. One of the great enigmas in finance is the question as to whether or not it is possible for a company to have an optimal capital structure so that its cost of capital represents the lowest possible cost. In a perfect capital market there is no such thing as an optimal capital structure but market imperfections suggest that a firm's overall share price is affected by its capital structure. For publicly quoted companies the problem for management is that the market's reaction to the news of raising additional debt finance is unknown until the announcement is made. As a general rule such announcements have a negative or at best a passive effect on the share price. In such cases it would suggest that the firm is moving away from an optimal capital structure whenever it seeks to raise new money by issuing debentures or additional loan stock. As the main strategic objective for the financial manager is to increase shareholder wealth, the timing and the reason of such announcements is important, as it will send a signal to investors who will make investment decisions which will affect the share price.

For non quoted companies debt finance is the main source of new capital and for small businesses it is often easier to raise short term money, even though it exposes the business to greater risk. Short term money should only be used to finance short term assets, unless management are confident that the short term finance can always be rolled over, thereby making it effectively a long term source of finance. The main sources of debt finance are explained below.

Main Sources of Debt Finance

Short-term Borrowing

1.   Bank Overdraft

This is the most popular form of business finance. It provides short-term money. In theory an overdraft is repayable on demand and so the money should only be used to finance additional current assets which can be quickly turned into cash. Overdraft finance is attractive as interest is only payable on the amount borrowed.   This can reduce the cost of capital if the account can quickly be returned to a credit balance.   Bankers often refer to an overdraft as a form of self liquidating finance.   This means that during the life of the overdraft facility the borrower will be overdrawn for some months and then in surplus before going back into overdraft.

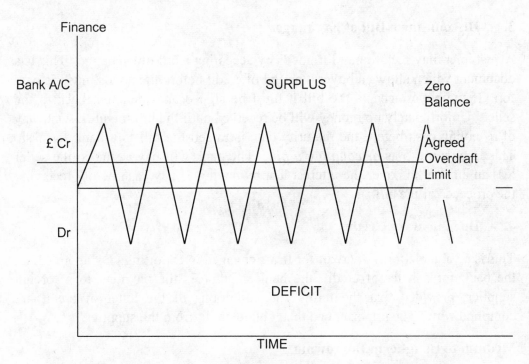

Figure 21:1 Using a Bank Overdraft as Self Liquidating Finance

When this happens the lender can see that the funds are being used to finance additional current assets which are later being turned into cash. If, on the other hand, this does not happen there is a danger that the overdraft is being used to pay the creditors. The business may be very short of cash and is having to borrow to pay its creditors. If there is no sign of this situation abating banks often call in the overdraft once the firm has reached its overdraft limit and continues to write cheques to meet its liabilities. Whilst this may protect the bank's position it will force the business into receivership.

2.   Factoring Debts

This is another method of raising cash to help firms which are short of working capital. The factoring house will purchase the invoices from the company, less a given percentage, and will credit the firm's bank account immediately. The factor will then collect the debt and pay any balance owing. In effect the business is selling its debts to raise cash. This is an expensive way of raising money but for small, fast growing firms it may still prove an attractive option as it ensures a constant flow of cash and reduces the need for internal credit control.

3.   Discounting a Bill of Exchange

A customer may seek to pay for goods by accepting a bill of exchange. This is a document which allows a buyer a period of credit before the goods must be paid for. If the buyer accepts the bill it must be signed and then sent back to the seller. Unfortunately no money will be received until the bill matures. One way of receiving cash before the maturity date is to sell the bill to a bank for cash. This is referred to as *discounting a bill*. The bank will pay a sum to the seller less an amount to cover the interest lost by having to pay cash before receiving the proceeds of the bill.

4.   Documentary Credit

This is a valuable form of credit for firms engaged in exporting. By approaching the bank for a letter of credit, the bank guarantees the payment to a foreign supplier, provided that the terms and conditions of the letter of credit are complied with. The importer can then obtain credit from the supplier.

Medium to Long-term Borrowing

5.   Hire Purchase

With the advent of leasing this has proved to be a less popular form of finance. The purchaser enters into a contract to hire the asset with an option to purchase it at the end of the contract. The borrower will normally have to place a deposit and then may repay the balance over a three to five year period. This allows time for the asset to earn funds which can be used to repay the loan.

6. Leasing

In recent years this has proved to be a very popular form of finance. The lessor (person leasing the equipment) allows the lessee to take possession of the asset if s/he agrees to make weekly or monthly repayments during the term of the lease. As with hire purchase the borrower can make the repayments out of earnings, thereby making the asset self financing. Although the asset will be owned by the lessor during the lifetime of the agreement, it is the use of assets which is important rather than the ownership of them.

7. Sale and Lease Back

Capital can be raised by selling the firm's buildings to a financial institution and at the same time entering into a leasing agreement. The business will gain capital for expansion and will still have the use of its premises but it will have lost a valuable freehold asset. Rent reviews, coupled with high rates of property inflation, can make this a very expensive form of finance and should only be considered after all other sources have been investigated.

8. Term Loan

These are loans which have a fixed life. The money can be borrowed for up to twenty years allowing it to be used to finance long-term investment projects. Often the interest rate can be fixed enabling the firm to budget its repayments and cost of capital. Term loans are attractive to small and medium sized businesses who do not have access to the capital markets and so cannot raise money by selling shares or debentures.

9. Foreign Currency Loans

Capital can be borrowed in foreign currencies. These loans may carry a lower rate of interest if interest rates are lower in other countries thereby making them, in the first instance, attractive. Unless the firm is able to earn foreign currency the borrower will be subject to exchange rate risk which could increase the size of the loan in sterling terms. This could make the loan a very expensive form of finance should the domestic currency depreciate against a stronger foreign currency.

Lending to the Commercial Borrower

Banks and other financial institutions make their profits by lending. They are always looking for what they call a *gilt edged lending opportunity* which can best be described as one where their money is safe and will be repaid with interest over the life of the loan. This does not mean that lenders are keen to avoid risk but they do tend to be risk averse. When they lend money they are, in effect, lending other customers' deposits, therefore, prudence demands that these balances are lent to borrowers who can repay. Before the loan is made the lender needs to know that the borrower can meet certain financial criteria which can be best summarised under the following headings.

Borrower

In some cases the lender will either not know or have only limited knowledge about the borrower. This is unfortunate for there is obviously greater risk in lending to commercial enterprises which have no record of borrowing and repaying money from the lender. The borrower's first task is to provide information which will inform the lender about the business and the people who manage it.

If the borrower is a company then a small report (often referred to as a *business plan*) should be submitted. This will contain a brief description about the business, its aims and objectives, together with a forecast outlining market opportunities. This should be presented together with the following documents:

a.   Certificate of Incorporation

b.   Copy of the Articles of Association

c.   Copy of the Memorandum of Association

d.   A recent set of audited accounts

e.   Copies of past bank statements

f.   A forecast cash budget

g.   A report outlining the purpose of the loan

h.   Business Plan

At this stage the borrower needs to provide as much information about the company as possible. Even if the borrower is known to the lender it may still be useful for it indicates that the borrower has thought about why the funds are needed and has already considered the cost and returns from the investment.

Amount

The lender will need to know how much capital will be required and for how long. It is far better to overestimate than to underestimate. Often the loan may be taken in tranches, thereby allowing a reduction in interest payments as interest will only be payable when the money is borrowed. If more money is needed at a later stage it suggests that the initial forecasts were inaccurate and, from the lender's view, there is no guarantee that the revised estimates will prove to be any more accurate. Often the additional working capital which will be needed to operate the new investment is understated leading to working capital problems at a later date. Ideally a breakdown should be given showing the amount of money needed to finance the capital investment together with a cash flow forecast showing the working capital costs of the project.

Repayment

Whatever is borrowed must be repaid. The aim is to make the repayments as painless for the borrower as possible, thereby increasing the probability of repayment. Repayments can only be made out of earnings and so the borrower will seek time to earn money from the investment before making repayments. Large early repayments can cause working capital problems, particularly if early earnings from the investment are small. In such cases it makes sense to ask the lender if interest only payments can be made at this stage. The capital repayments can then be made when the investment starts to yield higher earnings and cash flows.

The amount of money which must be repaid can be calculated by the following formula:

$$CI = \frac{PR}{1 - \frac{1}{(1+R)^n}}$$

where   CI   =   annual repayment of capital and interest

            P   =   the amount of the loan

            P   =   the flat rate of interest

            n   =   life of the loan

313

Example

A company wants to borrow £50,000 for 10 years at a fixed rate loan of 12 per cent per annum. What will its yearly capital and interest payments be?

$$\text{CI} = \frac{PR}{1 - \dfrac{1}{(1+R)^n}} = \frac{£50000 \times 0.12}{1 - \left(\dfrac{1}{1.12}\right)^{10}}$$

$$= \frac{£6000}{(1-0.3220)} = \frac{£6000}{0.678}$$

$$= £8,850 \text{ per annum}$$

The borrower must know the cost of credit. The interest rate is generally shown as an annual percentage rate (APR) for example 8% per annum. Different lenders will compound the interest charge according to different time periods. Some may charge interest monthly whilst others may only do so annually. This is why a borrower needs to calculate the effective annual rate (EAR) for comparative purposes. The effective annual rate shows the equivalent if the lender only compounded the interest rate being charged once per year. The formula is:

$$\text{EAR} = \frac{(1 + APR)^m - 1}{m}$$

Example

The owners of the curtain shop are intending to borrow money at an APR of 6% but interest on the loan will be compounded monthly. This means that the lender will charge interest on the sum borrowed at $\frac{1}{12}^{th}$ of the stated APR and so the real interest rate will be .005 or (½%) per month.

By calculating the future value at each year end per pound lent at the beginning of the year it is possible to calculate the effective annual rate. In this example it will be;

$$\textbf{FV} = \textbf{(1.005)}^{12} = \textbf{1.0616778}$$

$$\textbf{EAR} = \textbf{1.0616778} - \textbf{1} = \textbf{0.0616778 or 6.168\% per annum.}$$

It is worth remembering that if interest is compounded once a year then the effective annual rate is the same as the annual percentage rate. The more frequently the interest rate is compounded the higher the effective annual rate becomes compared to the annual percentage rate.

Security

The lender will often require some form of security before agreeing to lend the money. This really safeguards the lender against the worst possible scenario of the borrower being unable to repay the debt. If this happens the lender needs to be able to sell the secured asset so that the borrowed funds and accrued interest can be recovered. As far as the lender is concerned this is a last resort and security is only taken to protect their financial position. Ideally the lender will ask for assets which are likely to remain constant in value and which can quickly be sold for cash. Land, life assurance policies, stocks and shares and unit trusts are frequently offered as security but guarantees from people offering to repay the loan in case of default may also prove to be acceptable. Usually the lender will only lend two thirds of the assets' market value for then, if there is a decrease in its value, the lender's position is still secure.

A lender will generally only by prepared to lend without security if the business has a good credit rating and can repay the loan quickly. The firm must have a stable and regular cash operating cycle. There is no safe limit but most lenders are likely to be reluctant to lend more than 50 per cent of a firm's net assets without asking for some form of security.

Control

The lenders will want to be certain that their money is in safe hands. The management must be able to demonstrate that they have the necessary skills to run the business. They must be prepared to answer the lenders' questions and it is often a good idea to invite lenders to visit the business. Then the business can be discussed in detail and the lenders can be shown the firm's order books, its administrative facilities and the skills and expertise of the work force.

The borrower must satisfy the lender on all these points before being able to obtain the finance. The cost of the loan will be determined by the interest rate which will be made up of two parts. Firstly, there will be the cost of money, often referred to as *the bank's base rate*. Secondly, there will be a premium to cover the risk of lending. If the borrower can show the lender that the risk is in fact a small one then this will be reflected in the interest charged above the bank's base rate. Often the interest payments saved by good preparation more than compensate for the cost of providing all the necessary information.

QUESTIONS

Answers begin page 497

1. **The Wooden Window Company**. For over twenty years Peter Wright worked as a carpenter for a small building company. Last year the firm was taken over and, because the larger firm prefers to sub contract work, Peter and three other workers were made redundant.

   Peter and his colleagues decided to rent a small unit and make wooden windows as this was their main area of expertise. They set up the business with £10,000 in cash and the firm has been so successful that, if they are to meet their current order book, they now need new premises and more stock.

   Peter and his colleagues have decided to approach their local bank manager but are apprehensive as they have never borrowed finance for a business before. They estimate that they need a loan of £20,000. The business is currently profitable and has a positive and stable cash flow.

   Before seeing the bank manager Peter has decided to seek your advice and has asked you the following questions:

   a.   What information is needed when seeing a bank manager for a loan?

   b.   Should a loan or an overdraft be sought?

2. A company is considering taking out a loan at an APR of 12%. Interest will be compounded monthly. What is the effective annual rate of the loan?

Chapter 22

The Capital Markets and Financial Securities

Introduction

Business organisations invest in fixed and current assets with the aim of increasing cash flows and profitability. As markets become more competitive a firm's continued existence depends upon investing in new products and services which can earn a positive return. All of this investment has to be financed and in market economies the capital markets play a crucial role in channelling funds from net suppliers to net users of capital. As a result companies who cannot generate sufficient funds to finance their investment programmes can still invest because they can raise money in the financial markets by issuing shares or bonds.

The Capital Markets

Capital markets exist because households, companies and governments are unable to generate sufficient funds to finance all of their current spending plans. Households need money to finance their homes and consumer goods, companies require funds so that they can invest in additional fixed and current assets and governments need money to pay for their expenditure which is not currently covered by taxation receipts. The total amount of money required by the three sectors of the economy, households, business and government is referred to as the aggregate demand for loanable funds and the amount of money provided by savers to the capital markets is called the supply of loanable funds.

The capital markets provide two important functions for publicly quoted companies. Firstly, they provide new sources of finance and, secondly, they provide a secondary market in quoted securities be they shares or bonds. By creating a market in securities investors know that they can always sell their investment because the market makers who deal in securities must quote a price at which they are prepared to buy and sell a given security.

The Principle of Capital Market Efficiency

In finance the principle of capital market efficiency states that the price of financial securities fully reflect all available information. There are three different degrees of efficiency which are called weak form, semi-strong form and finally the strong form. Weak form efficiency describes a market where share prices reflect all past price information. There is a large amount of empirical evidence to support this proposition that future price movements are

317

not related to past information. In such a market share prices resemble a random walk and it is because the price movements are random that nobody can in the long term consistently predict correctly future stock prices.

In an efficient market which is said to be semi-strong current share prices reflect all publicly available information. In such a market an investor cannot earn abnormal gains by subscribing to specialist financial magazines.

The last form of efficiency strong form describes a market where all information both private and public is reflected in the share price.

As long as investors are able to make abnormal returns by "insider dealing" it suggests that the market is not strong form efficient but there is a large amount of evidence to support the weak and semi-strong form of efficiency.

In an efficient market security prices will, therefore, change as new information is received by the market and investors evaluate it by deciding to purchase or sell their securities. The problem for any investor considering buying a financial security is whether or not the price is a fair one. In a perfect capital market the answer is *yes*, but the question for any investor is 'How far do the capital markets represent a perfect capital market?'

For a capital market to be perfect or, to put it another way, one hundred per cent efficient, the following eight conditions would have to apply;

1. There must be no barriers of entry and so the market does not deny access to all suppliers and users of funds

2. No participant in the market is able to dominate and so the market is akin to the economic concept of perfect competition

3. A borrower or lender does not have to pay any transaction costs such as commission

4. Information is freely available to all investors

5. Taxation does not exist

6. Financial securities must be infinitely divisible

7. No government restrictions relating to trading

8. It is assumed that bankruptcy is costless

In such a market a firm's value must be the same as the total value of all its assets because the value of any combined assets must equal the sum of its individual parts.

Whilst there is a wealth of research which supports the assertion that stock markets such as the London Stock Exchange are efficient, they are not perfect because not all of the eight conditions apply. When a condition is absent it is referred to as a *market imperfection*, There are three main imperfections which mean that, in practice, the world's main capital markets can be said to be efficient rather than perfect. The first is called asymmetric taxes which is a financial term for explaining a situation where different participants in the market have differential tax rates. Secondly, not all information is costless and available to all as some subscribers will pay brokers or investment houses for advice as to which securities they should buy or sell. Finally, securities cannot be bought or sold without incurring transaction costs and so this is another important market imperfection. Despite these limitations the principle of capital market efficiency is important because it enables models to be developed which further increase our understanding of how the financial markets operate.

The Supply and Demand For Funds

Suppliers of funds currently have a surplus of cash. The largest supplier of funds will be the household sector but industry and sometimes government will also be suppliers of funds. This supply of funds represents foregone consumption and is rewarded by paying the owner of such funds interest. As a general rule suppliers of funds will be more willing to provide finance when interest rates are high, although there would still be a supply of funds even at very low interest rates. This is because a significant proportion of households are prepared to defer consumption even though interest rates are low.

The demand for funds will depend on household consumption patterns and the amount of industrial investment and government spending plans, all of which will be affected by the rate of interest and the level of aggregate demand in the economy.

The Capital Markets and the Firm

Large companies can borrow money directly in the capital markets which is generally cheaper than finance which can be raised from the banking sector. Publicly quoted companies can by pass the banking sector because they can issue commercial paper. Commercial paper should be thought of as an IOU. It will show the name of the organisation borrowing the money, the interest to be paid to the lender and the date when the loan will be repaid.

These loans are called bonds. During the lifetime of the bond the holder will receive interest payments on the due date and repayment of the principal at the end of the loan. Any purchaser is in effect buying a future income stream and the right to repayment of a capital sum at the end of a number of years. We have already seen that money has a time value because money invested now can earn interest and this principle affects the value of all commercial paper.

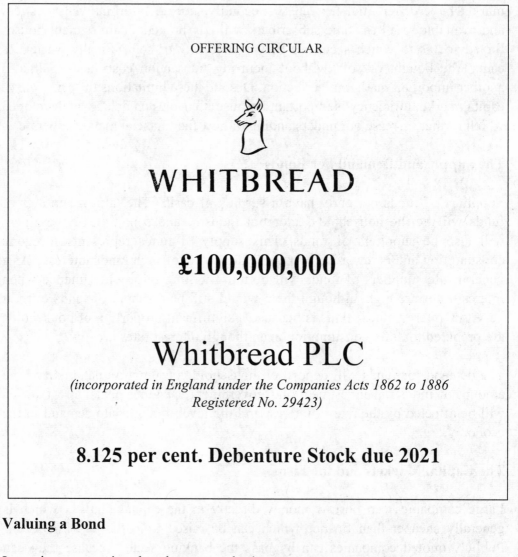

OFFERING CIRCULAR

WHITBREAD

£100,000,000

Whitbread PLC

*(incorporated in England under the Companies Acts 1862 to 1886
Registered No. 29423)*

8.125 per cent. Debenture Stock due 2021

Valuing a Bond

Investing money in a bond exposes the investor to a greater level of risk than if they simply invested the sum in a bank deposit account. This is because the bond's market value will be affected by many factors which, in turn, will affect an investor's return. In finance there are two different types of financial return.

The first is the *required rate of return* which reflects the investor's opportunity cost of capital in that it is the minimum rate of return required for investing in that type of security. The second is called the *expected rate of return* which an investor expects to earn should they decide to invest in that type of security.

Any bond can be seen as a financial security which offers its holder future cash flows. As these cash flows will not be paid immediately they are affected by the principle of the time value of money and so a bond's value should be a reflection of the present value of its expected future cash flows. Investors, therefore, need to know the yield to maturity before making investment decisions. Any change in the yield will affect the market value of the bond, thereby making the holder either a capital gain or loss should they decide to sell the security before the maturity date. This is why a bond exposes the holder to more financial risk than a bank deposit account because the initial capital deposited with the bank always remains the same, even though its real value will be affected by the rate of inflation.

Many investors would be unwilling to purchase commercial paper if they had to wait for the final repayment date of the loan. The capital markets not only raise funds but also provide a market for would-be buyers and sellers. The value of any bond will be affected by the following factors.

Default Risk

Whenever money is lent there is a danger that during the lifetime of the loan the borrower will default on the interest payments or fail to repay the amount borrowed. This is the risk in lending money because, although the amount lent is certain, the sum to be received in the future cannot be guaranteed. The default risk refers to the likelihood of the borrower not fulfilling the conditions of the loan. Government securities are deemed to be risk free because governments can always print money to repay their debts whereas this facility is not available to other borrowers. Commercial paper is graded by institutions, such as Moody's and Standard and Poor, who each offer a guide which ranges from the highest investment grade to the lowest speculative. These grades reflect the credit worthiness of the borrower and will be adjusted upwards or downwards should economic or business conditions alter. Examples of the grading criteria are shown in the appendix.

Liquidity and Term to Maturity

In finance the word liquidity refers to how easily an asset can be converted into cash. By its very nature commercial paper is less liquid than cash but it is the length of time till maturity which determines the degree of liquidity of the bond. Bonds which will repay the principal sum borrowed in 90 days are said to be more liquid than those which will not repay the sum borrowed for many years. This is called the *term to maturity*. As a general rule investors will require a higher return if they have to lend for long periods of time to compensate them for this loss of liquidity.

Change in Interest Rates

Interest is the reward for deferring consumption and the amount of the reward for postponing consumption will be affected by the rate of inflation, the supply of net funds to the capital markets, government economic policy and interest rates in other countries.

Most bonds confer on the holder a fixed rate of interest during the lifetime of the bond. This rate of interest may be equal to the current market interest rate or it may be higher or lower. A new investor will require the return currently offered by the market. If the rate of interest being paid on an existing bond differs from the current market rate, then the current market value of the bond will be a reflection of this difference. If the bond is paying a higher interest rate than the current market rate its value will increase and, if the interest is less, its value will fall. The price of a bond always moves in the opposite direction to a change in interest rates, and so, if interest rates rise, bond prices fall and, if interest rates fall, bond prices rise. This will be the case because the existing bond will always earn the current market rate for the new holder, even if this means a capital loss or gain for the original holder. An investor cannot, therefore, be certain of the exact capital value of their security from the date of purchase until it is redeemed as its value will fluctuate.

Tax Status

Interest is treated as income by the tax authorities and so the holder must pay tax on their interest payments, unless they have allowances which offset the tax owed. Some bonds issued by governments may be tax exempt and so the holder will pay no tax when they receive the interest. Whatever the tax position investors will consider the before and after tax yield before making any investment decisions.

Special Provisions

The issuer may insert any number of special features but two of the main ones are, firstly, the right to buy back the bond before maturity on a specified date. This is referred to as a call feature. The second main provision inserted in the terms of a bond is the right for the investor to convert the bond into ordinary shares. This right is called a *convertibility clause* and a bond which can be converted into shares is called *convertible loan stock*.

All of these factors will affect a bond's value and its yield to maturity.

Bond Values and Maturity

A bond's value is based partly upon the concept of the time value of money. If a person invested £1,000 in a bond which paid the holder 10% for one year, the holder would receive £100 interest in one year's time and their total assets would have increased from £1,000 to £1,100. The question is 'What is the bond's value should the holder wish to sell it now or, in other words, before it can earn the one year's interest. One way of valuing the bond is to say that its value is based on the present value of the future cash flows which it can generate.

Most bonds offer two different cash flow streams. The first is the interest paid each year, often called the *coupon* and, secondly, the repayment of the loan at the end of a certain period of time. A bond's coupon rate refers to the interest rate which applies to its face value. If a company issues a ten year bond with a face value of £100,000 which has an annual coupon rate of 8%, then the issuer must pay .08 x 100,000 which equals £8,000 as interest each year during the bond's life. On maturity the original sum borrowed, £100,000, must be repaid and this final payment is often called a 'bullet' payment. The holder is, therefore, purchasing the right to these two cash flow streams. The purchaser of a bond will receive these two cash flows at some date in the future and so the price they pay to acquire the bond should be based on the present value of those cash flows. This means that the future cash flows coming from the bond must be adjusted to show what they are worth now. This is what is meant by the principle of the time value of money.

The Structure of Interest Rates and the Yield Curve

Bonds are issued for different lengths of time but, whatever their maturity date, they are subject to the principle of the time value of money. Whenever the market price of a coupon bond is the same as its face value, it is said to be a par bond. In such cases the bond's yield will be the same as its coupon rate. It is most likely that the market price of a coupon bond and its face value, will not be the same. If the market price of the bond is higher than its face value it is called a *premium bond* and, if it is less, it is said to be *at a discount*. Whenever a bond has a market price which is higher than its face value the bond's yield to maturity will be less than its coupon rate. Similarly, a bond which has a market price which is lower than its face value will pay a return which is more than its coupon rate. This will be the case because the purchaser of a premium bond has paid a higher price for the asset than its face value and so, on maturity, the holder will suffer a capital loss. This loss will be reflected in the yield to maturity just as it would increase the return on a bond currently trading at a discount, because the purchaser has paid less than its face value.

The price of a bond in the market will only equal its face value if its yield to maturity equals investors' desired return for that class of security. This is why any bond's value is linked to its yield. Any change in the yield and the bond's market value will change.

As a general rule investors will require a bond with a long maturity date, say twenty years, to have a higher interest rate than a bond which only has a short term to maturity. As a result there is a relationship between interest rates and bond maturity dates. These can be plotted as a graph and in finance this is referred to as the term structure of interest rates or *yield curve*. The graph will generally be upward sloping, thereby showing that long term interest rates are higher than short term ones.

Figure 22:1 Typical Yield Curve

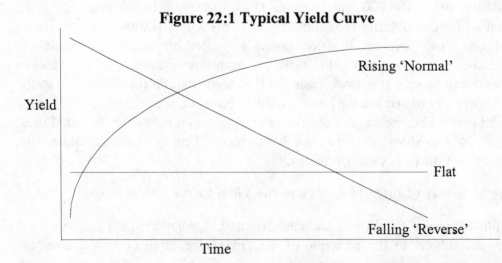

324

The yield curve can show three different patterns. The normal shape shows a rising yield curve because investors generally seek an increased interest rate with long term loans.

Sometimes the yield curve will be falling and is referred to as the 'reverse' yield curve. The graph shows a situation where the yield on short term government debt exceeds that on long term debt.

If the yield curve is flat, then the market expects no change in interest rates and so the cost of one month's money would be the same as six month's money.

The shape of the yield curve will be determined by investor's expectations about the level of future short term interest rates. If investors expect interest rates to fall, then they will seek to purchase long term debt in the market by borrowing at the current short term interest rate. This situation inevitably places upward pressure on short term interest rates and downward pressure on long term rates. In such a situation the yield curve will be said to be downward sloping. This can be seen in the diagram.

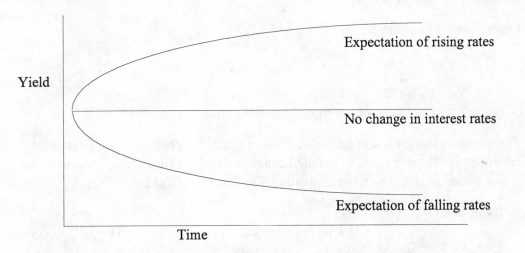

The yield curve also considers the relationship between a bond's interest rate and its maturity date. We have already seen that any change in interest rates will lead to a change in bond values. The expectancy theory states that the shape of the yield curve reflects investor expectations about future interest rates. When the yield curve is upward sloping, the expectancy theory holds that interest rates will be higher than today's rate. If the yield curve is flat, then future interest rates should be the same as today's rate but, if the yield curve is downward sloping, future interest rates should be lower than today's rate.

The yield curve is important to investors and financial managers because it reflects investor expectations about future interest rates. If investors can buy bonds which offer high yields over long periods of time, they can secure a good long term cash stream. Whilst this is good news for investors, it means that borrowers will be forced to pay high interest rates on their loans for many years. In the market the supply and demand for bonds will affect their yields and this is why it is important for financial managers to remember the old investor/ company maxim. Most investors only want to invest short term and prefer more liquidity to less, but companies need to borrow long term and so, although the capital markets will always be able to supply the necessary funds, the cost may be more than the business is willing to pay.

How to Calculate the Present Value of a Bond

An investor is considering purchasing a £100 corporate bond which has three years to run until it matures and which currently pays the holder 12% a year. The key question is what price should one pay now to own these future cash flows? The first task is to calculate the cash flows which the owner will receive and these are shown below;

Cash Flows From the Bond

Year 0	Zero
Year 1	£12
Year 2	£12
Year 3	£112 (£100 capital repayment plus £12 interest)

The current price of the bond will be based upon the present value of its future cash flows. These can be calculated mathematically or by using present value tables which are shown in the appendix. The mathematical formula is:

$$\text{PV of bond} = \frac{C}{(1+i)^1} + \frac{C}{(1+i)^2} + ... \frac{C+P}{(1+i)^n}$$

C = Coupon Payment or Interest Rate

P = Par Value the face value of the bond

i = the interest rate being used to discount the bond which, in this case, is 12% because that is the rate which the bond is paying to the holder

n = the number of years until the bond matures which, in this example, is three years.

$$\text{PV of bond} = £12/(1+.12)^1 + £12/(1+.12)^2 + £112/(1+.12)^3$$
$$= £10.71 + £9.57 + £79.72 = £100$$

Present Value tables are often used to calculate the present value of a bond because they remove the need for mathematical calculation. These tables are shown in the appendix, and an extract of the table is shown below:

Present Value Interest Factor of an Annuity

Period	10%	11%	12%
1	0.9091	0.9009	0.8929
2	0.8264	0.8116	0.7972
3	0.7513	0.7312	0.7118

Calculation of the Bond's Value

Year	Cash Flow	PVIFA	Present Value
1	£12.00	0.8929	£10.71
2	£12.00	0.7972	£ 9.57
3	£112.00	0.7118	£79.72
			£100.00

Note: £12 x 0.8929 =£10.71

In year 3 Bond £100 + interest £12 = £112

Valuing Bonds Which Pay Interest Half Yearly

Many bonds pay interest to the holder twice a year and so the annual discount rate should be halved, thereby reflecting the two six monthly payments. The formula for such a calculation is:

**Present Value of a Bond with = $\dfrac{C/2}{(1+i/2)^1} + \dfrac{C/2}{(1+i/2)^2} + \dfrac{C/2 + P}{(1+i/2)^{2n}}$
Half Yearly Payments**

Using the same figures as in the last example let us assume that the bond will now pay interest twice during the year.

PV of bond =	$\dfrac{£6}{(1.06)^1} + \dfrac{£6}{(1.06)^2}$ + $\dfrac{£6}{(1.06)^3} + \dfrac{£6}{(1.06)^4}$ + $\dfrac{£6}{(1.06)^5} + \dfrac{£106}{(1.06)^6}$		
	£5.67 + £5.34 + 5.04 + £4.75 + £4.48 + £74.72		
			£100
	Year One	Year Two	Year Three

The Investor's Required Rate of Return and The Value of a Bond

Changes in interest rates affect bond values. This is because the bond's valuation is a reflection of an investor's opportunity cost of future income. An investor will prefer to hold cash if interest rates are forecast to rise because bond prices will fall. By delaying the purchase an investor will earn a higher return and forego a capital loss. The opposite will be the case should interest rates be forecast to fall. In such cases an investor should purchase bonds before the rate cut for in this way they will make a capital gain and enjoy a higher rate of return.

This is a very important concept to both investors and the issuers of commercial paper because the value of these securities will alter with changes in interest rates. It is this principle which enables the issuer of commercial paper to issue bonds at either a premium or a discount so that they appeal to different classes of investors. Any bond which is issued below its par value is called a discount bond and a bond which pays no interest during its life is called a zero coupon bond. When a bond is issued at a price above its par value it is said to be issued at a premium.

It is partly because money has a time value and because the tax authorities distinguish between income and capital that bonds can be issued at either a discount or a premium. A person earning a high income will have to pay tax on their income and so will not seek investments which will increase their income and tax liability. If they can purchase a security which pays no interest but which will earn them a capital gain, they may be able to mitigate their tax liability, because small capital gains are generally free of tax. The advantage to an investor is that once the gain has been earned it can be spent just like any other income, except that the holder has mitigated their tax liability. Other investors, such as people who have retired, may be anxious to earn an income and so they may be willing to pay a small premium for a security which guarantees them a high one for future years. This will particularly be the case if investors believe that, in the long run, interest rates will fall.

In a market economy the price of anything and its allocation is determined by the price mechanism and the forces of supply and demand. Money is just another commodity and so the same principles apply in the capital markets. The market will determine the required rate by the actions of investors who make buy and sell decisions, after considering the returns and risks offered to the holders of other financial securities.

When a bond is issued, it generally carries a fixed rate of return in the form of interest which will be paid to its owner. This rate of interest or coupon may be higher, lower or the same as the market rate. Whenever the bond's rate and the market rate differ, the value of the security will change and so it is unlikely that the security's par value and its market value will be the same before the bond matures. This point is illustrated by the following example.

Five years ago Crabtree Estates issued a £100 bond which paid a 10% rate of interest. The bond currently has four more years until it matures but market interest rates have increased to 12%. Calculate the market price of the bond.

$$\text{PV of Bond} = £10/(1+.12)^1 + £10/(1+.12)^2 + £10/(1+.12)^3 + £110/(1+.12)^4$$
$$= £8.93 + £7.97 + £7.12 + 69.91$$
$$\text{PV} = £93.93$$

The bond's value is less than its par value because the market wants a higher rate of return. The bond can only pay the new holder this higher return by falling in value and so the holder will now earn the 12% return. By paying £93.93 for a bond which has a par value of £100 an investor will be able to earn a 12% return.

Whenever, a firm invests surplus cash in short term or long term financial securities it must consider future interest changes because this will affect the total value of its investment portfolio.

Investment Decisions and the Time Value of Money Concept

The time value of money is very important because it enables a value to be placed on a future cash stream which results from an investment decision. People make investments in real assets or financial securities because over time they expect to increase their future cash inflows.

The key investment question is whether or not these future cash flows will increase their owner's wealth.

One way of determining the value of an asset is to calculate the present value of its future cash flows. If their present value exceeds the asset's current cost as represented by the cash outflows to acquire it, there will be a financial gain to the buyer. This difference in finance is called a *net present value* (NPV) and a positive net present value will result in an increase in wealth, whereas a negative NPV will result in a reduction in wealth.

Any asset which has a positive net present value will increase the wealth of its owner because it has been acquired at a price which is less than its true value. Similarly, if an asset has a negative NPV, its owner has paid more for it than it is worth and so its acquisition has reduced its owner's wealth.

In a perfect capital market the current security price reflects all available information and so they are fairly priced or, in financial terms, they are assets which have a zero NPV. A zero NPV does not mean that a holder will not earn a return or a profit from its acquisition, but that the return earned will be commensurate with the risk. In such a perfect capital market an investor cannot earn an abnormal return, but market imperfections make it possible to earn abnormal returns in the short term.

Although the capital markets are not perfect, there is a large amount of empirical evidence which suggests that they are efficient, and so it is not possible in the long run to earn abnormal returns by investing in financial securities. In an imperfect market, such as the firm's business environment, it is possible to earn an abnormal return provided that business enjoys a competitive advantage over its competitors. It is these imperfections, together with the principle of valuable ideas, which enable a business to earn positive net present values for its shareholders.

The expected value of any future cash sum is dependent upon the discount rate used and this should reflect the cost of investment opportunities foregone. This is why the correct discount rate is the one which reflects the firm's opportunity cost of capital and will reflect the capital markets' current discount rate. Any change in the discount rate will alter the present value of any future cash flow and this explains why security prices change over time. When the capital markets increase the discount rate the present value of any future cash flow will be reduced, whereas a decrease in the discount rate will result in an increase in the cash flow's present value. The present value is, therefore, inversely related to the discount rate and any change in the rate will affect an asset's value and the return which its holder will earn.

The key to maximising shareholder value is to make strategic decisions which enhance shareholder wealth, because they have a positive net present value. The capital markets will always provide the necessary finance for such future investment decisions and this is one of the major advantages of being a publicly quoted company. Whilst managers may not like the high cost of this capital, there is no reason from a theoretical perspective why they should pursue policies of capital rationing because they lack the necessary money for investment. If shareholder wealth is to be increased, then all projects which will earn positive net present values should be financed before competitors seize the opportunity to earn the return for themselves.

From a business point of view, the time value of money is important because it affects the value of the firm's debt and equity securities, its cost of capital and the required rate of return which investors will expect to earn from owning a share in the firm's current and future investments in its fixed and current assets.

QUESTIONS

Answers begin page 497

1. If a company can invest its funds at a fixed rate of 10.5 per cent, how much must be invested now to get £50,000 in three years time?

2. What is the value of a three year bond, paying 6 per cent per annum, when the market rate for a bond of this type is 10 per cent?

3. Should an investor buy bonds or keep their money in a cash deposit account if it is believed that interest rates are about to rise. Give your reasons.

4. State two reasons why the required rate for a bond changes over time.

5. How would a period of low inflation affect bond prices?

6. Why should managers understand the relationship between interest rates and security prices before making investment decisions?

Chapter 23

Gearing

Introduction

All businesses need assets so that they can trade and make profits. The money to finance these assets will have been provided either by the owners or by lenders of funds to the business. If the firm wishes to increase its level of trading, it will require additional assets and these will have to be financed. One way of paying for them is to reinvest past profits but this takes a long time and often the management want the company to expand fast to take advantage of current market opportunities. There are two ways of acquiring more capital. One way is to raise additional money from the shareholders who are the owners of the business, the other is to borrow the money from lenders who then become long-term creditors.

Figure 23:1 Different Sources of Long Term Finance

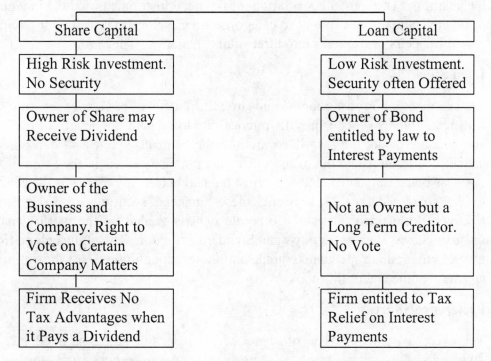

Ratio of Share to loan capital defines a firm's level of Gearing; the more debt, the more highly geared.

Gearing

The word *gearing* is used to define the capital structure of a firm. Companies can often choose how they will raise the additional capital they need. If they decide to raise more money by issuing additional shares, they are said to be increasing their equity capital while, if they chose to borrow the money, they are said to be increasing their debt capital.

The Cost of Capital

Any additional capital raised will have to be paid for and so the business must be able to generate a return from its capital employed which exceeds its cost. Shareholders will want to receive dividends from their investment and lenders will demand their interest payments. The percentage of profit paid as dividend and the rate of interest charged for the money borrowed will determine the business's cost of capital. The aim is to keep the overall cost as low as possible so that the maximum return can be made for the owners.

The cost which any business has to pay for capital will reflect the returns which investors in financial securities require as a return for investing their money in the business. There are a large variety of financial instruments and the ingenuity of financiers makes it difficult to categorise them. Nevertheless it is possible to put all financial instruments into three main categories. They are:

Loan Stock

The company borrows money and in return offers the lender of funds a certificate (bond) which states the interest rate to be paid, the length of the loan and whether or not the loan is secured on the company's assets. Loan holders are entitled to be repaid out of the sale of the company assets in the event of the business being liquidated, and they must be paid before any money is distributed to the shareholders. As a result, these financial securities offer investors relatively little financial risk. Corporate debt is graded by the world's major credit agencies, such as Moody's and Standard and Poor. The ratings range from investment grade to speculative grade and the exact definitions are shown in the appendix at the end of this book.

Preference Shares

These are a particular type of share which pays the holder a fixed rate of dividend so long as the business is profitable. A preference shareholder is an owner of the firm. There is a greater financial risk in buying this type of security because there is no legal duty to pay a dividend. Also in the event of the company being liquidated, a preference shareholder's claim ranks after any holder of loan capital. This increase in risk means that investors generally require a higher rate of return and so, to the company, this is a more expensive form of long-term finance.

Ordinary Shares

This is the riskiest of the three financial securities because the holder is not legally entitled to any dividend and the amount paid will vary with the company's earnings. Some years the holder may not receive a dividend and ordinary shareholders are also the last in line to benefit from the sale of the company's assets upon liquidation. Investors, therefore, require a higher rate of return than that paid to loan stock holders or owners of preference shares to compensate them for the additional risk.

Figure 23:2 Type of Financial Security

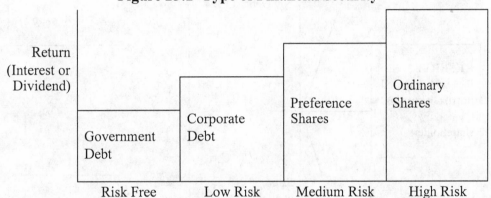

Companies are not the only users of funds which are provided by the financial markets. The government is also a large borrower and it too sells paper financial securities called *Gilts* or *Treasury Stock*. These securities are almost identical to the corporate debt issued by the country's top companies, with the exception that there is no danger of the government defaulting on the loan interest and capital repayment at the end of the loan. This is the case because only governments have the power to print money. As a result this debt is regarded as low risk and the rate of return paid reflects this.

Figure 23:3 Cost of Capital

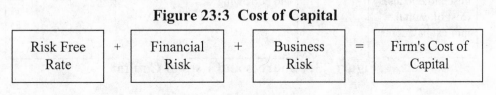

Government debt is usually regarded as risk free. If an investor is to be persuaded to take another form of financial security, a premium must be paid to compensate for the additional risk. Investing in a company exposes an investor to two further risks. They are the risks of holding the security offered by the firm, which is called *financial risk,* plus the *business risk* which refers to the variability of its earnings from trading. The more a company's earnings fluctuate with the level of economic activity, the greater the level of business risk.

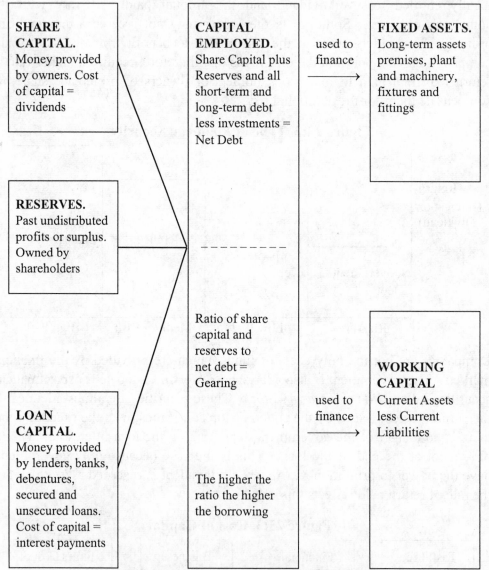

Figure 23:4 Sources and Uses of Capital

Factors to be Considered Before Borrowing Money

A firm should only increase its debt capital if it is certain that it can meet the additional interest costs and capital repayments out of its cash flows. Management must ensure that these additional interest and capital repayments can be met and that they will not place an intolerable burden on the business. Whilst, in some cases, it is possible to repay past borrowing by additional borrowing in the future, it is more likely that money will have to be set aside to meet the final redemption of the loan or to make capital repayments during the life of the loan. These capital repayments can have a severe effect on cash flow, particularly if sales and profits are closely affected by changes in the level of economic activity in the economy.

The current level of interest rates must also be considered. The rate of interest which the firm has to pay will be affected by two criteria. Firstly, the general level of interest rates for borrowed money and, secondly, the risk premium which has to be paid to the lender. The greater the risk, as assessed by the lender, the greater the premium required by the lender to compensate for that additional risk. The firm must assess what premium it will have to pay. In recent years this task has been made more difficult because interest rates have been very volatile.

The amount of money which the firm has already borrowed will also have a bearing on whether it should increase its borrowings. Firms which have borrowed a large proportion of their capital are said to be *highly geared*. These firms are often unpopular with investors because of the increased risk that one day they will be unable to meet their interest payments, should sales and profits decrease.

Lastly, the lender will often want some kind of security before granting the loan. Premises and other fixed assets offer a degree of security for the lender and the borrower must assess how much money the lender is likely to advance on the security value of the asset and at what rate of interest. Regardless of whether a lender is prepared to provide additional loan finance, a business should never raise additional debt finance if its use would be likely to increase the probability of the firm becoming insolvent.

The Advantages of Raising Additional Capital by Borrowing

The amount of profit which a firm can distribute as dividend will be determined by two main factors. Firstly, the amount of profit made and, secondly, the number of shareholders. It is not the amount of money which will be distributed as dividend which is important, but the number of shareholders who will receive a share of it. The fewer the number of shareholders, the greater the dividend per share that can be paid. One way of achieving this is to borrow money, thereby placing a limit on the number of shareholders.

Most companies only distribute a percentage of their after-tax earnings as dividends. This is the main reason why companies use debt capital as part of their long-term capital because it enables the firm to pay higher returns to ordinary shareholders. How a firm's capital structure affects shareholder wealth is the subject of great debate in finance, based on the model of perfect capital markets. A perfect capital market is a market where it is assumed that information is free, that there are no taxes and no costs involved in buying and selling financial securities. Although the capital markets are near examples of perfect markets, they are still imperfect markets and this is why the traditional view of financial management argues that there is an optimum capital structure for a company. In an imperfect market capital financing decisions are important because it is argued that there is an optimum capital structure which will increase shareholder wealth. In a perfect capital market, however, it is possible to show that a firm's capital structure will not affect shareholder wealth. This is because the value of a share in a perfect market is based on the firm's profitability and the present value of its future cash flows.

The Geared Company and the Equity Company

Let us assume that two companies sell similar products and have just published their annual results. They both have the same amount of capital employed and have both made a net profit after tax of £15,000. If the directors decide to distribute all of this profit amongst the shareholders, then the firm which has the fewer shareholders stands to receive the larger dividend payouts. This point can be seen by looking at two companies with different capital structures but with the same long-term capital base.

Example

Extract of the firm's balance sheets

	Geared Company £	Equity Company £
Ordinary shares £1 issued and fully paid	100,000	170,000
10% Debentures Stock	40,000	-
8% Unsecured Loan Stock	30,000	-
Total Capital	170,000	170,000
Earnings after interest and tax	15,000	15,000

Although both firms have declared the same amount of profit available for distribution, the Geared Company will be able to pay the larger dividend. This is because the dividend has only to be distributed to 100,000 ordinary shareholders as against the 170,000 of the Equity Return Company.

The Geared Company will also have a higher earnings per share ratio. Using the earnings per share ratio which is:

$$\frac{\text{Profit after Tax and Preference Dividend}}{\text{Number of Ordinary Shares}}$$

The figures for the Geared Company are:

$$\frac{£15,000}{100,000} \quad \text{x } 100$$

which give earnings per share of 15p.

The profits of the Equity Company have to be shared amongst 170,000 shareholders and so the figures show a lower earnings ratio:

$$\frac{£15,000}{170,000} \quad \text{x } 100$$

which result is earnings per share of approximately 9p.

This example shows that by increasing the level of gearing it is possible to increase the returns paid to shareholders. Once a company has introduced debt into its capital structure, its earnings per share will change to a greater extent than the change in its earnings before interest and tax.

If a company had no debt capital, being financed entirely by the shareholders, a twenty per cent increase in earnings would result in a twenty per cent increase in earnings per share. The reverse would also hold true, and so a twenty per cent decrease in earnings would reduce earnings per share by the same amount.

So long as a geared company can increase its earnings, it will be able to show a more than proportional increase in its earnings per share. Unfortunately the reverse is also true, and so, if earnings decline, the reduction in earnings per share will also be greater. As a result there is more financial risk to an investor in purchasing securities in a highly geared company, particularly if the firm is likely to suffer from erratic earnings brought about by the level of economic activity in the economy. This can be seen in the following diagram and numerical example.

How Earnings Per Share is Affected by a firm's Capital Structure

	Equity Company		Geared Company	
Increase in earnings	20% increase in earnings	20% increase in earnings per share	20% increase in earnings	Greater increase than 20 % in earnings per share
Decrease in earnings	20% reduction in earnings	20% reduction in earnings per share	20% reduction in earnings	Greater decrease than 20% in earnings per share
	Low Risk		**High Risk**	

Hrgadk Industries

Level of Gearing	0	25%	50%	75%
	£	£	£	£
Total Assets	500,000	500,000	500,000	500,000
Share Capital	**500,000**	**375,000**	**250,000**	**125,000**
Debt 10% interest	-	125,000	250,000	375,000
Capital employed	500,000	500,000	500,000	500,000
Earnings before interest & tax	150,000	150,000	150,000	150,000
Interest 10%	-	12,500	25,000	37,500
Earnings after interest	150,000	137,500	125,000	112,500
Tax at 50%	75,000	68,750	62,500	56,250
Earnings after tax	75,000	68,750	62,500	56,250
Earnings per share	**15%**	**18%**	**25%**	**45%**

If the company reports a 20 per cent reduction in earnings before interest and tax, its earnings per share will fall by an even greater percentage.

	£	£	£	£
Earnings before interest and tax	120,000	120,000	120,000	120,000
Interest 10%	-	12,500	25,000	37,500
Earnings after interest	120,000	107,500	95,000	82,500
Tax at 50%	60,000	53,750	47,500	41,250
Earnings after tax	60,000	53,750	47,500	41,250
Earnings per share	12%	14%	19%	33%
Reduction in earnings	20%	20%	20%	20%
Reduction in earnings per share	**20%**	**22%**	**24%**	**27%**

(Change in earnings as % of former earnings) £68,750 - £53,750 = £15,000 $\dfrac{£15,000 \times 100}{£68,750} = 22\%$

The risk to an investor is that, if earnings fall to a point where the company cannot meet its interest payments, the loan holders will appoint a receiver to sell the firm's assets so they can be paid. It is likely that ordinary shareholders will lose their investment. This is why most investors in Britain and the United States do not like to put their money into highly geared companies.

Most shareholders purchase shares with the aim of maximising the return on their investment. They hope to see the share price and the size of their dividends increase over time. The amount of money which a share can earn when it is invested in one company as opposed to another is generally reflected in its share price. The higher the earnings, the more expensive the share. This should enable the investor to make a capital gain and will ensure that the shares are popular with investors, thereby making it possible one day to sell more shares to existing investors should the company need additional finance. A high share price also makes the firm less vulnerable to a hostile takeover bid as the high price of the shares may deter prospective purchasers from trying to acquire a controlling interest. The high share price also acts as a signal to investors that the business is being effectively managed.

Reducing the Cost of Capital

A firm is sometimes able to reduce the overall cost of capital by borrowing. This is best explained by looking at the capital structure of the Geared and Equity Companies.

341

GEARING

The Equity Company's Cost of Capital:

	£
170,000 Ordinary £1 shares issued and fully paid	170,000
Dividend	15,000

Earnings per share, as previously calculated = 9p (approx.), thus the cost of capital for the company is 9p per £1 share or 9 per cent.

The cost of share capital is determined by the rate of dividend which the company pays to its shareholders. The shareholder will only be prepared to invest if there is the prospect of earning a reasonable return, either in the form of dividends or capital appreciation. The earnings per share ratio can, therefore, be used as the cost of using equity capital.

The Geared Company's Cost of Capital:

Capital Employed	£
100,000 Ordinary £1 shares issued and fully paid	100,000
£40,000 10% Debenture Stock 2020 - 2030	40,000
£30,000 8% Unsecured Loan Stock 2015 -2020	30,000
	170,000

Cost of Capital	£
Ordinary Shares (Dividends)	15,000
Debentures (10% interest)	4,000
Unsecured Loan Stock (8% interest)	2,400
Total Cost of Capital	21,400

The overall cost of capital now is $\dfrac{£21,400 \times 100}{£170,000} = 13\%$ (approx.)

The Geared Company has been able to reduce its total cost of capital from 15 per cent to 13 per cent by raising debt capital. It is important to remember that a firm's cost of capital can only be reduced, provided that the company does not increase the level of financial and business risk attached to investing in the firm's financial securities.

Reduction in Taxation Payable

Companies pay corporation tax on their profits. Some expenses, such as interest payments, are tax deductible and so the tax advantage will reduce the cost of capital. This is called the *tax shield* and the higher the rate of tax the greater the benefit to the company. If a company has borrowed £500,000 at an interest rate of 10 per cent, then its annual interest charges, before tax, will be £50,000. If the rate of corporation tax is 50 per cent, then the after tax cost of borrowing the money will only be £25,000. Dividend payments are not tax deductible and so no tax advantages are gained from employing additional share capital.

The Capital Puzzle

During the last fifty years the composition of a firm's capital structure has been the subject of a great deal of academic debate. At the centre of the controversy is whether a firm's total value is affected by its choice of capital structure.

Two American academics Modigliani and Miller (1958) wrote an article which challenged the conventional wisdom relating to gearing. This is now generally referred to as the traditional theory of finance. The traditional theory holds that it is possible for a company to have an optimum capital structure comprising a mix of debt and equity finance . The company gains from having this mix of capital by being able to minimise its weighted average cost of capital, thereby enabling it to maximise its market value. This optimum level of gearing will apply for any firm, and so a company which currently has no debt capital would be able to increase its market value by introducing some debt capital into its structure. Provided a firm can achieve an optimum capital structure, it will be able to minimise its weighted average cost of capital thereby enabling it to maximise its market value. This is only possible because debt is a cheaper form of long term finance than share capital. The problem for management is what constitutes an optimum level of debt for, should the company exceed this, the savings from using debt capital would be more than offset by the increase in the required rate of return on its equity capital. If this situation arose, the firm's weighted average cost of capital would rise, leading to a reduction in the firm's market value.

The Modigliani and Miller hypothesis was based on the assumption that a company's shares trade in a perfect market. In such a market managers cannot alter the firm's value by changing a company's level of gearing. In a perfect capital market a firm's capital structure has no bearing on its value because the share price is only affected by the company's expected future cash flows and the required rate of return by equity investors. The market value of a company in such a market is, therefore, based upon the present value of its cash flows and not on how they are divided between its shareholders and long term holders of debt capital.

Modigliani and Miller based their arguments on two important propositions. The first one was that an investor could always substitute personal gearing for corporate gearing by simply borrowing funds themselves for investment purposes. Secondly, that the financial principle of arbitrage would apply, thereby making it impossible in a perfect market for an investor to make a capital gain. Arbitrage is a financial term used to describe a situation where a security or an equivalent security trade at two different prices in two different markets. An investor is able to make an arbitrage gain by purchasing the asset at the lower price and immediately selling it in the other market for the higher price. In a perfect market, should the share price of two companies having the same earnings but different capital structures differ, then the action of arbitrageurs would ensure that the share price of the two companies would trade for the same price. Modigliani and Miller provided mathematical evidence to show that, if investors engaged in what they called home-made gearing and arbitrage activity, the end result would be that the two companies would have the same share price.

The problem for financial managers and investors is that the capital markets are not perfect. Taxes, transaction costs and the fact that information is not free and available to everyone are important and relevant market imperfections. In 1963 Modigliani and Miller wrote a second paper which addressed the question of corporate taxation as their original work ignored the effects of taxation. This article put forward the view that, whilst the capital markets are sufficiently perfect to make capital structure irrelevant to a firm's value, the position was distorted because of the tax advantages enjoyed by the corporate sector if they financed part of their long term capital finance with debt capital. Companies are allowed to treat interest payments as a tax deductible expense, thereby reducing the cost of debt capital. The higher the tax rate, the greater the saving. Modigliani and Miller's second article concluded that it was this tax advantage which created extra value for shareholders because the firm's value will rise linearly as management increase the amount of debt in the firm's capital structure.

The second article addressed the question of corporate taxation, but ignored personal tax, and this was considered by Miller in 1977. Companies pay corporation tax on their earnings before any payment is made to shareholders in the form of dividends. These dividend payments will generally incur a tax liability for their recipient just as interest payments do. The tax authorities, however, distinguish between income and capital for taxation purposes. Capital gains are usually only taxed when the gain is realised and a certain sum each year may be taken free of tax. Shareholders receive two possible financial gains from ownership. Firstly, dividend payments and secondly capital gains through share price appreciation. Shareholders will pay a lower rate of tax if they are able to take some of their income by way of treating it as a capital gain. Debt holders on the other hand must pay tax on all of their investment income and so, if the company was highly geared they would incur a greater tax liability. Miller's work shows that, at certain tax rates, the gain from corporate taxes was cancelled out by the extra liability incurred on personal taxes with the effect that a firm's value is unaffected by its capital structure.

Although Modigliani and Miller showed that from a mathematical perspective a firm's value is maximised whenever it is financed entirely with debt capital, other factors explain why in practice this does not happen. Even management buyouts, which are renowned for using high levels of debt finance, rarely have a ratio of debt to equity above eighty per cent. One factor which explains why companies are reluctant to use such high levels of debt was addressed by Miller when he looked at the role of personal taxation and its effect on a firm's capital structure.

Whilst tax is an important market imperfection, it is not the only one. The generic term transaction costs which covers such terms as agency costs and bankruptcy also has an important impact on a firm's level of gearing.

Whenever a company is highly geared, the shareholders stand to gain financially at the expense of the debt holders. Agency theory holds that managers, therefore, seek to employ a range of financial securities to balance the interests of those people such as shareholders, debt holders, managers and outside creditors who also have a claim over the firm's asset base.

The higher the level of debt, the more likely it is that the firm will face financial disasters because of the large cash outflows needed to meet interest payments. Firms which are highly geared face a greater possibility of bankruptcy, thereby making it undesirable to employ large amounts of debt capital.

Finally, there is the important financial principle of signalling which also has a bearing on a firm's level of gearing. Actions are signals and the raising of additional capital sends a signal to the market which must be interpreted by investors. The signal may be positive, in the sense that it shows that management have a range of projects which have a positive present value, or that the firm is having to raise money to fund liquidity shortages brought about by unprofitable trading. As a general rule share buy back schemes have a positive impact on the share price whereas, raising more money by issuing additional shares, reduces share values.

Capital structure decisions are very important because they have a bearing on the firm's market value. There is probably no such thing as an optimum structure in terms of a given percentage of debt to equity. This may explain why most companies in the United Kingdom are reluctant to increase the level of gearing beyond fifty per cent. Each company is different. Utilities, such as the water authorities, can afford to be more highly geared than construction companies, who face large differences in earnings because of changes in economic business cycles. No decision, however, should be taken without considering the tax advantages and the signalling effect brought about by the decision to raise outside finance. Indeed, this may explain why many companies seek to raise the money internally from their operations, thereby avoiding the rigorous scrutiny and appraisal of the business by the capital markets.

The Dangers of Raising Capital by Borrowing

Every time a firm borrows money it has to be able to meet the interest charges incurred. This means that a firm must always have sufficient cash to meet its interest payments. In business profits can never be guaranteed. High interest rates, coupled with a downturn in demand, can soon lead to reduced sales and profits. It is then that many companies (particularly small ones) are forced into liquidation as they can no longer meet the combined pressures of high interest rates, static profits and increased overheads. Even large companies are not immune as once-famous household names, such as Polly Peck, Coloroll, Sock Shop, Rush and Tompkins and British and Commonwealth, have had to apply to the Companies' Court for an administrator or have had to appoint a receiver.

When this happens, highly geared companies become unpopular with investors. Bankers are likely to become less keen to lend and financial analysts are likely to reduce the firm's credit rating. In extreme cases, the bank may call in its short-term loans and creditors may also be reluctant to continue trading on the same business terms. These actions can force companies into insolvency and so highly geared companies are always considered more risky investments.

It is, therefore, vital that the benefits of borrowing money outweigh the risks. It is not just the amount of debt to equity capital which must be considered but also the company's ability to repay the debt out of earnings. The higher the ratio of earnings before tax to interest charges, the smaller the risk of financial insolvency.

Companies are often forced into insolvency once they can no longer earn sufficient profits to service their debt. If the level of earnings can be increased, then the company can cope with a higher proportion of debt capital, but it is important that this ratio of debt to earnings is kept at a realistic level. One method of measuring this debt to earnings ratio is by calculating the total liquidity of the firm by the following calculation:

$$\frac{\text{Working Capital} + \text{Long-term Debt}}{\text{After Tax Earnings}}$$

This ratio shows how long it will take the firm to redeem all of its debt out of earnings. The quicker the debt can be repaid, the lower the risk, but it is for the management to decide what is an acceptable risk. This will inevitably be determined by estimated future earnings and whether or not these earnings are greatly affected by different levels of economic activity.

As a general rule firms which have stable sales can afford to borrow more money than firms with unstable sales, but ultimately it is the lenders who consider what is a safe level of debt. If the amount of debt increases too fast, they will either increase the interest charges or refuse to lend more money until the firm has increased the shareholders' stake in the business.

Before borrowing money, management must balance the benefits of increased earnings and possible lower capital costs with the dangers of a reduction in the company's credit rating and the possibility of insolvency if the business is unable to meet its interest and capital repayments from its earnings.

From an analytical stand-point successful businesses are ones which are good at generating cash from their trading activities and, therefore, have little need to borrow finance to fund their capital investment programmes. As a result high levels of gearing are generally taken as a bad sign for it is a principle of financial management that actions are signals. If investors interpret high levels of debt as a bad sign, then this will adversely affect the firm's share price, credit rating and future cost of capital.

References

Modigliani, F. and Miller, M. The Cost of Capital, Corporation Finance and the Theory of Investment. *American Economic Review* 48 (June 1958) : 261-297.

Modigliani, F. and Miller, M. Corporate Income Taxes and the Cost of Capital: A Correction. *American Economic Review* 53 (June 1963) : 433-43.

Miller, M. Debt and Taxes. *Journal of Finance* 32 (May 1977) : 261-75

QUESTIONS

Answers begin page 498

1. How can a company's level of gearing be measured?

2. A company has to pay £60,000 in interest charges and pays tax at 50 per cent. If the company has 150,000 ordinary £1 shares, calculate how much earnings per share will increase because of the tax shield.

3. Volos Ltd is an all equity company and has an authorised and issued capital of 200,000 ordinary £1 shares, which are currently quoted on the stock market at £2. The directors plan to raise £200,000 10 per cent debentures. Last year Volos' earnings, before interest and tax, were £180,000 and this year, after raising the additional capital, the directors expect earnings, before interest and tax, to rise to £260,000. The company currently pays tax at 40 per cent.

   Calculate Volos Ltd earnings per share and its earnings after interest and tax before and after the issuing of the 10 per cent debenture stock.

4. Fegan Ltd is an all equity company and has 300,000 ordinary £1 shares which are currently quoted on the stock market at £2.50.

   The directors intend to issue £300,000 12 per cent secured loan stock. Last year the firm's earning were £220,000 and this year they are expected to rise to £310,000. The company pays tax at 50 per cent. It is company policy to distribute 60 per cent of its after tax earnings as dividends.

   a. Calculate the firm's earnings per share and its earnings after interest and tax before and after the issuing of the 12 per cent secured loan stock.

   b. Calculate the firm's weighted average cost of capital before and after the issue of the loan stock.

5.

THE DIVERSE ENGINEERING GROUP

Robert Walters
Financial Correspondent

Any shareholder who bought shares in the company during the last eighteen months has seen the value of their investment drastically reduced. Yesterday the shares dropped another 10p to an all time low of £1.27 and most financial analysts are convinced that the company is not yet out of the wood.

The group's problems can be traced back to the time when it embarked upon a huge acquisition programme in Germany and the United States. Corporate borrowings rose dramatically as a whole range of engineering firms were purchased. For a while profits rose but a series of problems in North America, coupled with currency fluctuations, has dramatically reduced corporate profits.

Today corporate debts stand at 70 per cent of total assets and, although the company has not yet approached its bankers to reschedule its debts, many people in the City wonder how long the group can remain so highly geared.

Fortunately the company is still profitable and stringent cash control measures have helped to secure institutional support at least for the short-term. Still the shares remain only for the very brave but, if the Chair Linda Johnson is right, financial rewards could flow once the North American Market moves out of recession.

a. What are the dangers of pursuing an acquisition policy with debt capital?

b. Why might the firm need to restructure its debts in the future?

c. Why might Linda Johnson be right in thinking that the shares could perform well in the future?

Chapter 24

Managing Capital Investments

Introduction

Most business organisations seek to expand by increasing their sales and profits. In the short-term this may be possible by making greater use of existing assets, however, in the long-term new investment will be needed to increase the productive capacity of the business. Any new investment expenditure will have to be financed. This can be done either by investing past profits back into the business or by investing new share or loan capital. In either case the new investment must yield a return which will be higher than the cost of capital and consistent with the firm's present and expected return on capital employed.

Investment decisions are important for two reasons. Firstly, they usually involve substantial amounts of capital and, secondly, they will have a large effect on the future profitability of the business. Once management have started capital investment programmes, it is nearly impossible for them to be halted without the business incurring great losses. This is why it is so important to make the correct decision before commencing on a particular course of action.

Cost of Capital

Money is a scarce resource and the owners of capital require a return commensurate with the risks involved. The return which investors seek will affect the firm's cost of capital and the return which the new project must earn in order to meet investor's expectations.

The cost of capital will vary from one company to another and will be influenced by such factors as the company's capital structure, current interest rates, the project's risk and the returns which investors expect to earn.

There are two reasons why a firm should not use its historical cost of capital as shown in the balance sheet when evaluating the desired return from a new investment. Firstly, the cost of capital may have risen if investors require higher returns than previously for financing such investments. This is why the firm's cost of capital as shown in the balance sheet should not be used to calculate the firm's cost of capital for investment purposes. Secondly, the new project may expose the business to a different level of risk than its existing projects and, if this is the case, investors will demand a higher rate of return to compensate them for the extra risk. This is called the *risk premium*. Finally, management must remember that an investment will only increase shareholder wealth if it can earn the return which investors expect from financing this type of investment. Whatever a business' actual cost of capital, it is useful to consider the cost under the following headings.

Cost of Borrowing

If loan finance is required then the minimum return from the project must be above the cost of servicing the loan. This means that the investment must make a greater return than the current or expected interest rate being charged for borrowed funds.

Return on Capital Employed

Every pound that is invested in the business must make a return on its investment. The return which a business can earn on its own capital is referred to as the return on its capital employed. It can be calculated by the formula:

$$\frac{\text{Profit (before interest on debt)} \times 100}{\text{Capital employed}}$$

and this can be used as a yard stick when considering new investments. Many firms set a rate of return which new capital investments must earn based on their current return on capital employed. In accounting this is referred to as the *hurdle rate*.

Weighted Cost of Capital

We have already seen that companies have two main sources of finance, either the money can be raised from the shareholders or borrowed from long-term lenders. When firms raise money by borrowing it is usual to offer security to the lender. The lender's capital is then protected in the event of the firm defaulting

on the loan or interest payments. As a result lenders are usually prep
accept a lower return because they are exposed to less financial
Shareholders, on the other hand, have no legal right to receive a dividend a
may even lose their investment if the company ceases trading. This is why
shareholders expect a higher rate of return in the form of dividend payments to
compensate them for the additional financial and business risk.

Companies can reduce their overall cost of capital by mixing the amount of
share and debt capital in their capital structure. The weighted average cost of
capital seeks to average out the firm's costs of capital by adding up the amount
and cost of each type of capital and then calculating the weighted return. This
can be done as follows:

Capital	Amount	Cost	Return	Capital Structure	Cost	Weighted Average
Shares	£40,000	12%	£4,800	20%	12%	2.4%
Reserves	£80,000	12%	£9,600	40%	12%	4.8%
6% Pref. Shares	£40,000	6%	£2,400	20%	6%	1.2%
8% Loan	£40,000	8%	£3,200	20%	8%	1.6%
Capital Employed	£200,000		£20,000			10.0%

Note: Reserves are treated as share capital because they belong to the shareholders.
Share capital is 20% of total capital and so the weighted cost is 20% of 12% = 2.4%.

Whilst investors, be they shareholders or long term creditors, can share the risk
in any proportion they choose, the firm's opportunity cost of capital is always
the required rate of return required by an investor for investing in a project with
that level of risk.

Determining the Weighted Average Cost of Capital

In the above example the weighted cost of capital is 10 per cent and so, by
having different sources of capital, the firm hopes to be able to reduce its overall
cost. This is best illustrated by looking at how the business has calculated its
weighted average cost of capital.

le has put a cost of 12 per cent on share capital. This figure
oking at the rate of dividend paid to shareholders in the form
ts. The higher the dividend, the higher the firm's cost of

ve seen earlier, reserves belong to the shareholders because
past profits which have been kept by the company to be
isiness, rather than being paid out to shareholders. It,
therefore, follows that the reserves should earn a return equal to the dividend
paid on ordinary shares.

Preference Shares: These are shares which carry a fixed rate of dividend and so
the cost of capital is 6 per cent.

8% Loan: The 8 per cent refers to the interest rate which has to be paid for
borrowing the money. Interest payments are tax deductible and so, assuming a
tax on profits (Corporation Tax) of 50 per cent, the true cost of the capital to the
firm would be 4 per cent. To keep this example simple taxation has been
ignored.

Investment decisions should not be based on the firm's historical cost of capital,
because it reflects the firm's past cost of capital and will be wrong if there has
been a change in the market rate for capital, such as a change in interest rates.
Even if management use their existing cost of capital for investment evaluation,
they will be wrong should the project not have the same risks as its existing
activities.

Managers should invest with the aim of increasing shareholder wealth. The
return which the new investment should earn must be commensurate with the
return which a shareholder could earn, were it possible to invest in the shares of
another company undertaking a similar investment. This return which a
shareholder can expect to earn should be equal to systematic risk of the project,
because this is the risk which portfolio theory subscribes to shareholders
whenever they decide to purchase equity investments. When management make
capital investment decisions, they should use a cost of capital which is
commensurate with the risks of the project's cash flows and not the cost of its
financing. The return from any investment must equate with its risk and, whilst
the risk of an investment remains the same for all firms, different companies will
be able to earn higher returns and cash flows from their investment. The higher

the cash flows that can be generated for an investment, the greater its value. For practical purposes managers should grade their new investment proposals into different risk classes so that the hurdle rate is consistent with the company's opportunity cost of capital.

Capital Investment

This is the term used to define money invested in fixed assets such as machinery and buildings. These assets will all have a limited productive life greater than one year and the aim is to choose investment projects which will yield the greatest return. It is not easy to choose projects which will become the future profit earners for the business, but the aim is to avoid two types of errors which are often referred to as *drop errors* and *go errors*. *Drop errors* occur when the management decide not to proceed with an investment, even though it would have been profitable. They may decide against such a project because at the time of making the investment decision they failed to see its full opportunity, or they may decide against it because, in their view, the initial capital costs are too high. A *go error* occurs when the firm invests in a project which fails to make the required return and which may even lose the firm money, thereby reducing its overall return on capital employed. An investment decision should only be taken if it will increase the value of the businesses by generating more cash inflows than cash outflows.

The cost of the investment is not just the financial cost of using the money but the opportunity cost of foregoing one investment opportunity as opposed to another. Investment appraisal techniques provide management with information about the likely returns to be made and the level of risk from the investment. They cannot, however, select on their own the optimum investments. This can only be done by management who are able to take other factors into account, such as future market developments, before making their investment decisions. Before any investment decision is taken, it is essential to know the amount of cash which will be required to finance the new project and the amount of cash inflows which it will generate.

Future Cash Flows and the Investment Decision

Before management make an investment decision, they need to first evaluate the future net cash flows which will be earned from the new investment and determine what cash flows are relevant to the investment decision. In order for a cash flow to be relevant, it must satisfy two criteria, first, it must change the firm's overall cash flow, and second, it must be directly related to the investment decision currently under consideration. Any cash flow which is unaffected by the proposed new project is called a non-relevant cash flow and is usually referred to as a sunk cost. A project's net investment and its operating cash flow is calculated as follows:

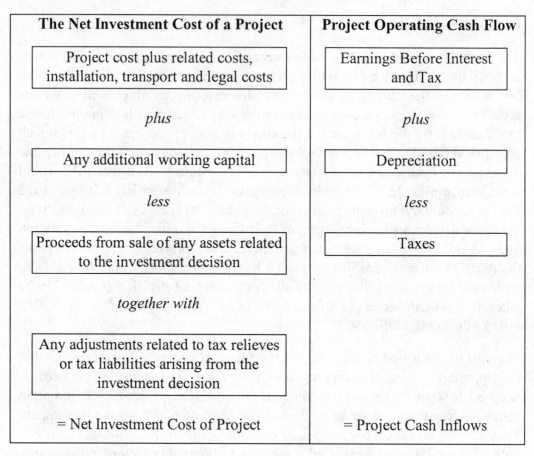

The Net Investment Cost of a Project	Project Operating Cash Flow
Project cost plus related costs, installation, transport and legal costs	Earnings Before Interest and Tax
plus	*plus*
Any additional working capital	Depreciation
less	*less*
Proceeds from sale of any assets related to the investment decision	Taxes
together with	
Any adjustments related to tax relieves or tax liabilities arising from the investment decision	
= Net Investment Cost of Project	= Project Cash Inflows

Cash Flow Tables

A cash flow table shows the cash inflows and outflows which are expected to occur from an investment. Cash will be needed to finance both the fixed assets and to provide the working capital which will be needed to pay for the day-to-day expenses. It is usually a mistake to assume that, once a fixed asset has been purchased, cash inflows will immediately follow. Often additional capital is needed to pay for new stock, training and spare parts and this, if not budgeted for, can put severe constraints on a business' working capital. The purpose of drawing up a cash flow table is to be able to determine the firm's net cash flow from the new investment. This is calculated by adding up all the inflows and subtracting all of the outflows.

Figure 24:1 Suggested Layout for a Cash Flow Table

Year	Capital outflows	Sales income	Costs	Profit	Tax on profits	Tax saved by allowances	Net cash flow
	£	£	£	£	£	£	£
0							
1							
2							
3							
4							
5							
6							
7							

Note: It is a good idea to construct separate columns for each cash inflow and cash outflow.

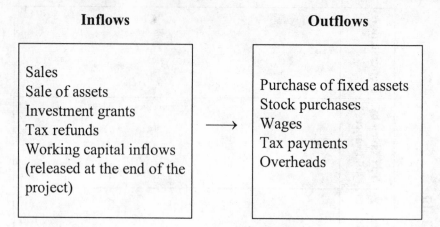

Constructing a Cash Flow Table

The following diagram shows examples of inflows and outflows of cash.

The cash flow table only shows receipts and payments of cash and so the following expenses are never included:

a.   Depreciation

b.   Bad debts

c.   Accruals (money owing but which does not yet have to be paid in cash)

d.   Profits or losses made on the sales of fixed assets

Example

A business which is profitable and which currently pays Corporation Tax on its profits is considering investing in a new electric saw which will cost £10,000 and which will have a life of five years. The firm has estimated that the cash inflows from the investment will be £4,400 per year and that the cost of running the machine will be £400 per year. The current rate of Corporation Tax is 40 per cent and the investment will not enjoy any write down relief (capital allowance). The firm's accountant has estimated that the machine will have a resale value in five years' time of £1,000.

Cash Flow Table

Year	Investment	Cash Inflow	Cash Outflow	Tax	Net Cash Flow
		£	£	£	£
0	(10,000)				(10,000)
1		4,400	(400)		4,000
2		4,400	(400)	(1,600)	2,400
3		4,400	(400)	(1,600)	2,400
4		4,400	(400)	(1,600)	2,400
5	1,000	5,400	(400)	(1,600)	3,400
6				(1,600)	(1,600)

Points to note:

a. Taxable income £4,400 - 400 = £4,000 per annum

b. Tax payments due £4,000 x 40% = £1,600

c. Corporation Tax (tax on company profits) is always paid 9 months after the tax liability is incurred. This means that effectively the tax will be paid the following year.

Taxation and the Investment Decision

Companies pay tax on their profits. If the government gives an allowance to firms investing in fixed assets the effect will be to reduce the amount of tax payable. These allowances are usually referred to as *capital allowances* or *write down allowances* and they enable a firm to offset part or all of the investment cost against profits. The higher the allowance the greater the tax saving.

MANAGING CAPITAL INVESTMENTS

Using the same figures as in the previous example, the directors have found out that the investment will qualify for the following allowances.

First Year Allowance (FYA)   60%

Write Down Allowance (WDA)   20%

Tax Effect

Year	Allowance	Cost £	Allowance £	Tax Saved £	Year Tax Payable
0		10,000			
1	FYA (60%)	(6,000)	6,000	2,400	2
2	WDA (20%)	4,000 (800)	800	320	3
3	WDA (20%)	3,200 (640)	640	256	4
4	WDA (20%)	2,560 (512)	512	204	5
5	Bal. allowance	2,048 (1,048)	1,048	420	6
		(1,000)	£9,000		

Note: The first year allowance provides a tax shield of 40 percent of £6,000. This results in a tax saving of £2,400 and is treated as a cash inflow.

The effect on the Cash Flow of the Project is:

Year	Original NCF £	Effect of Capital Allowance £	Adjusted NCF £
0	(10,000)		(10,000)
1	4,000		4,000
2	2,400	2,400	4,800
3	2,400	320	2,720
4	2,400	256	2,656
5	3,400	204	3,604
6	(1,600)	420	(1,180)
	£3,000		£6,600

Traditional Investment Appraisal Techniques

Businesses use a number of capital budgeting techniques for evaluating capital investment projects. One of the most popular with business people is the pay back method, even though it is widely criticised by academics in business schools.

Pay Back Method

Before businesses decide to invest in new machinery or other fixed assets, they need to consider how long the investment will take to pay for itself and the rate of return which will be earned on it. The return must be sufficient to cover the cost of using the money. This means that a return will be needed which is consistent with the firm's present return on capital employed and which is definitely higher than the current interest rate, which is effectively the cost of borrowed capital. In addition, a margin must be added to cover the cost of unsuccessful investments as not all new projects will turn out to be successful, and those that are must carry those that are not.

The pay back method is concerned with how quickly the firm will be able to recoup the money invested in a new project. It is calculated by the formula:

$$\text{Pay back} = \frac{\text{Net Investment}}{\text{Net Cash Flows per annum}}$$

The pay back time is very important if the investment is likely to become obsolete because of changes in technology or market demand. In such cases the quicker the pay back time, the lower the risk, although it should be remembered that business risks are not always time related and that the pay back method is not a good measure for risk analysis.

Pay back is a useful method as an initial screening process because it eliminates the least financially viable projects when making capital investment decisions.

Example

Let us assume that a business is currently considering investing a maximum of £50,000 in new fixed assets. The firm needs to expand quickly because the market is growing fast and this expansion is placing severe constraints upon its working capital. Ideally it would like projects which require a minimum amount of investment capital and which pay for themselves over a short period of time, thereby easing its cash flow problems. The management are currently considering three new projects which they expect will have a life of four years. After this time the assets will be worn out and additional investment will be required.

	Project A	Project B	Project C
Investment	£15,000	£25,000	£50,000
Life of investment	4 years	4 years	4 years
Year One cash inflow	£4,000	£8,000	£20,000
Year Two cash inflow	£6,000	£10,000	£30,000
Year Threecash inflow	£5,000	£12,000	£15,000
Year Four cash inflow	£4,000	£6,000	£9,000
Pay back time	**3 years**	**2 years & 7 months**	**2 years**

By adding up the inflows, which are the expected level of sales, and then dividing it by the initial investment, it is possible to calculate how quickly the investment will take to pay for itself. In this example Project C has the quickest pay back time which could well be a factor influencing the investment decision.

The calculation of the pay back time for Projects A and C was made easier because the cash inflows exactly equalled the initial investment. Project B's pay back time was 2 years 7 months and in such cases it is best to construct a cumulative cash flow table. Using the figures for Project B the cumulative cash flow table would be:

Year	Cash Outflow £	Cash Inflow £	Cumulative Cash Flow £
0	(25,000)	-	(25,000)
1		8,000	8,000
2		10,000	18,000
3		12,000	shortfall	7,000

Note: The pay back time is somewhere between year 2 and year 3. To find the exact pay back in years and months an assumption is made that the cash flows in year 3 are earned monthly and so the total is divided by 12 to find the monthly inflow. £12,000 ÷ 12 = £1,000.

The next step is to divide the monthly inflow into the shortfall.

$$\frac{\text{Shortfall}}{\text{Monthly inflow}} \qquad \frac{\text{£7,000}}{\text{£1,000}} \qquad = \qquad 7$$

Pay back time 2 years 7 months.

Advantages of the Pay Back Method

The pay back method is simple to calculate and shows how quickly the initial investment will be recovered from sales income. This probably explains why the method is so popular as it enables business people to see how long their investment is at risk. As a general rule, the quicker the pay back time, the lower the risk. The method also places great emphasis on liquidity and this may explain its popularity with managers who are worried about how large cash outflows will affect the firm's overall liquidity.

Disadvantages of the Pay Back Method

The main disadvantage of the pay back method is that it does not take into consideration the earnings that the investment yields after it has paid for itself. In the example, Projects A and B are rejected, even though they both yield greater returns than Project C after the pay back period. Finally, the method assumes that all receipts and payments occur within the period under consideration. Nevertheless, it is a useful investment appraisal technique for projects which have an initial capital investment followed by a steady flow of sales income. The method is best suited to investment decisions which do not involve a large amount of capital, but should not be used on its own for deciding whether or not to proceed with an investment decision.

Accounting Rate of Return

The accounting rate of return seeks to measure the future profitability of a proposed investment. It is a poor method because it is simply a ratio based on two sets of accounting data.

This method is used to select the project which will yield the greatest return on investment. It is calculated by the formula:

$$ARR = \frac{\text{Average Net Profit x 100 (after depreciation)}}{\text{Average Capital Investment}}$$

$$\text{Where Average Net Profit} = \frac{\text{Net Profit (after depreciation)}}{\text{Life of the Investment}}$$

$$\text{And where Average Capital Investment} = \frac{\text{Capital Investment}}{2}$$

Example

The managers of a business intend to invest £20,000 in a project which will have a life of five years. The annual estimated returns are shown below:

Net Cash Inflows	£
Year One	6,000
Year Two	8,000
Year Three	6,000
Year Four	10,000
Year Five	10,000
Total Inflows	40,000

How to Calculate Accounting Rate of Return

a. Calculate Annual Depreciation
   Annual depreciation is cost of the asset divided by life of the asset. Cost of asset: £20,000, life: 5 years. Therefore, annual depreciation £4,000 a year

b. Deduct depreciation from cash flow: £40,000 minus £20,000 = £20,000

c. Calculate Average Annual Return: Average annual return 20,000 divided by life of investment (5 years) = £4,000. Therefore, Accounting Rate of Return equals:

$$\frac{£4,000 \times 100}{10,000} = 40\%$$

This shows that the business will earn a return of 40 per cent on the original investment if management proceed with this project.

Advantage of Accounting Rate of Return

This method shows the return on the capital invested and it takes account of all profits earned throughout the project's life.

Disadvantage of Accounting Rate of Return

The main disadvantage of this method is that it does not take account of taxation payments and write down allowances which can greatly affect the net cash flows from a project. The method also considers accounting profits instead of cash flows and is, therefore, not a good investment appraisal technique. Finally the ARR takes no account of the time value of money.

The Principle of the Time Value of Money

If a person has a sum of money they can either spend it or save it. Assuming they choose to save it, they could either keep it in an envelope in a safe place or deposit their money with a financial institution, such as a bank, which will pay interest on the sum deposited. The opportunity cost of keeping the money in an envelope is the interest lost which the bank would have paid. This is why it is said that money has a time value, for money owned now can be lent to earn interest, whereas money received in the future cannot be so invested.

It is usual for interest to be added to capital and, as a result, it is possible to calculate the future value of a sum of money at the end of a set period, provided that the length of time and the interest rate payable are known. This is compound interest and is best illustrated by the following example.

Emma Harding has £5,000 to invest. She could place it in a three-year deposit account where the interest rate will be 10 per cent (compound per annum).

At the end of each year the investment will have grown as follows:

Year		£
0		5,000
1	£5,000 x (1.10) =	5,500
2	£5,000 x (1.10)^2 =	6,050
3	£5,000 x (1.10)^3 =	6,655

Emma has earned interest on her interest during the three years and this is known as the *principle of compound interest*. The formula for calculating compound interest is:

FV	=	PV		$(I+r)^n$	
$\downarrow$		$\downarrow$		$\downarrow$	$\searrow$
Future value		Present value of initial investment		Interest rate	Number of years

Let us now assume that Emma has been promised £5,000 in one year's time. If she had the money now, it could earn 10 per cent and so the time delay has deprived her of the interest. Emma, therefore, needs to know the current value (present value) of £5,000 to be received in one year's time assuming a 10 per cent return on money. This is known as the *principle of discounting* and is compounding in reverse.

£5,000 to be received in 1 years time

$$£5,000 \quad \text{x} \quad \frac{1}{1.10} \quad = \quad £4,545$$

The formula for discounting is:

$$PV \quad = \quad FV \quad \frac{1}{(I+r)^n}$$

It, therefore, follows that any money to be received in the future should be discounted so that the returns payable can be compared with the initial capital investment.

A business also enjoys three other major benefits by receiving money immediately rather than in the future. Firstly, the money can be invested in the business. Secondly, the risk of the investment is negated as soon as it has paid for itself and, lastly, the money received can be used to meet the business' immediate liabilities.

Inflation further erodes the value of money, and so an allowance for inflation should always be made before making any financial decision.

Discounted Cash Flow

The main limitations of both the pay back method and the accounting rate of return is that both methods ignore the time taken to receive the cash inflows.

The discounted cash flow method seeks to calculate the value of cash inflows received in the future, for money received immediately is worth more than money to be received in the future. This is so because cash invested in interest-earning deposits will increase in value because of the interest received. The interest can then be added to the capital and even more interest will accrue in the future. When money is received at a later date, the receiver has been deprived, in the meantime, of the use of the money and of the interest. This is why the future cash inflow should be discounted to ascertain its present value based on a specific interest rate. In this way future cash flows can be compared with the value of money invested at the start of the project. In the absence of a spread sheet, the easiest way of working out the time value of a sum of money to be received in the future is to construct a table and to use mathematical tables which are at the back of this book.

Year	Cash Outflow £	Discount Factor £	Cash Inflow £	Net Present Value £

Figure 24:2 Example of a Discounted Cash Flow Table Layout

Note:

1. The initial investment is always made in year 0.

2. Any additional working capital must be added to the capital cost at the beginning of the project. At the end it must be treated as an inflow and discounted.

3. Any residual value must be similarly treated as an inflow in the last year and discounted.

4. Any opportunity cost of capital should be treated as a cash outflow.

5. Any saving should be treated as a cash inflow.

Figure 24:3 How Compounding and Discounting Affects the Time Value of Money

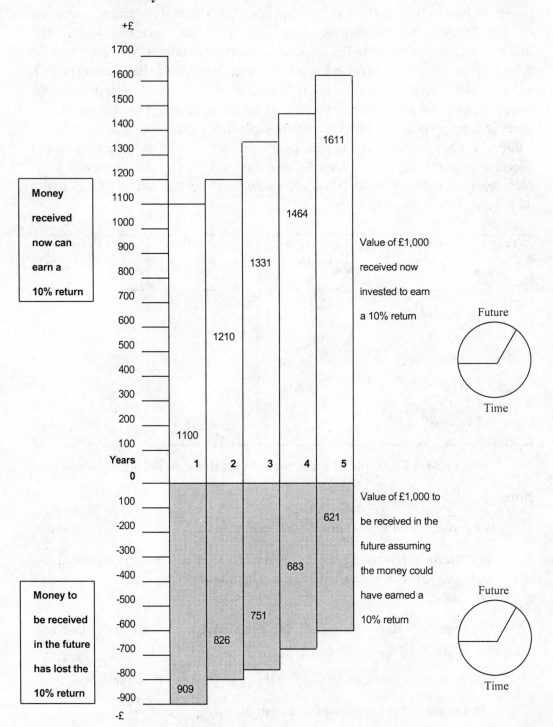

How to use the table

COMPOUNDING (Time makes money grow)

Year	10%	£1,000 (received now + invested)	Future Value £
0		1,000	1,000
1	1.100	1,000	1,100
2	1.210	1,000	1,210
3	1.331	1,000	1,331
4	1.464	1,000	1,464
5	1.611	1,000	1,611

Note: Please see tables in the appendix.

DISCOUNTING (Time makes money less)

Year	10%	£1,000 (received in the future)	Future Value £
0		1,000	1,000
1	0.909	1,000	909
2	0.826	1,000	826
3	0.751	1,000	751
4	0.683	1,000	683
5	0.621	1,000	621

Note: Please see tables in the appendix.

Example

Using the same figures as in the previous example, the management would like to know if the investment is still viable. At present the business earns a return of 15 per cent on its capital and so any investment must yield such a return. This is often called the hurdle rate.

369

How to Discount Cash Inflows and Calculate an Investment's Net Present Value

Year	Cash Outflow £	Cash Inflow £	Discount Factor	Net Present Value £
0	(20,000)	-	15%	(20,000)
1		6,000	0.870	5,220
2		8,000	0.756	6,048
3		6,000	0.658	3,948
4		10,000	0.572	5,720
5		10,000	0.497	4,970
	Total value of discounted inflows			25,906
	Less original investment			20,000
	Net present value			5,906

Points to Note:

a. The original investment of £20,000 is not discounted because money at the start of the project must be worth its original amount.

b. The discount figures are taken from the tables in the appendix.

c. By discounting the cash inflows, it is possible to see their value had the firm been able to receive the money immediately and earn a return of 15 per cent.

d. By adding up the discounted returns and subtracting them from the original investment, management know that the investment is financially viable. This is because all inflows have earned the required return of 15 per cent, thereby reducing them to their present day values. In this way the money received at different future dates can be compared with the value of the original investment.

Interpreting the Net Present Value of a Project

There are only three possible outcomes when calculating the net present value of a project. These are:

a. **Positive Net Present Value.**
    This happens when the total value of the discounted inflows is equal to or greater than the outflows. The project is, therefore, capable of earning a return equal to or greater than the firm's cost of capital and will increase shareholder wealth.

b. **Negative Net Present Value.**
    If the total discounted outflows exceed the discounted inflows, then the project is incapable of earning a return which is greater than the cost of capital and would not lead to an increase in shareholder wealth.

c. **Nil Net Present Value.**
    In this situation the total discounted inflows exactly equal the discounted outflows. This shows that the project is capable of earning a return which equals the cost of capital and is called the *internal rate of return* (IRR).

Example

A firm is considering investing £20,000 and is currently evaluating the returns from three investment opportunities which it has called Projects A, B and C. The cash inflows and their net present values, using a rate of return of 10 per cent, are shown below:

Year	DCF	Project A £		Project B £		Project C £	
0	10%	Cash Flow	NPV	Cash Flow	NPV	Cash Flow	NPV
		(20,000)	(20,000)	(20,000)	(20,000)	(20,000)	(20,000)
1	0.91	2,000	1,820	6,000	5,460	2,000	1,820
2	0.83	4,000	3,320	6,000	4,980	4,000	3,320
3	0.75	6,000	4,500	6,000	4,500	3,920	2,940
4	0.68	6,000	4,080	2,000	1,360	4,000	2,720
5	0.62	6,000	3,720	1,800	1,116	4,000	2,480
6	0.56	6,800	3,808	1,800	1,008	12,000	6,720
		NPV	1,248	NPV	(1,576)	NPV	Nil
		Positive NPV		Negative NPV		Zero NPV	

By discounting the cash inflows it can be seen that:

a.   Project A is capable of earning a higher return than that required.

b.   Project B is unable to earn the required rate of return.

c.   Project C can earn the return required.

If the firm can only invest in one project, it should choose Project A.

The Internal Rate of Return

The internal rate of return (IRR) is the discount rate which yields a zero net present value. This will be the case if the total discounted cash flows, less the initial investment, result in a zero net present value.

Example

I M Industries

The firm is considering investing £10,000 in new equipment and its required rate of return is 10 per cent. The net cash flows are shown below:

Year	Cash Outflow [£]	Cash Inflow [£]	DF 10%	NPV [£]
0	(10,000)	-		(10,000)
1		1,000	0.91	910
2		2,000	0.83	1,660
3		3,000	0.75	2,250
4		3,000	0.68	2,040
5		3,000	0.62	1,860
6		3,400	0.56	1904
			NPV	624

The investment can earn a positive net present value but the owner would like to know the investment's internal rate of return. The IRR of the project can be calculated by interpolation. The first step is to work out a number of net present values using higher discount rates than the 10 per cent already used.

Calculation of the project's IRR

D/F	10%	11%	12%	13%	14%
NPV	£624	£262	(£16)	(£408)	(£676)

Note: The net present values are calculated by discounting the cash flows by the discount factors.

At a discount rate of 11 per cent the project still has a positive NPV, but at 12 per cent the NPV is negative. The project's IRR lies somewhere between 11 per cent and 12 per cent. The exact rate is:

$$IRR = 11\% + \frac{(262 \times 1)}{278} = 11.94\%$$

[Note: 11% = 262£]   [262 + £16 = 278]

Whenever a firm is considering investing in only one project but is currently considering a number of investments, they are said to be *mutually exclusive*. In such cases the project which can earn the largest NPV should be selected, but sometimes the evaluation can be made more complicated because the NPV and the IRR give different returns. In such cases the project which can earn the highest NPV should be chosen. This is because the NPV and IRR are based upon different assumptions.

The IRR assumes that the net cash flows are reinvested at the IRR whereas the NPV method assumes that they are invested at the firm's required rate of return or hurdle rate. If the hurdle rate is correct, then it will reflect the firm's opportunity cost of capital and is, therefore, the correct reinvestment rate for the firm. This is so because in a competitive market the future returns earned from a similar investment will be zero, and so the reinvested cash flows will equal the hurdle rate. This is why NPV should take precedence over IRR whenever management are considering either mutually exclusive projects or single projects, should the two methods give rise to differing returns. Finally NPV is the only measure which shows whether shareholder wealth will be increased and this is why it is the best investment appraisal technique.

In a perfect capital market an investor's required rate of return will equal an investor's expected rate and that is why the net present value of any financial security in such a market is zero. Whenever management invests in real assets they operate in an imperfect market where the assets they are buying may or may not be correctly priced. This is why management should consider the present value of any future cash flows which will stem from a capital investment.

In chapter 1 we saw that many business organisations set themselves the goal of maximising shareholder wealth. The shareholders are the owners of the firm and they require a return on the money which they have invested in it by purchasing the company's shares. Whenever a business invests in a capital project, where the present value of the cash inflows discounted at the firm's cost of capital are greater than the present value of the cash outflows, it has made a sound investment. The investment has been a good one because the returns are worth more than the costs of undertaking the capital investment and, as a result, shareholder wealth has been increased. It, therefore, follows that a business should only invest if it can earn a positive net present value. This is why most people agree that discounted cash flow techniques are the best method for appraising capital investment programmes, because they take into account the principle of the time value of money.

Limitations of Investment Appraisal Techniques

The problem for management is that competitive forces in the market place make it ever harder to find investments which can yield a positive net present value. This is why the principle of new ideas is so important when making investment decisions. An asset can only yield a positive net present value if its true value has been incorrectly valued. This will have come about either because the seller valued it wrongly or because they failed to see its full investment potential. Any investment which is over valued will have a negative net present value. This is consistent with the principle of two-sided transactions because one person's gain must be another's loss. The entrepreneur's skill is to spot investments which have been either incorrectly valued or to invent new services or products or new ways of improving existing ones. This can be seen in the following example.

Example

Katong Construction

The Property Acquisitions Director has just seen a large Edwardian house close to the town centre. The property is currently derelict and in urgent need of repair.

The director believes that this property would make a suitable investment because it could be turned into six self-contained flats. The house is currently priced at £140,000 and conversion costs would be a further £60,000. In one year's time the flats could be sold for £55,000 each. The directors never invest unless they can earn a return of 18 per cent.

Solution

The property will only be a suitable investment if the discounted values of the cash inflows exceed the cash outflows. The director must have found a house whose true value has not been recognised by its current owners. If the original owner knew its true value, then this would be reflected in the selling price, thereby making it impossible for Katong Construction to earn a positive net present value from their investment.

Cash Flow Table

Year	Cash Outflow [£]	Cash Inflow [£]	DF 18%	NPV [£]
0	(200,000)	-		(200,000)
1	330,000	0.847	279,510	
			NPV	79,510

This investment can earn a positive return and so it is a suitable investment.

Time is the real problem in any investment decision. There are only three aspects to time. Time past, showing trends, which may or may not be relevant to the investment decision. Time present, which is already gone, and time future, which will prove whether or not the investment decision was a correct one. For the business person time is not a void as it is assumed to be in mathematics but an uncertain variable where new information can have a profound effect on any investment decision. As a result, all methods of appraising the return from investments are based upon forecast returns and expectations about the level of inflation, interest rates and cash inflows. If there is a sharp increase in the rate of inflation, a rise in interest rates or cost overruns, then the expected return or cost may well turn out to be very different from the estimated return. The National Westminster Bank Tower was originally forecast to cost £15 million, but the final cost was £115 million. Similarly, the Thames Barrier was budgeted to cost £23 million but, eventually, the cost was £461 million, and the cost of constructing the Humber Bridge spiralled from a planned £19 million to £120 million. All of these cost overruns have been dwarfed by the building of the Channel Tunnel where the final cost was in excess of £9 billion from the original estimate, making the initial calculations worthless. The real losers, however, are the shareholders who saw the price of their shares fall as the costs increased. These examples all highlight the risks involved in investing in projects which take a long time to complete and which will yield a return only after completion.

QUESTIONS

Answers begin page 500

1.   Calculate the pay back time of the following investment programmes.

Project	A	B	C
	£	£	£
Invested	75,000	55,000	120,000
Cash Inflows			
Year One	15,000	18,000	22,000
Year Two	28,000	25,000	36,000
Year Three	32,000	48,000	46,000
Year Four	36,000	44,000	52,000

2.   **The Investment Decision**. The directors of unit 22 are considering investing £40,000 in new machinery. They have looked at a couple of machines and have calculated that either of them will pay for themselves in just three years.

Before making their final decision they have decided to visit the suppliers once more. On their way they decided to listen to the radio and heard a programme about small businesses and investment. Unfortunately they had missed most of the programme but have been worried by the fact that one of the commentators stated that an investment which pays for itself quickly should not automatically be considered as a good investment opportunity.

a.   What at the dangers of applying the pay back method to an investment decision?

b.   Why is the method still popular with business people?

3.   Calculate the accounting rate of return for the following projects:

Project	A	B	C
	£	£	£
Investment	40,000	60,000	75,000
Cash Inflows			
Year One	25,000	30,000	15,000
Year Two	30,000	40,000	35,000
Year Three	35,000	46,000	50,000
Year Four	42,000	48,000	55,000

4.   A company has estimated that it will receive the following cash inflows in the future. Calculate the cash inflows' net present value, having taken into account the firm's cost of capital.

a.   £12,760 to be received in four years' time, assuming an 8 per cent cost of capital.

b.   £23,987 to be received next year, assuming a 12 per cent cost of capital.

c.   £17,540 to be received in eight years' time, assuming a 6 per cent cost of capital.

d.   £67,800 to be received in ten years' time, assuming a 16 per cent cost of capital.

5.   **Lee Valley Farm**. Ten years ago the owners of the Lee Valley Farm invested in a new milking parlour. The cost was £100,000 and the owners believe that it will have a life of 5 years. During the investment's lifetime it has earned £200,000 a year less £150,000 operating costs. The owners are pleased with the profits from the investment and are considering reinvesting so long as there is a reasonable probability of the investment earning similar profits.

a.   Calculate the profits and cash flows earned from the investment.

b.   When considering an investment is it better to consider the profits or cash flows which will result from the investment decision?

6.   **Woodland Nurseries**. The management at Woodland Nurseries are considering investing in more greenhouses. The cost of the new premises is £150,000 and this will be funded out of the firm's free cash flow. The firm's current return on capital employed is 16 per cent and the managers use this as the minimum hurdle rate when evaluating new investments. The forecast cash flows are shown below.

Year	Cash Inflows [£]
One	60,000
Two	85,000
Three	90,000
Four	102,000
Five	108,000

a. Calculate whether the proposed investment can earn a return of 16 per cent.

b. What is meant by the term free cash flow?

c. Why do many firms set a hurdle rate for new investment?

7. **The Chiltern Saw Mill**. During the last year there has been a big increase in the demand for wood, but the directors of the Chiltern Saw Mill have been unable to expand their business because of a lack of industrial capacity. The directors have borrowed £90,000 and are currently considering three different investment projects called A, B and C.

The forecast net cash inflows are shown below. The directors have set the hurdle rate at 10 per cent and can only afford to invest in one project.

Project		A	B	C
		£	£	£
Cash outflows	Year 0	(90,000)	(72,000)	(63,000)
Net cash inflows	Year 1	20,000	25,000	15,000
	Year 2	34,000	33,000	30,000
	Year 3	42,000	39,000	35,000
	Year 4	57,000	45,000	39,000
	Year 5	46,000	47,000	38,500
	Year 6	38,000	42,000	35,000

The directors would like you to calculate

a. the average net inflow

b. the annual depreciation

c. the average net profit

d. the average investment

e. the accounting rate of return

f. the pay back period in months

g. the net present value of each project.

Chapter 25

Valuation of a Business

Introduction

In accounting it is a convention that a business will trade for ever. This is known as the *going concern* concept and it is why a balance sheet is not prepared to reflect the market value of a firm's assets. Instead, the assets are shown at their cost price or valuation, less an allowance for depreciation. Nevertheless, if the owners wish to sell the company or some other party is interested in purchasing it, a value must be placed on the firm's assets.

Reasons for Valuing a Company

There are three reasons why a valuation of a going concern may be sought. Firstly, if a company is quoted on a recognised stock exchange, a would-be purchaser needs to know if the market place reflects the real worth of the business. Similarly, if the directors are seeking a stock exchange listing, an offer price will have to be set for its shares which will reflect its assets and their earnings capability.

Secondly, the owners of a private company may wish to sell their shares and this will necessitate a value being placed upon them. Unlike a public company, whose shares are quoted on a stock exchange, the shares in a private company do not have a market value. In this case there is no market valuation to guide a purchaser, therefore, a valuation must be calculated from the assets which the firm owns and on its ability to generate a return from them.

The last main reason for placing a value on a company's shares occurs during a takeover bid. Once a public company has its shares quoted on a stock exchange, it is possible for another outside party to try to purchase enough shares with the aim of acquiring a holding. This is how one company is able to take over another.

If the takeover bid causes the share price to rise, existing shareholders may be tempted to sell, making an immediate capital gain from their investment. In an attempt to defeat the bid from the would-be predator, the directors may seek to prove that the offer price is unrealistic and that even the higher share price does not reflect the company's true worth, because of the future earnings which its assets can generate. In such a situation it is to be hoped that the existing shareholders will not seek a short-term gain at the expense of a secure long-term return.

Methods of Valuing a Business

The real value of a business lies in its ability to use its assets profitably. An asset is only really worth what it can earn. Just as the market price of a fixed interest bearing bond is reflected by the current market rate of interest, a share price reflects the company's ability to earn a return on the shareholders' investment. As a general rule, the greater the earnings, the higher the share price and, similarly, if profits and earnings decrease, this will be reflected in a falling share price. The share price is, therefore, determined by the laws of supply and demand and will be influenced by investor confidence about projected returns as well as their expectations about future political and economic events.

Ultimately a business must be worth the value of its net assets for they could be liquidated and sold for cash. If this were done, the purchaser would be guaranteed not to lose any money. Once a higher price is paid, the difference must be compensated for by expected future earnings. In accounting the difference is called *goodwill*.

Value of Fixed and Current Assets £15,000	Amount of money paid to purchase the assets of the business £20,000
Goodwill £5,000	

Figure 25:1 How Goodwill is Calculated

Goodwill is treated as an intangible fixed asset and is shown in the acquiring company's balance sheet. By valuing the difference between the market value of the assets and the amount paid for them as goodwill, the total liabilities will equal the total assets in the balance sheet.

Methods of Valuing a Firm

There are four main ways of assessing the value of a business. Ultimately it is only worth what someone will pay for it, but the would-be purchaser needs some guidance as to its true worth. The following methods are used for assessment purposes for they provide a guide to the offer price which is likely to prove acceptable to the seller.

Method One: Stock Market Valuation Method

If shares are quoted on the stock market, the market valuation of the company will be the share price multiplied by the number of issued ordinary shares. For instance, if a company has 500,000 ordinary £1 shares with a market price of £2 per share, the company's market valuation will be £1,000,000. This does not mean that the business has assets worth one million pounds, but it does reflect the price which investors are prepared to pay for its shares. This will be influenced by the assets, investor confidence about the economy and the future earnings potential of the business. As the share price rises and falls, so does its market capitalisation. If the capital markets are efficient, then the share price will reflect all available information, and so the share price represents a correct valuation of the business. In such cases the investment will yield a zero net present value. The stock markets, however, are not perfectly efficient and so there will be times when the market price may overvalue or undervalue the business. It is then useful to use other methods of valuation which can assess the market valuation. A would-be purchaser will always have to offer a higher price than the market price, otherwise there is no financial incentive for the owner to sell the shares. This is why the share price rises during a takeover bid and generally falls when the bid fails. The purchase price, however, must allow the buyer to earn a positive net present value on the investment, if the acquiring company is to increase shareholder wealth.

Method Two: Valuation of Assets Method

In theory a company must be worth the value of its assets. If a business can be bought for just its asset value, no premium has to be paid for its earnings potential. This is why it is always cheaper to purchase a firm which has gone into liquidation than one which is currently trading. The business which has been forced to stop trading is only worth the value of its assets, while the going concern is worth its assets plus a certain amount for its future earnings potential. This is best illustrated by looking at an example.

Example

The Hotel Beautiful Isle is an established company. It is not quoted on a recognised stock market, therefore, there is no market valuation to guide a would-be purchaser. The lowest valuation of the Hotel Beautiful Isle must be the market value of its assets. Let us assume in this example that, at the time of preparing the last balance sheet, the owners declared that they no longer intended to continue running the business. As a result the assets were revalued and so, unusually, the balance sheet reflects its market valuation.

The Hotel Beautiful Isle Balance Sheet as at 5 April Year 6

Fixed Assets	Cost Valuation £'000	Depreciation to Date £'000		NBV £'000
Freehold Property	450	-		450
Fixtures and Fittings	125	25		100
Motor Vehicles	50	10		40
	625	35		590
Current Assets				
Stock		50		
Debtors		30		
Bank		40	120	
Less Liabilities (12 months)				
Creditors		20		
Taxation		15	35	
				85
Working Capital				675
Liabilities due after 12 months				
Bank term loan 12% 2015			50	50
Net Assets				625
Financed by				
350,000 Ordinary £1 shares issued and fully paid				350
50,000 £1 9% Preference Shares				50
Revaluation Reserve				100
Retained Profit				125
Shareholders' Funds				625

Notes to the accounts: The Hotel Beautiful Isle's earnings after tax over the last 5 years have been:

Year	£'000
One	80
Two	120
Three	90
Four	110
Five	115

The average return on capital for hotels in this sector is 12 per cent and the average earnings yield is 15 per cent. The yield on comparable preference shares is 7 per cent.

How to Calculate the Value of the Business

The assets of the business are shown under the headings Fixed Assets and Current Assets. These show the long-term and short-term assets. If the firm had no liabilities, the value of the fixed and current assets would be the value of the business. This is unlikely to be the case because most firms finance some of their assets by borrowing, allowing them to increase their assets and earnings potential.

By subtracting the liabilities from the total asset figure, the net assets of the business can be calculated. If the number of ordinary shares is then divided into the net asset valuation the asset backing per share can be calculated. In our example this is done as follows:

Method of calculating the asset valuation of the Hotel Beautiful Isle

Fixed Assets plus Current Assets = Total Assets

Total Assets less Liabilities = Net Assets

$$\frac{\text{Net Assets}}{\text{Number of ordinary shares}} = \text{Asset backing per share}$$

Using the figures in the example this can be seen to be:

$$\frac{\text{Net Assets}}{\text{Number of ordinary shares}} \quad \frac{£625,000}{350,000} = £1.79 \text{ (approx.)}$$

383

This means that each share represents £1.79 of the firm's total assets and is referred to as the *asset backing per share.*

This is the lowest possible valuation of the hotel as it does not take into account future earnings potential. What is needed, therefore, is a valuation which does take this into account.

Method Three: Valuation of Goodwill

The accounts show that every year the hotel generates a profit from its assets. The profits in our example are erratic in that they go up and down and, therefore, some way must be found of calculating the hotel's average profit. The simplest method is to calculate the simple average by adding up the total profit and then dividing it by the number of years. If the firm enjoys a steadily increasing profit, it may be more appropriate to use a weighted average.

Whichever method is used, an average profit must be calculated. We have already seen (Chapter 11: Interpreting Financial Statements) that data is available from analysts about the average return earned by companies operating within a sector. It is now necessary to compare the return which the hotel can earn from its own capital with that earned by the rest of the industry. If the return from the hotel's capital is higher, the purchase price will reflect this. The amount paid over the asset value is called *goodwill* and is really compensation to the owners in the form of a capital sum for the future earnings potential of the business.

Valuation of the Hotel Beautiful Isle's Goodwill

The first task is to calculate the average profit. This can be done by calculating the mean profit, i.e. adding up the five years' profit and dividing it by the number of years.

Calculation of the Average Profit

Year	£				
One	80,000				
Two	120,000	Total Profit	£515,000	=	£103,000 Average Profit
Three	90,000	Years	5		
Four	110,000				
Five	115,000				
	515,000				

Once the average profit has been calculated, any preference dividends paid and investment income earned must be deducted. This is because preference shares are regarded as being akin to debt capital as they pay a fixed rate of dividend, and so the amount is deducted from the average profit. Investment income is deducted because it does not reflect profits earned from the firm's trading assets.

	£
Average Profit	103,000
Less Preference Dividend (9% of £50,000)	4,500
Less Investment Income (if applicable)	-
Average maintainable profit	98,500

The last stage is to calculate whether or not the hotel can earn bigger profits than those earned by similar companies. If it can, the extra profit is called *super profits*. By applying a formula the super profits can be capitalised, thereby calculating the goodwill.

Calculation of Super Profits

	£
Average maintainable profit	98,500
Less revenue which trading assets should earn (£625,000 x 12%)	75,000
Super profits	23,500

$$\text{Goodwill} = \frac{\text{Super Profits} \times 100}{\text{Average return on capital in similar companies}} = \frac{23,500 \times 100}{12\%} = £195,833 \text{ (Goodwill)}$$

Value of the Business

	£
Net tangible trading assets	625,000
Add goodwill	195,833
Total tangible and intangible assets	820,833

VALUATION OF A BUSINESS

Value per share   = $\dfrac{\text{Total tangible and intangible assets}}{\text{Number of ordinary shares}}$

= $\dfrac{£820,833}{350,000}$ = £2.35

Method Four: Valuation of Earnings

This method seeks to value the business' future earnings by capitalising the earnings yield. This is done by the formula:

$\dfrac{\text{Average Profit x 100}}{\begin{array}{c}\text{Earning yield on ordinary}\\\text{shares in similar companies}\end{array}}$ = $\dfrac{£98,500 \times 100}{15}$ = £656,667

By dividing the capitalised value by the number of shares, a value can be placed on the firm's future earnings potential. The formula is:

$\dfrac{\text{Capitalised earnings value}}{\text{Number of ordinary shares}}$ $\dfrac{£656,667}{350,000}$ = £1.88 per share

The value of a preference share is similarly based upon what it can earn. If the fixed dividend payable is higher than the industry average, the value of the share will be higher than its nominal value. If the return is lower, the value will be less. The formula is:

Value = $\dfrac{\text{Nominal value x dividend payable}}{\text{Average dividend in the industry}}$ = $\dfrac{£1 \times 9p}{7p}$ = £1.29

Evaluating a Company's Worth

The four methods which have been outlined provide a guide as to a company's value. The purchaser will determine its value by offering a price which is acceptable to the seller for, until this happens, no one knows the true market value of any asset. The methods of valuing a business seek to assess the true worth of the assets by placing a value on them and on their earnings potential. By doing this the price offered should be both realistic and affordable to the acquiring company. There is always a danger that, if a price is paid which is in excess of the asset value and the earnings potential, the purchase may prove to be an expensive white elephant incapable of earning the expected return.

Financing the Purchase

There are three possible ways of financing a takeover. The most expensive method is a cash offer for the shares, which will probably necessitate raising additional loans or will run down cash reserves. In many cases existing owners seek cash bids and are not prepared to accept any other form of paper financial security as consideration for the purchase price.

If the purchase can be financed by offering some form of paper financial security, such as an offer of shares or some form of loan stock, the cost can be spread over several years. This will not only help the cash flow position, but also give the firm the chance to pay for the acquisition out of earnings. This can be done in one of two ways. Firstly, the purchaser could offer an exchange of shares based on some agreed weighting. This is likely to be acceptable if the acquiring company is a household name with a high share price which is likely to increase in value in the coming years.

Another method of financing the purchase is to offer the seller some form of fixed interest security, such as a debenture, or by borrowing the finance from a bank or finance house and then paying the cash to the seller. In either case the acquiring business will be increasing its debt capital so it must be able to service the additional debt interest payments out of future earnings.

The Dangers of Growth by Acquisition

There is always a danger that the acquiring company may pay too high a price for the assets, based upon an over-optimistic valuation of asset values and future earnings. This problem is often particularly acute during a boom when people's expectations about future values exceed realistic returns. Ultimately, the boom ends, with a fall in asset values leaving many purchasers saddled with over-valued assets, coupled with a mounting debt burden which has been used to finance the purchase. If earnings fall, the burden of servicing the debt can force an otherwise successful business into liquidation or force it to dispose of assets at unrealistic prices, as it struggles to raise cash to meet interest and debt repayments.

VALUATION OF A BUSINESS

The aim of these valuation methods, coupled with investment appraisal techniques, is to lessen the likelihood of overvaluing an asset. Earnings can never be guaranteed and, if the cost of the asset is high in relation to its earnings, potential investors should be cautious about investing. In the end an asset is only worth what it can earn and this is why the projected future earnings should be discounted at the firm's appropriate cost of capital, to see whether or not the proposed investment can yield a positive net present value.

QUESTIONS

Answers begin page 505

1. **Artistic Lights**. The company manufacture stage lighting. Over the years they have built a good reputation and the directors have asked you to:
   a.   value the company's asset backing per share, and
   b.   value its goodwill.

The relevant extracts from the company's accounts are shown below.

Balance Sheet of Artistic Lights as at 10th March Year 25

Fixed Assets	Cost [£]	Depreciation to date [£]	Net Book Value [£]
Land and Buildings	150,000	-	150,000
Fixtures & Fittings	40,000	5,000	35,000
Plant & Machinery	90,000	15,000	75,000
	280,000	20,000	260,000
Current Assets			
Raw Materials		40,000	
Work In Progress		60,000	
Finished Goods		25,000	
Debtors		35,000	
Bank		40,000	
		200,000	
Current Liabilities			
Creditors		80,000	
Working Capital			120,000
Net Assets			380,000
Financed By			
300,000 £1 Ord. Shares			
Issued and fully paid			300,000
General Reserve			50,000
Profit and Loss			30,000
Shareholders' Funds			380,000

Notes to the Accounts:
1. Harlequin Enterprises' earnings after tax, over the last five years have been £40,000, £55,000, £72,000, £67,000, £64,000.

2. All assets shown in the balance sheet reflect their current value except debtors. The firm has decided to provide a provision of 4 per cent for bad debts.

3. The average return for companies operating in this sector is 11 per cent.

389

2.   **The Original Postcard Company**. For over sixty years the company has marketed a range of postcards depicting some of Britain's finest scenery. The firm is still owned by the founding family. They have recently received an enquiry from a public company, but are not certain whether or not to accept the offer. The public company has offered £80,000 in cash plus £40,000 10 per cent loan stock 2010 and 80,000 £1 shares, which are currently valued on the Stock Market at £1.76. You have been asked to advise the owners of the Original Postcard Company as to its value.

Balance Sheet of The Original Postcard Company
as at the 10th March Year 25

Fixed Assets	Cost [£]	Depreciation to Date [£]	Net Book Value [£]
Land and Buildings	80,000	-	80,000
Fixtures and Fittings	20,000	5,000	15,000
Plant and Machinery	30,000	10,000	20,000
	130,000	15,000	115,000
Current Assets			
Raw Materials		12,000	
Work In Progress		20,000	
Finished Goods		30,000	
Debtors		40,000	
Bank		20,000	
		122,000	
Current Liabilities			
Creditors		60,000	
Working Capital			62,000
Net Assets			177,000
Financed By			
100,000 £1 Ord. Shares			
Issued and fully paid			100,000
General Reserve			40,000
Profit and Loss			37,000
Shareholders' Funds			177,000

Notes to the Accounts

1. The company's earnings after tax, over the last six years, have been £25,000, £30,000, £18,000, £30,000, £44,000 and £57,000.
2. The fixed assets shown in the balance sheet are not shown at market value. Land and buildings has been revalued at £120,000. The directors of the company would keep any bank balances.
3. The average return for companies operating in this sector is 9 per cent and the average earnings yield is 11 per cent.

Chapter 26

Working Capital

Introduction

Working capital is the term used to describe a firm's short-term use of funds. Part of the firm's capital will be locked away in fixed assets, but a certain sum must be left aside to finance the day-to-day business expenses. Money is needed to pay the wages, to purchase stock and to finance credit sales. If the firm lacks sufficient working capital to meet its short-term obligations, it will be unable to continue trading and so the management of the working capital cycle is very important. Indeed the long-term survival and growth of the firm is dependent upon management developing effective policies for controlling and monitoring working capital. Working capital comprises a high proportion of total assets for all firms but, as a general rule, it is higher for wholesaling and retailing than it is for manufacturing businesses.

The Working Capital Cycle

Imagine a business trader who purchases stock for cash and sells it in a market for cash. The trader must ensure that s/he has sufficient cash balances to meet all the expenses of the business, such as the cost of the stall, and sufficient investment in stock to attract customers. If the trader finds that in one month s/he is short of cash, additional stock will not be purchased and gradually the cash receipts from sales will improve the business' cash position. The working capital cycle is shown in the diagram below.

Figure 26:1 The effect of Credit on the Working Capital Cycle

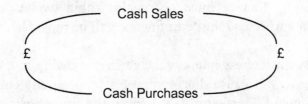

There are very few firms which only buy and sell for cash. Most transactions are done on credit which means that the buyer has a small period of time before the goods or service has to be paid for. As a result two new factors must be considered. These are time and money. The aim is to take longer to pay one's creditors and to receive payments from debtors as quickly as possible. Any delay in the cycle will mean that the firm risks not having sufficient cash deposits to meet its own liabilities. This new situation is shown below.

Figure 26:2 The introduction of Credit into the Working Capital Cycle

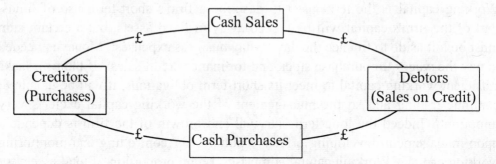

Figure 26:2, above, illustrates a firm's trading cycle which involves purchasing stock or raw materials, making a product (if applicable) and selling it.

Effective working capital management involves the appraisal and monitoring of two key components of a firm's net current assets (current assets less current liabilities). These are, firstly, the firm's total investment in current assets and the amount of money currently held in stock, debtors and bank and cash balances. Secondly, the ratio of the firm's short-term debt (current liabilities) to its long-term debt. The more short-term debt a firm has the greater the need for liquidity.

The Dangers of Using Short-term Finance

Accountants distinguish between short and long-term sources of finance. The difference between the two is in the time in which the borrowed funds must be repaid. Short-term finance must be repaid within twelve months from the balance sheet date whereas long-term finance will be repaid later than one year.

There is usually an interest rate advantage in borrowing money short-term as opposed to long-term because short-term rates are generally cheaper. However, excessive amounts of short-term debt expose the firm to greater risks. Long-term debt usually has a fixed rate of interest attached to it and so temporary upward fluctuation in interest rates do not affect cash flow. Short-term debt will generally be subject to a variable interest rate and so changes in rates will directly affect both costs and cash flow. Many firms later discover, to their dismay, that what they could afford at one rate of interest has suddenly become an enormous financial burden once rates rise. Often additional credit sources have to be used to finance these interest charges, such as bank overdrafts, which push businesses further into debt, thereby damaging their cash flow and liquidity.

Governments also use interest rates to regulate the level of activity within the economy. A rise in rates usually signals a slow-down in economic activity making it harder for businesses to sell their goods and services. When this happens sales decrease, which leads to a rise in stock levels, and the end result is a deterioration in the firm's liquidity levels.

The Management of Working Capital

Accountants define working capital as the difference between the current assets and current liabilities of a business. The manager's role is to ensure that the firm has sufficient current assets in order to meet its day-to-day financial obligations. The amount of money invested in current assets will depend upon the type of business which the firm is engaged in. For instance many service industries, such as hairdressing and small restaurants, need only a small amount of stock. Also most of the sales are for cash and so, in theory, they should not experience the same working capital problems as manufacturing businesses which need to keep large investments in stocks and to sell nearly all of their products on credit. The control of working capital is important because, generally, current assets represent sixty per cent of the total assets of any business. Unlike fixed assets, current assets are continually changing. Stock is constantly being sold and bought and the investment in debtors is constantly changing as the firm sells and collects it debts. As a result most firms have the majority of their assets in a very volatile form and so this area of the business needs constant attention.

Many small businesses find it difficult to raise long-term capital to finance their capital investment programmes. As a result the owners seek to minimise their investment in fixed assets and enter into hire and leasing agreements as the assets can be acquired without having to pay for them immediately. While it can be argued that the use of assets is more important than their ownership, this form of finance often causes cash flow problems because of the high interest rates charged by the hiring or leasing company. Inevitably this increases the risk of running the business and accounts for more than its fair share of business failures. It should be remembered that many firms are forced into liquidation, not because they are unprofitable, but because they simply do not have sufficient cash to meet their day to day expenses.

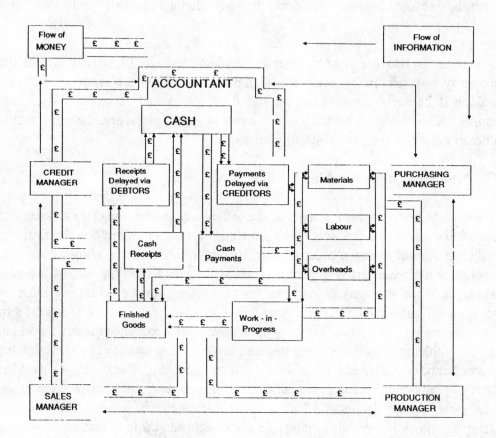

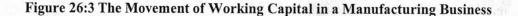

Figure 26:3 The Movement of Working Capital in a Manufacturing Business

The Perils of Lack of Control

The art of managing working capital is to control two variables, time and money. As far as time is concerned, it is necessary for money to flow from cash through stocks and from stocks through debtors so that it comes back again as cash as quickly as possible. Payment to creditors should be delayed for as long as reasonably possible so that the minimum amount of cash is tied up in stocks and debtors whilst maximising the amount of funds from creditors. In this way creditors provide short-term interest-free finance while the firm's own money is working hard to earn profits.

In many firms this situation does not occur. Instead of minimising the investment in stock and debtors, large amounts of cash are tied up in stock. This involves the firm in additional costs, as often it has to be financed by using expensive bank loans and there is always the danger of loss from pilferage, deterioration and obsolescence. Similarly, if large amounts of money are owed to it, the firm is being denied the use of its own funds. In effect it is making an interest-free loan to other businesses and, all the time that it waits for payment, it is running the risk of the debtors being unable to pay and bad debts being incurred which will reduce profits and cash flow.

The Benefits of Controlling Working Capital

If the working capital cycle can be controlled effectively, there will be an increase in profits. The less cash tied up in stock and debtors the more interest which can be earned by investing the money in short-term interest bearing deposits. Similarly, if overdraft finance is required, the amount of borrowed finance can be kept to a minimum, thereby minimising interest charges.

By controlling the amount of working capital it becomes possible to support more sales with the same amount of capital.

Once a firm can reduce the amount of capital it needs to generate each £ of sales, it can reduce the chances of overtrading by taking on more business than it is able to support with its available finances. If this situation occurs the firm is said to be overtrading and, once this happens, there are constant cash flow problems as the firm struggles to finance its day to day running expenses.

The Optimum Level of Working Capital

As a general rule, the more money a firm has invested in its net working capital, the greater the probability that it will be able to meet all of its short-term liabilities as and when they fall due. The optimum level of working capital is one which enables a business to increase its overall profitability without increasing the level of risk to an investor, because the firm has reduced its investment in net working capital. A firm's optimum level of working capital can only be determined by consulting:

1. The firm's current and future cash operating cycle.
2. The current level of sales and predicted sales.
3. How seasonal sales alter the firm's overall working capital position.
4. The firm's stock holding policies.
5. The firm's credit policies.
6. The current and forecast level of interest rates.
7. The firm's current credit rating.

This can be seen in the following example. Southwood Industries is considering expanding its sales during the coming year but the management are worried how this will affect the firm's working capital and profit margins. They have given you the following information:

	Present Position £	Budgeted Position £
Sales	120,000	170,000
Cost of goods sold	100,000	144,500
Purchases	66,000	99,000
Debtors	16,500	19,800
Creditors	9,200	22,000
Raw materials	16,800	32,000
Work in Progress	8,400	15,300
Finished goods	19,200	28,900

Calculation of Southwood Industries' Working Capital

	Present Position £	Budgeted Position £
Raw materials	16,800	32,000
Work in progress	8,400	15,300
Finished goods	19,200	28,900
Debtors	16,500	19,800
	60,900	96,000
Less Creditors	9,200	22,000
Working Capital	51,700	74,000

Calculation of Working Capital required to generate each £1 of sales

Working Capital   £51,700   = 43 p   £74,000   = 44p

Sales   £120,000   £170,000

Calculation of Profit Margin

Profit x 100   £120,000 - £100,000 x 100   £170,000 - £146500 x 100

Sales   £120,000   £170,000

                 = 17 per cent   = 14 per cent

Note: If actual sales are the same as budgeted sales, the company has succeeded in increasing the level of sales in a way which places no additional pressure on its working capital, but has had to reduce its profit margins to gain this new level of sales.

The Need for Forecasting and Communication

In order to control the working capital cycle, forecasts must be prepared so that future investments in stock and debtors can be determined. Good forecasting always starts by looking at the projected sales as this will determine both the firm's income and stock levels. In large companies the sales director will have this information and, from it, a production plan can be drawn up. Once this has been done, a production schedule can be ascertained so that the purchasing department can fix the minimum, maximum and re-order levels for stocks.

Once the sales, production and buying plans have been agreed, the next step is to calculate how much cash will be required to finance this estimated level of activity. The credit controller can then assess when customers are likely to pay for the goods, thereby allowing the accountant to determine how and when to pay the creditors. The whole financial picture can then be put together into a cash budget which is described in chapter 22.

It is essential for all managers involved in the working capital cycle to communicate with each other. The purchasing department cannot fix the minimum, maximum and re-order stock levels until the production forecasts and sales budgets have been determined, and the purchasing department needs up-to-date information from the production department to enable it to monitor stock levels constantly.

WORKING CAPITAL

Good planning and communication are the key to effective control of working capital in any business, because it is impossible to synchronise cash inflows and cash flows. This is why the firm must build a margin of safety into working capital positions. Regular meetings should be held where all the main participants can discuss the current levels of activity as these will all affect the firm's cash flows. If the level of business trading deviates from the budgeted level, the firm will experience working capital problems. For example, if a firm collects all its debts in thirty days and has credit sales of £1,000 per day at the end of a month it will be owed £30,000 from its debtors. If sales rise to £2,000 per day, its debtors will rise to £60,000, and so the business will need double the amount of money to finance its working capital requirements. This is why any deviation from the budgeted level of activity needs to be reported to management immediately, otherwise the firm may well find that its working capital requirements are insufficient. If unchecked, this could damage the financial reputation and solvency of the business.

QUESTIONS

Answers begin page 507

1. Calculate each hospital's working capital from the information given below:

	£	£	£	£
Firm	**A**	**B**	**C**	**D**
Current assets	43,000	37,000	22,500	18,000
Current liabilities	18,000	17,000	11,300	8,000
Working capital				

2. **Medical Supplies**. This company manufactures medical equipment and has enjoyed a rapid growth in sales, but has experienced cash flow difficulties and has, therefore, increased its overdraft facility at the bank. The owners cannot understand why the firm is so short of cash and have supplied the following information asking you to calculate the firm's cash operating cycle.

	Last Year £	This Year £
Sales	600,000	690,000
Cost of sales	504,000	594,000
Purchases	336,000	408,000
Debtors	75,000	114,000
Creditors	48,000	72,000
Stock of raw materials	84,000	144,000
Work in progress	42,000	72,000
Finished stock	96,000	102,000

3. **The Griffin Glass Company**. This company manufactures a range of glass bottles which are sold to hospitals. The company has just had its best year ever and has been so successful that, to keep pace with demand, new workers have been recruited and an extension has had to be built. The directors cannot understand why, when trade is so good, the firm is short of cash and is constantly in overdraft. You have been given the following information and have been asked to prepare the firm's cash

399

operating statement, together with a brief report outlining why the firm is so short of cash.

	Last Year £	This Year £
Sales	500,000	820,000
Cost of sales	350,000	660,000
Purchases	180,000	270,000
Debtors	50,000	134,000
Creditors	25,000	80,000
Stock of raw materials	60,000	125,000
Work in progress	35,000	66,000
Finished stock	48,000	78,000

4. **The Whole Wheat Bakery**. This company was started three years ago by Mr and Mrs Prescott who believed that there was a market for bread baked with organically-grown flour. The firm has been successful supplying both retail and catering companies.

For the last three months the firm has been in overdraft and each month the overdraft figure increases. Mr and Mrs Prescott cannot understand how this can be the case. The firm is selling 20 per cent more than the same quarter last year and credit sales to companies are up 14 per cent. Unfortunately the firm's cash shortage has led to problems in paying suppliers and many are now demanding cash with orders.

The owners have received a letter from their bank manager warning them that the firm must not exceed its overdraft position and inviting Mr and Mrs Prescott to visit the manager to discuss the current working capital problems. Mrs and Mrs Prescott have sought your advice and have asked the following questions.

a. What is working capital?

b. How can a profitable firm be short of cash?

c. What action should the firm take to improve its cash flow?

Chapter 27

Managing Current Assets

Introduction

Current assets are of a circulating nature. Unlike fixed assets they are constantly changing and it is by using these assets effectively that profit will be made. They are recorded in the balance sheet according to how quickly they can be turned into cash. The quicker an asset can be turned into cash the more liquid it is said to be. Stock is the most illiquid and so it is shown first. Debtors are shown next. This chapter is concerned with the effective management of stock and debtors. Cash management is explained in chapter 28.

The Need for Effective Management

Current assets are very volatile assets. Stock may become obsolete or deteriorate. Debtors may not be able to pay and idle cash bank balances have an opportunity cost for they could be either earning interest or be invested in the business. The more effectively a firm can use its current assets the greater its profitability. The amount of capital tied up in stock, debtors and cash needs to be constantly monitored, ensuring that the highest return on capital can be achieved.

The Management of Stock

Most people think of stock as goods for resale. In shops they see lines of merchandise waiting to be bought. The retailer's aim is to achieve the greatest level of sales from each square metre of floor space and to ensure that the shop is fully stocked.

In a manufacturing business stock is not just the finished goods being produced. The factory will have had to purchase raw materials and it will also have goods which are not yet completed. This work is called work in progress and, until it is finished, it cannot be sold. During the manufacturing process it is still stock but, unlike the retailer's stock, it will be impossible to sell until finished.

All stock has to be financed and, until it is sold, it soaks up the firm's precious cash reserves. The quicker the firm can produce and sell the goods, the quicker the cash can be released to purchase more stock, allowing the business to earn more profit.

The Need for Efficient Stock Control

Inefficient stock control policies reduce a firm's profitability and cash resources. Stock-holding costs can account for a large percentage of operating costs. These costs are often called *stock carrying costs* and include storage and handling costs, insurance, theft, obsolescence and stock deterioration. In addition there is the opportunity cost in that money tied up in unsold stock cannot be invested in more profitable projects.

In some businesses if you are out of stock the sale will be lost forever. Imagine a restaurant which has under ordered and cannot now serve certain meals. Customers cannot wait until a new order has been placed and so they may well choose to eat elsewhere. Similarly, there is no point in having stock which will not sell taking up valuable shelf space. It is far better to sell it a reduced price and invest that money in stock which will sell.

Accounting for Stock Control

A system must be designed to account for material costs and it is essential that management set up a procedure for collecting such costs as quickly and accurately as possible. This information will be needed so that costs can be determined but also to minimise the costs of holding stocks. Any reduction in stock levels which are not offset by the added costs of being out of stock will increase the firm's profitability and cash flow.

Money will also be wasted if too little stock is held. Apart from lost sales, the business will experience higher stock ordering costs and may also lose money if production has to be halted because of a lack of components or raw materials. Materials control procedures are designed to optimise a firm's investment in stock by determining economic order quantities and by setting stock levels.

The Economic Order Quantity

This is the quantity of material that should be ordered so that the cost of ordering, together with the cost of stock-holding, is minimised. The economic order quantity can be presented as a graph or calculated by using the formula:

$$EOQ = \sqrt{\frac{2MO}{C}}$$

where   M   =   Materials required
           O   =   Cost of placing order
           C   =   Stock holding cost per unit of stock.

Example

A gift shop knows that each month it sells 5,000 glass vases. The cost of placing the order is £18 and the cost of holding one vase for a year is £2. The shop's optimum order size is:

$$EOQ = \sqrt{\frac{2 \times 5000 \times 18}{2}} = 300$$

In order to minimise stock holding costs the shop should place orders for 300 vases. While the model is useful it should be remembered that the amount of stock held must take account of seasonal fluctuations. Most businesses experience seasonal demand and, if they stick rigidly to the model, they may occasionally be out of stock. The past sales records should be looked at before deciding how much buffer stock should be held to prevent lost sales caused by being temporarily out of stock.

The model shows that while some of the costs associated with holding stock, such as insurance and storage, will decline as stock holdings increase, other costs, such as theft, waste and obsolescence, will increase as stock holdings rise. The difference in these two costs will tend to balance each other and it is assumed that the total holding cost of stock is constant but that stock holding costs will increase proportionally to the rate of increase in stock held. Whilst this is true for traditional manufacturing companies, high tech manufacturers have found that these costs have increased greatly.

The major limitation of the EOQ model is that it does not take account of all the relevant costs in placing an order, such as quantity discounts or the total purchase price. Finally, the model assumes that usage is linear, but seasonal and demand changes may make the model curvilinear.

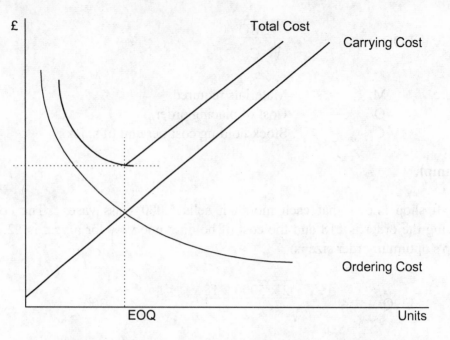

Figure 27:1 Graphical Presentation of Economic Order Quantity

These limitations, together with the introduction of Just in Time stock control systems which have reduced ordering costs, has meant that materials requirements planning (MRP) requires computer technology which can formulate models which include all of the important variables.

Stock Control Techniques

It is possible to ensure that stock levels are kept to their optimum for day-to-day trading by setting the following stock levels according to usage and the time taken to order new stocks, which is called *lead time*.

Re-order level: This is the level below which stock levels must not fall. The formula for calculating re-order level is:

Re-order level = Maximum Usage x Maximum Lead Time

Minimum Stock Level: This is the minimum amount of stock which must be held and it is an amount just below the re-order level. Once this level is reached, stock must be obtained quickly if production is not to be halted by a shortage of raw materials. The formula is:

Minimum Stock Level = Re-order Level - (Average Usage x Average Lead Time)

Maximum Stock Level: This is the maximum level of stock which should be held. The formula is:

Maximum Stock Level = Re-order level - (Minimum Usage x Minimum Lead Time) + Re-order Quantity

Average Stock Level:

Average Stock Level = Minimum Stock Level + ½ Re-order Quantity

The use of formula in stock control is shown in the next example.

Example

The Efficient Marketing Company

The managers at the Efficient Marketing Company have been assessing their stock levels. They predict the following usage:

	Units
January	300
February	300
March	500
April	600
May	800
June	1000
July	1000
August	1000
September	1000
October	900
November	600
December	400

The management has set the re-order quantity at 2000 units and the delivery times are as follows:

Maximum Delivery Time	4 weeks
Average Delivery Time	3 weeks
Minimum Delivery Time	2 weeks

Calculate the firm's re-order, maximum stock level, minimum stock level and average stock level for the next twelve months.

Re-order Level = Maximum Usage x Minimum Lead Time

1000 x 4 = 4000 units

Maximum Level = Re-order Level - (Minimum Usage x Minimum Lead Time) + Re-order Quantity

4000 - (300 x 2) + 2000 = 5400 units

Minimum Level = Re-order Level - (Average Usage x Average Lead Time)

4000 - (700 x 3) = 1900 units

Average Stock Level = Minimum Stock Level + ½ Re-Order Quantity

$$1900 + \frac{1}{2} \text{ROQ} \quad \frac{2000}{2} = 1000 = 2900 \text{ units}$$

The Just in Time Method of Stock Control

If a company can receive the stock it needs from suppliers as it is needed on the production line, it can eliminate its stock holding costs. The method was first developed by Toyota in Japan and is best suited to repetitive production processes, such as car assembly. Any delay is very expensive because in a just in time system the firm carries no buffer or safety stocks, and so production is halted. If this a frequent occurrence, then the costs of lost production can soon exceed the gains from reduced stock holding costs. This is why many firms which operate a just in time system of stock control still keep small buffer stocks, giving rise to the term *just in case* instead of just in time.

The Management of Debtors

When goods are sold on credit the purchasers are recorded as debtors. They are treated as short-term assets because it is expected that they will pay the amount they owe soon. There are three main reasons why firms sell on credit. Firstly, it enables a business to increase its sales because the buyer does not have to pay immediately. Indeed a firm's level of sales is often dependent upon the terms and amount of credit which it is prepared to give. Secondly, credit allows the buyer to inspect the goods and gives time for any faults or problems to be rectified before payment is made. Finally, collecting payment at the time of sale or delivery would be expensive as delivery vehicles would have to be fitted with security features to enable them to hold such large amounts of money.

Whenever credit is granted to a buyer, there is always some risk that the firm will not receive payment and, while it is owed, the seller is helping to finance the buyer's business. This is why a firm's investment in debtors should be kept to a minimum because the opportunity cost of this money is the return which it could earn should it be invested elsewhere.

The Firm's Credit Policy

Trade credit is one of the largest sources of short-term debt finance available to industry and commerce. As with any loan the granter of credit is lending a sum certain in return for a sum uncertain. This is why the decision to grant trade credit should be thought of as any other investment decision. The aim is to find debtors who are a good credit risk and who place large orders and pay regularly. A good credit policy is one which will increase the firm's level of sales without exposing it to the risk of large losses from bad debts.

Establishing a credit policy is expensive. Accounts must be opened for all customers and new accounts must be checked to see that the applicants are credit worthy. Managers must set credit standards and terms for all customers and then decide what level of the firm's resources are to be deployed into chasing overdue debts.

Granting Trade Credit

In most cases established customers will have a good credit rating. The fact that these debtors have in the past paid on time means that there is a reasonable probability that they will continue to do so. This means that the most important decisions are ones which must be made about new customers.

Large firms usually employ a credit manager whose job it is to assess the credit worthiness of each applicant. There is a large amount of information which can be used to assess the financial standing of any applicant. The credit manager may ask for a copy of the customer's latest accounts, a reference from another trade supplier, a bank reference or a report from a credit rating agency or all of these. The checking and collection of all this information is expensive and so the firm should begin by using the cheapest and most available sources. Ideally a decision should never be taken on the basis of one piece of information because it does not allow the granter of credit to build up a complete profile of the buyer's credit worthiness.

Credit managers often use what is called the *five C's* of credit management. It is generally accepted that the first two are the most important but credit should only be granted if the applicant can meet all of the criteria. The five C's refer to the applicant's character, capacity, capital, collateral and willingness to comply with the conditions which are attached to the granting of credit.

Monitoring Debtor Balances

Most credit managers state that their aim is to take two months' credit from their suppliers, whilst giving only one month's credit to their purchasers. If this can be achieved, the firm will have a very effective credit control policy but, in reality, it will depend on the type of business the firm is in, the size of the company and the general level of liquidity within the economy. If the monetary authorities are seeking to restrict credit within the economy, they usually raise interest rates to restrict the availability of bank credit. This has the effect of tightening all firms' credit control policies, making it harder to use supplier credit as a form of short-term finance.

Credit is an important marketing variable. Sometimes contracts can only be won by offering credit terms which are as good or better than competitors. This can put a large strain on any firm's working capital because increased credit terms will lengthen the cash operating cycle. Many a firm has been forced into financial problems because it could not pay its own bills because other people would not pay theirs.

Small firms often consider selling their invoices to a factoring house. Factoring houses are financial institutions which are prepared to lend money on a firm's invoices. The factor will charge a basic commission on the firm's level of sales and then advance a set percentage of the invoice value. It is even possible to seek facilities which protect the firm from the risk of bad debts. Factoring is an expensive form of finance and is generally more expensive than a bank overdraft. This cost can sometimes be offset by savings in credit control but, despite its cost, factoring is often used by small fast growing business who are constantly short of cash.

Whenever interest rates rise credit controllers find it harder to collect money owed. Firms with money try to maximise their interest earnings while others try to juggle their payments to conserve their cash resources. The higher the level of interest rates, the more vigilant a firm must be in its credit control policy and the greater the opportunity cost of investing in debtors.

Long delays in payment are often the first signs that a debtor is in financial trouble and the longer a debt remains unpaid the greater the probability that it will never be paid. This is why the firms should employ two precautionary devices when selling goods on credit. Firstly, all invoices should carry a printed warning that goods remain the property of the seller until paid for and, secondly, sales staff should only be paid commission once the debtor has settled the account.

A firm should continually appraise and monitor its credit policy so that the risks and returns from granting credit can be assessed, for any sudden increase in bad debts will adversely affect its liquidity.

QUESTIONS

Answers begin page 510

1. **Auto Factors**

Auto Factors is a small motor accessory shop which sells to the general public and the trade. Its best-selling line is filters. The firm is currently setting its stock levels for the coming year. The manager has asked you to calculate:

a.   the re-order level, maximum, minimum and average stock level for oil filters.

b.   the shop's stock turnover rate for oil filters.

Budgeted Sales

Month	Spark Plugs
January	1000
February	1400
March	1300
April	1600
May	1700
June	2200
July	1800
August	1900
September	1450
October	1550
November	1670
December	1200

Delivery Period	Spark Plugs [weeks]
Maximum	3
Average	2
Minimum	1
Re-order quantity	500

2. Johnstone Building Supplies

The company has just prepared its sales budget for the next five months. The budgeted sales are:

	£
July	50,400
August	52,920
September	57,960
October	60,480
November	65,520

The Sales Director believes that 10 per cent of the sales will be for cash, that two thirds of credit sales are paid for in the month after sale and the remainder during the following month.

The company prices goods to give a 33.33 per cent gross profit on cost.

Required:

a. Total sales

b. Cash sales

c. Credit sales

d. Cost of sales

Chapter 28

Cash Management

Introduction

Cash is any firm's most liquid current asset and its effective management has become more important because of volatile interest rates, the increasing rate of corporate failures and the new emphasis placed on a firm's ability to generate cash by financial analysts. Cash is the lifeblood of any business and management must consider how any decision will affect the firm's cash flow. The business must be able to generate cash from its trading activities so that it can meet all of its liabilities. Once a business has insufficient cash balances to cover its level of trading activity, it will be unable to trade, unless it can secure additional sources of finance. Many firms, even though profitable, have been forced into liquidation by their creditors because the business lacked the cash resources to meet its day-to-day financial obligations. This is why effective cash management is so important.

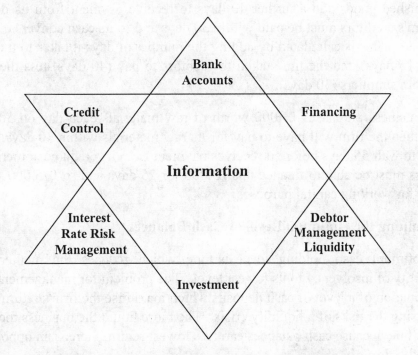

Figure 28:1 Key Factors in Cash Management

CASH MANAGEMENT

Why Firms Hold Cash

If a firm's cash receipts exactly balanced its cash outflows there would be no need to hold cash balances. These balances are used like a reservoir to store surplus cash and to release it as and when needed. There are three main reasons why firms hold cash. Firstly, money is needed to pay the day to day expenses of the business and is called the *transactionary motive*. Secondly, the *precautionary motive* where money is kept in case of an unexpected expense and, finally, management may decide to hold cash in case there is an attractive business proposition. This is called the *speculative motive* for holding cash.

The Payment Cycle

The amount of cash which any business needs to hold will depend upon its payment cycle. This is illustrated by the following example:

Example

Woodland Furniture

The company knows that it takes on average 15 days to turn its raw materials into finished goods and a further 40 days to receive payment from its debtors. The firm's creditors must be paid within 30 days and so its cash conversion cycle is 25 days. This is calculated by adding the number of days it takes to make the goods (15 days) and the time taken for debtors to pay (40 days) less the credit time from suppliers (30 days).

If the business purchases £3,000 worth of raw materials each day on 30 days' credit, then the firm will have to pay for its raw materials within 30 days, whilst having to wait 55 days before it receives payment from its credit customers. The business must be able to finance this £3,000 for 25 days and so £75,000 will be needed for working capital purposes.

Determining the Optimum Level of Cash Balances

The optimum cash holding level is one which reduces the mathematical probability of insolvency to its lowest level. The problem for management is the determination of a level of cash deposits which maximise the firm's return whilst minimising the risks of a liquidity crisis. The more liquid the business the lower the risk but, because cash balances earn the lowest return, there is an opportunity cost to the firm.

Before a business can set an optimum cash level, management must study the pattern of the firm's receipts and payments. Cash inflows will occur when customers pay for the firm's goods or services and is the most important source of cash. Cash will also be received if the business borrows additional capital or sells more shares to its shareholders, or disposes of fixed assets. These sources are not renewable and this is why so much emphasis is placed by financial analysts on the amount of cash generated from trading.

It is generally easier to predict cash outflows than inflows. Cash outflows occur every time the business purchases materials, pays its workforce and the day-to-day expenses of running the business. The key to having sufficient cash lies in accurate forecasting. Most businesses do not experience a stable level of sales throughout the year which would make cash forecasting easier. For most firms sales are seasonal, which means that the business cannot rely on a stream of sales each month and instead experiences peaks and troughs in its sales and cash flow.

Seven Rules For Conserving Cash

Even if a business is good at generating cash, poor management control can still lead to liquidity problems. This is why it is important to:

1. Keep the amount of money tied up in stock, whether it be raw materials, work in progress, or finished stock, at the minimum amount consistent with maintaining production and delivery.

2. Ensure that the business has an effective and efficient credit control system.

3. Negotiate the best credit terms from suppliers.

4. Conserve working capital by leasing or hiring assets instead of outright purchase which may damage cash flow.

5. Ensure that overheads and administrative costs are kept to their budgeted targets.

6. Audit the effectiveness of promotional and advertising campaigns.

7. Keep idle cash balances to the minimum for making day to day payments. Any cash balances not currently needed should be placed on deposit or invested in short term financial securities where the money will earn interest.

This is why cash budgets are so important because they seek to forecast future cash inflows with outflows and force management to consider whether they are making the best use of their current resources.

Cash Budgets

Cash budgets are an essential short term planning tool for they show how changes in cash flow will affect the firm's overall level of liquidity. A cash budget shows three things. Firstly the forecast cash flows for the coming months, the payments and finally the forecast monthly cash balance be it positive or negative.

Cash Budget for the Period January to June Year Seven

	Jan £	Feb £	March £	Apr £	May £	June £
RECEIPTS						
Cash Sales						
Credit Sales						
Sale of Fixed Assets						
New Share Capital						
New Loans						
TOTAL RECEIPTS						
PAYMENTS						
Suppliers						
Wages						
Rent and Rates						
Interest						
Dividends						
Loan Repayment						
Tax						
Purchase of Fixed Assets						
Any Cash Outflow						
TOTAL PAYMENTS						
BALANCE						
Opening Balance						
Plus Receipts						
Total Receipts						
Less Payments						
Closing Balance						

Note: The last month's closing balance is the next months opening balance.

Figure 28:2 Layout of a Cash Budget

Cash budgets are not based on the accruals concept and so cash receipts and payments are recorded only when they are received or paid. This means that if raw materials are bought in January on two months credit that the cash outflow will not be recorded in the cash budget until March. Similarly if goods are sold on one month's credit in January payment will not be received until February. Non cash expenses such as depreciation are not relevant as they do not involve a cash outflow and so they are not shown in the cash budget.

The preparation of a cash budget once all estimates have been made about forecast receipts and expenditure of cash is shown below.

Example

The Prudent Company's management have estimated their forecast receipts and payments of cash for the next six months from January to June. These are shown below:

	Dec	Jan	Feb	Mar	Apr	May	June
Sales (Units £9 per unit)	80	100	120	90	140	150	125
	£	£	£	£	£	£	£
Raw Materials	500	625	750	550	875	925	750
Direct Labour	248	310	372	279	434	465	372
Rent	100	100	100	100	100	100	100
Overheads	180	200	230	190	260	280	235
Bank Loan				3,000			
Purchase of Machinery			300			700	

The firm has an opening cash balance of £2,300. It gives one month's credit on its sales and pays for its materials one month after purchase. All other payments are made in the month in which they are incurred.

Prepare the firm's six months cash budget for the period January to June.

Note: Calculation of Sales and Payments.

Goods Sold on one month's credit in December 80 x £9 = £720 - Received January as cash

The purchaser receives one month's credit and so the cash from the sale will not be received until January. This is when the cash inflow will be shown in the cash budget. Payments are not shown when the goods are ordered but only when they are paid for. Materials are ordered but will not be paid until January.

415

Projected Cash Budget for the Prudent Company January to June Year Two

	January £	February £	March £	April £	May £	June £
Receipts						
Sales (units x £9)	720	900	1080	810	1260	1350
Loans			3000			
Total Receipts	720	900	4080	810	1260	1350
Payments						
Raw Materials	500	625	750	550	875	925
Labour Costs	310	372	279	434	465	372
Rent	100	100	100	100	100	100
Overheads	200	230	190	260	280	235
Purchase of Machinery		300			700	
Total Payments	1110	1627	1319	1344	2420	1632
Opening Balance	2300	1920	1193	3954	3420	2260
Total Receipts	3020	2820	5273	4764	4680	3610
Less Payments	1100	1627	1319	1344	2420	1632
Closing Balance	1920	1193	3954	3420	2260	1978

Note: The cash from sales made in December is not received until January because they are made on one month's credit. Similarly raw materials bought in December are not paid for until January.

Analysing the Cash Budget

Once prepared, management will know whether the business will have cash surpluses or whether it will need to seek additional credit because it has insufficient cash to meet its cash outflows. Cash surpluses can either be placed in interest bearing deposits, such as bank deposit accounts, or invested in short term government financial securities, such as Treasury Bills. Treasury Bills are a safe short term investment and the security can soon be sold and converted into cash.

Cash shortages must be funded for, unless this is done, the business will be unable to meet its short term liabilities. This type of finance is usually provided by bank overdraft which effectively means that the business is using the bank's money to pay its expenses. Such a situation cannot continue indefinitely for all the firm is doing is exchanging one creditor for another.

This is why banks sometimes refuse to provide overdraft finance, because in their view the firm is incapable of generating sufficient cash to meet its financial obligations. From the bank's point of view they are lending a sum certain with the aim of receiving uncertain cash inflows in the form of interest and capital repayments. Although banks can make good profits by lending to companies which are temporary illiquid, they incur bad debts should the loans not be repaid.

In order to protect the bank's position, bank managers often ask for a cash budget before they are prepared to grant a loan or arrange an overdraft facility. Bankers do not like to lend to companies who have run out of their own money, and who then wish to spend the bank's. Cash forecasts show that the firm's management are engaged in financial planning and that the lending of funds represents an acceptable business risk.

Controlling the Cash Cycle

The term cash cycle refers to the time period taken to receive cash after it has been invested in stock and debtors. Idle cash balances provide a safety buffer for any unexpected expense, even though there is an opportunity cost for holding such balances. The greater the return which the business can make from investing the money in additional current assets, the greater the opportunity cost of the idle cash balances. The foregone earnings must be balanced against the financial losses which will be incurred from cash shortages.

CASH MANAGEMENT

Most firms do not suddenly run out of cash but go through several stages. It is important, therefore, that management recognise these stages that generally lead to the business becoming illiquid and take the necessary action. These stages can be seen in the following diagram.

Figure 28:3 How Declining Levels of Liquidity Affect the Firm

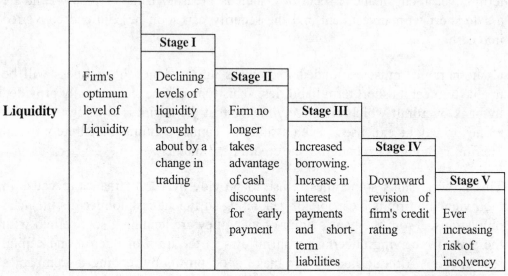

Cash balances will decline if any or all of the following events happen. A reduction in sales, increase in operating costs and poor working capital management will lead to the business experiencing reducing cash balances. This will mean that the firm can no longer take advantage of cash discounts for early payment and so it will be forced to borrow money from its creditors. This is a very expensive form of finance for the discount represents the interest cost of the money. The true cost of the goods is thus represented by the cash discount. This can be seen in the next example.

Example

The Music Store

The Music Store is currently very short of cash and can no longer afford to take advantage of cash discounts because the money is needed elsewhere. The firm has just ordered £100 worth of goods from a supplier who offers 30 days' credit or a 2 per cent discount if payment is made within ten days from the date of the invoice. Calculate the interest cost of not taking advantage of the discount.

418

Solution

The cost of trade credit is calculated by the formula:

$$\text{Annual Cost of Credit} = \frac{\text{\% Discount}}{\text{£100 - \% Discount}} \quad \frac{\text{365 Days}}{\text{Additional Days}}$$

$$\text{Annual Cost of Credit} = \frac{2}{\text{£100-2}} \quad \frac{365}{30-10}$$

$$= \frac{2}{98} \times \frac{365}{20} = \frac{730}{1960} \times 100 = 37\%$$

This example illustrates the high cost of this type of finance and would only be taken by an organisation desperately short of liquidity and other sources of finance.

As a business becomes less liquid it represents a greater risk to would-be lenders. Lenders can be assumed to be risk adverse and so they prefer to lend where they can earn a high return coupled with low risk. Those lenders prepared to accept the additional risk will demand a premium which will be reflected in a higher rate of interest. This will inevitably increase the firm's cost of capital and the higher interest payments will adversely affect cash flow.

Credit rating companies evaluate the ability of a firm to meet its obligations. As liquidity levels fall there is a greater probability that the business will be incapable of meeting these obligations and so the firm's credit rating will be reduced. A reduction in a firm's credit rating is a signal to the world that the business is experiencing financial problems and this will affect its ability to secure further credit.

The final stage arrives when a business cannot meet its financial obligations from its own cash resources and can no longer secure additional sources of finance. The business is now at the mercy of its creditors and they are likely to take action, which will lead to the liquidation of the business.

This is why cash management is so important for the very survival of the business depends on it. Indeed it may explain why many managers prefer to build a safety level based on past experience into their liquid balances even though the opportunity cost is a marginal decrease in earnings.

QUESTIONS

Answers begin page 511

1. **The Welsh Honey Farm**

The management of the farm have asked you to prepare their six monthly cash forecast. They have given you the following figures.

	Jan £	Feb £	Mar £	Apr £	May £	June £
Sales	65,000	73,000	120,000	140,000	110,000	130,000
Variable costs	33,000	40,000	70,000	85,000	65,000	80,000
Fixed costs	15,000	15,000	20,000	20,000	20,000	20,000
Taxation		8,000			22,000	
Dividends			35,000			

Note: On 1 January the firm has a credit balance at the bank of £15,000.

2. **The Woollen Rug Company**

The management of the company are preparing their six monthly cash forecast. The firm is already in overdraft and must not exceed a £99,000 overdraft facility. The directors have asked you to prepare the firm's cash budget and to advise them should they be in any danger of exceeding their overdraft limit.

	Jan	Feb	Mar	Apr	May	June
Sales	37,200	39,000	48,000	39,200	40,800	52,000
Raw materials	16,780	17,550	21,600	17,640	15,120	14,166
Labour costs	7,440	7,800	9,600	7,840	6,720	6,296
Variable overheads	2,790	2,925	3,600	2,940	2,520	2,361
Fixed overheads	9,000	9,000	9,000	9,000	9,000	9,000
New machinery		15,000		8,000		
Leasing payments	800	800	800	800	800	800
Taxation			33,000			

Note: On 1 January the firm's overdraft was £47,859.

3.   **The Griffin Paint Company**

At the main factory on the outskirts of Cardiff the firm manufactures specialist paints used by the aerospace industry. The budgeted costs and selling price for the coming six months are shown below. You have been asked to prepare the firm's cash budget for the next six months' trading.

Griffin Paint - costs per litre

	£
Direct materials	20
Direct labour	5
Variable overheads	2
Selling price	47

Additional information:

a. The firm has fixed costs of £15,000 per month.
b. All direct labour costs are paid in the month in which they are incurred.
c. The firm receives two months' credit for raw materials purchased.
d. The firm pays its variable overhead costs in the month in which they are incurred.
e. The firm has £800 leasing payments per month.
f. The firm must repay a £10,000 loan repayment in May.
g. The firm sells 20 per cent of its output for cash with the balance being received one month after sale.
h. On 1 January the company had a bank balance of £80,000.
i. Depreciation of plant and machinery equals £300 per month.

Budgeted Production and Sales Figures

PRODUCTION	Nov	Dec	Jan	Feb	Mar	Apr	May	June
Litres	1,000	1,200	1,400	1,400	1,100	1,250	900	850

SALES	Nov	Dec	Jan	Feb	Mar	Apr	May	June
Litres	900	1,000	1,200	1,500	800	950	700	800

4. **Leather Boots Ltd**

The company manufacture a range of boots for the industrial and leisure market. The budgeted production and sales are shown below. You work in the firm's Finance Department and have been asked to prepare the firm's cash budget for the following six months.

Budgeted Production and Sales Figures

PRODUCTION	Dec	Jan	Feb	Mar	Apr	May	June
(pairs)	4,200	3,400	2,100	2,400	1,750	1,500	1,400

SALES	Dec	Jan	Feb	Mar	Apr	May	June
(pairs)	3,500	3,000	1,800	2,000	1,900	1,300	1,100

The firm has the additional costs:

a. Raw materials used in production are £12 a unit.

b. Direct labour costs are £6 per unit.

c. All prime costs are payable in the month of production.

d. The firm pays leasing charges of £2,000 a month.

e. Variable overheads are £7,000 a month.

f. Factory rent is £8,000 a month.

g. All goods are sold one month's credit but past experience shows that 25 per cent of the firm's customers pay in the month in which the goods are sold. The remainder pay the following month.

h. The leather boots are sold for £39.

i. The company currently has a £60,000 cash balance.

Chapter 29

Foreign Exchange

Introduction

There are very few businesses which are immune from the effects of currency fluctuations, but some are more at risk than others. As soon as the value of the pound changes relative to the currencies of our major trading partners, there will be a difference in the price of goods and services expressed in foreign currency. Any business buying and selling goods from overseas knows that its transactions are subject to an exchange risk which could make the firm extra profits or cause it to make losses as a result of these movements in the exchange rate.

Exchange Rate Exposure

Any change in the exchange rate will result in a gain or loss to one of the contracting parties. The greater the likelihood of a fluctuation in the exchange rate the greater the risk involved. The main types of foreign exchange exposure are:

Translation Exposure

This is the term used to explain how a change in the exchange rate will alter the price of the goods or services being bought or sold. Translation exposure relates to the level of risk to a change in a firm's cash flows and realised profits from a change in the exchange rate. This can be seen from the following example.

Example

The Californian Wine Company

The company purchases American wines and sells them in the United Kingdom. On the first day of every month the firm buys $30,000 worth of goods from an agent in New York and settles its account in US dollars on the last day of each month. The goods are sold in the UK for twice their cost price. At the beginning of the month the exchange rate was £1.00 = $2.00 and so the goods cost the firm

£15,000. If the exchange rate does not fluctuate the firm stands to make a profit of £15,000. If the pound weakens against the US dollar during the month the goods will become more expensive and, if prices cannot be raised, profits will be reduced. When the firm comes to pay for the goods the exchange rate has moved to £1.00 = $1.90 and so the goods now cost the firm £15,789. This will reduce the firm's profits by £789 or five per cent. Similarly, if the pound rises against the US dollar the goods will become cheaper and the firm will make bigger profits, provided it can sell all of the merchandise.

In this example the profit margins are large and the time periods short. This may not be the case when contracts are entered into for capital goods and the delivery time may run into months or even years. One way of avoiding the risk of currency fluctuations is to ask to be invoiced or paid in your own currency. If this is done, the exchange rate risk (be it favourable or adverse) is passed to the other party who must then decide what action to take. The extent of the risk will depend upon the strength or weakness of the particular currency. If the currency is weak then one party stands to make losses as their currency moves lower against the stronger one. If, on the other hand, it is strong windfall profits will be made. In certain cases the movement in the exchange rate can turn what once seemed profitable contracts into loss making ones which can damage a firm's earnings and liquidity.

Profit Translation Exposure

When a British company has earned profits overseas these must be translated into sterling. This is done by using either the exchange rate at the end of the financial year or the average exchange rate for the year.

Net Assets Exposure

At the end of the financial year a company's net investments in foreign assets must be converted into the firm's group accounts by using the exchange rate at the end of the financial year. Any change in the rate will therefore affect the reserves which, in turn, affect the value of the net assets of the business. Financial managers must remember that any large change in the exchange rate, particularly where a business has large overseas investments in relation to its domestic assets, will affect the company's gearing ratio and possibly its cost of capital. If the level of investments is small, it is possible to argue that small short term fluctuations in the exchange rates can be ignored.

When a company owns assets such as investments or shares in an overseas subsidiary their value will be in a foreign currency. In order to prepare group accounts all of the firm's assets and liabilities must be consolidated and so a value in sterling must be placed on its foreign assets and liabilities. Any change in the exchange rate during the financial year will result in a gain or loss on consolidation. Whilst these accounting translations do not generate actual cash flows for the business, they still have an impact on the firm's profits and balance sheet.

How Exchange Rates are Determined

Exchange rates will be determined by the market makers according to political and economic news. Although the rates may change without any buying or selling, as when rates are set at the start of trading, the exchange rate will generally be determined by the forces of supply and demand.

During any business day some people will need to purchase foreign currency while others will want to sell it. Their transactions will determine the demand for the two currencies. When there are more buyers than sellers, the price will rise because of a shortage in supply and, if there are more sellers than buyers, the price will fall as supply exceeds demand. Exchange rates will then move upwards or downwards showing the price of one currency in terms of another.

Business transactions are not the only reason for changes in the exchange rate. Investment managers and speculators buy and sell currencies depending on how they believe their investment portfolio will be affected by exchange rate changes. Their decisions are influenced by political and economic news, such as forecast interest and inflation rates.

If one country has higher interest rates than another investors may be attracted to invest their money in that country, so long as a fall in the exchange rate relative to other currencies does not erode the gain made from the different interest rate.

This pool of investment funds is often referred to as *hot money* for it may suddenly be withdrawn from one country and invested in another because of expected changes in exchange rates. A sudden withdrawal of investment will affect the exchange rate and will have a dramatic effect on the business community. Some business transactions will appear more profitable while others could be turned into losses. It will all depend on how the exchange rate moves.

How Exchange Rates are Quoted

The exchange rate is quoted in one of two ways. Sometimes it is quoted as one unit of currency being equal to another, in which case it is referred to as an indirect quote. For example, £1 is worth $1.75. It can also be shown as what is called a direct quote when a number of units of currency are equal to one or more units of another currency. For example, 100 Swiss Francs are worth £25. The London Foreign Exchange Market uses the indirect method whereas New York uses the direct quote.

Example of Foreign Exchange Rates quoted on the London Market

Sterling Spot and Forward Rates

	Range	Close	1 Month	3 Months
New York	1.6135 - 1.6215	1.6155 - 1.6165	1.06 - 1.05 pr	2.90 - 2.88 pr
Tokyo	153.25 - 155.27	153.32 - 153.65	$1^{1}/8$ - 1 pr	$3^{1}/2$ - 3 pr
Zurich	2.3134 - 2.3262	2.3170 - 2.3202	$1^{1}/2$ - 1 pr	$3^{1}/8$ - $2^{7}/8$ pr

The table shows the exchange rates for different currencies and can be divided into two halves. The left-hand side shows how the rates have moved during the previous day's trading and the final rates at the end of trading are shown under the heading CLOSE. The right-hand side shows the forward margins for people wishing to purchase or sell a currency in one or three months' time.

The exchange rate at the close of business is always shown as two figures and they are referred to as the *bid* and *offer rate*. The bid rate is the bank's buying rate and the offer its selling rate. It is easier to remember that banks always buy high and sell low on each deal so that they can make profits on each currency exchange. When they purchase currency they buy as much as they can so the higher rate is used. In this way the customer must part with as much currency as possible in order to gain the new one. Similarly, when the bank sells, its aim is to exchange as little of its currency for the other by using the lower rate. Once again the exchange rate works to the customer's detriment allowing the bank to part with the smallest amount of the wanted currency. The difference between the buying and selling rate is called the *currency spread* and is really the bank's profit margin on the transaction.

Foreign currencies are always quoted to four decimal places and these are called pips. For example, £1 may be quoted as £1.7542 to £1.7584 and the difference between these two rates is the *currency spread*.

Purchasing or Selling Foreign Currency

Different rates will be offered for buying or selling a currency, depending upon the length of time required before making the exchange. There are three different types of foreign exchange transactions and they are designed to take account of timing differences as to when the currency is wanted. They are called the *spot rate*, the *forward rate* and the *swap rate*.

Spot Rate

This is the current rate offered by the dealers. It will fluctuate during the day but the bank will be able to offer a rate by telephoning a foreign exchange dealer and this can then be accepted or rejected. If accepted the currency transaction will be completed within two working days of the transaction, although it can be completed earlier if required.

Forward Rate

A customer may need to purchase 10,000 US dollars to pay for goods in three months' time. During that time the rate may change but it is possible to enter into a forward contract which will fix the rate, guaranteeing the exchange rate regardless of the spot rate in three months' time. This is a forward contract and, by entering into such an agreement, it is possible to limit the exchange rate risk. The contract may be for a specified date or it may allow the customer to choose a date during the length of the contract, in which case it is referred to as an option forward contract. This must not be confused with an option contract which is explained later in this chapter. Once again the forward rate is calculated by applying the old maxim that banks always buy at the high rate and sell at the lower one. An example will help to illustrate this point.

Example

The Import and Export Company have agreed to purchase $320,000 worth of goods from an American supplier. Payment is to be made in US dollars in three months' time. The rates are as follows:

US dollars Spot	1.7530 - 1.7550	Three months forward	0.07 - 0.05 cpm

FOREIGN EXCHANGE

The spot rate represents the exchange rate at the moment, whereas the forward rate must be calculated by deducting the premium from the current spot rate. Forward rates are quoted at either a premium or a discount. The premium is always subtracted from the spot rate and the discount is always added. A premium, therefore, makes the currency more expensive and a discount makes it cheaper. The forward rate will be at a discount whenever the interest rate of the foreign currency is higher than the base (domestic) currency and a premium will be payable when the interest rate of the foreign currency is lower than the base currency. Occasionally a forward rate will be the same as the spot rate. In such cases it is said to be at par.

Before calculating the forward rate care must be taken in applying the decimal point. Most currencies such as the US dollar, and sterling are shown in terms of one hundred division of their currency unit. This means that each American cent is divided into a hundred segments and so the premium 0.07 cents means 0.0007 US dollars. Some currencies only have one unit of currency, such as the Italian lire or the Japanese yen, which make the calculation easier as there is no decimal.

Calculation of the Forward Rate

US Dollars	Bank's Buying Rate	Bank's Selling Rate
Spot Rate	1.7550	1.7530
Less Premium	0.0005	0.0007
Three month forward rate	1.7545	1.7523

Note: The higher premium is deducted from the spot selling rate and the lower premium from the buying rate.

When buying or selling a currency the rate is always calculated from the bank's position. This means that when a customer wishes to buy foreign exchange the bank is selling it and, when the customer sells foreign currency, the bank purchases it.

Calculation of the Sterling Purchase Price

Amount	Spot Rate	Amount	Forward Rate
$320,000	1.7530	$320,000	1.7523

$$\frac{\$320,000}{1.7530} = £182,544.21 \qquad \frac{\$320,000}{1.7523} = £182,617.13$$

Although the forward rate will cost the firm £72.92 more than the spot rate the firm has locked itself into a fixed rate and can, therefore ignore exchange rate fluctuations.

Swap Rate

A transaction is called a swap when a customer wishes to purchase or sell a currency at the spot price and then simultaneously sells or purchases it in the forward market. The swap rate is calculated by taking the difference between the premium or discount rate at the time the parties enter into the forward contract. Swap agreements do not involve any currency exposure because the party entering into the swap transaction has matched either a spot sale or purchase with a forward purchase or sale. A swap transaction is best used whenever a party wishes to take a position on a change in the interest differential between two countries.

How Forward Rates are Calculated

The forward rate does not reflect the future expected exchange rate at maturity but simply reflects the difference between the interest rates of the two currencies being exchanged.

The difference in rate between the spot price and the forward rate is accounted for by the different rates of interest charged for money by different financial centres. In the absence of foreign exchange controls an investor may choose to invest in overseas paper financial securities. Different financial centres will offer a range of interest rates. International investors seek to earn the highest return relative to the exchange rate risk by investing in different financial centres by purchasing a range of financial securities.

It is this difference in interest rates which accounts for the forward premium or discount. Forward rates are calculated by taking the current spot rate and adjusting it by adding or subtracting an amount, called *forward points*, which compensate for the change in interest rates between two financial centres. The country which has the higher interest rate is said to be at a discount to the low interest rate currency, whilst the low interest rate currency will be at a premium to the high interest rate currency.

Example of Euro Currency Rates % Per Annum

	One Month		Three Month	
	Bid	**Offer**	**Bid**	**Offer**
Swiss Franc	2.75	3.00	3.00	3.25
Sterling	7.25	8.00	7.75	8.00
US Dollars	5.12	5.25	5.25	5.47

Note: The interest rate quoted always works to the bank's advantage. If a customer is lending funds they will receive the lower interest rate (bid) and, should the customer wish to borrow funds, the bank will quote the higher rate (offer).

Calculating Forward Points

The formula for an exchange rate quoted as base/currency is:

$$\frac{\text{Spot Rate} \times \dfrac{\text{Number of Days}}{360} \times \dfrac{(\text{Base Interest Rate} - \text{Currency Interest Rate})}{100}}{1 + \left(\dfrac{\text{Base Interest Rate}}{100} \times \dfrac{\text{Number of Days}}{360}\right)}$$

= Number of Forward Points of Currency

This is best illustrated by an example.

	Bid	Offer
US Dollar/Swiss Franc	1.5695	1.5705

Euro Currency Rate % Per Annum.

	Bid	Offer
Swiss Franc	4.19	4.31
US Dollar	4.12	4.25

Calculate the one month forward Swiss Franc against the US Dollar. Assume a thirty day month.

Swiss Franc Forward

$$= \frac{1.5695 \times 30 / 360 \times \left(\dfrac{0.0700}{100}\right)}{1 + \left(\dfrac{4.25}{100} \times \dfrac{30}{360}\right)}$$

$$\frac{1.5695 \times 0.08333 \times 0.0007}{1 + (0.0425 \times 0.08333)}$$

$$\frac{0.0000915}{1.0035415} = \text{SF } 0.0001 \text{ or 1 point}$$

The International Investment Trust

The trust managers have a large cash portfolio and they wish to invest it where the funds will earn the greatest return. The fund is in Swiss Francs but interest rates in Switzerland are currently 3 per cent, as opposed to Britain's 6 per cent. The company, like other investors, seeks to invest in Britain because of the higher return and so exchanges Swiss Francs for Sterling. By doing this the investor runs the risk that there will be no change in the exchange rates between the two currencies and that, if they wish to change their currency from Sterling to Swiss Francs, the exchange rate will be the same. If the exchange rates are thought by investors to be stable the exchange can be made in the spot market, but otherwise the investor must seek to hedge their foreign exchange exposure.

When interest rates are higher in one centre than another the monetary authorities are usually trying to attract an inflow of foreign currency by offering investors a higher return. This higher interest rate could be seen as a risk premium for being prepared to hold a weaker currency as opposed to a strong one.

In such a situation investors will seek to purchase pounds in the spot market and then immediately sell them forward for Swiss Francs. This will lead to an increase in the number of Swiss Francs being wanted and so the forward rate will rise relative to the spot rate. If the investor wishes to carry out a *'swap'* in Sterling against Swiss Francs more Sterling will be needed, the foreign exchange dealer will have had to pay more for Sterling to buy spot marks than will be received for the forward resale of Swiss Francs against Sterling.

A loss will then be made in selling spot and buying forward Swiss Francs and this loss must be offset against the interest gained from moving funds from Switzerland to Britain. By purchasing currency forward, the investor will sacrifice part of the gain made through changes in interest rates by having to pay a premium for the currency. During normal trading conditions the premium will be at a lower rate than the percentage gain in interest. If this is not the case there is no benefit in covering the gain forward.

The Cost of a Forward Contract

The cost of a forward contract can be calculated as an annual percentage. The premium or discount can be calculated by using this formula:

$$\frac{\text{Premium/Discount} \times 360 \times 100}{\text{Forward Rate} \times \text{Number of Days}}$$

Example

The Sterling US dollar forward rate is 1.7154 and the three month forward rate premium is 0.85c. The cost of entering into a forward contract is:

$$\frac{\text{Premium/Discount x 360 x 100}}{\text{Forward Rate x Number of Days}}$$

$$\frac{0.0085 \text{ x } 360 \text{ x } 100}{1.7154 \text{ x } 90}$$

$$= \quad \frac{306}{154} \quad = 1.99\%$$

Note: Financial year 360 days 12 x 30 day periods.

What is an Option Contract?

Whilst a *forward contract* provides the financial manager with a certain outcome, it does not enable the firm to gain should the exchange rate move in the company's favour. In certain circumstances the company may prefer to use an option contract because it enables the company to forego the opportunity loss of a forward contract.

An *option contract* is similar to a forward contract but gives the person entering into it the right, but not the obligation, to buy or sell a financial instrument or futures contract at a set price on or before a specified future date. The buyer is called the *option holder* and has to pay a premium to the seller, who is called the *option writer*.

The option can be either to buy or to sell a financial instrument or futures contract. A *call option* gives the buyer the right to purchase the option, while a put option confers on the buyer the right to sell to the option writer. A *double option* gives the buyer the right to sell or buy. Once the option has been bought and the premium paid, that is the maximum loss which the buyer can incur once the decision is taken to allow it to expire.

The Price of an option = intrinsic value + time value.

Intrinsic value is the term used to describe the difference between the *strike rate* (rate which the buyer of the option can exercise their right to buy or sell) and the outright forward rate. The time value of an option depends upon the number of days left before the option expires and the implied volatility of the spot rate.

Swan China

The company has just sold 1m US Dollars' worth of china to an American Discount Store. Swan China will receive payment in six months' time. The current Sterling/Dollar spot rate is 1.5800 and the forward rate is 1.5700

In six months' time Swan China will want to sell 1m US Dollars for Sterling. If the company purchases Sterling by selling US Dollars forward, the firm will be committed to the Sterling Dollar Forward Rate of 1.5700. Whilst there is certainty to the rate which the firm will receive in six months' time, there is still the risk that, if the spot rate falls, Swan China would have received more Sterling for their one million Dollars.

If the company hedges its exposure by purchasing an option, the firm will be able to elect the course of action which will earn it the most sterling. Should the spot rate rise during the six months, Swan China can exercise their option and buy Sterling at the rate of £1 : $1.5700. If, on the other hand, the spot rate falls the option can be allowed to expire unexercised because a better rate could be obtained in the spot market. Purchasing an option contract is less risky than entering into a forward contract because the maximum loss is the cost of the option contract. This is why an option always has a positive net present value because the right even to do nothing must have a value.

Currency Futures Contracts

A Currency Futures Contract is an agreement to purchase or sell a standard amount of foreign exchange at an agreed price at a future date. In Britain financial futures are traded on the floor of the London International Financial Futures Exchange (LIFFE).

Before entering into a currency futures contract, buyers and sellers have to deposit a margin with the clearing house to guarantee their credit worthiness, because profits and losses will be added or subtracted on the margin on a daily basis. The margin is made up of two parts – the *initial margin* and the *variation margin*. The initial margin reflects the volatility of the future contract and ranges from 0.1 per cent to 6 per cent of the face value of the contract, whereas the variation margin refers to any additional money which must be paid to cover losses made on the contract.

Financial futures are highly speculative but they are nevertheless useful to business people who wish to limit their risk by transferring it to speculators who seek high risks in order to make profits.

FOREIGN EXCHANGE

Example of a Currencies Futures Contract

Clothing USA

The company specialises in importing and distributing American clothing and has just entered into a contract with an American shoe manufacturer to purchase $45,000 worth of merchandise for delivery in 3 months' time. Payment will be made once the goods are delivered.

At the time of entering into the contract the exchange rate was £1/$1.80. The firm's treasurer believes that sterling will weaken during the next three months and the computer forecasts predict a future rate of £1/$1.60.

On the floor of the LIFFE a financial futures sterling contract can be purchased at the rate of £1/1.79. The company purchases one sterling contract for £25,000 for delivery in three months' time.

When the company has to pay for the goods, the sterling exchange spot rate is £1/$1.60 confirming the treasurer's predictions. The firm will have made a profit on its contract and this can be seen from the following calculations.

Calculations

Spot rate $1.60/£1
Futures Contract (right to sell) $1.79/£1

	$
$25,000 x $1.79	44,750

	£
$44,750 are worth in sterling with a spot rate £1/$1.60	27,969
Cost of futures contract	25,000
Profit in sterling	2,969

	$
This can also be calculated in dollars	
Future rate £25,000 x $1.79	44,750
Less spot rate £25,000 x $1.60	40,000
Profit in dollars	4,750

With a spot rate of £1/$1.60 $4,750 = £2,969.

Note: All calculations to nearest whole number.

This example shows that the firm has been able to make a profit by correctly forecasting the movement in the exchange rate. Had the firm been wrong, a loss would have been incurred. In this case the profit from the future contract will offset the extra cost of the goods brought about by the movement in the exchange rate.

Purchasing future contracts is, therefore, riskier than entering into forward contracts because the hedge will only be successful if the buyer is correct in both the timing and the price paid for the contract. For this reason professional advice should always be sought before entering into financial futures contracts, because of the risks involved.

How to reduce the Risk Involved in Foreign Exchange Transactions

Forward contracts and currency options allow business people to limit their exposure to exchange rate risk by developing hedging strategies. *Hedging* involves the simultaneous purchase and sale of a currency or commodity in two different markets at the same time, together with a further sale and purchase of the same currency or commodity at a later date. By developing hedging strategies, business people are able to concentrate on managing their business knowing that the risk or loss due to adverse exchange rate movements have been considerably reduced or eliminated. The whole principle of hedging is based on the fact that the hedger is risk averse and does not seek abnormal profits. Forward and option contracts provide a way of limiting risk exposure which is inherent in dealing in any non-domestic financial security because of fluctuations in exchange rates.

By entering into a hedging position, the firm can separate the contract into two parts. These are the price of the transaction and the transaction itself. By purchasing an option contract, the buyer is able to eliminate the market risk, but is still subject to the risk of how the market price compares with the hedged position. There will always be some risk. It is never possible to predict with certainty how financial markets will behave because of the large number of variables which influence them. Nevertheless, the risk averse firm can take a position which will enable it to be certain of the financial outcome. Forward and option contracts enable a firm to benefit from foreign trade while, at the same time, limit its exposure to loss.

When exchange rates fluctuate it is generally small firms that suffer most, because the owners or managers are unaware as to how to manage the exchange rate risk.

FOREIGN EXCHANGE

Many small firms try to solve the problem by adding a small percentage to their prices to cover fluctuations. Most large companies have their own treasury departments and access to foreign currency earnings which places them in a better position to manage the exchange risk. Once a firm can earn foreign currency, it can use that money to settle debts without having to exchange one currency for another if the rates are unfavourable. If this is not possible, forward contracts and currency options can help the firm limit its exposure to financial losses resulting from business transactions which necessitate the use of foreign currency.

QUESTIONS

Answers begin page 514

1. From the following information, what is the bank's buying and selling rate?

Currency		
Fr	8.1234	8.1576
$	1.6543	1.6743
CD	2.1021	2.1043
Dm	2.5670	2.5890

2. A firm is owed $75,000 from a US company. How much sterling will it receive at the following spot rates?

    (a) $1.69 - $1.70,   (b) $1.71 - $1.72,   (c) $1.80 - $1.82,

    (d) $1.50 - $1.52,   (e) $1.40 - $1.42,   (f) $1.30 - S1.32,

    (g) $1.28 - $1.29,   (h) $1.17 - $1.19,   (i) $1.24 - $1.26.

3. A firm has just contracted for components which cost $40,000. What is the sterling cost if the spot rates are as follows?

    (a) $1.64 - $1.66,   (b) $1.86 - $1.87,   (c) $1.52 - $1.54,

    (d) $1.45 - $1.46,   (e) $1.32 - $1.34,   (f) $1.16 - $1.18,

    (g) $1.22 - $1.24,   (h) $1.27 - $1.29,   (i) $1.05 - $1.07.

4. Calculate the exchange rate for a three month forward contract from the following information:

    US dollars Spot $1.6320 - $1.6430 three months 0.10 cpm.

5. **Holidays USA** have to book their holiday accommodation in February for the coming summer season. The payments must be made in US dollars three months after booking.

    Last year the company's profit margins were reduced by 10 per cent because of currency fluctuations. This year the company would like to eliminate as much uncertainty as possible because the holidays have been marketed using the theme of no surcharges. As a result, any adverse change in exchange rates will bite into already hard-pressed profit margins.

At the moment the sterling dollar exchange rate is as follows:

Sterling Spot and Forward Rates				
	Range	**Close**	**1 Month**	**3 Month**
New York	1.7032-1.7140	1.7120-1.7130	0.06pr	0.85pr

The firm will have to pay $600,000 for its accommodation in May.

a.   Calculate the current cost of the accommodation, using the spot rate.

b.   What would be the sterling cost if the firm chose to enter into a one month or three month forward contract?

c.   What is meant by the term *exchange rate risk* and what action could the firm take to mitigate such risks?

6.   **IMD Engineering**

The company have just sold a machine to an American company for $200,000. Payment is to be made in US Dollars in three months' time.

The current spot rate between sterling and Dollars in London is:

£1 = $1.5D - 1.51.

The premium for the Dollar for a three month forward contract is:

1.20 -1.15 premium.

Calculate the amount of sterling which the company will receive if it decides to enter into a forward contract.

Glossary of Financial Terms

Absorbed cost
Costs which have been spread over operational units, e.g. job, batch unit or contract.

Accounting
The system of recording accounting information using double entry book-keeping.

Accounting equation
The assets of a firm are equal to its liabilities. Assets are things which the firm owns, even if it has not yet paid for them, and liabilities are claims against the firm.

Accounting period
The amount of time covered by the financial statements of a business.

Accounting policies
The specific accounting bases chosen and followed by a firm which the management believe are the most appropriate and which will present its results and financial position fairly.

Accounts Receivable
A firm's credit sales to customers.

Accrual
An amount owing at the time the annual accounts are prepared. The sum owing will be shown in the balance sheet under current liabilities.

Accrued expenses
Expenses which are recognised when goods received or services provided during a given accounting period have not been invoiced, or when wages have been earned but not paid by the end of that period.

Acid test ratio
Current assets less stock/current liabilities. This ratio shows the firm's ability to meet its short-term liabilities out of its cash and near cash assets, such as debtors.

Activity based costing
Costing method which takes account of how costs change with activity.

Annual accounts
The set of accounts comprising a balance sheet together with a profit and loss account and a cash flow statement together with directors' report and other information as required by Companies' Act 1985 and 1989. (*See* chapter 9).

Apportioned costs
Costs which have been spread over cost centres.

Appropriation account
A financial statement which shows how the firm's net profit after taxation has been used.

GLOSSARY

Assets	Anything of value owned by a business.
Authorised share capital	This is the amount of money which the company took power to raise when it was formed.
Avoidable cost	A cost not incurred if an action is not taken, or is discontinued.
Bad debt	A debt which has not been paid. It is an expense to the firm and the amount will be shown in the profit and loss account.
Balance sheet	A statement showing the assets and liabilities of a business at a particular date.
Basis	The cash price less the futures price.
Basis point	The smallest increment for measuring price.
Bear	A person who believes that a share price will fall.
Bid price	The price a buyer will pay for a financial security or futures contract
Bond	A financial security (certificate) showing the indebtedness of an organisation, together with the rate of interest payable and the date, if applicable, when it will be repaid.
Bonus issue	The issuing of shares to existing shareholders by distributing a company's reserves as shares. No monetary payments are made. Sometimes called a *scrip issue*.
Book value	The historical cost of an asset, less depreciation accumulated over the asset's life.
Break-even	The amount of sales needed to cover a firm's fixed and variable costs. Above the break-even point the firm makes a profit and below it makes a loss.
Bull	A person who believes share prices will rise.
Business risk	The risk from investing in a business
Called up capital	This refers to shares issued by the company but not yet fully paid for by the shareholders.
Capital	The long-term money which is financing a business.

Capital employed	The long-term capital which finances a firm. It includes share capital, reserves and loan capital (debentures, secured loan stock and unsecured loan stock).
Capital expenditure	Money spent by the company on purchasing fixed assets.
Capital loss	Losses made on the sale of fixed assets.
Capital profit	Money made on the sale of fixed assets.
Capital receipts	Money received by a company on the issue of shares and debentures.
Capital reserve	Reserves which are not available for distribution as dividends, e.g. any surplus arising as a premium on the issue of shares or debentures.
Carriage inwards	The cost of having goods delivered. It increases the cost of purchases and the amount paid is shown in the trading account.
Carriage outwards	The cost of delivering goods to customers. The amount is treated as an expense and is shown in the profit and loss account.
Cash budget	Budget drawn up to enable the firm to forecast future cash receipts and payments.
Cash flow	Accounting term used to describe the cash generated and used during a given financial period.
Cash flow statement	Accounting statement showing sources and uses of cash during an accounting period.
Cash operating cycle	Length of time a firm has to wait before it receives cash.
Contingent liability	Obligation which may arise in respect of past events. Such as the outcome of a law case.
Contribution	Sales less variable costs = contribution.
Convertible loan stock	A loan which give the holder the right to convert to other securities, normally ordinary shares, at a pre-determined rate and time.
Corporation tax	Tax calculated on a company's profits.
Cost centre	A location, individual or item of equipment for which costs may be ascertained and used for purposes of control or product costing.

Cost driver	A cost which increases with activity, e.g. a variable cost.
Cost unit	Item of product (usually of output or service) to which costs can be allocated or attributed.
Coupon	The interest paid on a bond.
Cumulative preference shares	These shares allow the owners to receive arrears of dividend before dividends are paid to the ordinary shareholders.
Current assets	These are assets of a circulating nature which are acquired by a business in order to trade with other companies or individuals. They are shown in the balance sheet in order of liquidity, with the least liquid shown first. The order is stock, debtors (people who owe the firm money), bank and cash balances.
Current worth	*See* Net worth.
Debenture	Normally a secured loan over the assets of a company. The debenture holders do not own the company but they are entitled to interest payments. If the interest is not paid, the debenture holders can sell the firm's assets so that they can recover their money.
Debt capital	A financial term for loan capital.
Deferred taxation	An amount provided to equalise the timing differences which arise between the tax charge based on the pre-tax profit in the profit and loss account and the actual tax liability, as separately computed in accordance with tax legislation. Transfers are made to a deferred taxation account, the balance of which is shown separately in the balance sheet.
Depreciation	Most assets wear out as they are used. Machinery wears out and buildings deteriorate. An allowance, called depreciation, for this fall in value must be included in the firm's accounts.
Direct cost	A cost which can be associated wholly and specifically with a cost unit, e.g. machine, department or individual.
Discount allowed	The cost of allowing a debtor to pay a smaller sum than the original bill if the debt is settled early. The cost is shown as an expense in the profit and loss account.

Discount received   Money given off a bill for settling it early. It is treated as income and added to gross profit.

Discretionary cost   A programmed cost which is subject to management discretion and control.

Dividend   A distribution to shareholders out of profits, usually in the form of cash.

Equity   The share capital of the business plus reserves.

Factoring   The technical term used to describe selling credit sales (debtors) to a factoring house or bank for cash.

Fixed assets   Assets acquired for retention in a business for the purpose of providing goods or services. Fixed assets are not held for resale in the normal course of business. Examples are land and buildings, plant and machinery.

Fixed cost   A cost unaffected by a change in activity during a given period of time.

Free cash flow   Cash flow left after a firm has invested in all projects capable of yielding a positive net present value.

Gearing   The ratio of a firm's debt to equity capital. In the USA it is called leverage.

Goodwill   Sum of money paid for the goods of a business. When a business is purchased any amount paid in excess of its net assets (total assets less liabilities) represents the value placed on goodwill.

Gross profit   The profit made on goods and services sold before expenses are deducted. The percentage of profit can be calculated by the following formula:

$$\frac{\text{Profit} \times 100}{\text{Cost Price}}$$

Historical cost   The original cost of acquiring the fixed asset.

Hurdle rate   The rate of return required from a capital investment.

Incremental cost   Additional cost of one course of action over another

Indirect cost   A cost which cannot be directly allocated but can be apportioned to cost centres and cost units, e.g. overhead costs.

GLOSSARY

Intangible asset   Assets which do not have a physical identity, e.g. goodwill.

Internal rate of return   A discount rate which will give a zero net present value.

Issued share capital   The number of shares which have been issued to shareholders and which have been fully paid for.

Leverage   *See* Gearing

Liquid asset   Cash and other financial security which can be converted quickly into cash.

Liquidity   Financial term for describing how much cash and near cash (debtors) a business has to meet its short-term financial obligations.

Listed investment   An investment which is quoted on a recognised stock exchange, e.g. London, Tokyo, New York.

Loan capital   Debt capital

Marginal cost   The amount of cost incurred at a given level of output by increasing the volume of output by one.

Minority interest   Shares held in a subsidiary company by shareholders other than a holding company or its nominees.

Net present value   The discounted value of an investment's net cash flow.

Net profit   The gross profit less expenses.

Net worth   A concept denoting the excess of the book values of all assets over liabilities. In a company it represents the interests of shareholders, i.e. the paid-up share capital and reserves. If the assets are taken at current values, instead of book values, the concept is known as current worth.

Nominal value   The face value of a share or loan stock.

Off balance sheet finance   A source of finance not shown on the balance sheet because there is no corresponding asset, e.g. an operating lease.

Ordinary shareholders   These are the owners of the company. They are entitled to a dividend which is a share of the firm's profit.

Paid up capital   This refers to shares which have been issued by the company and which have been fully paid for by the shareholders.

444

Pay back	The time taken for inflows from an investment to equal its cost.
Preference shareholders	Owners of these shares enjoy preferential rights over the ordinary shareholders. Their dividend is normally at a pre-determined rate and they receive it before the ordinary shareholders are paid. The Articles of Association sometimes make special provision for the preference shareholders by allowing them to be repaid in full before the ordinary shareholders in the event of the company being wound up. If there is not such provision then all shareholders share equally the remaining assets of the company.
Present value	The discounted value of a future cash flow.
Prime cost	Total of direct material, direct labour and direct expenses. Always a variable cost.
Provisions	Amounts written off or retained by way of providing for depreciation, renewals or diminution of assets, or retained to provide for a known liability the extent of which cannot be expressly determined, e.g. provision for bad debts.
Relevant cost	Those costs which are pertinent to the decision being made.
Reserves	These are unappropriated profits (not distributed to shareholders as dividends or surplus funds made possible by the revaluation of fixed assets or the issue of shares for more than their nominal value.
Retained profits	These consist of undistributed profits and can be used to pay dividends, maintain the business or absorb losses. The revenue reserve is made up of the general reserve and the profit and loss account as shown in the balance sheet.
Returns inwards	Sales returned to the firm by customers. The amount reduces sales and is shown in the trading account. Sometimes referred to as net sales.
Returns outwards	Purchases returned by the firm to suppliers. The amount reduces purchases and is shown in the trading account. Sometimes referred to as net purchases.
Rights issue	The raising of new capital by inviting existing shareholders to subscribe for shares on preferential terms. The shares can generally be bought for less than their stock market price.

GLOSSARY

Secured creditors Creditors whose claims are wholly or partly secured on the assets of the business.

Share premium This shows that the shares were once sold for more than their nominal value, the surplus is shown in the balance sheet as a capital reserve.

Signalling Conveying information through actions such as making dividend payments. Shows investors that a company is profitable and that it can afford to make such payments.

Sinking fund A fund created for the redemption of a liability. The aim is to set aside a certain sum which will, at a set date in the future, be sufficient to meet a liability.

Source and application of funds statement A financial statement which shows the external and internal sources from which funds have been obtained to finance a business during a given accounting period and the manner in which the funds have been deployed.

Standard cost A predetermined cost, calculated on the basis of a desired level of operating efficiency and activity level.

Stocks Raw materials, work in progress, finished goods and goods in transit or on consignment at the end of an accounting period.

Sunk cost Those costs invested in a project which will not be recovered even if the project is discontinued.

Tangible assets Assets having a physical identity, e.g. land and buildings, plant and machinery.

Trading account A financial statement which shows the revenue from sales, the cost of those sales and the gross profit arising during a given accounting period.

Unappropriated profits Profits which the company has reinvested in the firm instead of distributing them as dividends to the shareholders.

Unlisted investment An investment which is not quoted on a recognised stock exchange.

Unsecured loan Loan stock which carries interest but is not secured on any of the assets of the company.

Variable cost Costs which vary directly with the level of activity (output), e.g. direct labour and direct materials.

Variance   A difference between the standard cost and the actual cost. The variance may be adverse, in which case the actual cost was more than the standard cost, or favourable, in which case it was less. In either case the reason for the variance must be analysed by management.

WACC   Weighted Average Cost of Capital.

Work in progress   Materials, components or products in various stages of completion during a manufacturing process. The term also applies to partly completed contracts.

Working capital   The difference between a firm's current assets and its current liabilities.

Zero coupon bond   A bond where the holder is only entitled to one payment of interest and principal.

Zero sum game   A financial term used to describe a situation where one party can only make a financial gain at the expense of another.

Ratings

The following two tables show the 1989 comparative ratings for corporates and banks. The rating scale can be interpreted as follows:

RATING SCALE

Long Term Ratings

AAA Obligations for which there is the lowest expectation of investment risk. Capacity for timely repayments of principal and interest is substantial such that adverse changes in business, economic, or financial conditions are unlikely to increase investment risk significantly.

AA Obligations for which there is a very low expectation of investment risk. Capacity for timely repayment of principal and interest is substantial. Adverse changes in business, economic, or financial conditions may increase investment risk, albeit not very significantly.

A Obligations for which there is a low expectation of investment risk. Capacity for timely repayment of principal and interest is strong, although adverse changes in business, economic, or financial conditions may lead to increased investment risk.

BBB Obligations for which there is currently a low expectation of investment risk. Capacity for timely repayment of principal and interest is adequate, although adverse changes in business, economic, or financial conditions are more likely to lead to increased investment risk than for obligations in higher categories.

BB Obligations for which there is a possibility of investment risk developing. Capacity for timely repayment of principal and interest exists, but is susceptible over time to adverse changes in business, economic, or financial conditions.

B Obligations for which investment risk exists. Timely repayment of principal and interest is not sufficiently protected against adverse changes in business, economic, or financial conditions.

CCC Obligations for which there is a current perceived possibility of default. Timely repayment of principal and interest is dependent on favourable business, economic, or financial conditions.

CC Obligations which are highly speculative or which have a high risk of default.

C Obligations which are currently in default.

Short Term Ratings
including Commercial Paper
(Up to 12 months)

A1+ Obligations supported by the highest capacity for timely repayment.

A1 Obligations supported by a very strong capacity for timely repayment.

A2 Obligations supported by a strong capacity for timely repayment, although such capacity may be susceptible to adverse changes in business, economic, or financial conditions.

B1 Obligations supported by an adequate capacity for timely repayment. Such capacity is more susceptible to adverse changes in business, economic, or financial conditions than for obligations in higher categories.

B2 Obligations for which the capacity for timely repayment is susceptible to adverse changes in business, economic, or financial conditions.

C1 Obligations for which there is an inadequate capacity to ensure timely repayment.

D1 Obligations which have a high risk of default or which are currently in default.

* * * * * * * * * * * * * * * * * * * *

Long term ratings of BB and below are assigned where it is considered that speculative characteristics are present.

"+" or "-" may be appended to a long term rating to denote relative status within major rating categories.

Rating Watch highlights an emerging situation which may materially affect the profile of a rated corporation.

Reproduced with permission from
The Treasurer's Handbook, 1990
(Association of Corporate Treasurers).

DCF TABLES

Compound Sum of £1 (CVIF) $S = P(1 + r)^N$

Period	1%	2%	3%	4%	5%	6%	7%	8%	9%	10%	12%	14%	15%	16%
1	1.010	1.020	1.030	1.040	1.050	1.060	1.070	1.080	1.090	1.100	1.120	1.140	1.150	1.160
2	1.020	1.040	1.061	1.082	1.102	1.124	1.145	1.166	1.186	1.210	1.254	1.300	1.322	1.346
3	1.030	1.061	1.093	1.125	1.158	1.191	1.225	1.260	1.295	1.331	1.405	1.482	1.521	1.561
4	1.041	1.082	1.126	1.170	1.216	1.262	1.311	1.360	1.412	1.464	1.574	1.689	1.749	1.811
5	1.051	1.104	1.159	1.217	1.276	1.338	1.403	1.469	1.539	1.611	1.762	1.925	2.011	2.100
6	1.062	1.126	1.19	1.265	1.340	1.419	1.501	1.587	1.677	1.772	1.974	2.195	2.313	2.436
7	1.072	1.149	1.230	1.316	1.407	1.504	1.606	1.714	1.828	1.949	2.211	2.502	2.660	2.826
8	1.083	1.172	1.267	1.369	1.477	1.594	1.718	1.851	1.993	2.144	2.476	2.853	3.059	3.278
9	1.094	1.195	1.305	1.423	1.551	1.689	1.838	1.999	2.172	2.358	2.773	3.252	3.518	3.803
10	1.105	1.219	1.344	1.480	1.629	1.791	1.967	2.159	2.367	2.594	3.106	3.707	4.046	4.411
11	1.116	1.243	1.384	1.539	1.710	1.898	2.105	2.332	2.580	2.853	3.479	4.226	4.652	5.117
12	1.127	1.268	1.426	1.601	1.796	2.012	2.252	2.518	2.813	3.138	3.896	4.818	5.350	5.926
13	1.138	1.294	1.469	1.665	1.886	2.133	2.410	2.720	3.066	3.452	4.363	5.492	6.153	6.886
14	1.149	1.319	1.513	1.732	1.980	2.261	2.579	2.937	3.342	3.797	4.887	6.261	7.076	7.988
15	1.161	1.346	1.558	1.801	2.079	2.397	2.759	3.172	3.642	4.177	5.474	7.138	8.137	9.266
16	1.173	1.373	1.605	1.873	2.183	2.540	2.952	3.426	3.970	4.595	6.130	8.137	9.358	10.748
17	1.184	1.400	1.653	1.948	2.292	2.693	3.159	3.700	4.328	5.054	6.866	9.276	10.761	12.468
18	1.196	1.428	1.702	2.026	2.407	2.854	3.380	3.996	4.717	5.560	7.690	10.575	12.375	14.463
19	1.208	1.457	1.754	2.107	2.527	3.026	3.617	4.316	5.142	6.116	8.613	12.056	14.232	16.777
20	1.220	1.486	1.806	2.191	2.653	3.207	3.870	4.661	5.604	6.728	9.646	13.743	16.367	19.461
25	1.282	1.641	2.094	2.666	3.386	4.292	5.427	6.848	8.623	10.835	17.000	26.462	32.919	40.874
30	1.348	1.811	2.427	3.243	4.322	5.743	7.612	10.063	13.268	17.449	29.960	50.950	66.212	85.850

Present Value of £1 (PVIF) $P = S(1+r)^{-N}$

Period	1%	2%	3%	4%	5%	6%	7%	8%	9%	10%	12%	14%	15%
1	0.990	0.980	0.971	0.962	0.952	0.943	0.935	0.926	0.917	0.909	0.893	0.877	0.870
2	0.980	0.961	0.943	0.925	0.907	0.890	0.873	0.857	0.842	0.826	0.797	0.769	0.756
3	0.971	0.942	0.915	0.889	0.864	0.840	0.816	0.794	0.772	0.751	0.712	0.675	0.658
4	0.961	0.924	0.889	0.855	0.823	0.792	0.763	0.735	0.708	0.683	0.636	0.592	0.572
5	0.951	0.906	0.863	0.822	0.784	0.747	0.713	0.681	0.650	0.621	0.567	0.519	0.497
6	0.942	0.888	0.838	0.790	0.746	0.705	0.666	0.630	0.596	0.564	0.507	0.456	0.432
7	0.933	0.871	0.813	0.760	0.711	0.665	0.623	0.583	0.547	0.513	0.452	0.400	0.376
8	0.923	0.853	0.789	0.731	0.677	0.627	0.582	0.540	0.502	0.467	0.404	0.351	0.327
9	0.914	0.837	0.766	0.703	0.645	0.592	0.544	0.500	0.460	0.424	0.361	0.308	0.284
10	0.905	0.820	0.744	0.676	0.614	0.558	0.508	0.463	0.422	0.386	0.322	0.270	0.247
11	0.896	0.804	0.722	0.650	0.585	0.527	0.475	0.429	0.388	0.350	0.287	0.237	0.215
12	0.887	0.788	0.701	0.625	0.557	0.497	0.444	0.397	0.356	0.319	0.257	0.208	0.187
13	0.879	0.773	0.681	0.601	0.530	0.469	0.415	0.368	0.326	0.290	0.229	0.182	0.163
14	0.870	0.758	0.661	0.577	0.505	0.442	0.388	0.340	0.299	0.263	0.205	0.160	0.141
15	0.861	0.743	0.642	0.555	0.481	0.417	0.362	0.315	0.275	0.239	0.183	0.140	0.123
16	0.853	0.728	0.623	0.534	0.458	0.394	0.339	0.292	0.252	0.218	0.163	0.123	0.107
17	0.844	0.714	0.605	0.513	0.436	0.371	0.317	0.270	0.231	0.198	0.146	0.108	0.093
18	0.836	0.700	0.587	0.494	0.416	0.350	0.296	0.250	0.212	0.180	0.130	0.095	0.081
19	0.828	0.686	0.570	0.475	0.396	0.331	0.276	0.232	0.194	0.164	0.116	0.083	0.070
20	0.820	0.673	0.554	0.456	0.377	0.312	0.258	0.215	0.178	0.149	0.104	0.073	0.061
25	0.780	0.610	0.478	0.375	0.295	0.233	0.184	0.146	0.116	0.092	0.059	0.038	0.030
30	0.742	0.552	0.412	0.308	0.231	0.174	0.131	0.099	0.075	0.057	0.033	0.020	0.015

Present Value of £1 (PVIF)P = S(1 + r) – N Continued

Period	16%	18%	20%	24%	28%	32%	36%	40%	50%	60%	70%	80%	90%
1	0.862	0.847	0.833	0.806	0.781	0.758	0.735	0.714	0.667	0.625	0.588	0.556	0.526
2	0.743	0.718	0.694	0.650	0.610	0.574	0.541	0.510	0.444	0.391	0.346	0.309	0.277
3	0.641	0.609	0.579	0.524	0.477	0.435	0.398	0.364	0.296	0.244	0.204	0.171	0.146
4	0.552	0.516	0.482	0.423	0.373	0.329	0.292	0.260	0.198	0.153	0.120	0.095	0.077
5	0.476	0.437	0.402	0.341	0.291	0.250	0.215	0.186	0.132	0.095	0.070	0.053	0.040
6	0.410	0.370	0.335	0.275	0.227	0.189	0.158	0.133	0.088	0.060	0.041	0.029	0.021
7	0.354	0.314	0.279	0.222	0.178	0.143	0.116	0.095	0.059	0.037	0.024	0.016	0.011
8	0.305	0.266	0.233	0.179	0.139	0.108	0.085	0.068	0.039	0.023	0.014	0.009	0.006
9	0.263	0.226	0.194	0.144	0.108	0.082	0.063	0.048	0.026	0.015	0.008	0.005	0.003
10	0.227	0.191	0.162	0.116	0.085	0.062	0.046	0.035	0.017	0.009	0.005	0.003	0.002
11	0.195	0.162	0.135	0.094	0.066	0.047	0.034	0.025	0.012	0.006	0.003	0.002	0.001
12	0.168	0.137	0.112	0.076	0.052	0.036	0.025	0.018	0.008	0.004	0.002	0.001	0.001
13	0.145	0.116	0.093	0.061	0.040	0.027	0.018	0.013	0.005	0.002	0.001	0.001	0.000
14	0.125	0.099	0.078	0.049	0.032	0.021	0.014	0.009	0.003	0.001	0.001	0.000	0.000
15	0.108	0.084	0.065	0.040	0.025	0.016	0.010	0.006	0.002	0.001	0.000	0.000	0.000
16	0.093	0.071	0.054	0.032	0.019	0.012	0.007	0.005	0.002	0.001	0.000	0.000	
17	0.080	0.060	0.045	0.026	0.015	0.009	0.005	0.003	0.001	0.000	0.000		
18	0.089	0.051	0.038	0.021	0.012	0.007	0.004	0.002	0.001	0.000	0.000		
19	0.060	0.043	0.031	0.017	0.009	0.005	0.003	0.002	0.000	0.000			
20	0.051	0.037	0.026	0.014	0.007	0.004	0.002	0.001	0.000	0.000			
25	0.024	0.016	0.010	0.005	0.002	0.001	0.000	0.000					
30	0.012	0.007	0.004	0.002	0.001	0.000	0.000	0.000					

Cumulative Present Value Factors

The table gives the present value of 'n' annual payments of £1 received for the next 'n' years with a constant discount of x% per year. For example, with a discount rate of 5% and with 5 annual payments of £1 the present value is £4.329.

Years 0 to	1%	2%	3%	4%	5%	6%	7%	8%	9%	10%	11%	12%	13%	14%	15%	16%	17%	18%	19%	20%
1	0.990	0.980	0.971	0.962	0.952	0.943	0.935	0.926	0.917	0.909	0.901	0.893	0.885	0.877	0.870	0.862	0.855	0.847	0.840	0.833
2	1.970	1.942	1.913	1.886	1.859	1.833	1.808	1.783	1.759	1.736	1.713	1.690	1.668	1.647	1.626	1.605	1.585	1.566	1.547	1.528
3	2.941	2.884	2.829	2.775	2.723	2.673	2.624	2.577	2.531	2.487	2.444	2.402	2.361	2.322	2.283	2.246	2.210	2.174	2.140	2.106
4	3.902	3.808	3.717	3.630	3.546	3.465	3.387	3.312	3.240	3.170	3.102	3.037	2.974	2.914	2.855	2.798	2.743	2.690	2.639	2.589
5	4.853	4.713	4.580	4.452	4.329	4.212	4.100	3.993	3.890	3.791	3.696	3.605	3.517	3.433	3.352	3.274	3.199	3.127	3.058	2.991
6	5.795	5.601	5.417	5.242	5.076	4.917	4.767	4.623	4.486	4.355	4.231	4.111	3.998	3.889	3.784	3.685	3.589	3.498	3.410	3.326
7	6.728	6.472	6.230	6.002	5.786	5.582	5.389	5.206	5.033	4.868	4.712	4.564	4.423	4.288	4.160	4.039	3.922	3.812	3.706	3.605
8	7.652	7.325	7.020	6.733	6.463	6.210	5.971	5.747	5.535	5.335	5.146	4.968	4.799	4.639	4.487	4.344	4.207	4.078	3.954	3.837
9	8.566	8.162	7.786	7.435	7.108	6.802	6.515	6.247	5.995	5.759	5.537	5.328	5.132	4.946	4.772	4.607	4.451	4.303	4.163	4.031
10	9.471	8.983	8.530	8.111	7.722	7.360	7.024	6.710	6.418	6.145	5.889	5.650	5.426	5.216	5.019	4.833	4.659	4.494	4.339	4.192
11	10.368	9.787	9.253	8.760	8.306	7.887	7.499	7.139	6.805	6.495	6.207	5.938	5.687	5.453	5.234	5.029	4.836	4.656	4.486	4.327
12	11.255	10.575	9.954	9.385	8.863	8.384	7.943	7.536	7.161	6.814	6.492	6.194	5.918	5.660	5.421	5.197	4.988	4.793	4.611	4.439
13	12.134	11.348	10.635	9.986	9.394	8.853	8.358	7.904	7.487	7.103	6.750	6.424	6.122	5.842	5.583	5.342	5.118	4.910	4.715	4.533
14	13.004	12.106	11.296	10.563	9.899	9.295	8.745	8.244	7.786	7.367	6.982	6.628	6.302	6.002	5.724	5.468	5.229	5.008	4.802	4.611
15	13.865	12.849	11.938	11.118	10.380	9.712	9.108	8.559	8.061	7.606	7.191	6.811	6.462	6.142	5.847	5.575	5.324	5.092	4.876	4.675
16	14.718	13.578	12.561	11.652	10.838	10.106	9.447	8.851	8.313	7.824	7.379	6.974	6.604	6.265	5.954	5.668	5.405	5.162	4.938	4.730
17	15.562	14.292	13.166	12.166	11.274	10.477	9.763	9.122	8.544	8.022	7.549	7.120	6.729	6.373	6.047	5.749	5.475	5.222	4.990	4.775
18	16.398	14.992	13.754	12.659	11.690	10.828	10.059	9.372	8.756	8.201	7.702	7.250	6.840	6.467	6.128	5.818	5.534	5.273	5.033	4.812
19	17.226	15.678	14.324	13.134	12.085	11.158	10.336	9.604	8.950	8.365	7.839	7.366	6.938	6.550	6.198	5.877	5.584	5.316	5.070	4.843
20	18.046	16.351	14.877	13.590	12.462	11.470	10.594	9.818	9.129	8.514	7.963	7.469	7.025	6.623	6.259	5.929	5.628	5.353	5.101	4.870
21	18.857	17.011	15.415	14.029	12.821	11.764	10.836	10.017	9.292	8.649	8.075	7.562	7.102	6.687	6.312	5.973	5.665	5.384	5.127	4.891
22	19.660	17.658	15.937	14.451	13.163	12.042	11.061	10.201	9.442	8.772	8.176	7.645	7.170	6.743	6.359	6.011	5.696	5.410	5.149	4.909
23	20.456	18.292	16.444	14.857	13.489	12.303	11.272	10.371	9.580	8.883	8.266	7.718	7.230	6.792	6.399	6.044	5.723	5.432	5.167	4.925
24	21.243	18.914	16.936	15.247	13.799	12.550	11.469	10.529	9.707	8.985	8.348	7.784	7.283	6.835	6.434	6.073	5.746	5.451	5.182	4.937
25	22.023	19.523	17.413	15.622	14.094	12.783	11.654	10.675	9.823	9.077	8.422	7.843	7.330	6.873	6.464	6.097	5.766	5.467	5.195	4.948
26	22.795	20.121	17.877	15.983	14.375	13.003	11.826	10.810	9.929	9.161	8.488	7.896	7.372	6.906	6.491	6.118	5.783	5.480	5.206	4.956
27	23.560	20.707	18.327	16.330	14.643	13.211	11.987	10.935	10.027	9.237	8.548	7.943	7.409	6.935	6.514	6.136	5.798	5.492	5.215	4.964
28	24.316	21.281	18.764	16.663	14.898	13.406	12.137	11.051	10.116	9.307	8.602	7.984	7.441	6.961	6.534	6.152	5.810	5.502	5.223	4.970
29	25.066	21.844	19.188	16.984	15.141	13.591	12.278	11.158	10.198	9.370	8.650	8.022	7.470	6.983	6.551	6.166	5.820	5.510	5.229	4.975
30	25.808	22.396	19.600	17.292	15.372	13.765	12.409	11.258	10.274	9.427	8.694	8.055	7.496	7.003	6.566	6.177	5.829	5.517	5.235	4.979

ANSWERS

CHAPTER 2   RECORDING FINANCIAL INFORMATION

1.   **Cash Book**

DEBIT ENTRIES	£	CREDIT ENTRIES	£
Opening balance	100	Stamps	20
Cash sales	10	Rent	15
Cash sales	30	Wages	20
Cash sales	25	Petrol	12
		Stationery	5
		Bank	15
		Balance	78
	165		165

2.   Credit balance = £100.

3.
a.	Debit	Bank,	Credit	Cash;
b.	Debit	Stationery,	Credit	Bank;
c.	Debit	Purchases,	Credit	Cash;
d.	Debit	Cash,	Credit	Sales;
e.	Debit	Motor Van,	Credit	Bank;
f.	Debit	Purchases,	Credit	Bank;
g.	Debit	Petrol,	Credit	Cash;
h.	Debit	Drawings,	Credit	Cash;
i.	Debit	Khan,	Credit	Sales;
j.	Debit	Insurance,	Credit	Bank;
k.	Debit	Rent,	Credit	Bank.

4.
a.	Debit	Cash,	Credit	Capital;
b.	Debit	Bank,	Credit	Cash;
c.	Debit	Purchases,	Credit	Bank;
d.	Debit	Cash,	Credit	Sales;
e.	Debit	Computer,	Credit	Bank;
f.	Debit	Bank,	Credit	Sales;
g.	Debit	Stationery,	Credit	Cash;
h.	Debit	Cash,	Credit	Capital;
i.	Debit	Cash,	Credit	Bank;
j.	Debit	Cleaning,	Credit	Cash.

5.

	Ledgers	Account	Dr/Cr
b.	Bank	Real	Debit
	Cash	Real	Credit
c.	Purchases	Real	Debit
	GH Ltd	Personal	Credit
d.	Wages	Real	Debit
	Bank	Real	Credit
e.	Premises	Real	Debit
	Bank	Real	Credit
f.	Cash	Real	Debit
	Sales	Personal	Credit
g.	Telephone	Real	Debit
	Cash	Real	Credit
h.	Computer	Real	Debit
	KL Supplies	Personal	Credit
i.	H Ltd	Real	Debit
	Sales	Personal	Credit
j.	Purchases	Real	Debit
	Cash	Real	Credit
k.	Cash	Real	Debit
	Bank	Real	Credit
l.	Insurances	Real	Debit
	Bank	Real	Credit
m.	Cash	Real	Debit
	Asset Disposal	Real	Credit

Note: To distinguish between Real Accounts and Personal Accounts – Real Accounts are Assets and Expense Accounts found in the Nominal Ledger, Personal Accounts are Individual Accounts found in the Purchase or Sales Ledgers.

6.

a.	Credit	b.	Credit	c.	Debit	d.	Debit	e.	Credit
f.	Credit	g.	Debit	h.	Debit	i.	Debit	j.	Debit
k.	Debit	l.	Debit	m.	Debit	n.	Debit	o.	Debit
p.	Debit	q.	Debit	r.	Debit	s.	Credit	t.	Debit
u.	Credit	v.	Debit	w.	Debit	x.	Debit	y.	Debit
				z.	Credit				

7. The Tool Box

Trial Balance as at 5 April Year 1

	Dr [£]	Cr [£]
Sales		45,890
Commission received		1,540
Freehold premises	73,000	
Purchases	22,583	
Motor Van	800	
Heat and light	300	
Wages	7,000	
Carriage inwards	200	
Office cleaning	340	
Rent and rates	1,350	
Discount received		400
Discount allowed	230	
Fixtures and fittings	2,560	
Debtors	8,300	
Creditors		22,000
Bank loan	1,500	
Motor expenses	400	
Returns inwards	100	
Capital		48,833
	118,663	118,663

Chapter 3 Understanding Financial Statements

1.	a.	Asset	b.	Liability	c.	Asset
	d.	Liability	e.	Asset	f.	Asset
	g.	Asset	h.	Asset	i.	Liability
	j.	Asset	k.	Liability	l.	Asset
	m.	Liability	n.	Liability	o.	Liability
	p.	Asset	q.	Asset		

2.	a.	Liability	b.	Fixed asset	c.	Fixed asset
	d.	Current asset	e.	Fixed asset	f.	Capital
	g.	Current asset	h.	Liability	i.	Liability
	j.	Fixed asset	k.	Fixed asset	l.	Current asset
	m.	Fixed asset	n.	Current asset		

3. a. £5,000 b. £15,000 c. £80,000 d. £25,000 e. £62,000

4. a. £20,000

    b. £80,000

	c.	Current assets	£26,000	Net assets	£40,000
	d.	Capital	£36,500	Net assets	£36,500
	e.	Current liabilities	£6,500	Net assets	£23,000

5. a. £14,000 b. £23,000 c. £30,000 d. £35,000

6. a. £15,000 b. £22,000 c. £37,000 d. £42,000

7.	a.	Net assets	£17,000	Capital	£17,000
	b.	Net assets	£24,000	Capital	£24,000
	c.	Net assets	£37,000	Capital	£37,000
	d.	Net assets	£53,000	Capital	£53,000

8.
a.	Trading account	b.	Profit and loss	c.	Trading account
d.	Trading account	e.	Profit and loss	f.	Profit and loss
g.	Profit and loss	h.	Profit and loss	i.	Profit and loss
j.	Profit and loss	k.	Profit and loss	l.	Trading account
m.	Profit and loss	n.	Trading account	0.	Profit and loss
p.	Profit and loss	q.	Trading account	r.	Profit and loss
s.	Profit and loss				

9.
a.	Income	b.	Expense	c.	Expense	d.	Expense
e.	Asset	f.	Income	g.	Income	h.	Expense
i.	Asset	j.	Expense	k.	Liability	l.	Expense
m.	Expense	n.	Expense	o.	Asset	p.	Asset
q.	Asset	r.	Expense	s.	Liability	t.	Asset
u.	Asset						

10.
a.	Trading	b.	Balance sheet
c.	Profit & loss & Balance sheet	d.	Balance sheet
e.	Balance sheet	f.	Balance sheet
g.	Profit and loss	h.	Profit and loss
i.	Balance sheet	j.	Balance sheet
k.	Balance sheet	l.	Profit and loss
m.	Trading account	n.	Trading account & Balance sheet
o.	Profit and loss	p.	Balance sheet
q.	Trading account	r.	Trading account
s.	Profit and loss	t.	Balance sheet
u.	Profit and loss	v.	Profit and loss

11.
a.	£42,000	b.	£72,000	c.	£70,000	d.	£62,500

12.
a.	£21,500	b.	£16,500	c.	£33,300	d.	£41,200

13. a. £15,100   b. £32,800   c. £43,600   d. £39,421

14. a. £11,000   b. £48,000   c. £56,000   d. £79,000

15. a. £20,000   b. £44,000   c. £27,500   d. £40,000

16. a. £45,000   b. £91,000   c. £83,000   d. £130,000

17.

		Net sales	COGS	G.P.
Net sales	a.	£33,000	£17,500	£15,500
Net sales	b.	£44,000	£23,800	£20,200
Net sales	c.	£82,000	£52,200	£29,800
Net sales	d.	£70,500	£37,300	£33,200

18.

a. Revenue	b. Capital	c. Revenue	d. Capital
e. Revenue	f. Capital	g. Revenue	h. Revenue
i. Revenue	j. Capital	k. Capital	l. Revenue

19. Mountain Biker

Trading, Profit and Loss Account for Mountain Biker for the year ending 31 March Year 1

	£	£
Sales		60,000
Purchases	35,500	
Less closing stock	7,000	
Cost of goods sold		28,500
Gross profit		31,500
Less Expenses		
Wages	10,000	
Lighting and heating	3,000	
Postage and telephone	1,500	
Cleaning	1,000	
Motor expenses	700	
Repairs to shop	500	
General expenses	800	
Total expenses		17,500
Gross Profit		14,000

20. Gardens and Lawns

Trading, Profit and Loss Account and Balance Sheet for Gardens and Lawns for the year ending 5 April Year 1

	£	£
Sales		101,160
Add purchases	54,225	
Less closing stock	13,275	
Cost of goods sold		40,950
Gross profit		60,210
Less Expenses		
Wages	31,230	
Office expenses	4,410	
Motor expenses	2,565	
Office cleaning	855	
Advertising	2,025	
Insurance	1,125	
Total expenses		42,210
Net Profit		18,000

Balance Sheet as at 5 April Year 1

Capital	£	Fixed Assets	£
Capital	20,000		
Add profit	18,000		
Current Liabilities		*Current Assets*	
Creditors	14,445	Stock	13,275
Bank overdraft	7,000	Debtors	46,170
	59,445		59,445

CHAPTER 4   ACCOUNTING CONCEPTS AND CONVENTIONS

1.   **R and J Builders**

    Gain on Revaluation

    The gain has not been realised it, therefore, cannot be included in the firm's profit and loss account. Breach of the Realisation Principle. If the property were sold then the gain could be included in the profit and loss account but would have to be shown separately from the trading profit.

    Advertising Expenditure

    If the firm can show that there is a future benefit to be gained from advertising then some of the cost can be spread forward, otherwise the total cost of the advertising should be charged to the final accounts. Breach of the Prudence Concept.

    Loss on Contract

    The loss should be charged against this years accounts for it is a foreseeable loss. Breach of the Prudence Concept.

2.   **Executive Stationery Supplies**

    a.   A van is a fixed asset which will have a working life of several years and so it would be wrong to write off the cost of the van against one years profit.

    b.   Historical Cost Concept and the Going Concern Concept. Assets are shown at their cost price rather than their current market value because there is an assumption that they will be used for several years.

    c.   The legal cost is part of the cost of acquiring the premises and so the cost is treated as capital expenditure and shown in the balance sheet rather than treating it as revenue expenditure.

CHAPTER 5   FINAL ACCOUNTS - ACCOUNTING FOR ADJUSTMENTS

1.

Woodland Furniture Trading Profit and Loss Account
for the year ending 30 September Year 3

	£	£
Sales		162,740
Less returns inwards		5,200
Net sales		157,540
Opening stock	12,260	
Add net purchases	93,800	
	106,060	
Less closing stock	11,160	
Cost of goods sold		94,900
Gross profit		62,640
Add discount received		1,560
		64,200
Less Expenses		
Wages	25,640	
Discount allowed	2,480	
Insurance	1,600	
Advertising	6,320	
Travelling	6,980	
Depreciation fixtures	284	
Depreciation vehicles	960	
Sundry expenses	4,620	48,884
Net profit		15,316

Woodland Furniture's Balance Sheet as at 30 September Year 3

Fixed Assets	Cost	Depreciation to Date	Net Book Value
	£	£	£
Premises	40,000	-	40,000
Furniture and fittings	2,840	284	2,556
Motor vehicles	6,400	960	5,440
	49,240	1,244	47,996
Current Assets			
Stock		11,160	
Debtors		12,880	
Bank		5,620	
		29,660	
Less Current Liabilities			
Creditors		14,900	
Working capital			14,760
Net Assets			**62,756**
Financed by			
Capital			56,000
Add net profit			15,316
			71,316
Less drawings			8,560
Capital employed			**62,756**

2.

RJ Landscapes Trading Profit and Loss Account
for the year ended 31 December Year 3

	£	£
Sales		182,400
Opening stock	20,100	
Add purchases	145,050	
	165,150	
Less closing stock	24,750	
Cost of goods sold		140,400
Gross profit		42,000
Add discounts received		2,952
Reduction in provision for bad debts		210
		45,162
Less expenses		
Discount allowed	3,945	
Wages	20,340	
Rent	5,847	
Insurance	654	
Advertising	429	
Rates	1,800	
Depreciation	372	
Bad debts	1,701	
Total expenses		35,088
Net profit		10,074

RJ Landscapes Balance Sheet as at 31 December Year 3

Fixed Assets	Cost	Depreciation to Date	Net Book Value
	£	£	£
Furniture and fittings	3,720	372	3,348
Current Assets			
Stock		24,750	
Debtors		16,062	
Bank		7,554	
		48,366	
Less Current Liabilities			
Creditors		15,210	
Working capital			33,156
Net Assets			36,504
Financed by			
Capital			35,400
Add net profit			10,074
			45,474
Less drawings			8,970
Capital employed			36,504

Note: Debtors £16,290 – £390 + £162 = £16,062.

3.

Jonquil Fashions Trading, Profit and Loss Account
for the Year Ended 31 December Year 8

	£	£
Sales		2,071,600
Less Returns Inwards		29,200
Net Sales		2,042,400
Opening Stock	137,200	
Add Purchases	1,473,600	
	1,610,800	
Less Returns Outwards	24,800	
	1,586,000	
Add Carriage Inwards	88,800	
	1,674,800	
Less Closing Stock	127,200	
Cost of Goods Sold		1,547,600
Gross Profit		494,800

	£	£
Gross Profit		494,800
Add Discount Received		33,600
Commission		77,800
Interest		4,800
Gross Profit Plus Additional Income		611,000
Less Expenses		
Discount Allowed	40,800	
Advertising	32,400	
Rates	19,920	
Wages	151,600	
Insurance	42,000	
Depreciation Fixtures & Fittings	600	
Bad Debts	1,600	
Provision for Bad Debts	2,800	
Stationery and Printing	13,400	
Carriage Outwards	41,200	
Heating and Lighting	66,400	
Total Expenses		412,720
Net Profit		198,280

Jonquil Fashions

Balance Sheet as at 31 December Year 8

Fixed Assets	Cost	Depreciation to Date	Net Book Value
	£	£	£
Buildings	184,000	-	184,000
Fixtures & Fittings	10,000	4,600	5,400
	194,000	4,600	189,400
Treasury Stock at Cost			80,000
			269,400
Current Assets			
Stock	127,200		
Debtors (less provision)	176,400		
Prepayments	9,400		
Bank	70,600		
Cash	5,000		
	388,600		
Less Current Liabilities			
Creditors	228,400		
Accruals	7,720	236,120	
Working Capital			152,480
Net Assets			421,880
Capital			£
Capital			280,000
Add Net Profit			198,280
			478,280
Less Drawings			56,400
Capital Employed			421,880

CHAPTER 6   CONTROL ACCOUNTS

1.   Locating errors
      Preventing fraud
      Management control
      Credit control
      Reconciliation with sales and purchases ledgers.

2.

Sales Ledger Control Account

		£			£
Nov 1	Balance b/d	11,448	Nov 1	Balance b/d	66
	Sales	21,270		Cash	1,312
	Cash refund	198		Bank	17,717
				Bad debts	700
				Discount allowed	1,112
				Returns inwards	492
	Balance c/f	120		Balance c/d	11,637
		33,036			33,036

3.   **Runa Ltd**

Sales Ledger Control Account

Yr 7		£	Yr 7		£
Dec 1	Balance	38,984	Dec 31	Cash	168,016
Dec 31	Sales	183,280		Discount allowed	3,280
				Bad debts	120
				Balance	50,848
		222,264			222,264

Purchase Ledger Control Account

Yr 7		£	Yr 7		£
Dec 31	Cash	145,520	Dec 1	Balance	19,200
	Discount received	2,808	Dec 31	Purchases	148,400
	Balance	19,272			
		167,600			167,600

ANSWERS

4. Solfana

Sales Ledger Control Account

Yr 6		£	Yr 6		£
Dec 1	Balance	16,068	Dec 31	Cash	12,912
Dec 31	Sales	10,032		Returns inwards	378
	Dishon. cheque	480		Discount allowed	678
				Bad debts	384
				Balance	12,228
		26,580			26,580

Purchase Ledger Control Account

Yr 6		£	Yr 6		£
Dec 31	Cash	7,776	Dec 1	Balance	11,274
	Returns outwds	222		Purchases	8,796
	Discount rec'd.	372			
	Bill/exch. payable	990			
	Balance	10,710			
		20,070			20,070

5. Kalliopi Ltd

Sales Ledger Control Account

Yr 5		£	Yr 5		£
Dec 1	Balance	32,136	Dec 31	Cash	25,824
Dec 31	Sales	20,064		Discount allowed	1,356
				Bad debts	768
				Bill/exch. receivable	2,400
				Balance	21,852
		52,200			52,200

Purchase Ledger Control Account

Yr 5		£	Yr 5		£
Dec 31	Cash	15,552	Dec 1	Balance	22,548
	Discount rec'd	744		Purchases	17,592
	Bill/exch. payable	1,980			
	Balance	21,864			
		40,140			40,140

CHAPTER 7   BANK RECONCILIATION

1. a.   Payments by standing order or direct debit.
         Deposits paid directly into the bank account.
         Bank charges.
         Dishonoured cheques.
    b.   Unpresented cheques.
         Presented cheques not yet credited.

2.

Cash Book

Yr 7		£	Yr 7		£
30 May	Balance	1,876.00	30 May	Bank charges	13.60
	Mutual Ins.	360.80		General leasing	400.00
				Balance	1,823.20
		2,236.80			2,236.80

Bank Reconciliation Statement as at 30 May Year 7

	£
Balance as per cash book	1,823.20
Add unpresented cheques	1,052.80
	2,876.00
Less uncollected cheques	628.00
Balance as per bank statement	2,248.00

3.

Cash Book

Yr 2		£	Yr 2		£
1 June	Direct credit	600.00	1 June	Current balance	1,347.60
				Bank charges	56.40
				Interest	2,500.00
	Balance	6,364.00		Ret'd cheque	3,060.00
		69,64.00			6,964.00

Bank Reconciliation Statement

	£
Balance on cash book	6,364.00
Add uncollected cheque	5,682.00
	12,046.00
Less unpresented cheque	4,889.28
Balance on bank statement	7,156.72

4.

Cash Book

Yr 2		£	Yr 2		£
1 June	Direct credit	200.00	1 June	Current balance	449.20
				Bank charges	78.80
				Interest	800.00
	Balance	1,128.00			
		1,328.00			1,328.00

Bank Reconciliation Statement

	£	£
Balance on cash book		1,128.00
Add unpresented cheque		1,894.00
		3,022.00
Less outstanding cheques	1,210.96	
	418.80	1,629.76
Balance on bank statement		1,392.24

CHAPTER 8   CORRECTION OF ERRORS

1. a. Failure to record the transaction in the ledgers.

    b. The financial transaction, although recorded in the appropriate subsidiary book, is recorded at more or less than the correct amount.

    c. Normally brought about by a lack of knowledge, e.g. treating capital expenditure as revenue expenditure. The entry is, therefore, made on wrong account.

2. a. Error will affect trial balance.

    b. Error will not affect trial balance.

    c. Error will not affect trial balance.

    d. Error will affect trial balance.

    e. Error will not affect trial balance.

3.

Journal

			£	£
June 1	Motor Vehicle Repairs Account Motor Vehicle Account Correction of error in posting.	Dr	110	110
June 7	Discount Allowed Account Discount Received Account Correction of error in posting	Dr	200	200
June 10	Motor Van Account Bank Account Motor vehicle purchased by cheque	Dr	3,000	3,000

4.

Ashby Traders' Journal

			£	£
a.	Welcome Traders Cash received from Welcome Traders posted wrongly to debit side of their account. Error now corrected.	Cr		400

b.	Returns Outwards
	  Returns Inwards
	  Cleo Ltd
	Credit note issued to Cleo Ltd wrongly entered in returns Outwards Book. Entry now corrected
		Dr
		Dr
			80
			80
				160

c.	Sales Account Sales book overcast. Entry now corrected	Dr	400	
d.	Mansell Traders Sales Invoice issued to Mansell Traders for £462 recorded in Sales Book as £426. Error now corrected	Dr	36	36

CHAPTER 9   COMPANY ACCOUNTS

1. **The General Trading Company Limited**

   a. **Income**:

Turnover	Income from Investments
Rental income received	Profit or loss on the sale of fixed assets.

   b. **Expenses:**

Staff costs	Directors' emoluments
Employees' emoluments	Interest payments
Hire of plant	Auditing fees
Depreciation	Reduction in the value of investments

   c. **Appropriation of profit:**

Taxation	Transfers to reserves
Reduction in goodwill	Dividends paid

2. **Plumbing Supplies Limited**

   ### Value Added Statement for Plumbing supplies Limited
   ### for 31 March Year 4

	£
Sales	324,000
Less cost of goods sold	120,000
Value added by the company	203,500
To employees:	
Wages and benefits	75,000
To providers of capital:	
Interest	14,000
Dividends	22,000
To government:	
Taxation	40,000
To finance and maintain fixed assets:	
Depreciation	17,000
Retained profit	35,000
Value added	203,000

3. **Transic plc**

Increase in turnover (sales) of 21 per cent. Trading profits have increased by 14 per cent. There has been an increase in interest payments. This may be because interest rates are now higher than last year but it is more likely that the company has increased its borrowing. Interest charges have risen by 63 per cent.

The company is able to increase the amount of profit available for distribution as dividend and has increased its earnings per share. Unfortunately retained profits which will be used to finance new investment have fallen slightly. Nevertheless a share holder would be pleased with these results particularly from a company operating in a recession.

CHAPTER 10   CASH FLOW STATEMENTS

1. a. Source   b. Application   c. Application
   d. Application   e. Application   f. Source
   g. Source   h. Application   i. Application
   j. Source   k. Source   l. Application
   m. Source   n. Application

2. S & J's Cash Flow Statement for the year ended 31st December Year 8

	£
Net Cash Flow From Operating Activities (Note 1)	7,570
Returns on Investment and Servicing of Finance	
Interest Paid	(500)
Corporation Tax Paid	(300)
Capital Expenditure	(6,670)
	100
Equity Dividends Paid	(700)
Decrease in Cash	(600)

Notes to the cash Flow Statement
Note 1. Reconciliation of operating profit to Net Cash Inflow from:

	£
Operating Profit	9,300
Depreciation Changes	1,500
Increase in Stock	(3,000)
Increase in Debtors	(500)
Increase in Creditors	270
Net Cash Inflow From Operating Activities	7,570

ANSWERS

CHAPTER 11   INTERPRETING FINANCIAL STATEMENTS

1. a. **Acid Test**

Current Assets less Stock/Current Liabilities
– Measures a firm's liquidity.

b. **Primary Ratio**

Profit x 100/Capital Employed
– Calculates the return on capital employed.

c. **Gearing**

Debt/Equity
– measures ratio of borrowed capital to share capital.

d. **Interest Cover**

Profit before interest and tax/interest paid
– Calculates the number of times a firm can meet its interest charges out of profits.

e. **Current Ratio**

Current Assets/Current Liabilities
– measures a firm's liquidity.

f. **Dividend Yield**

Ordinary dividend per share x 100/market price per share
– Calculates the real return a shareholder receives when a dividend is paid by taking into account the market price of the share and not the shares nominal value.

g. **Earnings Per Share**

Profit after tax and preference share dividend/number of issued ordinary shares
– Calculates the return a company can earn with its share capital.

h. **Stock Turnover**

Cost of Goods Sold/Average Stock x 365
– Calculates the number of times stock is sold during a financial year.

i. **Debtors' Collection Period**

Debtors x 365/Sales
– Calculates the time taken to collect debts.

j. **Price to Earnings**

Present market price per ordinary share/Annual earnings per share
– Calculates the number of times it would take for the firm's earnings to equal the current share price.

2. **Wine Grotto**

    a. **Current Ratio**

Current Assets	£600,000	=	2:1
Current Liabilities	£300,000		

    b. **Acid Test Ratio**

Current Assets less Stock	£520,000	=	1.73:1
Current Liabilities	£300,000		

    c. **Stock Turnover**

Cost of Goods Sold	£220,000	=	2.75:1
Average Stock	£80,000		

    d. **Debtors' Turnover**

Debtors x 365	£120,000 x 365	=	95 days
Sales	£460,000		

    e. **Return on Capital Employed**

Net Profit	£160,000 x 100	=	23%
Shareholders' Funds	£700,000		

3. **Traditional Kitchens Ltd**

Liquidity	This Year		Last Year	
Current Ratio	£110,000	= 1.67:1	£114,000	= 1.68:1
	£66,000		£68,000	
Acid Test	£60,000	= 0.9:1	£46,000	= 0.68:1
	£66,000		£68,000	

Profitability	This Year		Last Year	
Gross Profit/Sales	£80,000 x 100	= 40%	£70,000 x 100	= 50%
	£200,000		£140,000	
Net Profit/Sales	£35,000 x 100	= 18%	£15,000 x 100	= 11%
	£200,000		£140,000	

ANSWERS

Use of Assets

Debtors' Turnover $\dfrac{£56,000 \times 365}{£200,000}$ = 102 days $\dfrac{£44,000 \times 365}{£140,000}$ = 115 days

Return on Capital $\dfrac{£35,000 \times 100}{£160,000}$ = 22% $\dfrac{£15,000 \times 100}{£120,000}$ = 13%
Employed

Forty-three per cent increase in sales. Improvement in liquidity. Declining gross profit margin but improved net profit margin. This shows that the firm is controlling its costs effectively even though the level of sales is increasing. The firm is earning a greater return on its capital employed.

CHAPTER 12   ACCOUNTING FOR THE EFFECTS OF INFLATION

1. **Plumbing Supplies**

   a. Inflation affects monetary values

   the replacement cost of fixed assets

   the value of loans is reduced in real terms by the rate of inflation

   more working capital will be needed to finance the same volume of sales

   profits are overstated

   need for stock adjustment – holding gain and operating gain

   b. Accounts are prepared under the historical cost accounting convention.

   c. Adjustment for depreciation.

   Adjustment for cost of sales.

   Adjustment for monetary working capital.

   Adjustment for gearing.

CHAPTER 13   INTRODUCTION TO COST ACCOUNTING

1. a.   Direct   b.   Indirect   c.   Direct
    d.   Indirect   e.   Indirect   f.   Indirect

2.   The variable cost is always £5.40.

3.   The material cost is always £2.25.

4.   The direct labour cost is always £6.30.

5.   £4.00.

6.   £5.00

7.   £500,   £1,000,   £1,500,   £2,000.

8.   **Zolan Limited**

a.	50%	60%	70%	80%	90%	100%
Output	10000	12000	14000	16000	18000	20000
	£	£	£	£	£	£
Materials	60,000	72,000	84,000	96,000	108,000	120,000
Labour	40,000	48,000	56,000	64,000	72,000	80,000
Variable O'hds	15,000	18,000	21,000	24,000	27,000	30,000
Fixed costs	40,000	40,000	40,000	40,000	40,000	40,000
Total cost	155,000	178,000	201,000	224,000	247,000	270,000

9. The Electric Motor Company

Output per month	Total fixed cost	Fixed cost per unit	Total variable cost	Variable cost per unit
	£	£	£	£
0	250,000	250,000	-	-
500	250,000	500	39,000	78
1,000	250,000	250	78,000	78
3,000	250,000	83	234,000	78
6,000	250,000	42	468,000	78
10,000	250,000	25	780,000	78
15,000	250,000	17	1,170,000	78
30,000	250,000	8	2,340,000	78
45,000	250,000	6	3,510,000	78
50,000	250,000	5	3,900,000	78
60,000	250,000	4	4,680,000	78

Note: Numbers to the nearest £.

10. Zoraq Limited

Output	Fixed Cost £	Variable Cost £	Sales £	Profit £
1,000	20,000	3,000	8,000	(15,000)
2,000	20,000	6,000	16,000	(10,000)
3,000	20,000	9,000	24,000	(5,000)
4,000	**20,000**	**12,000**	**32,000**	**Break even**
5,000	20,000	15,000	40,000	5,000
6,000	20,000	18,000	48,000	10,000
7,000	20,000	21,000	56,000	15,000
8,000	20,000	24,000	64,000	20,000
9,000	20,000	27,000	72,000	25,000
10,000	20,000	30,000	80,000	30,000
11,000	20,000	33,000	88,000	35,000
12,000	20,000	36,000	96,000	40,000
13,000	20,000	39,000	104,000	45,000
14,000	20,000	42,000	112,000	50,000
15,000	20,000	45,000	120,000	55,000

CHAPTER 14   ACCOUNTING FOR OVERHEADS

1.   a.   Floor area.

   b.   Plant value.

   c.   Floor area.

   d.   Number of employees.

   e.   Number of quotations.

   f.   Number of employees.

   g.   Machine hours.

2.   **Ramal Engineering**

   a.   Historical overhead rate per direct labour hour
   $$\frac{£30,000}{6000 \text{ hrs}} \quad = \quad £5.00$$

   b.   The Conference overhead should be charged as follows:

			£
Job A171	700	hrs at £5	3,500
A191	400	hrs at £5	2,000
B200	1500	hrs at £5	7,500
B242	1000	hrs at £5	5,000
C314	1800	hrs at £5	9,000
C318	600	hrs at £5	3,000
			30,000

   c.   Overheads cannot be charged to the job until the work has been completed.

Overhead rates may change with activity from one period to another because some of the overheads will be fixed whilst others will be variable. Any change in activity will alter the Conference Centre's overhead rate.

ANSWERS

3.   **Alpine Skis**

Departments	Customer Service £	Engineering £	Machinery £	Assembly £
Overheads	800,000	200,000	600,000	200,000
Allocation of customer service costs	(800,000)	160,000	240,000	400,000
Allocation of Engineering costs		(200,000)	80,000	120,000
Total costs			920,000	720,000
Machine hours			30,000	
Labour hours				20,000

Absorption rates   £30.67 per machine hour

£36.00 per labour hour

The firm should allocate its overheads according to activity.

Machinery costs should be allocated on machine hours.

Assembly costs should be allocated on labour hours.

CHAPTER 15   PROFIT AND OUTPUT DECISIONS

1.

	A £	B £	C £	D £
Contribution	50,000	50,000	30,000	51,000
Profit	35,000	25,000	-	16,000

2.

	A £	B £	C £	D £
Contribution	15,000	101,000	5,900	22,000

3.

	A £	B £	C £	D £	E £
Contribution	45,000	31,000	8,000	11,000	7,000

4.

	£	£	£	£
Units to break even	9,000	3,000	3,000	4,000

5.

	A £	B £	C £	D £
Margin of safety	31,600	66,000	41,000	14,000

480

6. Product A because it makes the biggest contribution.

7. **5,000**

8. **Geoff's Garage**

    a. Break even is the term used by accountants to describe the point where total sales equal total costs. At this level of sales the firm makes neither a profit not a loss but merely covers its costs.

    b. Calculation of break even point:

	£	£
Selling price		14.50
Less variable costs:		
Oil	5.00	
Filter	3.50	
		8.50
Contribution		6.00

Calculation of fixed costs	£
Ramp	1,000
Wages	12,000
Overheads	5,000
Total fixed costs	18,000

    Break even = $\dfrac{\text{Fixed costs}}{\text{Contribution}}$ $\dfrac{£18,000}{£6}$ = 3,000 services to break even

9. **Metal Forge Masters**

    a.
Marginal cost:	£
Direct materials	200
Direct labour	75
Variable Overheads	30
	305

    b.
	£
Selling price	630
Less variable costs	305
Contribution	325

    c. Break even:

    $\dfrac{\text{Fixed costs}}{\text{Contribution}}$ $\dfrac{£25,000}{£325}$ = 77 units

    Note: Break even to nearest whole number.

10. The Interior Door Company

Quantity for month	Average Revenue £	Total Revenue £	Total Cost £	ATC £	Profit (Loss) £	MC £	IMR £
0	48	-	75,000	-	(75,000)	-	-
1000	45	45,000	105,000	105.00	(60,000)	30,000	45,000
2000	42	84,000	123,000	61.50	(39,000)	18,000	39,000
3000	39	117,000	135,000	45.00	(18,000)	12,000	33,000
4000	36	144,000	141,000	35.25	3,000	6,000	27,000
5000	33	165,000	147,000	29.40	18,000	6,000	21,000
6000	30	180,000	156,000	26.00	24,000	9,000	15,000
7000	27	189,000	171,000	24.42	18,000	15,000	9,000
8000	24	192,000	195,000	24.38	(3,000)	24,000	3,000
9000	21	189,000	237,000	26.33	(48,000)	42,000	(3,000)
10000	18	180,000	300,000	30.00	(120,000)	63,000	(9,000)

The most profitable level of output is 6,000.

CHAPTER 16   ABSORPTION AND MARGINAL COSTING

1.   Leaded Lights

	May £	June £	July £	Aug £	Sept £	Oct £
Glass	4,500	5,580	6,300	7,560	8,100	8,460
Units	500	620	700	840	900	940
Cost per unit	9	9	9	9	9	9
Labour	2,315	2,871	3,241	3,889	4,167	4,352
Units	500	620	700	840	900	940
Cost per unit	£4.63	£4.63	£4.63	£4.63	£4.63	£4.63

Calculation of Variable Overhead:

	Cost [£]	Output
Highest	12,416	940
Lowest	11,285	500
Change cost/output	1,131	440

Therefore, variable cost of overhead per unit is £2.57. (£1,131 ÷ 440).

Calculation of Fixed Overhead:

	May £	June £	July £	Aug £	Sept £	Oct £
Overhead	11,285	11,593	11,799	12,159	12,313	12,416
Variable cost per unit x output	1,285	1,593	1,799	2,159	2,313	2,416
Fixed cost	10,000	10,000	10,000	10,000	10,000	10,000

a.

Variable cost	**£**
Glass	9.00
Labour	4.63
Variable overhead	2.57
Unit variable cost	16.20

b.   Fixed costs £10,000 per month.

2.   Bridge Hotel

	Jan	Feb	Mar	Apr	May
Food	£94,800	£118,500	£156,420	£189,600	£213,300
Output	20,000	25,000	33,000	40,000	45,000
Cost per meal	£4.74	£4.74	£4.74	£4.74	£4.74
Labour	£25,800	£32,250	£42,570	£51,600	£58,050
Output	20,000	25,000	33,000	40,000	45,000
Cost per meal	£1.29	£1.29	£1.29	£1.29	£1.29

ANSWERS

Calculation of variable overhead:

	Cost £	Activity
Highest	129,150	45,000
Lowest	82,400	20,000
	46,750	25,000

$$\frac{\text{Cost}}{\text{Activity}} \qquad \frac{£46,750}{25,000} \quad = \quad £1.87$$

Therefore, variable cost of overhead is £1.87 per meal.

Calculation of fixed overhead:

	Jan £	Feb £	Mar £	Apr £	May £
Overhead	82,400	91,750	106,710	119,800	129,150
Variable o'hd x output	37,400	46,750	61,710	74,800	84,150
Fixed cost	45,000	45,000	45,000	45,000	45,000

a. Variable costs of the restaurant:

	£
Food	4.74
Labour	1.29
Variable overhead	1.87
Total variable unit cost	7.90

b. Fixed costs £45,000 per month.

c. Contribution = selling price less variable cost.

	£
Selling price per meal	12.50
Less variable cost	7.90
Contribution per meal	4.60

d. Break even = fixed costs divided by contribution.

$$\frac{\text{Fixed costs}}{\text{Contribution}} \qquad \frac{£45,000}{£4.60} \quad = \quad 9783 \text{ meals to break even}$$

484

3.   **Hi Slope Skis**

	October	November	December
Materials	£255,000	£289,000	£340,000
Output	15,000	17,000	20,000
Cost per unit	£17	£17	£17
Labour	£180,000	£204,000	£240,000
Output	15,000	17,000	20,000
Cost per unit	£12	£12	£12

Calculation of variable overhead:

	Cost £	Activity
Highest	113,500	20,000
Lowest	93,500	15,000
Change in cost/activity	20,000	5,000

$$\frac{\text{Cost}}{\text{Activity}} \quad \frac{£20,000}{5,000} \quad = \quad £4$$

Therefore, variable cost of overhead is £4 per unit.
Calculation of fixed cost of overhead:

	October £	November £	December £
Total overhead	93,500	101,500	113,500
Variable overhead £4 x output	60,000	68,000	80,000
Fixed cost	33,500	33,500	33,500

a.   Unit variable cost of manufacturing skis:

	£
Materials	17
Labour	12
Variable overheads	4
	33

b.   Output x unit variable cost plus fixed cost:

25,000   x £33 =   £825,000 + £33,500 =   £858,500

c.   Break even:

	October £	November £	December £
Fixed costs	33,500	33,500	33,500
Contribution	20	20	20
Break even points-units	1,675	1,675	1,675

4.   Manakos Limited

Calculation of Prime Cost:

	January £	February £	March £
Prime cost	83,000	99,600	106,240
Output	25,000	30,000	32,000
Prime cost per unit	3.32	3.32	3.32

Calculation of production overhead into fixed and variable elements:

	Cost	Level of Activity	Unit Cost
March (highest level of activity)	52,940	32,000	1.65
January (lowest level of activity	44,750	25,000	1.79

The production overhead cost is, therefore, partly fixed and partly variable because as output increases unit costs fall.

	Cost £	Level of Activity
March	52,940	32,000
January	44,750	25,000
	£8,190	£7,000

If the change in cost is divided by the change in output the variable cost can be ascertained:

$$\frac{£8,190}{7,000} \quad = \quad £1.17$$

	January £	February £	March £
Production overhead	44,750	50,600	52,940
Variable cost per unit £1.17 x output	29,250	35,100	37,440
Fixed costs	15,500	15,500	15,500

The firm now knows what it costs to make one unit of production in each of the three months.

	January	February	March
Prime cost	£3.32	£3.32	£3.32
Variable production overhead	£1.17	£1.17	£1.17
Fixed costs (divided by output)	0.62	0.51	0.48
	£5.11	£5.00	£4.97

Order can be accepted as it earns a contribution.

5. Firework Party

Activity	50%	60%	70%	80%	90%	100%
Members	120	144	168	192	216	240
Non members	50	60	70	80	90	100
Total	**170**	**204**	**238**	**272**	**306**	**340**
Receipts	**£**	**£**	**£**	**£**	**£**	**£**
Members	720	864	1008	1152	1296	1440
Non members	350	420	490	560	630	700
Total receipts	**1070**	**1284**	**1498**	**1712**	**1926**	**2140**
Less variable costs						
Food	340	408	476	544	612	680
Drinks	68	82	95	109	122	136
Programme	109	131	152	174	196	218
Total variable costs	**517**	**621**	**723**	**827**	**930**	**1034**
Less fixed costs						
Bonfire	70	70	70	70	70	70
Disco	120	120	120	120	120	120
Insurance	50	50	50	50	50	50
Hire of equipment	70	70	70	70	70	70
Fireworks	400	400	400	400	400	400
Total fixed costs	**710**	**710**	**710**	**710**	**710**	**710**
Surplus/Deficit	**(157)**	**(47)**	**65**	**175**	**286**	**396**

Note: Calculations to nearest whole number.

ANSWERS

CHAPTER 17   ACCOUNTING FOR DECISION MAKING

1.   The Potter's Wheel

    a.   Marginal cost - Small £3.25;   Medium £4.35;   Large £6.00

    b.   Contribution - Small £3.75;   Medium £4.65;   Large £5.00

    c.   In the absence of any other constraints the firm should make the product which will yield the greatest contribution. This can be calculated by dividing the time to make each pot into the contribution earned from each sale.

	Small	Medium	Large
Contribution	£3.75	£4.65	£5.00
Time (hours)	2	3	4
Contribution per hour	£1.88	£1.55	£1.25

The firm should make the small pot because it makes the largest contribution.

2.   Central Theme Parks

	Attraction		
	Shark	Swamp	Tunnel
	£	£	£
Sales	130,000	90,000	225,000
Less:			
Variable costs	50,000	35,000	70,000
Direct labour	35,000	15,000	40,000
Total variable costs	85,000	50,000	110,000
Contribution	45,000	40,000	115,000
Less Fixed costs	65,000	20,000	55,000
Profit/(loss)	**(20,000)**	**20,000**	**60,000**

Profit = £60,000

488

Proposal to close Shark Ride:

	£
Contribution	155,000
Less fixed costs	140,000
Profit	15,000

Closure would reduce profits by £45,000.

3.   Southern Cross Hotel

	Docklands £	City £	Waterside £
Sales	80,000	150,000	197,000
Less variable costs:			
Food	25,000	45,000	63,000
Labour	25,000	35,000	45,000
Variable o'hd	12,000	12,000	12,000
Total variable cost	**62,000**	**92,000**	**120,000**
Contribution	80,000	58,000	77,000
Less fixed costs	28,000	28,000	28,000
Profit/(loss)	**(10,000)**	**30,000**	**49,000**

Total profit = £79,000 less £10,000 loss = £69,000.

Proposal to close the Docklands Restaurant:

	£
Contribution	135,000
Less fixed costs	84,000
Profit	51,000

£18,000 reduction in profit because in the short-term the hotel still has to meet the fixed costs.

Note: In the short-term, so long as a department or product makes a contribution towards fixed costs, it should be kept.

ANSWERS

CHAPTER 18   BUDGETARY CONTROL

1.   The South West Brewing Company

Flexible Budget for South West Brewing Company

Activity	70% £	80% £	90% £	100% £
Rent	70,000	70,000	70,000	70,000
Rates	15,000	15,000	15,000	15,000
Prime Cost	63,000	72,000	81,000	90,000
Insurance	10,000	10,000	10,000	10,000
Indirect Labour	20,000	20,000	20,000	20,000
Advertising	5,000	5,000	5,000	5,000
Total cost	183,000	192,000	201,000	210,000

Note: The company has high fixed costs and these remain fixed regardless of the level of activity.

2.   The Wooden Fencing Company

Activity	70% £	80% £	90% £	100% £	110% £
Rent	100,000	100,000	100,000	100,000	100,000
Rates	20,000	20,000	20,000	20,000	20,000
Direct materials	420,000	480,000	540,000	600,000	660,000
Direct labour	315,000	360,000	405,000	450,000	495,000
Power	84,000	96,000	108,000	120,000	132,000
Insurance	20,000	20,000	20,000	20,000	20,000
Indirect labour	30,000	30,000	30,000	30,000	30,000
Total cost	989,000	1,106,000	1,223,000	1,340,000	1,457,000

3. Electric Motors Limited

	80% £	Per Unit £	90% £	Per Unit £	100% £	Per Unit £
Direct material	115,600	17	130,050	17	144,500	17
Direct labour	74,800	11	84,150	11	93,500	11
Overhead	143,800	21.1	146,775	19.2	149,750	17.6
Sales	353,600	52	397,800	52	442,000	52
Units	6,800		7,650		8,500	

Overhead

	80%	90%	100%
Cost	143,800	146,775	149,750
Units	6,800	7,650	8,500
Incremental cost		2,975	2,975
Incremental units		850	850
Variable cost per unit		3.5	3.5

Overhead cost	146,775
Less: 7650 units @ £3.50	26,775
Fixed cost	£120,000

a. **Statement showing profit @ 70% activity**

Units	Per Unit £	5950 £
Sales 5950 @	52	308,400
Less Variable cost (£17 + 11 + 3.5)	31.5	(187,425)
Contribution		121,975
Less Fixed cost		(120,000)
Profit		1,975

b. The overhead absorption rate is derived by dividing the overheads at the budgeted activity level by the associated budgeted hours or units.

c. The budget relating to the actual activity achieved is used for comparison with actual costs to help in cost control.

ANSWERS

4. R and H Metal Manufacturers

	£	£
Sales		948,300
Less variable costs:		
Raw materials	162,750	
Wages	139,100	
Variable overheads	39,220	
Total variable cost		341,070
Contribution		607,230
Less fixed costs		50,440
Profit		556,790

5. The Malaysian Restaurant

	£	£
Sales		112,000
Less variable costs:		
Food	31,200	
Wages	26,525	
Variable overheads	7,000	
Total variable cost		64,725
Contribution		47,275
Less fixed costs		22,000
Profit		25,275

b. Three main benefits:

Management must set objectives for the business.

It ensures that management consider the best way of using the firm's limited resources.

Staff become part of the decision making process.

6. Ankar Limited

	Present Budget	Budget for Productivity Deal	Budget for 10% pay rise
Sales quality	400,000	450,000	400,000
	£'000	£'000	£'000
Sales	1,600	1,710	1,600
Variable costs			
Direct materials	320	360	320
Direct wages	480	552	528
Production overhead	72	81	72
Selling overhead	80	85.5	80
Distribution overhead	64	72.0	64
Total variable cost	1,016	1,150.5	1,064
Contribution	584	559.5	536
Total fixed cost	371	371.0	371
Profit	213	188.5	165

The productivity scheme shows a profit of £188,500 which is £23,500 better than the 10 per cent pay rise alternative.

Note: All numbers rounded to nearest whole number.

7. Rolan

Materials Budget

	January £	February £	March £
Opening stock	3,000	6,200	8,200
Add purchases	6,000	8,000	10,000
	9,000	14,200	18,200
Less production	2,800	6,000	12,000
Closing stock	6,200	8,200	6,200

Production Budget

	January Units	February Units	March Units
Opening stock	200	20	80
Add production	140	300	600
	340	320	680
Less sales	320	240	600
Closing stock	20	80	80

Note: Opening Stock £10,800 ÷ 54 = 200 units

Production Cost Budget

	January £	February £	March £
Materials	2,800	6,000	12,000
Labour	3,360	7,200	14,400
Variable overhead	1,400	3,000	6,000
Fixed overhead	3,600	3,600	3,600
	11,160	19,800	36,000

Note: (VC per unit x output)

Creditors Budget

	January £	February £	March £
Opening balance	4,000	6,000	8,000
Add purchases	6,000	8,000	10,000
	10,000	14,000	18,000
Less payments	4,000	6,000	8,000
Closing balance	6,000	8,000	10,000

Debtors' Budget

	January £	February £	March £
Opening balance	14,600	51,200	38,400
Add sales	51,200	38,400	96,000
	65,800	89,600	134,400
Less receipts	14,600	51,200	38,400
Balance	51,200	38,400	96,000

Cash Budget

	January £	February £	March £
Opening balance	12,000	14,240	45,640
Debtors	14,600	51,200	38,400
Total receipts	26,600	65,440	84,040
Less payments			
Materials	4,000	6,000	8,000
Labour	3,360	7,200	14,400
Var. overheads	1,400	3,000	6,000
Fixed overheads	3,600	3,600	3,600
Total payments	12,360	19,800	32,000
Closing balance	14,240	45,640	52,040

CHAPTER 20   VARIANCE ANALYSIS

1.   Material Usage Variances

a.   [1000kg - 1200kg] x 30p
= [200 kg] x 30 p
= £60 Adverse.

b.   3000 bricks - 2700 bricks x 40p
= 300 bricks x 40p
= £120 Favourable.

c.   [8000 litres - 9000 litres] x 46p
= [1000 litres] x 46p
= £460 Adverse.

2.   Direct Labour Variances

a.   £51 - £30   =   £21 Favourable
b.   £3 - £3   =   –
c.   £50 - £99   =   £49 Adverse

3.   Material Price Variances

a.   1,200 x 0.3 = £36 Adverse
b.   2,700 x 0.2 = £54 Favourable
c.   9,000 x .01 = £90 Adverse

4. Executive Traveller

Profit and Loss Account

	Budgeted £	Actual £
Sales	1,125,000	950,000
Less		
Materials	500,000	450,000
Labour	250,000	300,000
Variable overheads	175,000	175,000
Fixed overheads	100,000	112,500
	1,025,000	1,037,500
Profit (Loss)	100,000	(87,500)
Budgeted profit		100,000
Sales Variance Adverse	(175,000)	
Materials Favourable	50,000	
Labour Adverse	(50,000)	
Fixed O'hd Var. Adverse	12,500	
		187,500
Actual Loss		87,500

5. The Kitchen Mouldings Company

Profit and Loss Account

	Budgeted £	Actual £
Sales	150,000	130,000
Less		
Materials	45,000	48,500
Labour	30,000	27,000
Variable overheads	15,000	15,000
Fixed overheads	15,000	14,000
	105,000	104,500
Profit (Loss)	45,000	25,500
Budgeted profit		45,000
Sales Variance Adverse	(20,000)	
Materials Adverse	(3,500)	
Labour Favourable	3,000	
Fixed O'hd Var. Favourable	1,000	
		(19,000)
Actual Profit		25,500

CHAPTER 21   RAISING FINANCE

1.   **The Wooden Window Company**

a.   Borrower's   -   CV experience

Amount   -   The amount of the loan

Repayment   -   How the money will be repaid

Security   -   What security will be offered

Account   -   Loan or overdraft

Control   -   Business plan, budgets forecasts.

b.   Overdraft for short-term financing, e.g. stock. Term loan to finance fixed assets.

2. $$EAR = (1 = [0.12/12]^{12}) - 1 = 12.68\%$$

CHAPTER 22   THE CAPITAL MARKETS AND FINANCIAL SECURITIES

1. $$PV = \frac{£50,000}{(1 + 0.105)^3} = £37,064.49$$

2. $$PV = \frac{6}{(1 + 0.10)^1} + \frac{6}{(1 + 0.10)^2} + \frac{6 + 100}{(1 + 1.10)^3}$$

$$= \frac{6}{1.10} + \frac{6}{1.21} + \frac{106}{1.33}$$

$$= 5.45 + 4.96 + 79.70$$

$$= £90.11$$

3.   If interest rates rise bond prices will fall. If the bonds were purchased prior to the rise in interest rates a capital loss will be made. It would be wise to keep the money invested in a cash deposit until the investor believes that interest rates have peaked.

4.   Change in interest rates or a change in the credit worthiness of the organisation which has issued the bond.

5.   One would expect to see a decline in interest rates during periods of low inflation. Long term bonds paying high rates of interest would, other things being equal, increase in value.

6.   The market value of bonds is very sensitive to changes in interest rates and so capital gains or losses will be made by investing at the most opportune time. This is why managers must understand the relationship between interest rates and bond prices.

CHAPTER 23   GEARING

1.   a.   Nominal value of debt to nominal value of share capital.

      b.   Market value of debt to market value of share capital.

      c.   Total debt (long and short-term) to shareholders' funds (share capital plus reserves).

      d.   Number of times interest is covered.

      e.   Ratio of the change in earnings before interest and tax to change in earnings per share.

2.   Interest   £60,000   £30,000
           Tax   30,000   150000   shares
                         30,000

                        = 2p Increase in EPS

3.

	Before	After
	£	£
Earnings before interest and tax	180,000	260,000
Less interest	-	20,000
Earnings after interest	180,000	240,000
Tax	72,000	96,000
Earnings after interest and tax	108,000	144,000
Calculation of EPS	£108,000	£144,000
	200,000 shares	200,000
	EPS 54p	EPS 72p

4a.

	Before £	After £
Earnings before interest and tax	220,000	310,000
Less interest	-	36,000
Earnings after interest	220,000	274,000
Tax	110,000	137,000
Earnings after interest and tax	110,000	137,000
Dividend	66,000	82,200
Retained earnings	44,000	54,800
Calculation of EPS	£44,000	£54,800
	300,000	300,000
	15p (appx)	18p

4b.   Calculation of firm's weighted average cost of capital

	Before £	After £
Dividend	22.0p	27.0p
Loan capital	-	12.0p
Weighted average cost of capital	22.0p	19.5p

Note: Calculation of dividend   = $\dfrac{\text{Total dividend payments}}{\text{No of ordinary shares}}$

5.   The Diverse Engineering Group

a.   The additional debt will increase interest payments. If sales and profits fall the increased debt may have an adverse effect on cash flow. If a company cannot meet its interest payments it may be forced into liquidation. Increased debt capital will increase the firm's gearing ratio which could adversely affect the share price and reduce its credit rating, thereby increasing the cost of any future borrowings.

b.   If a firm is unable to meet its interest payments or repay the sum borrowed it may need to restructure its debts. This can take the form of either lengthening the time period of the loan or the lender agreeing to turn current interest payments into additional debt. Sometimes the lender may seek both of these options.

c.   A highly geared company is a more risky investment particularly if sales and profits fall. So long as the firm is profitable it should, in theory, be able to pay higher dividends than a lowly geared company because it has fewer shareholders. If the company can increase its profits and solve its current problems it should be able to increase its dividend payments, thereby leading to an increase in its share price.

ANSWERS

Chapter 24   INVESTMENT APPRAISAL

1.   **Project A** = 3 years.

     Project B

Year	Cash Outflow £	Cash Inflow £	Cumulative Cash Flow £
0	(55,000)	-	(55,000)
1		18,000	18,000
2		25,000	43,000
			Shortfall 12,000

$$\frac{£48,000}{12} = £4,000 \qquad \frac{Shortfall}{Monthly\ inflow} \qquad \frac{£12,000}{£4,000} = 3$$

Payback = 2 years 3 months

     Project C

Year	Cash Outflow £	Cash Inflow £	Cumulative Cash Flow £
0	(120,000)	-	(120,000)
1		22,000	22,000
2		36,000	58,000
3		46,000	104,000
4		48,000	Shortfall 16,000

$$\frac{£48,000}{12} = £4,000 \qquad \frac{Shortfall}{Monthly\ inflow} \qquad \frac{£16,000}{£4,000} = 4$$

Payback = 3 years 4 months approx.

2.   a.   The method does not consider all of the cash flows and no distinction is made over their timing. As a result cash inflows in later years are treated the same as those received in earlier ones.

       b.   Managers facing liquidity problems tend to favour pay back. Many investment decisions do not warrant vast amounts of analysis, so investment appraisal techniques would be a waste of management time.

           The method can be used as a screening device for any investment which cannot pay for itself it should not, therefore, be proceeded with.

           Finally the method is simple to use and to understand.

3.

	Project A £	Project B £	Project C £
Total inflows	132,000	164,000	155,000
Less investment	40,000	60,000	75,000
Profit	92,000	104,000	80,000
Years	4	4	4
Average profit	23,000	26,000	20,000
Average investment	20,000	30,000	37,500

ARR = $\dfrac{\text{AP} \times 100}{\text{AI}}$ $\dfrac{£23,000 \times 100}{£20,000}$ = **115%** $\dfrac{£26,000 \times 100}{£30,000}$ = **87%** $\dfrac{£20,000 \times 100}{£37,500}$ = **53%**

Where AP = Average Profit
AI = Average Investment.

4. a. £12,760 x 0.735 = £9,378.60

b. £23,987 x 0.893 = £21,420.39

c. £17,540 x 0.627 = £10,997.58

d. £67,800 x 0.227 = £15,390.60

5. a. **Lee Valley Farm**

Year	Profit £	Cash Flow £
0	-	(100,000)
1	30,000	50,000
2	30,000	50,000
3	30,000	50,000
4	30,000	50,000
5	30,000	50,000
Total	150,000	250,000

501

Calculation of Yearly Profit/Cash Flow

	Profit £	Cash Flow £
Sales	200,000	200,000
Less cost of sales	150,000	150,000
Profit before depreciation	50,000	50,000
Less depreciation	20,000	NIL
Profit/Cash flow	30,000	50,000

Note: Depreciation is a non cash expense

b.   Best to consider cash flows. If the cash flows are discounted at the firm's opportunity cost of capital then they reflect an economist's definition of profit which considers the change in cash flows which result from an investment decision. Accountants seek to show the profits earned by a firm by matching expenditure against revenue. Accounting profits, therefore, do not measure the change in value which has resulted from the investment decision.

6.   Woodland Nurseries

a.

Year	Cash Outflow [£]	Cash Inflow [£]	D/F	NPV [£]
0	(150,000)	-	16%	(150,000)
1		60,000	0.862	51,720
2		85,000	0.743	63,155
3		90,000	0.641	57,690
4		102,000	0.552	56,304
5		108,000	0.476	51,408
			NPV	130,277

b.   Cash flow left after a firm has invested in all projects capable of yielding a positive net present value.

c.   the hurdle rate represents the return which the business must earn on any new investment and should reflect the firm's opportunity cost of capital.

7. The Chiltern Saw Mill

a. Average Net Inflow

Project	A	B	C
Inflows	£237,000	£231,000	£192,500
Time	6 years	6 years	6 years
Average inflow	£39,500	£38,500	£32,083

b. The Annual Depreciation

Project	A	B	C
Investment	£90,000	£72,000	£63,000
Time	6 years	6 years	6 years
Depreciation	£15,000	£12,000	£10,500

c. Average Net Profit

Project	A	B	C
Inflows	£237,000	£231,000	£192,500
Less expenditure	£90,000	£72,000	£63,000
Profit	£147,000	£159,000	£129,500
Time	6 years	6 years	6 years
Average profit	£24,500	£26,500	£21,583

d. Average Investment

Project	A	B	C
*Investment	£90,000	£72,000	£63,000
	2	2	2
	£45,000	£36,000	£31,500

* assumes investment occurred in the middle of the year.

e. Accounting Rate of Return

Project	A	B	C
Average profit	£24,500 x 100	£26,500 x 100	£21,583 x 100
Average investment	£45,000	£36,000	£31,500
ARR	54%	74%	69%

f. The Pay Back Period

Project	A	B	C
Investment	£90,000	£72,000	£63,000
Inflows			
Year 1	£20,000	£25,000	£15,000
2	£34,000	£33,000	£30,000
Total	£54,000	£58,000	£45,000
Shortfall	£36,000	£14,000	£18,000
Year 3	£42,000	£39,000	£35,000
Months	12	12	12
Monthly inflow	£3,500	£3,250	£2,917
Shortfall divided by	£36,000	£14,000	£18,000
Monthly inflow	£3,500	£3,250	£2,917
=	10 months	4 months	6 months
Pay back time	34 months	26 months	30 months

g. Net Present Value

Project A

Year	Outflow £	DF £	Inflow £	NPV £
0	90,000	10%		(90,000)
1		0.909	20,000	18,180
2		0.826	34,000	28,084
3		0.751	42,000	31,542
4		0.683	57,000	38,931
5		0.621	46,000	28,566
6		0.564	38,000	21,432
			NPV	£76,735

Project B

Year	Outflow £	DF	Inflow £	NPV £
0	72,000	10%		(72,000)
1		0.909	25,000	22,725
2		0.826	33,000	27,258
3		0.751	39,000	29,289
4		0.683	45,000	30,735
5		0.621	47,000	29,187
6		0.564	42,000	23,688
			NPV	90,882

Project C

Year	Outflow £	DF	Inflow £	NPV £
0	63,000	10%		(63,000)
1		0.909	15,000	13,635
2		0.826	30,000	24,780
3		0.751	35,000	26,285
4		0.683	39,000	26,637
5		0.621	38,500	23,909
6		0.564	35,000	19,740
			NPV	71,986

CHAPTER 25   VALUATION OF A BUSINESS

1.   Valuation based on net assets

	£
Net assets	380,000
Less provision for bad debts	1,400
Revised net assets	378,600

Net Assets   £378,600   = £1.26 Asset backing per share
Ord. Shares   300,000

ANSWERS

Valuation of goodwill

Calculation of Average Maintainable Profit

£		
40,000		
55,000	Total Profit	£298,000
72,000	Time	5 years
67,000		
64,000	Average Profit	£59,600
298,000		

Calculation of Super Profit

	£
Average profit	59,600
Less revenue which trading	
Assets should earn £378,600 x 11%	41,646
Super Profits	17,954

$$\text{Goodwill} = \frac{\text{Super Profits x 100}}{\text{Average return on Capital in similar companies}} \qquad \frac{£17,954 \times 100}{11}$$

Goodwill £163,218

2. **The Original Postcard Company**

Market Valuation of the Company:

100,000 ordinary shares x £1.76 = £176,000

Valuation based on net assets:

	£
Net assets	177,000
Add Revaluations:	
Land and buildings	40,000
	217,000
Less bank balance	20,000
Revised value of net assets	197,000

$$\frac{\text{Net Assets}}{\text{Ord. shares}} \quad \frac{£197,000}{100,000} \quad = £1.97 \text{ Assets backing per share}$$

506

Valuation of Goodwill

Calculation of Average Maintainable Profit

£		
25,000		
30,000	Total Profit	£204,000
18,000	Time	6 years
30,000		
44,000		
57,000	Average Profit	£34,000
204,000		

Calculation of Super Profit

	£
Average profit	34,000
Less revenue which trading	
Assets should earn £197,000 x 9%	17,730
Super Profits	16,270

$$\text{Goodwill} = \frac{\text{Super Profits x 100}}{\text{Average return on Capital in similar companies}} \qquad \frac{£16,270 \times 100}{9}$$

Goodwill £180,778

Valuation based on firm's earnings

$$\frac{\text{Average profit x 100}}{\text{Shares in similar companies}} \qquad \frac{£34,000 \times 100}{11} \qquad = £309,091$$

Capitalised Value of Future Earnings = £309,091

CHAPTER 26   WORKING CAPITAL

1.   A.   £25,000

    B.   £20,000

    C.   £11,200

    D.   £10,000

2.

	Last Year	**This Year**
STOCK TURNOVER		
Raw Materials		
=Stock of Raw Materials x 365	£84,000 x 365	£144,000 x 365
Purchases	£336,000	£408,000
	91 days	129 days

	Last Year	**This Year**
PRODUCTION TIME		
= Work in progress x 365	£42,000 x 365	£72,000 x 365
Cost of sales	£504,000	£594,000
	30 days	44 days

	Last Year	**This Year**
FINISHED GOODS		
= Finished goods x 365	£96,000 x 365	£102,000 x 365
Cost of sales	£504,000	£594,000
	70 days	63 days

	Last Year	**This Year**
DEBTORS' COLLECTION TIME		
= Debtors x 365	£75,000 x 365	£114,000 x 365
Sales	£600,000	£690,000
	46 days	60 days

	Last Year	**This Year**
CREDIT RECEIVED		
= Creditors x 365	£48,000 x 365	£72,000 x 365
Purchases	£336,000	£408,000
	(52 days)	64 days

Calculation of Cash Operating Cycle:

	Last Year [Days]	**This Year [Days]**
Holding time of raw materials	91	129
Time to make goods	30	44
Time to sell finished goods	70	63
Credit terms given to debtors	46	60
	237	296
Less credit time from suppliers	52	64
Cash operating cycle	185	232

3.

	Last Year	**This Year**
STOCK TURNOVER		
Raw Materials		
=Stock of Raw Materials x 365 / Purchases	£60,000 x 365 / £180,000	£125,000 x 365 / £270,000
	122 days	169 days
PRODUCTION TIME		
= Work in progress x 365 / Cost of sales	£35,000 x 365 / £350,000	£66,000 x 365 / £660,000
	37 days	37 days
FINISHED GOODS		
= Finished goods x 365 / Cost of sales	£48,000 x 365 / £350,000	£78,000 x 365 / £660,000
	50 days	43 days
DEBTORS' COLLECTION TIME		
= Debtors x 365 / Sales	£50,000 x 365 / £500,000	£134,000 x 365 / £820,000
	37 days	60 days
CREDIT RECEIVED		
= Creditors x 365 / Purchases	£25,000 x 365 / £180,000	£80,000 x 365 / £270,000
	(51 days)	(108 days)

Calculation of Cash Operating Cycle:

	Last Year [Days]	**This Year [Days]**
Holding time of raw materials	122	169
Time to make goods	37	37
Time to sell finished goods	50	43
Credit terms given to debtors	37	60
	246	309
Less credit time from suppliers	51	108
Cash operating cycle	195	201

Insufficient stock control

Increase in credit terms to debtors

Large increase in the time taken to pay creditors.

ANSWERS

4. a. Working capital is the short-term money used to finance a business. A firm's working capital can be calculated by subtracting its current liabilities from its current assets.

b. In the short-term a firm's profits and cash are not the same because a sale is recorded when it is made and not when the cash is received - realisation concept.

c. Reduce stocks. Set minimum and maximum stock levels. Economic order quantity. Improve debtor collection times. Prepare cash budgets and monitor the cash operating cycle.

CHAPTER 27   MANAGING CURRENT ASSETS

1. **Auto Factors**

a. *Re-order level =*

Maximum Usage x Maximum Lead Time =

2200 x 3   = 6600 units

Maximum stock level =

Re-order level - (Minimum Usage x Minimum Lead Time) + re-order quantity

6600 (1000 x1) + 500 = 5600 + 500   = 6100 units

Minimum stock level =

Re-order level - (Average Usage x Average Lead Time) =

6600 (1564 x 2) = 6600 - 3128   = 3472 units

Average stock level =

Minimum stock level + ½ re-order quantity =

3472 + 250   = 3722 units

b. *Turnover rate =*

Quantity issued   18770

Average stock   3122   = 6.0 times

2. Johnson Builders Merchants

Month	Total Sales	Cash Sales 10%	Credit Sales 90%	Receipts 2/3	Receipts 1/3	COS 3/4 SP
July	50400	5040	45360	30240	15120	37800
August	52920	5292	47628	31752	15876	39690
September	57960	5796	52164	34776	17388	43470
October	60480	6048	54432	36288	18144	45360
November	65520	6552	58968	39312	19656	49140

CHAPTER 28   CASH MANAGEMENT

1. The Welsh Honey Farm

Receipts	Jan	Feb	Mar	Apr	May	June
	£	£	£	£	£	£
Sales	65,000	73,000	120,000	140,000	110,000	130,000
Payments						
Var. Costs	33,000	40,000	70,000	85,000	65,000	80,000
Fixed costs	15,000	15,000	20,000	20,000	20,000	20,000
Taxation		8,000			22,000	
Dividends			35,000			
Total	**48,000**	**63,000**	**125,000**	**105,000**	**107,000**	**100,000**
Balance						
Op. bal.	15,000	32,000	42,000	37,000	72,000	75,000
Receipts	65,000	73,000	120,000	140,000	110,000	130,000
Less Payments	48,000	63,000	125,000	105,000	107,000	100,000
Cl. Bal	**32,000**	**42,000**	**37,000**	**72,000**	**75,000**	**105,000**

Note: In this case receipts are total sales but if there are any other inflows, such as an issue of shares or sale of fixed assets, then these other items would be included in the total receipts.

2. The Woollen Rug Company

Receipts	Jan	Feb	Mar	Apr	May	June
	£	£	£	£	£	£
Sales	37,200	39,000	48,000	39,200	40,800	52,000
Payments						
Raw Mat.	16,780	17,550	21,600	17,640	15,120	14,166
Lab. costs	7,400	7,800	9,600	7,840	6,720	6,296
Var. o'hd.	2,790	2,925	3,600	2,940	2,520	2,361
Fixed o'hd.	9,000	9,000	9,000	9,000	9,000	9,000
Machinery		15,000		8,000		
Leasing	800	800	800	800	800	800
Taxation			33,000			
Total	**36,770**	**53,075**	**77,600**	**46,220**	**34,160**	**32,623**
Balance						
Op. bal.	(47,859)	(47,429)	(61,504)	(91,104)	(98,124)	(91,484)
Receipts	37,200	39,000	48,000	39,200	40,800	52,000
Payments	36,770	53,075	77,600	46,220	34,160	32,623
Cl. bal.	**(47,429)**	**(61,504)**	**(91,104)**	**(98,124)**	**(91,484)**	**(72,107)**

Note: This company is overdrawn and, therefore, has a negative cash position. Until the company has a positive cash flow any receipts merely reduce the deficit and so payments increase it again.

3. The Griffin Paint Company

Receipts	Jan	Feb	Mar	Apr	May	June
	£	£	£	£	£	£
Sales						
Cash	11,280	14,100	7,520	8,930	6,580	7,520
Credit	37,600	45,120	56,400	30,080	35,720	26,320
Total	**48,880**	**59,220**	**63,920**	**39,010**	**42,300**	**33,840**
Payments						
Fixed costs	15,000	15,000	15,000	15,000	15,000	15,000
Raw mat.	20,000	24,000	28,000	28,000	22,000	25,000
Dir. lab	7,000	7,000	5,500	6,250	4,500	4,250
Var. o'hd.	2,800	2,800	2,200	2,500	1,800	1,700
Leasing	800	800	800	800	800	800
Loan rep.					10,000	
Total	**45,600**	**49,600**	**51,500**	**52,550**	**54,100**	**46,750**
Balance						
Op. bal.	80,000	83,280	92,900	105,320	91,780	79,980
Receipts	48,880	59,220	63,920	39,010	42,300	33,840
Total Receipts	128,880	142,500	156,820	144,330	134,080	113,820
Less Payments	45,600	49,600	51,500	52,550	54,100	46,750
Cl. bal.	**83,280**	**92,900**	**105,320**	**91,780**	**79,980**	**67,070**

Note: Depreciation is a non-cash expense and so it is not shown in a cash budget.

4.   Leather Boots Ltd

Receipts	Jan	Feb	Mar	Apr	May	June
Sales	£	£	£	£	£	£
Cash	29,250	17,550	19,500	18,525	12,675	10,725
Credit	102,375	87,750	52,650	58,500	55,575	38,025
Total	**131,625**	**105,300**	**72,150**	**77,025**	**68,250**	**48,750**
Payments						
Raw mat.	40,800	25,200	28,800	21,000	18,000	16,800
Dir. lab.	20,400	12,600	14,400	10,500	9,000	8,400
Var. o'hd.	7,000	7,000	7,000	7,000	7,000	7,000
Leasing	2,000	2,000	2,000	2,000	2,000	2,000
Rent	8,000	8,000	8,000	8,000	8,000	8,000
Total	**78,200**	**54,800**	**60,200**	**48,500**	**44,000**	**42,200**
Balance						
Opening Bal.	60,000	113,425	163,925	175,875	204,400	228,650
Receipts	131,625	105,300	72,150	77,025	68,250	48,750
Total Receipts	191,625	218,725	236,075	252,900	272,650	277,400
Less Payments	78,200	54,800	60,200	48,500	44,000	42,200
Cl. Balance	**113,425**	**163,925**	**175,875**	**204,400**	**228,650**	**235,200**

CHAPTER 29   FOREIGN EXCHANGE

1.   **Note:** Banks buy high and sell low.

	Buying Rate	**Selling Rate**
Fr	8.1576	8.1234
$	1.6743	1.6543
CD	2.1043	2.1021
DM	2.5890	2.5670

2. **Note:** The company is selling dollars so the bank is buying dollars. The bank will buy at the high rate.

    (a) $75,000 ÷ $1.70   = £44,117.65

    (b) $75,000 ÷ $1.72   = £43,604.65

    (c) $75,000 ÷ $1.82   = £41,208.79

    (d) $75,000 ÷ $1.52   = £49,342.11

    (e) $75,000 ÷ $1.42   = £52,816.90

    (f) $75,000 ÷ $1.32   = £56,818.18

    (g) $75,000 ÷ $1.29   = £58,139.53

    (h) $75,000 ÷ £1.19   = £63,025.21

    (i) $75,000 ÷ $1.26   = £59,523.81

Note: All calculations to nearest whole number.

3. **Note:** The company wants to buy dollars so the bank is selling. The bank will sell at the low rate.

    (a) $40,000 ÷ $1.64   = £24,390.24

    (b) $40,000 ÷ $1.86   = £21,505.38

    (c) $40,000 ÷ $1.52   = £26,315.79

    (d) $40,000 ÷ $1.45   = £27.586.21

    (e) $40,000 ÷ $1.32   = £30,303.03

    (f) $40,000 ÷ $1.16   = £34,482.76

    (g) $40,000 ÷ $1.22   = £32,786.89

    (h) $40,000 ÷ £1.27   = £31,496.06

    (i) $40,000 ÷ $1.05   = £38,095.24

4.

	Buying	**Selling**
US dollar spot	$1.6430	$1.6320
Less premium	0.0010	0.0010
Forward rate	1.6420	1.6310

5.   a.   **Note:** The Company wants to buy and so the bank is selling. Bank sells at the low rate.

$$\$600{,}000 \div \$1.7120 = \pounds35{,}0467.28$$

b.

	Buying	**Selling**
US dollar spot	$1.7130	$1.7120
Less premium	0.0006	0.0006
One month forward rate	1.7124	1.7114

	Buying	**Selling**
US dollar spot	$1.7130	$1.7120
Less premium	0.0085	0.0085
Three month forward rate	1.7045	1.7035

c.   Ask to be invoiced in sterling.

Buy the dollars spot and invest them in interest earning deposits.

Enter into a forward contract.

Enter into an option contract.

Exchange Rate Risk means that a change in the exchange rate could result in a profit or loss.

6.   Forward Contract to Sell $200,000

Rate   =   Bank buts at the high rate $1.51
              Less Premium   (1.15)
              Forward Rate   1.4985

              200,000 / 1.4985   =   £133,467 in 3 months

Index

This index is arranged in alphabetical order.
Items explained in the Glossary have the letter G at the end of the entry.

C

T

U

V

International Business Culture, second edition

Terry Garrison

This book is an ambitious and unusual attempt to meet a need in an increasingly important management field: cross cultural teamwork. Its focus is not on the popular aspects of different behaviours typically exhibited in teamwork involving people from different nations, but on the rationales for those behavioural stances. The book throws little light on the question *what ?*, but strongly illuminates the question *why?* It distinguishes between the super-structure of a nation's business culture and the bedrock.

The bedrock is difficult to pin down. It deals with what we call the issue of *where these people are coming from.* It focuses on key factors, often invisible, and always difficult for a foreigner to make out, which shape and predetermine the visible superstructure, like those of a nation's politics, economics, even its religions, which tend to be under-researched, yet are of vital importance for those involved in international management.

The book's main aim is to show why an understanding of a nation's business culture bedrock is vital, to indicate which factors are of major importance in cross-cultural work and to offer contemporary case studies that illustrate clearly how bedrock factors impact. It is a book for the practitioner. An original feature is the Triangle Test ©, a method for use by members of international teams to help raise questions with their partners about important differences of attitude, viewpoint and values.

The 21 case studies range widely, from European mergers to economic crises, from business corruption to government restructuring and cover, literally, the entire business world. Useful for MBA students doing inter-culture analysis courses and for executives in cross-national project teams.

Sewn paperback   352 pages   ISBN 1 85450 232 8   1998

European Business Strategy, sixth edition

Terry Garrison

Twenty-four real-life, topical case studies which increase knowledge about the strategic moves being made by European businesses in the context of the economic and political changes in Europe.

Chapter on international strategy analysis, including major theorists and researchers.

Contents

Banesto	EMU	Groupe Bull
Barings Bank	Air Europe	Ikarus
The Berlin Wall	The ERM	Irish Distillers
British Aerospace	Europe PLC	Klöckner
BSE	European Fighter	Perestroika
Cable & Wireless	Aircraft	Pirelli
Canary Wharf	European Space	Plessey
The Channel Tunnel	Agency	Renault
Crédit Lyonnais	France Télécom	The Port of St
Daf	GATT	Petersburg

Sewn paperback, 552 pages, ISBN 1 85450 250 6, £16.95, Autumn 1997

Tutor's Manual, 6th edition

Two-volume set of notes, chronologies and other material to support the case studies.   ISBN 1 85450 407 X   A4 looseleaf   1998

Case Studies in Business Law, second edition

Jeffrey Young
Twenty topical and interesting case studies on a range of issues in business law
from liability to description, from property to personal problems.
Illustrated and appealing to young people studying business.
Level beginners plus to post-experience general business and management
courses. A4 looseleaf binder with pockets, carrying photocopying rights for
student materials.
Includes case studies, tutor materials, colour OHPs, notes,
model answers. ISBN 1 85450 270 0

Exercises in Business Law, revised edition

Fiona Golby
Lots of varied, user-friendly exercises, crosswords and puzzles, for
first-level, post-experience students.
BTEC Nat.HND Business Law, GNVQ advanced level, A level.
Tutor's Manual (with copying rights), ISBN 1 85450 268 9

European Leisure Businesses: strategies for the future
Brian Eaton
Leisure has been the largest growth sector in the United Kingdom economy
over the past decade. Major organisations, operating in the UK, in Europe and
beyond have emerged. This book covers strategies for the future of leisure
businesses by studying individual business organisations in the context of an
expanding European leisure industry. It is invaluable to those who run leisure
businesses, study business and leisure as part of a course and who seek an
understanding of the growth of the private sector in leisure provision.
Contents: history & development of leisure businesses; strategic issues and the
customer; growth, expansion; annotated list of market research statistics and
sources of information;
conclusions, review; illustrations, photographs, charts and tables
Organisation Profiles Rank, Stakis, First Leisure, Eurocamp,David Lloyd,
Allied Leisure, Ladbrokes, VCI
ISBN 1 85450 230 1

Travel and Tourism, third edition - Patrick Lavery

People in Organisations - fifth edition

Pat Armstrong & Chris Dawson

Book

A comprehensive, well-written guide to managing people which assumes no previous knowledge of personnel management or organisational structure and behaviour. Useful for GNVQ and a range of introductory post-experience business and management courses. Written in an accessible and yet authoritative style, it covers the main areas of personnel management and development and encapsulates a large amount of research and writing on organisations as well as the psychology of individuals and groups.

The authors write with clarity and brevity, using their experience teaching and training a wide variety of learning and practising managers and professionals.

Section 1 - Organisations Goals Determinants of structure Variations in structure Human resource planning **Section 2 - Individual/Group Behaviour** Personality Attitude formation & change The motivation to work Communication & perception Groups Leadership **Section 3, Assessing/monitoring employees** Acquiring new employees Psychological testing The interview Performance management	**Section 4 - Developing employees** Learning Training **Section 5 - Rewarding employees** Rewards **Section 6 - Employee relations** Human resource management and employee relations Legislation affecting employee relations **Section 7 - The organisation in context** Systems The impact of technology Organisational change *Figures, charts, references, readings and index*

ISBN 1 85450 240 9   472 pages   (free to tutors with 10 books direct)

Tutor's Manual - fifth edition

Copyright free exercises, case studies and other materials for tutors to use in the training room. Tested on a variety of professional and management trainees, individual, group and inter-group exercises allow practical skills to be developed.

ISBN 1 85450 426 6, A4 looseleaf binder   (free to tutors with 15 books direct)